A HISTORY OF ORTHODOX
THEOLOGY SINCE 1453

A HISTORY OF
ORTHODOX THEOLOGY
SINCE 1453

by

George A. Maloney, S.J.

NORDLAND PUBLISHING COMPANY
BELMONT, MASSACHUSETTS 02178
1976

By the Same Author

The Cosmic Christ (1972)
Russian Hesychasm (1972)
Man — The Divine Icon (1973)
The Breath of the Mystic (1974)
*Hymns of Divine Love by St. Symeon
    the New Theologian* [translator] (1975)

Library of Congress Catalog Card Number 75-27491
ISBN 0-913124-12-5
© Copyright 1976 by NORDLAND PUBLISHING COMPANY
All Rights Reserved

Dedication

TO REVEREND FREDERICK WILCOCK, S.J., FOUNDER OF THE JOHN XXIII CENTER FOR EASTERN CHRISTIAN STUDIES AT FORDHAM, PIONEER IN ECUMENISM AND A FATHER TO ME.

Acknowledgements

I would like to express my deepest appreciation to Dr. Richard S. Haugh, presently Fellow in Residence at Harvard University, who helped immensely in preparing the manuscript for final publication as well as Miss Kristine Massari who helped in proofreading, and in preparing the Index of Names. Thanks to my secretary, Mrs. Ann Kemble, who typed the manuscript, and also Mr. Paul Fekula for his invaluable loan of material from his library stored at General Theological Seminary, New York City, Miss Anne Murphy, librarian at Fordham University for obtaining material for me from other libraries throughout the U.S. and in Europe and Mr. Declan Murphy for his many suggestions. Finally, an expression of gratitude to Nordland Publishing Co. for patiently seeing this work to its final stages of publication.

GEORGE A. MALONEY, S.J.

About the Author

Fr. George A. Maloney, S.J. received his licentiate from the Gregorian Pontifical University in 1958. He received his doctorate *summa cum laude* in 1962 from the Pontifical Oriental Institute. Fluent in several languages, Fr. Maloney has traveled extensively in Russia, Greece, Egypt, Lebanon, Jordan, Israel and Turkey in an attempt to meet the Eastern Christian groups and to understand their religious background. He spent two summers on Mt. Athos.

Fr. Maloney, a member of the Pope John XXIII Center for Eastern Christian Studies, is Associate Professor of Theology at Fordham University.

Founder and editor of the ecumenical quarterly *Diakonia*, Fr. Maloney is the author of *The Cosmic Christ: from Paul to Teilhard; Russian Hesychasm; Man — The Divine Icon;* and *The Breath of the Mystic*. He is also the translator of *Hymns of Divine Love by St. Symeon the New Theologian*.

Contents

PART ONE

The Russian Church*

WHEN Mohammed II's picked reserves, the Janissaries, scaled the walls of Constantinople on May 29, 1453 and brought the imperial city to a humiliating surrender, it was more than merely another Ottoman victory. Constantine the Great brought the Byzantine Empire into being in erecting his city along the shimmering shores of the Bosphorus. Constantine XI, the last defender of Constantinople, saw Byzantine sovereignty collapse and cease to exist.

But more than Byzantine military prowess had crumbled. Byzantine theology, which had flourished under the spiritual leadership of the emperors and patriarchs of Constantinople for a full millennium, now became locked within the pages of printed manuscripts and sung liturgies. Some of these spiritual riches passed to the Renaissance West. But Byzantine culture and theology were transported mostly to Russia via the southern Slavic countries. This process of assimilating Byzantine theology into Russian cultural modes of expression did not begin in 1453 with the sacking of Constantinople, for it had been going on for many centuries prior to this break. What took place then in Russian thinking was the psychological awareness of Russia's messianic mission to preserve and to develop the Orthodox faith.

---

*The L of C transliteration has been used in this section as often as possible.

When Ivan III married Sophia, the niece of the last Paleologos emperor of the Byzantine Empire, the imperial two-headed eagle passed from Byzantium to Moscow. The ancient Rome had fallen to heresy; the second Rome of Constantinople had fallen to the Islam enemy. It remained for Moscow, the "Third Rome," to carry on the traditions of faith, theology and political aspirations of the Byzantine Empire. To see how Russia fulfilled its theological mission, we need to see briefly what it had already received from the West and from Byzantium prior to 1453.

WESTERN INFLUENCE

The theological influence of the West upon Christian Russia up to the middle of the 15th century is almost negligible. Although Ol'ga, ruling Kiev for her son Sviatoslav, the future father of Vladimir, had been baptized in Constantinople, probably about 957, upon her return to Kiev, she turned towards Germany for a bishop.[1]

The monk Adalbert of the Monastery of St. Maximus in Trier was consecrated bishop and resided in Kiev near Queen Ol'ga from 961 to 962 until he was driven out by a pagan mob. Probably through Adalbert's intervention in Magdeburg, Iaropolk, son of Sviatoslav and ruler of Kiev, received legates from Pope Benedict VII (977-983). Around Novgorod also there lived pockets of Western Christians, the Varangians from the newly Christianized Scandinavian countries. Christianity therefore had entered Russia from the West to a certain degree before the reign of Vladimir, but the bonds with the West were vague and juridical rather than deeply cultural in influence.[2]

With the fall of the Germanic ruling house of the Ottos, both in Germany and in Italy, the influence from the West upon Russian Christianity decreased. The language barrier of Latin clearly lessened the possibility that Western Christianity would play a leading role in shaping Christian Russia. When Vladimir (reportedly about 988) became a Christian as a necessary condition for the hand in marriage of Anna, the sister of two Byzantine emperors, the religious thought of Russia focused primarily on the theological riches of the Byzantine Empire that were made available to Russian thinkers as Western thought never had been, through the medium of translations into their own primitive Slavonic tongue by the Bulgarian, and later still the Serbian, Slavs.

SLAVIC BYZANTINISM

The fact that the literature and culture of the Byzantine Empire was handed to newly converted Christian Russia in a language known to the native Russians was due primarily in origin to the missionary efforts of Cyril and Methodius. Patriarch Photios had entrusted the mission of Pannonia in the middle Danube region of Moravia to these two brothers from Salonika. Traditionally Cyril is credited with the invention of the Slavic alphabet which is still today called the Cyrillic alphabet. Scholars generally tend today to attribute to Cyril the more primitive, transitional Glagolitic alphabet while pupils of Methodius are supposed to have developed the Cyrillic or Slavic alphabet.[3]

Until the Germans invaded Moravia and prohibited the use of the Slavic language in the liturgy, Cyril and Methodius and their disciples labored to translate a basic treasury of Biblical and liturgical works from Greek into Church Slavonic which thus became the mother tongue for all the Slavic countries.[4] Under German persecution the disciples of Cyril and Methodius fled to Bulgaria, bringing to the Bulgars the Slavic written word from where it passed into Serbia and ultimately to Russia.

SLAVONIC TRANSLATIONS

George Fedotov asks the question: Why with so many
translations from Greek into Slavonic pouring into Russia
from Bulgaria, Moravia and Serbia did not Russia witness
a blossoming of medieval culture borrowed from Byzantium
such as the Western countries of France, Germany and England at the same time were undergoing in regard to Latin
culture?[5] The answer, he points out, why for seven centuries
Russia produced no really original, creative work in literature
or dogmatic theology until the 17th century was due precisely
to the riches of Slavonic translations that fed Russian thought
with the highest cultural achievements of the Byzantine
Empire. The Russian mind could hardly at the beginning
stages of Russian cultural development compete with the
theology of the golden patristic age of Byzantine Christianity.
"The bulk of this literature was more than sufficient for
the needs of a newly converted people...The available
Slavonic literature had an overwhelmingly practical and
didactic character. Theoretical interests had not been awaken-
ed. And the Russian intellect was dwarfed in its development for a long time...because of the absence of external
occasion for exercise."[6]

Practically all the Russian literature between the 11th
and the 15th centuries is of a translated nature coming to
Russia from the southern Slavic countries through Slavonic
translations.[7] Ikonnikov gives a list of the major Byzantine
writers, almost exclusively ascetical writers, whose works were
translated either on Mt. Athos or in Constantinople, Bulgaria
or Serbia.[8]

E. Golubinskii has devoted almost an entire volume
to research into the intellectual life of early Russia.[9] He
gives a description of the extant manuscripts found in the
Russia of his day of Slavonic translations made between the
invasion of the Mongols (1238) and the church reforms
of Metropolitan Makarii (1551).[10] His list also shows a

predominance of Byzantine ascetical works and lives of saints interspersed by some individual books from the Bible with a rare treatise on dogmatic theology from Pseudo-Dionysios, Basil the Great or Gregory of Nyssa. In general, the heavy emphasis on the ascetical and moral life in early Russian Christianity dictated the dominating preference for such Byzantine writers who wrote in a similar vein, while the almost complete absence of dogmatic treatises from patristic theologians shows a total lack of interest in speculative theology. Golubinskii gives only a few manuscripts devoted to the theological works of Basil the Great, Gregory of Nyssa, Athanasios and Cyril of Alexandria; a few more of a practical, didactic nature, e.g. St. Cyril of Jerusalem's catechetical sermons and St. John Damascene's exposition of the Orthodox Faith.[11] The bases of early Slavonic translations were the Byzantine hagiographical compilations and ascetical treatises produced between the 5th and 7th centuries.[12] During the Moslem invasions of the Byzantine Empire, collections called *pandectes* were written in Greek to provide an encyclopedia on the ascetical life in one volume.

Two of the most famous collections translated into Slavonic found their way to Russia and enjoyed continued popularity: the *Pandectes* of the monk Antiochos of the 7th century and the *Pandectes* and *Taktikon* [*Book of Discipline*] of Nikon of Montenegro of the 11th century.[13] *Catenae* and *Pateriki* were usually collections of quotations often without giving the author or the work cited. *Palaea* were collections of Biblical history mingled with apocryphal and even non-religious writings.

It is only in the 16th century that we find in Russia a canon of the books of the Bible, but even this indicates the low level of scholarship in Russia up to that time. S. Sol'skii gives a typical ancient Russian Bible canon with the first books of Genesis through Proverbs inclusively with selections of the book of Wisdom, followed by sections on the life of Alexander the Great and an apocryphal vision of a specious prophet called Daniel.[14]

With the renaissance of hesychastic monasticism that took place in the 14th century on Mt. Athos under the inspiration of St. Gregory Sinaite, not only a steady stream of Russian monks travelled to take up residence in Greek-speaking parts of the Byzantine Empire but a great deal of the ascetical and mystical writings of the hesychastic tradition of the Fathers of the desert, of Mt. Sinai and of Mt. Athos was translated into Slavonic and formed a part of Russia's inheritance from Byzantine spirituality. Typical of both those Russians who lived on Mt. Athos and who in Russia translated the classical Byzantine spiritual writings into Slavonic was Nil Sorskii (d. 1508). A. S. Arkhangelskii traces the patristic sources quoted by Nil in his two main works, *Ustav* and *Predanie,* and shows that such authors as Klimacos, Isaac the Syrian, Gregory Sinaite, Simeon the New Theologian, Basil the Great, John Chrysostom, Ephrem the Syrian, Hesychios Sinaite and Maximos the Confessor are cited most frequently.[15]

ORIGINAL THEOLOGICAL WRITINGS

Occasionally, like a flaming meteor lighting up the darkness, there appeared in this period of Russian culture before the fall of Constantinople a few original thinkers who have produced, mostly by way of sermons or letters, a beginning of theological writings. The first and perhaps the greatest preacher and religious thinker of Kievan and even Muscovite times is Illarion, the first native, non-Greek metropolitan of Kiev (c. 1051). His *Confession of Faith* seems to be a free adaptation of a Greek work. It shows no great creative thought but indicates by the author's incisive dogmatic formulations a mind well grounded and disciplined in theology.[16]

Illarion's classical sermon *"On Law and Grace,"* probably delivered before Iaroslav and his court in St. Sophia in Kiev on the occasion of an eulogy in honor of St. Vladimir, ranks equally with any Byzantine work of its kind. With force and eloquence presented in the highest rhetorical style that employs perfect proportion, Illarion gives a rapid review of salvation history. He contrasts the Old Testament dispensation with the New Law of love and inserts the Christianity of *Rus'* into the stream of world salvation. He presents human history and above all Russia's position within that history from an eschatological point of view. Drawing heavily from St. John's theology of grace, Illarion presents salvation as a gradual process growing into fuller realization until the final *eschaton.* The sermon breathes an incarnation and resurrectional optimism that is rooted at the same time in a concrete sense of man's history.

Klimentii Smoliatich, metropolitan of Kiev (1147-1155), has left us only one work, a letter addressed to the priest of Smolensk, Foma, who had accused Klimentii of introducing the pagan philosophies of Homer, Plato and Aristotle into his scriptural exegesis.[17] Klimentii shows himself to be no original thinker but rather an eclectic gatherer and imitator of the humanism found in the Byzantine Empire in the 10th and 11th century.[18] Klimentii answers Foma's accusations against his method of scriptural exegesis by appealing to the examples of other noted Fathers of the Church[19] and by imitating in particular Theodoret of Cyrus and Nicetas of Heracleia in their use of exegetical allegory. We see the beginnings in Russia of two different schools of scriptural interpretation: one a more literal interpretation favored by the Smolensk and later the Novgorod school while Kiev, permeated by Hellenism, sought to reduplicate, in almost slavish imitation, the allegorical types used in Byzantium.[20]

Kirill, bishop of Turov (1130-1189), not far from Kiev, is famous for his sermons, prayers and letters. Showing a possible Bogomil influence from Bulgaria, Kirill stresses the sternness of the Godhead and man's helplessness. The abyss separating man from God is stressed and in his impersonal manner of writing, Kirill takes little pains to bridge the gulf.[21] His sermons delivered on the great feasts of the liturgical year follow the panegyric style of Byzantine oratory. These ranked him with Illarion as one of the leading preachers in Russia. His writings are permeated by the spirit of the Fathers, yet he does not slavishly string the patristic texts into a disconnected series. We find no original thought, yet there is an orderly mind at work in the organization of his patristic sources. A tone of anti-Semitism permeates many of his works, but this merely demonstrates again his fidelity to his Byzantine sources. An interesting point in his soteriology is his presentation of Christ as a warrior pitted against the demonic powers. His theology can be called one of Holy Saturday with the emphasis on Christ conquering the powers in Hades and thus redeeming the world rather than one of paschal, resurrectional joy.

Kirill has produced some moving prayers that reveal the depths of his spirituality but at the same time the prayers remain quite impersonal. Again man's sinfulness and need to cry out for mercy and forgiveness to a majestic, all-powerful God are stressed.

In Kirill as in Klimentii we find nothing original to Russian theological thought. Illarion does show an independent mind that looks upon Christian Russia as a country developing itself into a strong creative nation. Other early spiritual writers would add their contributions to produce a theology that was kenotic as well as eschatological in emphasis.

THE KENOTIC IDEAL

Kenoticism was a spirit that entered into Russian piety

with the recorded life of St. Boris and St. Gleb and permeated Russian monasticism and theological thought. Boris and Gleb, violently murdered by their cruel brother, Sviatopolk, became for Russian believers an ideal of non-resistance to persecution and ultimately to death.[22] Suffering of any kind, borne with meekness for love of Christ, blossomed into the kenoticism of St. Feodosii, founder with St. Antonii of the Pecherskii Lavra. St. Feodosii can be regarded as the father of coenobitic monasticism in Russia and through his biography written by Nestor[23] the model of Palestinian asceticism was concretized for Russians of all times. Feodosii, in his "uncouth garb," bearing sufferings through physical labors in the service of his neighbor in imitation of the meek and humble Jesus Christ, became the ideal for all Russians to imitate. The *Paterikon* of the Kiev-Pecherskii Lavra with its thirty miniatures of the lives of holy monks who imitated Feodosii and St. Sergii of Radonezh transported the kenotic ideal of Feodosii to the northern "thebaid" where monasticism intensified its social activity in creating a northern culture that was transfused by the humble example of Sergii.[24]

A strange note is introduced into the formation of early Russian spiritual thought by the prophetic figure of Avraam of Smolensk. Although his personality is unique in this early history of Russia, his particular eschatological emphasis became an important feature of Russian thought in the following centuries. Efrem, his disciple, wrote the life of St. Avraam in which we see Avraam presented as an intense, vehement ascetic, overcome by the eschatological vision of the end of the world.[25]

He obtained this view of the world by meditating at length on the eschatological, metanoetic sermons of St. Efrem the Syrian and the apocalyptical (often apocryphal) literature which he read in Slavonic translation. It is disputed by scholars whether the *"Sermon of the Celestial*

Powers" should be attributed to him or to St. Kirill of Turov.[26]

Its lack of affected eloquence and general tenor of ideas coincide with Avraam's general personality. The vision that the author bequeathes to succeeding generations of Russians is one of a final, purifying judgment that transfigures the cosmos into a new heavenly Jerusalem.

MONASTICISM

Monasticism, probably more than any other single factor, was the mother which fed and developed theological thought in Russia. Monasteries were the only centers of intense moral and intellectual life. In the monasteries there were harbored the precious books which contained the theological riches of Byzantium and the southern Slavic countries. Six of the most eminent libraries in the 15th century were found in the Troitsko-Sergievskii, Chudovskii, Kirillo-Belozerskii, Rostovskii, Soloviets and Volokolamsk monasteries. But even among the 2,673 Slavonic manuscripts found there, one thousand dealt purely with asceticism.[27] Few theological works are available.

In the 12th century monasticism began to spread like a consuming fire. Of the twenty monasteries known up to the 12th century, only four were found in northern Russia.[28] Of fifty new establishments in the 12th century, forty-eight were in the north. Novgorod and Moscow quickly took over as the centers of monasticism. Each prince felt it his duty to decorate his city-residence with at least one monastery. In the 14th century, a new phenomenon occurred. Up to then, nearly all monasteries were built in cities. Frequent Mongol raids dictated such a practice. But in the 14th century, monasticism moved into the wooded "deserts" both to seek solitude and to avoid the frequent battles between city dynasties. This movement did more than any other social phenomenon to colonize the vast forests, to build cities and eventually to develop centers of learning. There developed three types of monasticism: the coenobitic or community-life; a strictly hermitical life; and the skete-type with two or three monks living together with a spiritual father and coming together with other brother monks from neighboring sketes or cells for communal services on Sundays and feastdays. Even though the interest of monks in these times was of a more ascetical nature, nevertheless, they, by their industry in copying manuscripts and by gifts from wealthy princes and boyars of precious books, spread indirectly the tools for a theological development.[29]

INTERNAL PROBLEMS AND HERESIES

In the region around Novgorod, the center of the commercial crossroads where West met East, there grew up in the 14th and 15th centuries a spirit of rugged individualism, a thirst for freedom, self-expression and personal enterprise. Its remoteness from Moscow, the controlling center of political and religious power, plus its rapid development as a rich commercial city fostered in the people a spirit of criticism against authority. The first serious heresy in Russia, that of the Strigol'niki (meaning, shorn-heads) began in Novgorod and Pskov. It began in 1375, not as a heresy but as a schismatic movement of reform led by two deacons, Nikita and Karp, and an unnamed third layman in protest against the dissolute morals of northern Russia and more particularly against the simony of priests and bishops. Since we have no extant writings of the Strigol'niki, our chief sources about their teachings are from the attacks of Stefan of Perm against them and the document of the Patriarch of Constantinople, Nilos, condemning them.[30] From these secondary sources we learn that the *Strigol'niki* rejected the hierarchy and priesthood along with the sacraments that were chiefly administered by the clergy. They denied the Holy Eucharist and refused to pray for the dead since they rejected the resurrection of the dead. Metropolitans Kiprian (1390-1406) and Photios (1406-1433) fought this heresy but it was principally the erudite and zealous Bishop Stefan of Perm who in his writings not only defended the Orthodox faith but developed positively the true doctrine concerning the priesthood, the Eucharistic sacrifice, confession and the other sacraments as well as the efficacy of prayers on behalf of the dead.

Again in Novgorod in the 15th century another controversy broke out concerning the practice of singing two or three Alleluias in the Liturgy. Metropolitan Photios favored the practice followed in many Russian churches of that time of the triple Alleluia. The monk Eufrosimos traveled to Constantinople where Patriarch Joseph II favored the double Alleluia according to the Byzantine custom. This caused great concern among many in Russia to the point that the Patriarch of Constantinople was accused of having defected from Orthodoxy. In the 17th century Nikon's reforms brought the Russian liturgical practices in conformity to the Byzantine usages except for the Old Believers who staunchly held to the triple Alleluia.

The first true heresy which attacked the teaching and ecclesiastical structure of the Russian Church was that of the Judaizers. Historians who treat of the Judaizers are divided into three groups: those who, relying entirely on Iosif of Volokolamsk's writings, see it as a clearcut form of Judaism against Christianity; the second group, led by N. A. Rudnev, modifies the Judaism as a mélange with Christian rationalism; while the third group links up the heresy with the cultural movements that entered into Russia through the southern Slavic countries, especially from Bulgaria and Serbia.[31] A view that embraces all three seems to be the right one if one is to judge from the assertions of Archbishop Gennadii of Novgorod who saw not just one species of Judaism but a whole complexity with various shades of "Marcionism and Messalianism." Iosif too speaks of "many heresies."[32]

The Judaizers' heresy split the intellectual class of latter 15th century Russia into two factions, not doctrinally, but rather in regard to methods to be used in extirpating heresy. The Trans-Volga *Startsi* (*starets* is the Russian word for a spiritual father) followed the hesychastic spirituality of Nil Sorskii (d.1508) and favored mercy rather than the use of torturing force towards heretics. The Josephians followed the monastic spirituality of Iosif of Volokolamsk who favored inquisitional methods in order to restore orthodoxy. Both Nil Sorskii and Iosif of Volokolamsk, however, have greater importance in the impact that they had on spirituality and the intellectualism in Russia of the 15th and 16th centuries.

REFORMERS

Nil Sorskii and Iosif of Volokolamsk stand out as the leading thinkers in this transitional period of the latter part of the 15th century when Russian thought, cut off from a lively intercourse with Byzantium, sought to develop its own source of creative theological thought. Nil had spent some time on Mt. Athos where he had learned Greek and had thoroughly grounded himself in the hesychastic spirituality of the Greek Fathers. Returning to Russia and dissatisfied with the decadent state of monasticism, he sought to develop the *skete* type of idiorrhythmic monasticism along the Sora River. Here he wrote his *Predanie* and *Ustav,* a rule of *skete* life based on the writings of the Greek Fathers, and gathered around him a group of intellectual monks who engaged in translating and critically amending manuscripts.[33] Nil was responsible for introducing into the northern "thebaid" of Russia a renaissance of hesychastic tradition of interior prayer and a love for solitude and poverty that clashed violently with the social monasticism as propounded by Iosif of Volokolamsk.

Iosif Sani, abbot of Volokolamsk (1439-1515), earnestly sought also to reform monasticism but along the strictly coenobitic lines. In contrast to the inner freedom and intellectual self-activity enjoined by Nil Sorskii, Iosef's spirituality favored a rigid, legalistic obedience to the letter of the law and the authority of the final arbiter, who was, according to his sycophantic way of thinking, the Tsar of "Third Rome." Iosif's chief writings are his *Prosvetitel'* [*Enlightener*][34] and his *Ustav* or *Dukhovnaia Gramota* [*Monastic Rule*].[35]

The Trans-Volgian *Startsi,* followers of Nil, found a most articulate supporter of their views against the Josephians in the person of Maxim the Greek. Russian theology begins with him, although he was not an original thinker nor one who worked out a complete system of theological thought.[36] A monk of the Vatopaedi Monastery of Mt. Athos, Maxim had studied in Paris and in Italy, especially in Florence where he was thoroughly grounded in the Renaissance of the *Cinquecento.* Vasilii, Grand Prince of Moscow, in 1517 requested a Greek monk to do translations from Greek into Slavonic. Not knowing Slavonic at first, Maxim translated the Psalter and other liturgical books from Greek into Latin while a Russian, Dimitrii Gerasimov, retranslated from Latin into Slavonic.[37] Gradually he learned the Slavonic tongue well enough to translate directly from Greek to Slavonic. Still, mistakes were unavoidable. This gave ground for the Josephians to press accusations against Maxim of distorting Orthodox traditions and doctrine.

Golubinskii lists all the extant manuscripts of Maxim and divides his works into the general categories of polemical-moral works, those that dealt with church problems, liturgical services, exegesis of Holy Scripture, liturgical texts and the lives of the Saints, works on the correction of books, defense of the Orthodoxy of the Greeks, history, letters, natural history, panegyrics of Saints and translations.[38] His polemical writings were aimed against Jews, pagans, Muslims, Armenians, Roman Catholics and Lutherans. He also wrote polemically against astrology and Slavonic apocryphal books. His polemical style consisted mainly in citing from texts of Holy Scripture and the early Fathers along with some commentary which, however, was not original but taken chiefly from Byzantine polemicists. It is mainly through his polemical works that the Byzantine diatribes against the Latins became a rather permanent feature in Russian theology.[39]

His moral works were not only directed to monks for a renewal of monasticism but they also aimed at legitimate authorities in the Church and State and were addressed to all Christians in general. He corrected the *Triod, Horologium,* and the *Menea* of the main liturgical feasts and the epistles read in the divine services.

His honesty and intense asceticism made him protest against the depravity of morals in the monastery and in the palace. He became involved with Vassian Patrikeev, one of the ardent followers of Nil Sorskii, in protesting the second marriage of the Grand Prince Vasilii. He was accused in the synod of 1525 of taking too great a freedom in correcting liturgical books, exalting the ecclesiastical authority of the patriarch of Constantinople and of some dogmatic errors. He was sentenced to prison and retired in 1531. He finally was moved to Troitsko-Sergievskii Monastery where he died in 1556.[40]

Another learned writer of this period is Metropolitan Daniil of Moscow. He was a bitter enemy of Maxim the Greek and a faithful follower of Iosif of Volokolamsk in his sychophancy towards the Grand Prince Vasilii. Still, he was a zealous pastor who strove by his writings to instill a true knowledge of theology and a love of divine services.[41]

One of the leading reformers of the 16th century and undoubtedly one of the great literary figures of the early

Russian Church was Makarii, first, archbishop of Novgorod and then metropolitan of Moscow for twenty-one years.[42] For twelve years he worked on his immense undertaking of twelve tomes, one for each liturgical month, the *Velikiia Chet'i-Minei*.[43] He called two synods in Moscow (1547 and 1549) in order to give a liturgical and hence national "status" to Russian saints who had hitherto enjoyed only a local devotion. His greatest ecclesiastical work was done in organizing the synod of 1551, called the *Stoglav* (meaning 100 chapters or decrees) which has proved to be the most important of the early Russian Church councils. The decrees are arranged in haphazard fashion in a list of thirty-seven questions posed by Ivan the Terrible to the bishops. These decrees touch mostly ecclesiastical disciplinary problems such as the education of clergy, benefices of monasteries, widowed priests, etc., but contain no important dogmatic theological statement. The synod decreed the chanting of two Alleluias in the Liturgy followed by "Glory to Thee, O Lord," while the sign of the Cross was to be formed with two fingers. These two simple declarations one century later would have sufficient authority to make the Old Believers break in schism from the national Church.[44]

Theologically we find nothing new in *Stoglav*. Canonists are in disagreement as to the importance of this synod. Golubinskii exaggerates its reforming effects on the Russian Church in comparing it to the Counter-Reformation Council of Trent.[45] The decades and even centuries that followed the synod of *Stoglav* showed that the reforms decreed on paper were hardly realized in actual practice.

CHURCH CANON LAW

Besides a rich library of theological and ascetical works bequeathed to Russian thought through Slavonic translations of Byzantine works, a one book library of canon law entered into Russian ecclesiastical life to give it, even in its beginning stages, a solid legal structure. This book was the famous *Kormchaia Kniga.*[46] Already in the 11th and 12th centuries Slavonic versions of the principal Byzantine canonical collections such as the *Synagogue 50* and the *14 Nomocanons* were found in Russia. Various ecclesiastical documents of Russian origin had been collected such as responses of various bishops or metropolitans and the two apocryphal writings on civil law of St. Vladimir and Iaroslav.[47]

In the 13th century various Slavonic manuscripts of the *Kormchaia Kniga* entered Russia. These can be divided into various manuscript families such as the Great Moravian or *Ustiuzhskaia Kormchaia,* the Bulgarian or *Efremovskaia,* the Serbian or *Riazanskaia,* the Russian or *Novgorodskaia* and some special kinds such as that translated by Vassian Patrikeev.[48] The manuscript family of the Serbian archbishop of Sava, brought to Russia in 1262, was approved in the Synod of Vladimir (1274) and in 1649 was the source for the first printed Russian version. The contents contain the early "apostolic" canons, those of the first seven ecumenical councils (counting Trullo (691-692) as the 6th and 2nd Nicaea (787) as the 7th), canons approved in the regional synods of Ancyra (314-315), Neo-Caesarea (314-325), Gangra (343), Antioch (c.332-340), Laodicea (343-381), Sardica (343-344), Carthage (419), Constantinople (394, 861, 880), various writings of the Holy Fathers, civil laws such as the *Novellae* of Emperor Alexis Comnenos and the *14 Nomocanons,* regulations on penances and church discipline along with anti-Latin polemical tracts such as those of Nicetas Stethatos, the *"Donation of Constantine"* and the *"Account of the Apostasy of the Roman Church."*[49]

The *Kormchaia Kniga,* therefore, included all laws on ecclesiastical matters issued in Russian by both the ecclesiastical and the civil authorities. It became the *"Constitution"* of the Russian Church. Along with Holy Scripture, the canonical parts of the *Kormchaia Kniga* were considered as unchangeable sources for norms regulating ecclesiastical discipline. This is one principal reason why the Russian Church, in spite of so many political and even religious upheavals throughout the centuries, remained unchanged.

CHURCH AND STATE

The *Kormchaia Kniga* and other canonical documents, however, did not work out in detail the harmony that was supposed to exist between Church and State. The working out of this mutual relationship was not left to theologians either but became in practice the domain of the most powerful prince. As Muscovy unified and the authority of its grand duke centralized in the persons of Ivan III and Vasilii III, new melodies were introduced to complicate the hitherto relatively harmonious symphony.

Ivan III took to himself the title of "Sovereign of all Russia." With the establishment of the Russian Church as autocephalous in 1448 and the destruction of the Byzantine Empire in 1453, the Grand Duke of Russia became aware of his unique religious mission to the world. God had given him his power. As the only remaining Orthodox ruler, Ivan felt it was only right in the late 1490's to assume unto himself the double eagle of Byzantium. He was the State and therefore, as the unique Orthodox ruler, he was the Church. Religious writers, as Iosif of Volokolamsk, Spiridon, metropolitan of Kiev, and Abbot Filofei of Pskov developed theories of the divine character of Moscow's Tsar.[50] Filofei's letter to Vasilii III in 1510 did much to concretize the growing ambition of the Tsar: "Two Romes fell, the third is still standing; and there will be no fourth."[51] Moscow was that Third Rome.[52] Ivan IV, the Terrible, would push this theory to extremes and prepare the way for Peter the Great's complete control of the Russian Church by liquidating the patriarchate of Moscow and setting up his Holy Synod. The symphony between Church and State was over.

REACTION TO THE UNION OF FLORENCE

In 1440 Metropolitan Isidor, newly made a cardinal and apostolic delegate of Pope Eugene IV, charged with the task of enforcing in the East Slavic countries the union of Florence, returned to Russia. He met with some success in Kiev but when in 1441 he read the declaration of church unity in Moscow, Tsar Vasilii II and the Russian bishop openly rejected the union. Isidor was imprisoned in the Kremlin monastery of Chudov.[53] Isidor went to Tver' where Duke Boris imprisoned him in 1442. He fled to Lithuania where he also met opposition from Prince Casimir who favored the Basel anti-pope, Felix V. Isidor finally returned to Rome.

After Russian ecclesiastical authorities were persuaded that Constantinople did not likewise reject the union immediately, they took the first step towards Russian independence from the mother Church of Constantinople. On December 5, 1448, Iona was elected metropolitan of all Russia. There was no immediate intention among the Muscovites to set up an independent Church against Constantinople but the overthrow of Constantinople as the political and spiritual leader of all Orthodox countries made it politically and psychologically impossible for the Russian Church to continue as anything but autocephalous. Thus, lack of communications made *de facto* the Church of Russia independent and autocephalous.

ESTABLISHMENT OF THE MOSCOW
PATRIARCHATE

Ivan IV, the Terrible, utilized the growing religious estrangement between Constantinople and the Russian Church to develop to full bloom the concept of sacred autocracy promulgated by Iosif of Volokolamsk, Filofei and the adherents of the Slavophile doctrine of Moscow as the Third Rome. When he drove towards the east in 1552, capturing Kazan' and thus breaking the Tatar bondage over Russia, Ivan IV strengthened the autonomy of the Russian Church. Now established as the only Orthodox country, both freed of the oppressive yoke of Islam and possessing the only remaining Christian emperor capable of defending true Orthodoxy, Russia still felt humiliated as long as its Church was ruled over by only a metropolitan.

Attempts were thus made to promote Moscow to an independent patriarchate. Patriarch Joachim of Antioch arrived in Moscow in June 17, 1586 to beg alms but refused to grant the wish of the Russian Church.[54] It was due to the plotting and diplomacy of Boris Godunov, brother-in-law of the sick tsar, Feodor, that finally gained Russia its patriarchal dignity. After staying in Moscow for two years, Patriarch Jeremias of Constantinople finally was worn down by gifts and flattery. On January 26, 1589, he consecrated Iov as the first Russian patriarch.[55]

Upon his return to Constantinople Jeremias persuaded the other Oriental patriarchs to recognize the validity of his action. Moscow was placed fifth in honor, after Jerusalem, thus retaining the pentarchical structure that had been shaken by what the Orthodox had conceived as the defection of Ancient Rome.

Before Jeremias, however, returned to Constantinople, he visited Western Russia where he deposed Metropolitan Onisifor and appointed Mikhail Ragoza as the new metropolitan. Kirill Terletskii was appointed by Jeremias as his exarch to supervise the Orthodox in Western Russia. Jeremias' support of the brotherhoods, especially of L'vov, over the control of the local bishops, embittered the latter and thus prepared for the union with Rome.

UNION OF BREST-LITOVSK

The second half of the 16th century witnessed in Russia a shift of theological ferment from Moscow to Western Russia. There where the Orthodox Church found itself a political subject of the Polish-Lithuanian King Sigismund III, Orthodox theology developed a strong polemical note of defense against the doctrines of Protestants, especially the Calvinists, and the Roman Catholics.

Two of the outstanding defenders of Orthodoxy were the Archimandrite Artemii and Prince Andrei Kurbskii. Artemii had been hegumen of the Troitskaia Lavra, but fled to Lithuania after having been judged in Moscow for heresy. He stresses in his writings the same deep interiority taught by the Trans-Volgian school of Nil Sorskii.[56] Kurbskii (1528-1583), having found disfavor with Ivan IV, fled to the Polish-Lithuanian Empire where he exhorted, chiefly by pen, his fellow Orthodox to remain firm in their traditional faith against Western theological innovations from Protestantism and Roman Catholicism. A scholar well-versed in the Greek Fathers, he set up a school to translate the patristic writings from Latin translations into Russian. He was not only interested in bringing Byzantine theology into Western Russian thought but also sought to overcome Western culture by a revival of Byzantine humanism.[57]

Kurbskii found in Prince Konstantin Ostrozhskii (1526-1608) a nobleman of means and a similar champion of Orthodoxy, who carried on the work of Byzantine humanism. Ostrozhskii was, however, much more Western in orientation and in the school of Ostrog, which he established, Latin was taught as well as Slavonic and Greek. His greatest contribution to religious thought was the translation and printing of the first complete Bible in Church Slavonic (1581). He had gathered at Ostrog leading Biblical scholars who worked on the Gennadii Slavonic text as well as other translations such as the Aldine and the Kompliotenskii texts to produce a Slavonic version that even today is the standard text for most Russian translations.[58]

Under the influence of Ostrozhskii, brotherhoods were established in Western Russian cities to support and defend Orthodoxy against Western influences through the establishment of schools, printing presses and hospitals. Typical of these were the brotherhoods founded in L'vov (1586) and in Vil'na (1588). But like Ostrozhskii, besides furthering the traditional Byzantine culture, these schools taught also in Latin and Polish and thus acted as a powerful transmitter of Western thought into traditional Orthodox theology.

Another factor that prepared for the *Unia* (union of the Orthodox Church with Roman Catholicism through the retention of the Byzantine rite) was the active apostolate of the Jesuits among the intellectual and noble classes. After entering Poland in 1555, they spread rapidly into Galicia. Two such Jesuits, both of Galicia, were Peter Skarga and Stanislaus Herbst. Skarga wrote *O Jednosci Kosciola Bozego* [*On the Unity of God's Church*][59] which favored reunion of Orthodoxy with Rome through the retention of the Eastern rite and ecclesiastical customs. The Jesuit Antonio Possevino was sent from Rome on various papal commissions to Poland and Russia to effect the conversion of Russian Orthodox to Roman Catholicism but he failed to realize his plan.[60]

All these were leading factors that led to the decision in 1591 of four Western Russian bishops under the leadership of Kirill Terletskii, appointed patriarchal exarch by Patriarch Jeremias II of Constantinople, to unite with Rome. This idea grew more strongly under the writing and persuasive oratory of Ipatii Potei, bishop of Vladimir-in-Volynia. Finally the Council of Brest was called by Sigismund III on October 5, 1596. The Uniates, headed by Ipatii Potei, Kirill Terletskii and Peter Skarga, accepted union with Rome while the Orthodox opposition under the leadership of Prince Ostrozhskii, Cyril Lukaris, representative of the patriarch of Alexandria, and Nicephoros, exarch of the patriarch of Constantinople, met and condemned the Uniate movement.[61]

From thence the Uniate Church became by favor of the Polish king the only Church of Russians in the Polish-Lithuanian Empire. This, however, divided the Churches into Uniates and Orthodox, a condition that grew worse because of the increased social opposition of peasants and Cossacks fanned to a new pitch of hatred for their Western lords by an enforced religious union.

PETER MOGILA

Besides the two extreme camps, one favoring a return to Byzantine Orthodoxy and the other favoring a Westernization through union with Rome, there was a mounting group of influential thinkers and writers who mingled both traditions. Chief representative of this class is Peter Mogila.

Mogila was born in Moldavia (1597) and educated in the Latinized Polish school of the Confraternity in L'vov. He traveled to the West and studied at the Sorbonne in Paris. Approved as archimandrite of the Kievan Lavra by Sigismund III because he gave promise for further union of Orthodox with Rome,[62] Mogila transformed an insignificant monastic school into what would soon after become the leading Kievan Academy. He modeled his school on the Jesuit Latin schools of Poland, teaching in Latin and using Western Roman Catholic sources of theology. Seeking to combat in Western Russia the influence of Calvinism and

in Hellenistic Orthodox countries the Calvinistic influence of
Cyril Lukaris' *Confession of Faith,* Mogila composed in
1640 his own *Confessio Fidei* which he hoped would offset
the errors of Lukaris and still provide a succinct catechism
of Orthodoxy that would be modeled on the Tridentine
Catechism in outline but in content would give the Orthodox doctrine.

The synod of Kiev approved of it in 1640 and submitted
it for approval to Parthenios, patriarch of Constantinople,
in a meeting of Russian and Greek theologians at Jassy,
Rumania in 1642. Meletios Syrigos not only translated it
from Latin into Greek but corrected and appended many
of the teachings. It should be noted that the version approved
was Syrigos' amended version in Greek.[63] A Malvy and M.
Viller[64] have edited a Latin manuscript (*Codex Parisinus
1265*) of the *Confessio* which is not the primitive Latin text
submitted for Greek approval at Jassy (this text has been
destroyed) but which contains the corrections of Syrigos
and his additions and is perhaps in other details the closest
to the primitive text of Mogila.

The *Confession* of Mogila approved by Patriarch Parthenios in 1643 and three other Oriental patriarchs was therefore the revised edition of Syrigos. Its contents, after a short
introduction of three questions on the necessity of faith and
good works for salvation (evidently setting the tone in
opposition to the tenets of Protestantism), are divided into
three parts, artificially constructed according to the three
theological virtues of faith, hope and charity. In question
and answer form, the first and longest part (126 questions)
lays the dogmatic truths to be believed, patterned after the
twelve articles of the Nicene-Constantinopolitan Creed. The
second part (63 questions) deals with the means of salvation, the necessity of grace and prayer, the corporal and
spiritual works of mercy along with an explanation of the
Lord's Prayer and the Beatitudes. The last section (72 questions) gives a summary of Christian morality, the virtues and

the capital sins, concluding with an explanation of the Decalogue.

Chrismation or Confirmation must be repeated in reinstating apostates into the Orthodox community (Q. 105); transubstantiation is brought about by the *Epiclesis* (Q. 107) and there is no intermediate state of temporal punishment (purgatory) between heaven and hell (Q. 64, 65). Essential happiness is granted to the saved only after the final judgment (Q. 68, 126). The Holy Spirit proceeds from the Father alone (Q. 9, 71). The primacy of the pope of Rome is denied and Christ alone is the Head of the Church while local bishops are His mere representatives (Q. 84, 85). If any Church is given an honor of precedence it should be the Church of Jerusalem, the mother of all Churches (Q. 84).

This famous *Confession* of the Orthodox faith through the centuries received the highest approbation from all of the Orthodox autocephalous Churches as a true presentation of the Orthodox faith. In 1643 the four patriarchs of the East in an official act stated that the Confession "conforms to the dogmas of the Church of Christ, is in full accord with the holy canons and there is nothing in it that the Church cannot accept."[65] Patriarch Ioakim (1685) approved the Slavonic translation which was published in Moscow in 1696 by order of Peter the Great and approbation of Patriarch Adrian who called it "a book divinely inspired."[66]

The *Confession* has authority to the degree that it accords with the dogmatic definitions of the first seven ecumenical councils. Many doctrines expressed in this confession had never received approbation in the early councils; hence such teachings have been accepted by many Orthodox theologians as mere theological opinions with some theologians such as Makarii Bulgakov, Sil'vestr Malevanskii, Antonii Amfiteatrov, Filaret, Gumilevskii, N. Damalas, C. Androutsos, D. Balanos, I. Mesoloras, actually teaching opposite doctrines as those propounded in this confession.[67] Therefore Mogila's *Confession of Faith* has a very relative authority. Even Peter Mogila

seemed to have resented the changes made by Syrigos and
did not print the Confession in Kiev where he certainly
possessed the facilities.[68]

In 1645 Mogila printed his *"Small Catechism"* in Kiev.
In this work, according to Georges Florovskii, Mogila corrected the emendations made upon his original text of his
Confession by Syrigos. Especially strong in the *Small Catechism* is the Roman Latin sacramentology with its clear-cut
distinction in each of the seven sacraments of matter and
form. A sacrament, he defines, "is a visible thing instituted
by the Lord Christ which, where it is hallowed by a priest
and given to men to be used, effects and signifies the
invisible grace of the Lord God who sanctifies man and
helps him to eternal life" (Q. 101). The indicative formula,
almost a direct translation from the Roman Latin (*"Ego te
absolvo..."*) is used in administering the sacrament of
Penance; Chrismation is called the sacrament of Confirmation
and the moment of Consecration occurs at the pronouncing
of the Lord's words (Q. 113). In explaining the 11th article
of the Creed ("I look for the resurrection of the dead"),
Mogila clearly teaches the bodily Assumption of the Mother
of God into Heaven (Q. 136).

The publication of Mogila's *Trebnik or Euchologion,* a
ritual for administering the sacraments and its acceptance in
1757 by the Russian Orthodox Church, was another step
away from the more ancient Byzantine customs towards the
introduction of more Latinisms into Russian liturgical practices.[69] Besides the Latinisms found also in his *Small Catechism,* Mogila introduces other teachings that are in evident
contradiction to the *Confession* approved at Jassy. Mogila
accepts the Baptism of Roman Catholics and Protestants
as valid, rejects the practice of reconfirming apostates, denies
the *Epiclesis* as essential in effecting the Eucharist, insists
on the mutual contract of two spouses in matrimony as
the essence of the sacrament and teaches the doctrine of

Purgatory as an intermediate stage of satisfaction for temporal punishment after death.[70]

E. Picot in his listing of Mogila's writings[71] attributes to Mogila, or possibly to a group of Kievan theologians under his guidance, under the penname of Eusebios Pimen (meaning in Greek, the Orthodox pastor) the polemical work: Λίθος: *abo kamen z proshy pravdi Tserkvei svietei pravoslavnei Ruskiei*[72] wherein the author seeks to defend not only the Orthodox faith but the Western innovations introduced by the new ritual against the polemical writings of the Uniate theologian, Cassian Sakowicz.

Mogila left a large group of disciples who continued, as rectors of the school of Kiev, to exert a continuing Westernizing influence upon Russian theology. Such theologians and academy administrators as Sil'vestr Kossov (d. 1657), the first rector of the Academy of Kiev and successor of Mogila as metropolitan of Kiev, Innokentii Popovskii (rector, 1704-07), Khristofor Chiarnutskii (1706-10), Iosif Volchianskii (1721-27), Illarion Levitskii (1727-31), Amvrosii Dubnevich (1731-35), Archimandrite Illarion Negrebetskii (1733-35), Sil'vestr Kuliavka (1740-45), the monk, Varlaam Liashchevskii (1747), Sil'vestr Liaskoronskii (1746-51), by their writings and teachings continued the infiltration of Western theology into Russian theological thought.[73] St. Thomas Aquinas and Duns Scotus became, through dependence upon Latin theological manuals, the great masters for the Kievan theologians while Western compendia cited frequently were those of Cajetan, Valencia, de Ariaga, Molina, Amici, Suarez, Vasquez, Perez, de Lugo, Martinez and Hurtado. The course of studies offered in the academy of Kiev did not differ greatly, at least in method, from a Latin Roman seminary. Theses were proposed (in Latin) and the various theological opinions were presented. Proof of the stated thesis flowed from argumentation presented from Holy Scripture, the Fathers (these included often

Augustine, Jerome, Hilary, Optatus and Arnobius) and noted theologians.

Such training, although it sought to avoid Roman extremes, especially in papal primacy and the *Filioque,* was bought at a price and the more traditional Orthodox teachings were obscured and even forgotten. After the indecisive war between Russia and Poland that ended in 1667 the Ukraine was divided and Kiev became a part of Moscow

Theology in Moscow had reached a nadir during the development of Kievan "baroque" theology. Cut off since the 13th century from any lively contact with Western thought, Moscow, theologically, distrusted both the West and the East. Constantinople had been reduced theologically through the Turkish invasion to a static repetition of the glorious patristic age of yesteryears. The Tsar, as the sole defender of Orthodoxy after Constantinople accepted the union of Florence, was supported by the Moscow patriarch and clergy in his political and theological self-awareness of being head of the Third Rome.

Now scholars, with their well-developed theological manuals, came from Kiev to Moscow to set up the Moscow Academy, modeled along the Western lines of the Academy of Kiev.

OLD BELIEVERS

After Mikhail Romanov was crowned Tsar, all of Russia moved out of the dark "Time of Troubles" into a new era. Reform on all levels was the cry of the day. In Moscow zealous clerics such as Patriarch Nikon (1605-1681), and priests Avvakum (1630-1682) and Ivan Neronov (1591-1670) began a religious revival that had the support of Tsar Aleksei (1645-1676). Soon the reformers split into two camps, those favoring Nikon's reforms, especially the liturgical ones patterned on the ritual used in Constantinople and those who insisted on the Russian usages that dated from the 11th century. The split was not merely a question of liturgical practices but there were deep political issues also at stake. Both Aleksei and Nikon saw the need to accept the Greek ritual to insure an Orthodox uniformity through the Slavic and Byzantine world for the return of Russian political ascendancy among the Slavs in the Ukraine, Serbia, Bulgaria and the Greeks in the Ottoman Empire.

For Avvakum and his followers, this was to deny that Moscow was truly the Third Rome after the defection of Constantinople. How could the citadel of Orthodoxy yield to the Westernizing Ukrainians or to the Greeks who were being educated mostly at this time in Italy because of Turkish oppression? Avvakum, one of the most talented Russian writers and the first Russian to have written his autobiography, was exiled with his followers to Eastern Siberia.[74]

STEFAN IAVORSKII

A small band of theologians in Moscow resisted this westernization in theological thought. Epifanii Slovenetskii (d. 1676) was one of the few Kievan theologians sent to Moscow by Tsar Aleksei who knew well the Greek Fathers. Two Greeks sent by Patriarch Dositheos of Jerusalem to offset the influence of Western theology in Moscow were the brothers Joannikos and Sophronios Likhoudes. Both had been trained in Western theology in Venice and Padua and in Moscow engaged in anti-Latin polemics, chiefly concerning the problem of the *Epiclesis.*

A westernizer of considerable influence among the nobility was Simeon Polotskii (d. 1680) of the Mogila school. He greatly impressed Tsar Aleksei with his eloquence and urbanity, a novelty not found among the clergy of Moscow and he taught the Tsar's children. He had great ability as a preacher in the baroque Western style, had written dog-

matic tracts, chief among them a *"summa theologica"* entitled, *"Corona fidei"* and polemical treatises against the
Raskol'niki or Old Believers.[75] Other "Westernizers" of this
period who fought against Byzantine theology were Sil'vestr
Medvedev (d. 1691), Lazar' Baranovich (d. 1693), Innokentii Ghizel (d. 1683), Antonii Radivilovskii (d. 1688)
and Ivan Galiatovskii (d. 1688), all equally known for
their sacred oratory and theological treatises that were cast
in Western thought categories.

Dimitrii Tuptalo, later bishop of Rostov and canonized
saint of the Russian Church, came also from the Ukraine
of the College of Kiev. He must be classified among the
great Russian spiritual writers for his prolific and scholarly
works of asceticism, apologetics against the Old Believers
and his principal work that occupied him for twenty years,
the *Menei* or the Lives of the Saints for the twelve months
of the liturgical year. He was an eminent preacher, also,
and presented through his sermons and writings proof of his
Western education.[76]

Tsar Peter (1682-1725) was happy that Great Russia,
not only industrially, militarily, culturally, but also theologically, was turning Westward away from Byzantine influence. Early in childhood, having witnessed the bloody
revolutions in the Kremlin, Peter developed a hatred for
Moscow and all of its ancient traditions. He was pragmatic
and technical by character and schooling. After much time
spent in Europe, he returned to Russia in 1699 to begin in
earnest a complete westernization of all Russia. The autocratic, absolute monarchy, modeled on Sweden, replaced
the ancient familiar dialogue between Tsar and Patriarch.
The Church for Peter was a mere instrument of service to
the State.

To further the theological break from Byzantium, Peter
appointed Stefan Iavorskii (1658-1722) bishop of Riazan'
in 1700, and in 1701 administrator of the vacant patriarchal
throne upon the death of Patriarch Adrian (d. 1700). Peter

sent back to their homeland the Greek Likhoudes brothers and placed for twenty years in the leading episcopal sees and the Moscow Academy theologians from the Kievan Academy.

The most outstanding of these Kievan theologians was Stefan Iavorskii. Born in Galicia in 1658, he studied in Kiev, then in L'vov, Lublin, Vil'na and Poznan'. While outside Russia he became a Roman Catholic, a practice quite common among Orthodox students of this period while they studied abroad. Upon returning to Kiev in 1689 he became Orthodox and was tonsured, taking the monastic name of Stefan. Having greatly impressed Peter by his oratory and Western ideas, he rose quickly to become the patriarchal exarch. He brought many theologians from Kiev, such as Palladii Rogovskii and Feofilakt Lopatinskii who had great influence in modeling the Moscow Academy along Kievan and Jesuit lines, an influence that would have an impact on Russian theological thought for centuries.[77]

Iavorskii's chief theological work is entitled *Kamen'very* [*Rock of Faith*], written in 1713. Essentially a polemical work against the Protestants, this work proved an embarrassment to Peter the Great who had earlier granted religious liberties to all Protestants in Russia and had even set up in St. Petersburg a central administration for Protestants. Peter did not expect to find in the leader whom he chose to guide the Russian Church such independence of thought and conviction as Iavorskii demonstrated in his treatise.

Kamen'very was forbidden to be printed by Peter and only in 1729 was it published to be immediately suppressed again until 1749. I. Morev has pointed out the influence of Western theologians, especially of the Jesuit, Robert Bellarmine, upon not only the ideas expressed by Iavorskii but even the very words used.[78] His method is Western scholastic in argumentation and in proof of proposed theses against Protestant innovations in Orthodox traditions. Dividing his material into 12 treatises, he vigorously defends holy icons, the cult of the saints and veneration of their relics, belief in the Holy Eucharist, efficacy of prayers for the dead, tradition as a source of revelation, the need for fasting and good works. Other writings of Iavorskii include a polemical work against the Old Believers[79] and a collection of his sermons published in Moscow (1804-05).[80]

FEOFAN PROKOPOVICH (1681-1738) AND HIS INFLUENCE

Disillusioned with the anti-Protestant tendencies of Iavorskii and his disciples, Peter turned to Feofan Prokopovich to set up the Russian Church upon a new theological basis that would accommodate itself with greater fluidity to Protestant thought. Born in Kiev in 1681, as a youth Feofan became a Roman Catholic and entered the Uniate Basilian Order. He studied in Rome and, upon his return to Russia, he became Orthodox and a bitter opponent of Roman Catholicism. He had great sympathy for Protestant ideas and was well read in Lutheran theology. Peter the Great, under Feofan's learned supervision, wrote _Ecclesiastical Regulations_ which was published in 1721 and set up the Russian ecclesiastical structure along administrative lines found in Lutheran countries.[81]

The patriarchate was replaced by the "Holy Governing Synod," composed of a president, two vice-presidents and eight other members. In substance the Tsar held absolute power over the Church, for he nominated the members and could remove them at whim. His direct supervision was accomplished by his hand-picked procurator who, although he lacked voting power, actually proposed candidates as members of the Synod and above all prepared the agenda for each meeting.

The Church had now lost its influence over the Tsar and over society in general. The state was supreme and for

two hundred more years the administrational side of the
Russian Orthodox Church was ruled by the Tsar, even
though the lower clergy and faithful never accepted the
Tsar's dominance over the Church.

Theological thought, mainly under the powerful influence of Feofan Prokopovich, veered away now from Roman
Catholicism as a source of inspiration and moved towards
Western Protestantism. Although he taught theology in Kiev
for only a few years (1707-1711) and had never worked
out his theological thought into a complete system, yet
through sympathetic followers, such as Samuil Mislavskii,
his theological works were published after his death.[82]

Prokopovich was born in Kiev in 1681 and, as previously
stated, in his youth professed to be a Roman Catholic. He
became a Basilian monk and studied theology in Rome.
Upon his return to Kiev, where he began to teach the
humanities in the Kievan Academy, he professed Orthodoxy.
In 1711 he became rector and professor of theology and in
1710 he became bishop of Pskov. In the works emended by
his disciples from class notes, we gather that not only the
method used by Prokopovich had changed from a Western
Latin Catholic scholasticism to a Latin Protestant scholasticism but, above all, his theological tenets had veered away
from Roman Catholic influence and reflected very fundamental Protestant positions.

Although Prokopovich did not openly use formulas taken
from his Lutheran, Calvinist and Anglican sources, he nevertheless succeeded in bringing into Russian theology both a
method and some basic Protestant teachings that clearly
were innovations in Russian Orthodox thought. Platon A.
Cherviakovskii in several works has shown the influence of
Protestantism on the thought and writings of Prokopovich.[83]

Prokopovich wanted clearly to crush from Russian theological thought the heavy Kievan influence of Roman
Catholic theology. To do this he relied heavily on the authority, method and ideas of the Protestant theologians,

Quenstedt, Pfeiffer, Gerhard, Hollas, Buddaeus, Chemnitz and Carpzov.[84] J. E. Gerhard, especially, provided Prokopovich with his main theological divisions.[85] In his work, *Introductio ad Theologiam,* Prokopovich divided theology into two parts: theology from beliefs and theology from action. He looked at God from faith *ad intra* and *ad extra.* God *ad intra* is viewed in His absolute essence, His attributes and His Person, while God's actions *ad extra* touch the divine decrees of creation and conservation. God has a providential relation to spirits, men and the world which touches such questions as fallen man, original sin, the incarnation, redemption and divine mediation. Fruits of redemption are applied through faith and the sacraments among which he lists justification, divine adoption, sanctification and glorification. The Church of Christ is the subject of predestination and has operated in four steps: the Church before the Law, under the Law, the Church in grace and in glory.[86]

Prokopovich is the first to bring into Russian theology the Protestant insistence on the Hebrew canon of the Old Testament with the rejection of the seven books of the Deuterocanon of the Septuagint. Although he does acknowledge some authority to traditions as handed down by the seven ecumenical councils and the Holy Fathers, Prokopovich, nevertheless, explains their value only as faithful interpreters of Holy Scripture, which constitutes for him the unique font of dogma.

In his tract, *De Gratuita Peccatoris per Christum Justificatione,* Prokopovich seeks to avoid any Protestant formula that would deny free will and exclude good works by using his own formulation: *"fides sola sed non solitaria."* He admits that true faith produces good works, but the latter arise not from faith but from the object of faith, Jesus Christ.

His ecclesiology shows the greatest dependence upon Protestant sources.[87] In his *Prima Instructio pro Pueris* he defines the Church in terms that show a Protestant influence: "The Church is the uniformity of sense among Christians observing the doctrine of Christ as handed down by the Fathers and the ecumenical councils." Perhaps no other Russian thinker can be responsible for the Caesaropapism and the submission of Church to State that entered into Russian Church life at this time than Prokopovich. In his *Regulamentum Ecclesiasticum* which he co-authored with Peter the Great and in his other writings, Prokopovich insists that the Church is to be submissive to the Tsar "who is submissive only to God." To the Tsar belongs the right and office to control ecclesiastical matters and is called by God to be a true *"episkopos"* in the primary sense of the Greek word, meaning an overseer of the Church.[88]

Prokopovich became archbishop of Novgorod in 1725 and died in St. Petersburg in 1736. His last task was to set up a seminary in St. Petersburg, modeled on the Lutheran seminary in Halle. It was mainly through this center that his ideas were to spread after his death and hold the dominating theological influence in Russia until 1836.

His ideas met some opposition from the theologians faithful to the Kievan tradition of Peter Mogila. Stefan Iavorskii had written his *Kamen'very* in 1712, which aimed in general at combating the growing influence in Russian theology of Protestantism, but through the influence of Prokopovich on Peter the Great, this book was suppressed in 1732.

Feofilakt Lopatinskii[89] and Gideon Vishnevskii, both theology professors of the Moscow Academy, collected eleven heretical teachings found in Prokopovich's writings and presented them to the Tsar and the bishops who were about to consecrate Prokopovich bishop of Pskov in 1710. But the latter's influence over Peter the Great succeeded in crushing any opposition for one century after Prokopovich's death. His influence spread throughout the Russian seminaries through professors of theology who had been taught personally by him or who had been influenced through his many writings.

Georgii Koniskii (d. 1795),[90] Arsenii Mogilianskii, Samuil Mislavskii (d. 1796)[91] and Irenei Falkovskii (d. 1827), all served as professors or rectors of the Kievan Academy and both in their teaching and writings propagated the ideas of Prokopovich. But it was in Moscow that not only Prokopovich's ideas received maximum acceptance, but among the Moscow theologians protestantization of Russian theology reached its apogee.

Kirill Florinskii (d. 1744), professor in the Moscow Academy and later bishop of Tver', and M. Volkhovskii, first rector of the new St. Sergii Seminary of the Troitskaia Lavra, both prepared the way for Prokopovich's ideas in Moscow. Florinskii used the scholastic method moderately in his work *Theologia Positiva ac Polemica* and fought vehemently against Latins, Protestants and unbelievers.[92] Volkhovskii wrote a *Summa Theologiae*[93] that is more a transcription of Prokopovich's ideas than an imitation. He, however, does dispute his master's traducianism concerning the origin of the human soul.

The principal theologian of this period is Platon Levshin, rector of the Moscow Academy (1761) and later metropolitan of Moscow (1775). His chief dogmatic work is entitled: *Theologia Christiana super Fundamentum Verbi Dei Exstructa ad Praxin Pietatis et Promotionem Fidei Jesu Christi Unice Directa.*[94] He avoids in his work many of the traditional scholastic problems and seeks to create a theology that would be relevant for the piety of his time. A sincere believing Christian and a famous preacher, he was more a lover of learning that could be used as a tool for better living than an erudite theologian. G. Florovskii characterizes Platon's theology as more catechetical than theological whose "theological doctrine differs little from the vague and moralistic Lutheran emotionalism of the times."[95] He was guided by the Protestant thought of

Quenstedt and Prokopovich. In 1765 he published his most famous and most widely known work: *Pravoslavnoe uchenie ili sokrashchennoe khristianskoe bogoslovie.*[96] Perhaps his fame as an orator and his reputation as counselor to the court enhanced the merits of this work, and it was soon printed in Latin, Greek, French, German, English, Dutch, Armenian and Georgian.

This work is divided into three parts: natural knowledge of God, revelation and finally Christian moral or ethical doctrine. Although he claims that the three devastating heresies in the Christian Church are the "papists, Calvinists and Lutherans" (Part II, ch. 28), nevertheless, as Gass points out, he must be listed among the Lutheranizing theologians of Russia as far as his doctrine on the Church and Sacred Scripture is concerned.[97] He defines the Church simply as a "Congregation of believers in Christ."

Levshin, pastorally orientated as he was, wanted very much to make theology, as taught in the Russian seminaries, not only more intelligible but also more relevant for Russian life. He met the greatest obstacle in achieving this end from the fact that theology was taken still in the 18th century from Western Latin sources, both Roman Catholic and Protestant, but also that theology was being taught in Latin. Russian seminarians could write and speak Latin fluently but could not write Russian. A Latin theology which grew up in other countries and cultures had been transplanted into Russia and hence could never become a living theology.

Other followers of Prokopovich[98] were Gavriil Petrov, rector of the Moscow Academy (d. 1801),[99] Feofilakt Gorskii (d. 1788),[100] Sil'vestr Lebedinskii (d. 1808), rector of the Kazan' Academy,[101] Iakinth Karpinskii (d. 1798) and Iuvenalii Medvedskii (d. 1809); the latter was the first to compose in Russian a scholarly theological system.[102] All these Prokopovian theologians wrote in the spirit of their master and greatly used Protestant sources to develop Prokopovich's doctrines. Almost all dispute Prokopovich's theory of traducianism and teach the traditional Orthodox doctrine on the procession of the Holy Spirit from the Father only, the Eucharist and sacraments in general, as well as the veneration of sacred icons. On justification and their doctrine of the Church they tend more than Prokopovich towards that of the Protestants, using even the same formulas.

Two other importations from the West that colored greatly the religious life, especially of the Russian intelligentsia were Masonry and Western pietism. The ground for receiving the first into Russia was perhaps prepared by the general doubt in the Muscovite administrative circles of Russian society in general that the ancient traditions, especially religious, had given a sufficient measure of resources for successful existence in the new future of industrialization that Peter's reforms had just begun to unfold.[103] Contact with the West shook the educated Russians in their naive chauvinism and old national self-complacency. Kliuchevskii characterizes the mood of the 17th and 18th centuries: "A declining faith in native antiquity and the forces of the people gave way to a despondency, a distrust of the natural capacity which opened wide the door to foreign influence."[104] Through Peter's reforms, a pragmatic utilitarianism infected the money class of Russia with a correspondent loss of religious values. The Masonry of the West, encouraged greatly by Catherine, offered a new religion of material value with a secret ritualism and asceticism that favored philanthropy and a sentimental humanism.

The other Western influence, pietism, flowed also from the diminution of religious values and the stress on a worldly humanism. The more the Russians became absorbed in the material concerns of the world, the more they sought to build up an interior piety based on the quietistic mysticism of the ancient Fathers of the desert, Pseudo-Dionisios, Palamas and the Western mystics, Meister Ekhardt, Arndt, Boehme and Weigel.

Two personages most responsible for integrating the surge of the 18th century towards pietism into a patristic perspective and still open theology to a fresh development were St. Tikhon Zadonsk (1724-1783)[105] and Paisii Velichkovskii (1722-1794).

ST. TIKHON ZADONSK AND PAISII VELICHKOVSKII

St. Tikhon had taught in the Latin School of Novgorod and Tver where he had developed a love not only for the early Greek Fathers but also for such Western writers as Augustine and Arndt. He was consecrated coadjutor bishop of Novgorod and occupied the see of Voronezh for four years when he withdrew to the monastery of Zadonskii where he lived until his death in 1783.

He read constantly Holy Scriptures and the early Fathers and meditated continually on the passion and sufferings of Jesus Christ. He strove towards a social doctrine of mercy towards one's neighbor that stemmed from his asceticism and mystical ethics. His voluminous writings show a great influence from Latin writers, especially in his many Latin expressions as well as a very precise style of writing. He attempted to write theology in terms that flowed out of a personal experience.[106]

Paisii was born in Poltava in the Ukraine and, after spending some time on Mount Athos in assimilating the hesychastic spirituality of the early Byzantine ascetical writers, he settled in Niamezh in Moldavia.[107] He brought back the ancient tradition of the *"starets,"* the spiritual father type of spiritual tradition familiar in Byzantine monasticism. He set up in his new monastery a group of writers and translators who formed an outstanding literary center of theological and ascetical ferment. He translated into Old Slavonic the *Philokalia* that had been compiled from the early hesychastic fathers by the Greek Athonite monk Nikodem and Bishop Makarios of Corinth.[108] This translation which he called *Dobrotoliubie* [*Love of the Good*] brought back again into Russia not only the "Jesus Prayer" but introduced a spirituality that offset the pietism of Aleksandr's age by a solidly Christian, traditional personalism that would initiate in Russia a more patristic theology. His ideas and methods were developed in Russia by Starets Feofan (d. 1829),[109] abbot of Kirillo-Novozerskii monastery, who began a religious movement that resisted the empty "supra-confessional" Christianity fostered by Tsar Aleksandr and Prince Golitsyn.

However, the influence of Tikhon and Paisii was to come only after Russia had felt the pietistic storm of Tsar Aleksandr I (1801-1825). Highly influenced by the Protestant "mystic" of Livonia, Frau von Krudener, Aleksandr and his cortège were introduced to the pietistic mystical writers of Boehme, Fenelon, Madame Guyon, St. Augustine, Swedenborg, Eckartshausen and Jung-Stilling. During the "apocalyptic" months of 1812, Aleksandr saw Napoleon as the beginning of the end. He sought comfort in reading Holy Scripture and the mystical literature that fostered a Protestant type of Christianity.

THE INFLUENCE OF GOLITSYN
AND PROTASOV

This interest in Holy Scripture encouraged his minister and head-procurator of the Holy Synod, Prince A. Golitsyn, to found in 1813 a Russian version of the English Bible Society. He was responsible in 1816 for the translation and publication of the Bible into Russian and all other languages found within the Russian Empire, but, however, there were to be no notes or commentaries. The "pure" word of Holy Scripture was sufficient. This had a great influence in creating a sense of indifference to the traditional Orthodox and

Roman Catholic Churches, while it succeeded in spreading the persuasion that all religions were equal. This tended to separate Christianity from its traditional roots; above all, from its theological heritage as well as from the teaching hierarchy.

Aleksandr accepted also the plan of Golitsyn to reform the seminary educational system in Russia and encharged him with both the supervision of the Holy Synod and the ecclesiastical schools. These latter were a network of schools beginning with the parochial schools through the seminaries and the four academies of St. Petersburg, Moscow, Kiev and Kazan'. Such are known also in the West but this innovation made the seminary no longer a school in which only to prepare priests but rather a cultural center open to any intellectual desirous of living a good Christian life; it was a prefiguring of the Russian universities.

It was not long, however, before the bishops complained about the "secularism" and the vague Christianity that Golitsyn had been introducing into various levels of Church life. Under Tsar Nikolai I (1825-1855) they chose Count Nikolai A. Protasov (1798-1855) to supervise the Holy Synod.[110] From 1836 onwards, Protasov studiously waged a war to eradicate all Protestant tendencies, especially of Prokopovian vintage, from Russian theology. Seeking to return to a more "orthodox" approach to doctrine, he favored the earlier theology of Mogila, Iavorskii and the Kievan Academy of two centuries earlier. He reformed the educational system and in the seminaries for the nebulous Christian culture offered by Golitsyn he substituted a return to the early Church Fathers. He had reprinted Stefan Iavorskii's *Kamen'very* along with the *Confession of Faith* of Peter Mogila and that of Patriarch of Jerusalem, Dositheos, which he had freely distributed to all priests and seminarians. Theologians were encouraged to produce original expositions and in this way he prepared for the classical period of Russian theology as a science that blossomed forth in the second half of the century.

He ordered Filaret Drozdov, metropolitan of Moscow, to compose a new catechism. Filaret (1782-1867) proved to be the most eminent and versatile theologian in the first half of the 19th century.[111] He was first professor of theology at the Academy of Moscow and then rector of St. Petersburg Academy. He became metropolitan of Moscow in 1821. He was an extraordinarily prolific writer. His earlier teaching and writings showed a decided tendency towards the protestantizing theology of Prokopovich and the "cultural" Christianity of Tsar Aleksandr.[112]

Perhaps Protasov sought, in ordering Filaret to compose a catechism, that in such a way he would be able to combat this tendency. Filaret wrote his *Catechism*[113] in 1823 on the order of the Holy Synod which suppressed it immediately, not because of any overt Protestant opinions, but chiefly because of the scandal that arose because Filaret had translated the Creed and the Our Father into the Russian vernacular. The second edition in 1827 was called *Prostranyi Katekhizis [The Expanded Catechism]*. But the current that Protasov had started, of a return to the theology of Mogila, forced Filaret to revise even the doctrine to conform more to that of the earlier Kievan theology. It is this edition, printed in 1839, which became considered as part of the symbolic books of the Orthodox faith by many within the Slavic Churches.[114]

Filaret's *Catechism* follows the general plan used by Mogila. The first part on faith is a commentary on the Nicene-Constantinopolitan Creed; the second on hope develops the Beatitudes while the third on charity discusses the divine commandments. He frequently describes the Church in terms of the Mystical Body of Christ and he accepts Prokopovich's canon of the Old Testament.

Editions in other languages such as Rumanian, Serbian, Bulgarian, Greek and others were soon made and thus provided material not only for commentators but for theologians who wrote compendia by using Filaret's basic doctrines and exposition. Such commentators were A. Gordkov,[115] F. Titov,[116] and A. Tsarevskii.[117]

Filaret's *Catechism* has always enjoyed great authority among the Slavic Churches although even among the Russians N. Barsov[118] and Filaret Gumilevskii criticize it for a lack of precision in formulating basic doctrines. In the universal Orthodox Church it has not been received with any authority as was declared in the Congress of Athens in 1936; and before that the Greeks declared the same in the Lambeth Conference of 1930.

Protasov encouraged the writing of theological compendia, the first of which was written in Russia by Peter Ternovskoi, but it proved to be too brief and superficial.[119] But the first serious treatise of theology in Russia was the manual published by Antonii Amfiteatrov (d. 1879), rector of the Kievan Academy, who published in Kiev in 1848, his *Dogmaticheskoe bogoslovie pravoslavnoi katolicheskoi vostochnoi tserkvi.*[120] It was criticized for its dependence upon Latin Catholic authors such as Libermann, Perrone and Migne.

History records another Filaret whose theological works did not have the authority of Filaret Drozdov's *Catechism* but nonetheless they became the spark for a new liberal and more creative theology of the latter half of the 19th century. Filaret Gumilevskii (d. 1860) taught theology at the Moscow Academy and is known as a church historian as well as a theologian.[121] Filaret wrote a famous history of the Church[122] and strove through his treatise on the Holy Fathers[123] to place the theological doctrines of the Fathers in their historical perspective—an innovation among Russian theologians who until Filaret were content to cite the Fathers, usually from Western textbooks, as a subsidiary proof only for an already formulated thesis.

Protasov requested that he write a compendium which Filaret entitled: *Pravoslavno-dogmaticheskoe bogoslovie.*[124] He shows much more individual thought than his other contemporary theologians. In this work we see his efforts to break away from the static concept of the Church by a greater emphasis on the charismatic working of the Spirit on all levels of the Church, especially in the interpretation of Holy Scripture. Filaret is known also for his twelve volumes on the Saints venerated in the Orthodox Church.[125]

MAKARII BULGAKOV

But the most celebrated theologian of the 19th century and the author of the classical compendium of theology in Russia is Makarii Bulgakov (1816-1883). He studied and taught in Kiev before he was made rector of the St. Petersburg Academy. Besides writing prodigiously in Church history and theology, he performed episcopal duties as bishop of Tambov, Khar'kov, Vil'no and finally as metropolitan of Moscow. His twelve volumes on the history of the Russian Church provided a pioneer study in going back to original fonts. Although Makarii lacks critical originality, his history, aided by the efforts of A. Gorskii who catalogued the ancient manuscripts of the Synodal Library of Moscow, reads often like a mosaic of unending citations.[126]

Makarii's fame rests primarily on his three theological *opera:* his introduction to theology: *Vvedenie v pravoslavnoe bogoslovie;*[127] his dogmatic treatise in five volumes: *Pravoslavnoe dogmaticheskoe bogoslovie;*[128] and his synopsis: *Rukovodstvo k izucheniiu khristianskogo pravoslavno-dogmaticheskogo bogosloviia.*[129] These works established him, not only in Russia but in the entire Slavic, Rumanian and Greek Orthodox world, as the leading theologian.[130]

He was the ideal type sought by Protasov as far as Makarii's orthodoxy went. However, he cannot be classified as an original thinker and both Orthodox and Roman Catholic scholars are agreed that Makarii depended greatly on

Roman Catholic sources such as H. Klee for the history of dogma, and on the theological treatises of P. Perrone as well as Protestant theologians for other areas. His citations of the Fathers often are drawn directly from these Western sources as well as his scholastic method of defending a doctrinal thesis by amassing arguments from holy Scripture, then tradition and finally from human reason.

In spite of the overwhelming success of Makarii's theological compendia throughout all the Orthodox countries, nevertheless, his methodology and thought content were heavily criticized by his fellow Russians. G. Florovskii summarizes well this criticism: "Indeed this intrinsic indifference or detachment in Makarii's books disturbed many even at the very time of their public actions. Khomiakov found Makarii's *"Vvednie"* 'alarmingly stupid' and so also Filaret Gumilevskii passes judgement on him: 'a silly maze,' 'no logical order, no powerful proofs.' About the theological books of Makarii we can say . . . that 'the dogmatic' tract of Makarii has all the appearance of a theological book but it is not theology but only a book'."[131]

Makarii paved the way and the format for a plethora of theological compendia that appeared in the latter half of the 19th century. Among the many authors must be listed the names of N. Favorov,[132] S. Nikitskii,[133] N. Anichkov,[134] A. Kudriavtsev,[135] P. Gorodtsev,[136] A. Rudakov,[137] N. Tikhvinskii,[138] K. Bretkevich,[139] A. Pokrovskii,[140] B. Dobrotovorskii,[141] and I. Vinogradov.[142]

The leading manuals among these many were the two written by Nikolai Malinovskii, rector of the seminary at Podolsk: *Pravoslavnoe dogmaticheskoe bogoslovie* (4 volumes)[143] and his two volume compendium for use in seminaries: *Ocherk pravoslavnogo dogmaticheskogo bogosloviia.*[144]

All books of theology before being printed had to receive the approval of the ecclesiastical censorship of books. A. Kotovich has described the severity of this censorship and how it favored a uniformity in both doctrine and method-

ology.[145] In the first half of the 19th century the official
ecclesiastical censorship refused publication to 46 theological
works while allowing only 82 to be actually printed.

A successor to Protasov who continued his own military
tactics in running the Church was Konstantin Petrovich
Pobedonostsev (1827-1907). For him the medieval Josephite
period of Church in submission to a God-fearing State was
the ideal, and he wished to return to that Church and the
devotion of the masses of the Middle Ages.

NEW DEVELOPMENTS IN THE 19th CENTURY

But in spite of such strong-minded procurators as
Protasov and Pobedonostsev ruling the Church of Russia in
the 19th century there soon developed schools other than
those of official censored policy. Peter Chaadaev published
in 1836 his *First Philosophical Letter* which crystallized the
first tendency: Latinophilism. Chaadaev favored an openness
to Western ideas and saw the Russian Church's salvation
to lie in a greater assimilation into the Latin culture, pietism
and theology of the Roman Catholic Church. He turned
more to France than Germany; he turned to the Roman
Catholic social writers for his ideas because he felt that
Roman Catholicism and socialism were not irreconciable as
they would be adapted, so he thought, in Russia. De Maistre,
but above all, Lamennais, Saint-Simon and Prospère Enfantin
fed ideas to Chaadaev and the other Latinophiles of Russia.[146]

The second new tendency in Russian thought was inspired by the German Romantic idealists such as Kant,
Fichte, Schelling, Oken and finally Hegel. This school of
thought, of the Occidentalists or Westernizers, was not concerned with a renewal of religious life through greater contact with Western thought, but rather looked to the West to
provide Russian thought with a new philosophy.[147] It was
especially the philosophy of Hegel that provided an instru-

ment of revolution against the oppressive regime of Nikolai I for such Russian thinkers as Herzen, Bakunin, Belinskii and Stankevich. The historical dialectic required the total destruction of the present structure of society. Such thinking easily tended to associate the Church and the traditional theological thought with a time past that necessarily had to be plowed under in order that a new age might begin.[148]

The third and more permeating tendency which constituted a reaction to the two preceding currents of thought was that of Slavophilism. The Slavophiles were mainly Russian thinkers imbued equally as the Westernizers with German and French idealism, who, however, sought the future of Russia not in an openness to the West which they considered as totally decadent, but, rather, in a return to the Muscovite ideology of Ivan IV. Everything about Peter the Great and the St. Petersburg society that he and his successors built up was rejected in a fierce chauvinism centered around Moscow. Basically conservative and traditional, the Slavophiles supported the Orthodox Church as synonymous with Russian native culture in opposition to Western Catholicism or Protestantism. Leaders of this movement, such as K. S. Aksakov, I. V. Kireevskii, M. P. Pogodin, F. I. Tiutchev, Iu. Samarin, and A. S. Khomiakov, fought for a spiritual and political isolationism from the contagions of the West by finding in the Slavic culture, especially that of the 16th century Muscovite Russia, the inspiration for all that would make Russia of the 19th century truly great.[149]

ALEKSEI KHOMIAKOV

The outstanding theologian of the Slavophile movement was Aleksei Stepanovich Khomiakov (1804-1860).[150] Without exaggeration Khomiakov can be called the most influential Russian lay theologian of the modern age. Born of middle class landed gentry, Khomiakov ventured into a military career, but he turned to the intellectual pursuits of history, philosophy and theology. Well versed in the writings of the early Fathers, he believed in a return to the unity in love that formed the bond of community in the early Church.

He had travelled widely throughout Europe and knew personally and through letters many of the leading intellectuals of his day. Yet such Western contacts only strengthened his conviction of the corruption of the West and the superiority of Russian culture and thought to that of the rest of Europe.

Khomiakov reacted violently against the Occidentalists' excessive use of Hegelian philosophy and German liberalism, and yet he drew heavily from the German idealism of Schelling who provided him with a mystical philosophy of the spirit which Khomiakov complemented by drawing also from the spiritualism of Cousin, Bordas-Demoulin, F. Ravaison-Mollier and C. Secretan.[151]

Universal history as sketched by Khomiakov is divided into two movements, the force of the principle of spirit and moral freedom, Iran, and the principle of nature and logical necessity, Kush. Kush dominates in the Old Testament and in the West, especially in the Roman Catholic Church, while the Iranian principle typifies Russian Orthodoxy.

Upon these principles, Khomiakov discovers two different ecclesiologies; one typical of the West and the other that of Eastern Orthodoxy. Khomiakov's first development of ecclesiology is found in his dissertation, published only after his death, *Opyt Katekhizicheskogo izlozheniia ucheniia o tserkvi.*[152]

Other leading ecclesiological ideas are found in his *Tserkov' odna* and the French collection, *L'Église latine et le Protestantisme au point de vue de l' Église Orient.* Iuri Samarin, Khomiakov's disciple and editor of his works, defended as Khomiakov's thesis that Iavorskii, typifying the Roman Catholic Church, preached a unity in the Church founded on external authority but having no liberty; Prokopovich, typifying Protestant ecclesiology, strove for internal liberty but lost the visible unity; it was the Russian Orthodox Church that combined (in Hegelian-styled synthesis) both liberty and unity in its ecclesiology.[153]

For Khomiakov, Church unity is achieved through the intrinsic element, immutable and firm which resides in concord of spirit and not in any apparent extrinsic bond. This catholicity or universality he calls by the term attributed thereafter to his form of ecclesiology, *Sobornost'*. He claimed that what SS. Cyril and Methodius had in mind when they translated the Greek word καθολικὴν in the Nicene Symbol by the Slavonic term *Sobornaia* [synodal or conciliar] was not the Roman Catholic sense of geographical extension of the Church over all the world (not καθ' ὅλα), but rather in the intensive sense (καθ' ὅλον).[154] The Church is truly Catholic because *Sobornost'*, a mystical charism of the Holy Spirit, conserves the unity and faith in the Church, not by extrinsic authority, but through the intimate life of the Church shared by all the members.

Infallibility in the Church therefore can never be a prerogative possessed by only one person, the pope, or by a group, the bishops united in an ecumenical council, but it resides, through *Sobornost'* in all the members united together in unity and faith through love. Khomiakov alludes to the Encyclical of 1848 of all Oriental Patriarchs[155] which rejected the invitation of Pope Pius IX for reunion with the Roman Catholic Church as proof that the patriarchs approved of his doctrine, namely, that ecumenical councils, to be valid and obliging upon all, must be received by the whole people of the Church. The following classical text describes Khomiakov's unique position on how *Sobornost'* functions within the Church:

How, therefore, is this to be done, namely, some councils are to be rejected even though they apparently differ in no way from the ecumenical councils? The reason is that their decisions have not been recognized, as they should be, as the voice of the Church by the whole ecclesiastical body, by this people in whom in the question of faith there is no difference between the learned and the ignorant, the ecclesiastic and the layman, man and woman, king and subject, lord and servant among whom, when it is necessary according to the will of God, a youth receives the gift of vision and a boy the word of wisdom and an ignorant shepherd discovers and refutes heresy held by his own learned bishop in order that all may be one in the free unity of a lived faith which is the manifestation of the Spirit of God. This dogma has been placed as the foundation of the very idea of a council.[156]

Much truth is mixed with false teaching in Khomiakov's ecclesiology, which clearly went against the traditional teaching among the Orthodox on the Church. It is true that the Church is a community of unity in liberty and love. But to achieve this Khomiakov denies, through an exaggerated opposition between internal and external authority, all hierarchical teaching authority in the Church. It is also true that in the Church not only bishops are obligated to defend the faith from heresy and error, but each baptized member. But Khomiakov's denial of a *magisterium,* authentically instituted by Christ in His Church as distinct from the laity, clearly negates eighteen centuries of Christian tradition. His ultimate criterion that conciliar decrees are infallible only when they have been received by the faithful fails to serve as a criterion because of its vagueness and its impossibility of being applied.[157]

Khomiakov's doctrine, especially of eccleciology, caused great dissent in Russia. His works were censored and were allowed to be printed in Russia only in 1879, but with due warning to the readers that Khomiakov's works contain errors, due to Khomiakov's lack of education in theological matters.[158] In 1894, theologian Akvilonov along with P. Svetlov sought to establish Khomiakov as an officially approved Russian theologian. Other more traditional theologians as well as those of the Westernizing tendency who opposed in general the Slavophiles fought against Khomiakov's basic idealistic principles which denied the ancient traditional teaching of the Orthodox Church on the teaching hierarchy and the visible structure of the Church. Through the following century theologians such as Florenskii, Bulgakov, Florovskii, Zenkovskii, Grabbe, Berdiaev, Karsavin, Kartashev, Arseniev, and Zankov have taught a moderate Khomiakovian position that sought to reconcile the traditional ecclesiology with the main lines of Khomiakov's thought.

Among the Greek Orthodox Khomiakov's theology was ignored at first for the most part. Reacting against an overly patronizing hierarchy, some theologians sought a measure of democracy and appealed to Khomiakov's ideas, for example, in the first Congress of Orthodox Theologians in Athens in 1936, as Balanos, Bratsiotis and Alivisatos demonstrated. Dyovuniotis and Trempelas remained staunch opponents of Khomiakov's innovating ideas.

VLADIMIR SOLOV'EV AND SOPHIOLOGY

Vladimir Sergeevich Solov'ev (1853-1900) became the moving force in the second half of the 19th century in Russia to counteract both the nebulous, unstructured theology of Khomiakov and the mounting influence of Marxist materialism. He himself had passed through various stages of becoming atheistic in his teens through the reading of the lives of Christ by Strauss and Renan, then materialistic and nihilistic through the writings of Buchner and Pisarev.

During his Moscow University years he underwent a religious crisis which created in him an interest in mysticism and theosophy. From 1881 to 1891 he moved gradually away from Khomiakov and the narrow religious and nationalistic views of the Slavophiles to search for a *"Weltanschauung"* that would provide a unity of the human race in a pan-theocracy. He read and traveled widely and was deeply influenced by Comte's philosophy as well as the religious philosophies of Spinoza, Schopenhauer, von Hartmann, Schelling, Hegel and the mystical writings of Jacob Boehme, von Baader and the seventeenth century English mystic, John Pordage.

He reports that at the age of nine and later in London and again in Egypt he had visions of the divine woman, whom he later called *Sophia,* who gradually became for Solov'ev the feminine principle of cosmic unity. Influenced by Boehme's feminine principle and Comte's goddess, the *"vierge positive"* of humanity as well as the traditional Byzantine sapiential principle of wisdom permeating all of reality, Solov'ev developed the beginnings of the mystical philosophy called *Sophiology.* We will summarize its basic tenets in dealing with the writings of S. Bulgakov. Solov'ev in his lectures on the humanity of God, found in the third part of his most famous work, *La Russie et l'Église universelle,* describes *Sophia* as a woman of singular beauty, his eternal friend. She is the unity produced in the divine body of Christ; the created unity, the principle, uniting and giving meaning to humanity. *Sophia* is the "idea which God has before Him as Creator and which He realizes in His creation."[159] Again he describes her as the ideal, perfect humanity that is found from eternity in the mind of God that includes Christ as the fulfillment of the created order.

Man's quest and activity on this earth should consist in realizing this union between *Sophia* and the world through the principle of *vseedinstvo,* the "all-unity" which pervades God's created world. Christ's mission through His humanity is to effect the union between God and man, not by any abstract thought but by the concrete attraction to the *Sophia* in Christ, i.e. to His beauty and goodness and harmony that reflect perfectly the mind of God.

Preoccupied with what man must do to effect the "all-unity" in the world around him, Solov'ev became ever more persuaded of the necessity of an ultimate authority in the universal Church, which led him to defend explicitly papal primacy in his tracts, *The Great Dispute and Christian Polity* (1883) and *The History and Future of Theocracy* (1884).[160] In 1896 he made a confession and profession of faith to a Roman Catholic priest, and yet he considered himself as not leaving the Orthodox Church but as entering into the fullness of the universal Church by joining together the traditions of the Christian East and the West. He maintained that the two Churches, the Orthodox and the Roman Catholic, had remained mystically united despite the extrinsic, legalistic separation. Even this estrangement would be overcome, Solov'ev taught, if both sides, East and West, would be convinced that each had something to learn from the other.

He sought a new Christian era which would come about through Christ's three earthly vicars: the Tsar, the Pope and the Prophets within the Church. The Tsar would be the ideal for all rulers, the Pope would unify the Church and the Prophets would hold out the echatological unity of the world to come. Not through coercion but through man's freedom to discover through *Sophia* the "all-unity" would unity come about.

Solov'ev played a leading role in reviving idealism in Russian theological thought as a respectable philosophical framework in which to form a theology of union, not only of the Eastern and Western Churches but of the entire human race. Those influenced by Solov'ev, especially by his theory of *Sophia*, were Pavel Florenskii (d. 1943), Petr Struve (d. 1944), the two brothers, Sergei and Evgenii

Trubetskoi (d. 1905, d. 1920), the Symbolist poets, especially V. Ivanov (d. 1949) and the philosophers, N. Berdiaev (d. 1948), L. Karsavin (d. 1952) and Antonii Kartashev (d. 1960).

Florenskii places spiritual beauty as the criterion of truth which for him is Solov'ev's *Sophia*.[161] He likens *Sophia* to a "fourth hypostasis" which participates in the life of the Holy Trinity. From its relationship to the hypostasis of the Father, *Sophia* is the ideal substance, the foundation of all creatures, the power and force of their existence. In relation to the hypostasis of the Son it is reason, meaning, truth, justice of any given creature. Considered in relationship to the hypostasis of the Holy Spirit, it is spirituality, sanctity, purity, integrity, the beauty of every creature. More concretely, as seen in the salvific order, *Sophia* analogously is the body or the individual humanity of Christ; or again it is His social body, the Church; and finally, it refers within the Church to that creature who mirrored forth most perfectly virginal beauty, Mary, the Mother of God.

It is Sergii Bulgakov who, after Solov'ev, is most directly linked with the thought-structure of Sophiology. At first he wrote in a philosophical strain about Sophiology[162] and later, after having been deported in 1922 from Russia and having begun to teach theology at Saint Sergius Orthodox Seminary in Paris, he developed it into a theological system.[163]

Bulgakov associated *Sophia* with the substance of God, shared equally by all three divine Persons. *Sophia* is the same as the idea of God, the eternal prototype of the created world that exists in the mind of God. Accused by his ecclesiastical superiors of introducing into God a fourth hypostasis,[164] he distinguished between *hypostasis* and *"hypostaseitas,"* i.e. personification. *Sophia* in Bulgakov's system appears both as an intermediate between God and creatures and as identical both with God and with creatures. It possesses a "double face," one turned towards God as the image of God and the other turned toward the world and hence the eternal foundation of the world. Bulgakov argues from Russian iconography, especially citing the three icons found in Iaroslavl', Kiev, and Novgorod: "In the beauty of nature as in the works of art, we feel the world being transfigured in time. We feel *Sophia* appears through beauty, and by means of this beauty and love for it man is elevated to the world of eternal ideas."[165]

Sophiology as a system had received great criticism both within and outside of Orthodoxy. Any intuitional method always lacks clarity in terms. This vagueness in using words, especially the key word, *Sophiology,* led to a misunderstanding that Solov'ev and Bulgakov were holding either pantheism or a position that held four hypostases in the Trinity. Yet they insist that they avoid pantheism, that Sophiology is a *"pan-en-theism"*—God in all things, to use Solov'ev's expression. One strong point in the system of Sophiology is the unity given to the relationship of God and His cosmos through the recapitulating concept of *Wisdom* whereby, through the unfolding of divine energy in the creative world, God's idea of creation unfolds gradually in the creative order and thus a unity is effected by means of this energizing wisdom that is both in God and in creatures at the same time.

THEOLOGICAL JOURNALS IN THE 19th CENTURY

A very productive medium for advancing theological thought in Russia reached its peak in the second half of the 19th century, namely, the theological journals. The most important of these were published by the four theological academies of St. Petersburg, Moscow, Kiev, and Kazan'. The earliest to appear was the *Khristianskoe Chtenie* [Christian Reading], first published in 1821 in St. Petersburg.[166] Originally a quarterly, it contained a vast collection of articles on Church history and Russian theology, especially of the

19th century. *Pravoslavnyi Sobesednik* [*Orthodox Lecturer*] was begun in 1855 on the request of Protasov to the archbishop of Kazan' to publish a journal that would counteract the Old Believers. It has specialized studies on Islamic culture, history and theology besides important works on the Old Believers.[167]

The Academy of Kiev began publishing its journal, *Trudy* [*Works*] in 1860 which specialized in the Orthodox and Roman Catholic history of Western Russia.[168] Moscow Academy began in 1892 the publication of *Bogoslovskii Vestnik* [*Theological Messenger*], which enjoyed the reputation of not only being the most serious theological periodical but also the most adventuresome in writing about Russian culture and religious reforms. It became the *bête noire* of the censorship and of the more rigidly Orthodox partisans.

In 1943 the same Academy of Moscow launched a quarterly *Pribavleniia k tvoreniiam sv. otets v russkom perevodie* [*Additions to the Works of the Holy Fathers in Russian Translation*], which more than any other source gave an impetus to a renaissance in patristic studies. Each of the above-mentioned journals from time to time produced important monumental patristic supplements. *Khristianskoe Chtenie* produced translations of the Greek Fathers and published them as supplements while *Trudy* specialized in the Latin Fathers. The Academy of Kazan' published the Acts of the ecumenical councils and particular synods of general ecclesiastical importance. Under the general title of *"Pamiatniki drevnerusskoi dukhovnoi pis'mennosti"* [*Monuments of Ancient Russian Ecclesiastical Literature*], it also published a rich collection of old Slavonic texts of the lives of Saints, letters of bishops, discourses and polemical works, especially those of Maxim the Greek.

Under the leadership and scholarship of Professor Nikolai Nikolvskii the Academy of St. Petersburg in 1906 published invaluable documents from early Russian thinkers in the collection *Materialy dlia povremennogo spiska russkikh pisatelei i inkh sochinenii.*[169]

There were other influential journals in the field of Orthodox theology besides those directed by the theological academies. The Holy Synod had its official organ, *Tserkhovnye Vedomosti [Ecclesiastical Notices].*[170] *Tserkovnyi Vestnik [Ecclesiastical Messenger]* was published in St. Petersburg beginning in 1875 and was directed to the interests and continued the theological education of the diocesan priests. Other journals that sought to promote a more contemporary relevant theology were the *Strannik [Traveler]*, *Tserkovnyi Golos [Ecclesiastical Voice]* and *Zvonar' [Bell-Ringer]*. Khar'kov's most famous theological contribution was in its philosophical and theological journal called *Vera i Razum [Faith and Reason]*, begun in 1884. It contained outstanding articles on the history of Russian theological and philosophical thought.

THE ORTHODOX THEOLOGICAL ENCYCLOPEDIA

An important contribution to Russian theology was the launching in 1900, under the editorship of A. Lopukhin, of the Orthodox theological encyclopedia *Pravoslavnaia bogoslavskaia Entsiklopediia.* P. A. Alekseev (d. 1801) had much earlier prepared the way by his theological dictionary, *Tserkovnyi Slovar',*[171] the first of its kind in Russian theological thought. Upon the death of Lopukhin in 1905, N. Glubokovskii took direction of the encyclopedia and gave it a more scholarly orientation. This work contains thirteen volumes but due to the First World War and the Russian Revolution Glubokovskii was unable to finish it. Although it never reached the quality of other European theological encyclopedias such as the French *Dictionnaire de Théologie catholique* or the *Kirchenlexicon* of Fribourg, nevertheless, it assembled invaluable articles on Biblical, historical, theological, canonical, liturgical and homiletic themes written by the foremost Russian theologians at the turn of the century.

THE NEW SCHOOLS OF THEOLOGIANS

The great influence of historical and Biblical criticism as well as the liberal theology from German universities upon Russian theological thought gradually produced a school of liberal theologians who were quite different from the Orthodoxy of the Makarii-type compendia as well as from the non-traditional Slavophilism of Khomiakov. Greater contact also with Old Catholics and Anglicans who avidly sought union with the Russian Orthodox opened these liberal theologians to new examinations of traditional Orthodox theological positions.

A turning point for this new school of liberal theologians was effected at the Bonn Conference of 1874 and 1875. Although little concrete results followed by way of creating a union among the Old Catholics, the Anglicans and the Orthodox who attended, nevertheless, it ignited a movement of controversial writings about the *Filioque* and the concept of unity in the Church. Ivan L. Ianyshev, professor of moral theology at St. Petersburg Academy, was one of the leading participants at Bonn and continued his interest to effect a rapprochement with the Old Catholics and the Anglicans,[172] along with amateur theologian, General A. Kireev and Church historian, V. V. Bolotov.

In 1892 the St. Petersburg Commission was appointed by the Holy Synod to deal with the dogmatic questions raised by the Old Catholics. Bolotov opposed strongly the rigid position of the Commission, especially in regard to its denunciation of the Roman Catholic teaching of the *Filioque*. Bolotov's work on the *Filioque* was first published in Germany under the patronage of A. Kireev and later appeared in Russia.[173] In this work the author distinguishes the terms *dogma, theologoumenon* and *theological opinion.* He maintains that the teaching of the Holy Spirit proceeding from the Father [ἐκ Πατρὸς] is dogma. It is a *theologoumenon,* taught by the majority of the early Greek Fathers that the Spirit proceeds from the Father through the Son [διά]. The position of Roman Catholics and Old Catholics that the Holy Spirit also proceeds from the Son [*Filioque*] is for Bolotov a mere theological opinion. The West can hold it and still be united with the Orthodox East as long as all hold in unity dogmas enunciated in the first seven ecumenical councils. Bolotov emphatically denies the 9th century position of Photios that the Spirit proceeds *only* from the Father as being against the universal testimony of the Holy Fathers.

The period of the latter decades of the 19th century up to the 1917 Russian Revolution must be considered as one of the most productive times in the history of Orthodox thought. A brief summary of the main theologians and their works during this period, therefore, must be presented.[174] Of all the areas developed in the second half of the 19th century by Russian theology, dogmatic theology remained the weakest in originality and depth. The professional theologians of this period were still influenced greatly by Protestantism and showed this attraction in a greater preference for Biblical exegesis, church history, patrology and canon law rather than speculative theology. Courses that touched dogma were taught in the seminaries as separate courses of dogmatic, moral, fundamental, pastoral and polemical theology. The basic dogmatic truths covered in such courses followed generally those treated in the *Catechism* of Filaret Drozdov.

Besides the dogmatic compendia already cited above of Makarii, Filaret and Sil'vestr Malevanskii, other writers who composed dogmatic compendia were N. Malinovskii, noted for his patristic citations as well as those of Russian writers,[175]

Antonii Amfiteatrov,[176] N. Favorov,[177] K. Bretkevich,[178] B. Dobrotvorskii,[179] T. Sigonskii,[180] and Ivan Sokolov.[181]

The common characteristics of such compendia only reflect what has been already said about Makarii's manual. They constituted basically works of classification and unification of all dogmatic material into a systematic presentation. The common basic weakness is their strong scholastic apriorism and bookish dryness, removing dogmas from the living Christian experience.

A reaction movement developed in Russian dogmatic theology at this time in the specific area of soteriology. Archpriest Pavel Svetlov (1861-1942) developed as a reaction to the compendists' legalistic presentation of redemption the soteriological lines found earlier in the writings of Khomiakov. In his tract on redemption[182] Svetlov insists that redemption must not be conceived according to the limitations of human reason. He insists that the redemption flowing from the Cross must be interpreted not in juridical terms but in terms of the infinite love of God for men. Metropolitan Sergii Staragorodskii (later patriarch of Moscow, 1943-1944)[183] and Metropolitan Antonii Khrapovitskii pursued this thinking more radically in their attempts to eliminate all trace of juridicism from soteriology. They insisted strongly on the subjective and moral application to human living of the Redeemer's sacrifice. Khrapovitskii goes so far as seemingly to deny an objective redemption, that is, the satisfaction and merits of Christ, independent of man's individual response in love to Christ.[184]

Influenced by the *kenosis* found in the writings of Feodor Dostoevskii, theologians such as V. Ekzempliarskii,[185] and A. Vvedenskii,[186] by their "genetic method," strove to present dogmatic truths both as speculative as well as living truths. Dogmas are a divine response to a human exigency which the Church recognizes in Holy Scripture and tradition. Moving this development further, V. Nikolskii[187] and F. Golubinskii[188] interpret, as did P. Florenskii much earlier, living experience as the unique means of dogmatic expression. The Orthodox faith shows itself by its life, not by any rational, dogmatic statement. The kingdom of God is reached not by rational means of our own concepts but rather through true Orthodox experience wherein God manifests Himself in His intimate existence and redemptive actions.

Still a strong need was felt for the manual type of dogmatic statements in order to defend Orthodoxy from the Western Christian confessions as well as from the Russian Old Believers. In 1884 a course of apologetics was introduced into the curriculum of theological seminaries aimed at the Old Believers and the Western Christian bodies. Thus a group of Russian theologians at the turn of the century began to write books of apologetics, especially in an attempt to preserve Russian Orthodoxy from the innovations of Roman Catholicism, e.g. the declaration in 1854 of the Immaculate Conception of the Mother of God and in 1870 of the infallibility of the Roman pope. Archimandrite Augustin and I. Nikolin wrote works that were widely used throughout Russia as well as did A. A. Lebedev,[189] P. Svetlov, A. M. Ivantsov-Platonov, N. Beliaev and A. Gusev.

Moral and ascetical theology developed as a theological science complementing at first dogma in the writings of the "scholastic" orientated theologians.[190] But under the strong reaction to make dogmatic theology a living experience in the daily life-response of individuals, I. Ianychev represents a breakthrough. He was the first to study the notion of morality and its elements in relation to human nature, tying it up with man's supreme good, salvation, as wrought through the person of Jesus Christ.[191] M. Olesnitskii enlarged upon Ianychev's central idea of the Kingdom of God alone being capable of giving to moral good its total plenitude.[192] This life of morality studied from the ascetical viewpoint of a daily struggle to acquire virtues was synthesized chiefly by Professors P. Ponomarev and S. Zarin.[193]

Scriptural exegesis in Russia of this period showed mainly

a great dependence upon that of German and English scholars and remained by and large only an elaboration of these foreign importations. Biblical exegesis, however, as taught in the seminaries remained rigidly traditional. One specific problem concerned the authority of the Septuagint Greek over the Masoretic Hebrew text. This became acute between 1858 and 1875 when a translation into Russian was being produced. Some theologians as P. Gorskii-Platonov admitted only the Hebrew text while others as V. Myshtsyn and Feofan Gonorov (Zatvornik) rejected the Masoretic text and preferred the Septuagint Greek version as more authentic, for they held that the Hebrew text had been corrupted by succeeding generations of Jewish scholars to cover over the evident Messianism in the Old Testament. The manner of writing Hebrew without punctuation and vowels, they felt, also facilitated arbitrary interpretation. Filaret Drozdov laid down the fundamental principles that were to guide Russian theologians in this matter up to the present time: (1) the Septuagint has a dogmatic value at times equal, at times superior, to the Hebrew text; (2) however, respect for the Septuagint must not allow one to neglect the Hebrew text which also enjoys great authority; (3) in order to preserve intact the full meaning of the original text, severe rules of hermeneutics are needed.[194] Thus both the Hebrew text and the Greek Septuagint equally enjoy great authority but in Messianic passages, greater value is attributed to the Septuagint from the tradition of the Church and arguments of reason.

Bishop Porfirii Uspenskii (d. 1885) began a translation into Russian from the Greek text but his work was never finished even though P. A. Iugerov succeeded in completing the translation of the Deutero-canon, the prophets and Genesis. Any new Slavonic editions usually have been made from the so-called Bible of Elizabeth, prepared in the time of Peter the Great and printed in 1751. But there exists to date no truly critical study of the entire Bible. Scholars, such as A. Gorskii, K. Nevostroev, G. Voskresenskii, I. Iakimov, V. Lebedev, A. Mikhailov, and I. Evseev, have worked on a commission established in St. Petersburg in 1915 to pour over the more than 4,000 Slavonic manuscripts of the Old Testament and an even more numerous collection of New Testament versions in an attempt to produce a definitive Slavonic text. Stopped by the Revolution, they succeeded to produce only six books of the Old Testament and three of the New.

The consistent traditionalism in Russian theology came forward in this period as a reaction to Protestant influences to create a patristic renaissance. Archimandrite Porfirii Popov and A. Lebedev struggled to establish the authority of the Holy Fathers as constituting a general voice of tradition to serve as a sure guide in theological development. But it was Archbishop Filaret Gumilevskii who saved patrology in Russian theological thought from becoming an auxiliary science to function merely as a repetitor of static, outdated patristic theology. He held in his three volume monumental work on the Holy Fathers[195] that they commanded special authority in theology because of the unique role they played both in exposing the purity of faith in their theological speculation as well as in their personal piety which were both fed by their interpretation of Holy Scripture.

LAY THEOLOGIANS

In the latter part of the 19th century Russian theology also benefited from the insights of lay theologians. These men were not theologians by profession or training but were, like the first Slavophiles, inclined by their literary pursuits and also by their own dispositions towards theological questions. V. V. Rozanov (1856-1919), like L. Tolstoi, was primarily a philosopher, a writer and literary critic. Attracted to theology by his great love for Dostoevskii's writings,

Rozanov highlighted the problem of spiritual freedom as the key to Dostoevskii's theological ideas. Rozanov also was very much preoccupied with the problem of sex which he understood as a mystical experience that demanded to be sanctified. From such interests he developed views on a "naturalistic" religion that differed greatly from his native Orthodoxy. He also wrote on the relationship of Christianity to the modern world; yet in this area his answers were not too successful. His writings, due to equivocal views on the Orthodox Church, made him suspect to Russian religious leaders.[196]

D. S. Merezhkovskii, like Rozanov, was a writer (poet and novelist) and a literary critic. By writing historical fiction he developed his new religious thought by synthesizing classical pagan religious ideas with those of Christianity. The faith of flesh meets the faith of the spirit, as he expresses it in his trilogy entitled *Khristos i Antikhrist*.[197]

THE REVOLUTION AND THE EMIGRATION

When the crack of the bullet brought down the last Russian Tsar on July 16, 1918 at Ekaterinburg, the Russian Revolution of the proletariat masses was declared a *fait accompli*. The revolutionists under Lenin who swept away the Kerenskii regime had also declared an end to theological speculation and religious education. But before January 20, 1918, when the Council of Commissaries of the People had approved the decree with its "separation of Church and State and the separation of schools from Church," the Communist Party allowed a modicum of freedom to the Russian Orthodox Church before it snuffed out all religious freedom.

This fleeting flash of Church freedom from the tentacles of the *ancien régime* allowed the Russian Church to hold the Moscow Synod from August 15, 1917 until August, 1918. The patriarchate was re-established and Metropolitan Tikhon of Moscow was elected patriarch. A new constitution for the Church was drawn up that allowed bishops to be elected by the dioceses along with greater laity participation both on parish and diocesan councils as well as in the higher administration of the patriarchate.

But once the decree of 1918 enforced separation of schools from Church influence, all religious instructions in both public and private schools came to a halt. Seminaries were closed from 1918 until 1944. The Bolsheviks deported or put into prison the theological thinkers who were reckoned by the atheists as the most dangerous thinkers, obstructing the building of a completely classless society.

Some of the best thinkers escaped to European centers of learning where they were well received by groups interested in unionistic plans or in Eastern Christianity as such. Russian theologians soon took up their usual academic life as before the Revolution; but now instead of the theological academies and seminaries of Russia, they lectured and wrote in Berlin, Prague, Warsaw, Munich, Paris, London and finally in America.

It would be untrue to say that these émigré theologians continued the traditional theology of Russia in the late 19th century. No longer subjected to the rigid censorship of the fatherland, their new-found intellectual liberty opened these thinkers to develop more original systems of theological thought. Not only did Western thinkers find a charm in their writings but the Russian émigrés also were exposed personally to new ideas and approaches of Western scholars that before were learned only through the medium of short written accounts. Cut off from a juridical ecclesiastical structure that controlled theological speculation and writing, these theologians now in Western Europe developed the ideas that they had earlier inherited from Khomiakov, Dostoevskii and Solov'ev. The doctrine of Khomiakov on *Sobornost'* mingled with an emphasis on St. John's mysticism gave their writings a great popularity among Roman Catholic, Protestant and

Anglican circles where the sword of Peter hung too heavily already after Vatican Council I.

Nikolai A. Berdiaev (1874-1948) proved to be an outstanding figure of the Russian lay intellectual émigré. After deportation in 1922 by the Soviets, he first carried on his intellectual activities in Berlin where he founded the anti-Communist *Religious Philosophical Society*. He moved to Paris in 1924 and published the theological-philosophical journal *Put'* (1925-1940). He was active in ecumenical conversations with Orthodox, Protestant and Roman Catholics, although he was more a "left" in regard to the traditional Russian theological positions of the Orthodox Church. His religious thought was very eclectic, combining ideas from Alexandrian gnosticism, medieval exemplarism, Lowland mysticism, German romanticism and idealism along with the eschatological emphasis of 19th century Russian thought. Rebelling against the stultifying effects of excessive logic and Western rationalism, he expressed his apocalyptic vision of the future Kingdom of God in prophetic and mystical language.[198]

A center of émigré Orthodoxy developed in Sremski-Karlovtzy on the Danube in Yugoslavia where Metropolitan Antonii Khrapovitskii of Kiev had gathered a group of exiled bishops together to form the Russian Synodal Church in Exile. This group claimed to be the sole representative of the true Russian Orthodox Church. Any other group outside of Russia not accepting its authority was labeled schismatic. The Synodal Church has produced no leading theologians, restricted by its rigid conservatism and refusal to encounter the West.

Most of the leading Russian émigré theologians in Bulgaria, Germany, Yugoslavia and Czechoslovakia gradually migrated to Paris where Metropolitan Evlogii, exarch of the Ecumenical Patriarch for Russian Orthodox Churches in Western Europe, opened the renowned St. Sergius Institute. Evlogii had been named in 1921 by Patriarch Tikhon as metropolitan for Western Europe but soon refused to recognize Tikhon's authority as well as that of the Karlovtzy Synod. He was then accepted under the patronage of the patriarch of Constantinople.

In 1925 Metropolitan Evlogii, as rector, opened the *Orthodox Theological Institute* in Paris which, until the Moscow Academy was reopened in 1944, was the only Russian theological academy of university level in the world and surely the first completely free Russian theological academy in history.[199]

It was not founded by the Holy Synod as other academies in Russia had been but by the émigré Russian society in Paris. Hence it devoted itself to academic freedom as well as to the promulgation of the liberal ideas that formulated the post-Revolution constitution of the Church in Russia which unfortunately had remained a mere dream under the Soviets. Soon an outstanding faculty was teaching, writing and in general making an impact upon not only Orthodox in the New World but upon other leading Christian groups. A list of the professors who over the decades distinguished themselves at St. Sergius would necessarily include Sergii Bulgakov, Bishop Kassian (Bezobrazov), Archimandrite Kiprian (Kern), George Fedotov, Georges Florovskii, V. N. Il'in, A. V. Kartashev, P. Kovalevskii, K. Mochulskii, F. G. Spasskii, V. P. Vysheslavtsev, V. V. Weidlé, L. A. Zander, V. V. Zenkovskii, N. Afanas'ev, A. Kniazev, B. I. Sove, S. Verkhovskoi, A. Schmemann, and J. Meyendorff.

Bulgakov (1871-1944) easily stands out as the leading intellectual and spiritual force sparking St. Sergius. His doctrine on sophiology has already been mentioned. He had been a leading layman in the Moscow *Sobor* of 1917-18 and was ordained priest shortly after. Exiled to the Crimea by the Communists, he fled to Prague and finally in 1925 to Paris where he became the first dean of St. Sergius. He taught dogmatic theology and interpreted traditional beliefs in a most original, liberal way, influenced as he was by the

Sophiology, of Solov'ev and Florenskii as well as by German idealism. His lecturing and writing soon made him a *cause célèbre* in the Russian Orthodox world. Metropolitan Antonii of Karlovtzy denounced him in 1924 as heretical, and in 1927 Antonii issued a letter condemning the "modernism" both of Bulgakov and the faculty of St. Sergius. Sergii, metropolitan of Moscow, also condemned Bulgakov in 1935, and the Bulgarian Archbishop Serafim published a large work against Bulgakov's *Sophia* doctrine. Bulgakov defended his theories before Evlogii, declaring his belief in all the dogmas taught by Orthodoxy and affirming his theories as personal interpretations of dogmas.

Bulgakov was a most prolific writer, producing a great number of creative, speculative, theological works that have been unequaled by any Orthodox writer in modern times.[200] His main theological works are: *The Burning Bush, The Friend of the Bridegroom* and *Jacob's Ladder,* which form his small trilogy (1927-29); *The Lamb of God, The Comforter* and *The Bride of the Lamb* make up his large trilogy (1933-46).

One of the outstanding theological contributions of the faculty of St. Sergius was in the area of ecumenism. These Russian theologians were among the participants of all the important ecumenical gatherings in Europe beginning with the first meeting of the *Life and Work Conference* called at Stockholm by the pioneer of the ecumenical movement, Archbishop Söderbloom. Father Georges Florovskii, especially, along with Bishop Kassian and L. Zander, represented St. Sergius and the Russian Church since no participation was possible by theologians within Soviet Russia. They took a leading part in the Oxford and Edinburgh Conferences of 1937 and in the initial conference of the World Council of Churches in Amsterdam in 1948.

The Parisian theologians also took a leading role in the first Conference of Orthodox Theologians from the academies of Bulgaria, Greece, Yugoslavia, Poland, Rumania and Paris who met to discuss Orthodox theology in the light of modern developments.[201]

A leading modern theologian who has had great influence in developing the ecclesiology of many young theologians of St. Sergius was Archpriest Nikolai Afanas'ev (d. 1966). In a reaction against the "universal" ecclesiology of the Roman Catholic Church, he developed his "Eucharistic" ecclesiology.[202] He maintains in his writings that a "universal ecclesiology" is found in the writings of St. Cyprian and consequently in the practice of Roman Catholicism which stress the authority and power of bishops and the importance of councils leading eventually to papal infallibility. Eucharistic ecclesiology begins with the local church found in all its fullness in the Eucharistic celebration by the bishop who presides over the church in love. The local Eucharistic assembly is not a part of the Body of Christ; it is the fullness of the Body. All churches are hence fundamentally equal and preeminence is gained not by exercise of power or authority of one church over others but by merit through services in love of others. Afanas'ev, in his exclusive stress placed upon the Khomiakovian principle of *Sobornost'*, departed from the traditional Orthodox teaching on the hierarchy and its authority, especially as exercised in the collegiality of an infallible ecumenical council.

Archpriest Georges Florovskii, one of the best known modern Orthodox theologians both in Europe and America, represents the link of Russian Orthodox theology from Europe to the United States. Born in Odessa in 1893, he studied at the University of Odessa and taught philosophy there for a short time. He emigrated to Prague in 1920 and finally in 1926 to Paris where he taught patristics at St. Sergius Institute. He was ordained priest in 1936 and in 1948 he moved to New York where he taught theology and patristics at the newly opened St. Vladimir's Orthodox Seminary where he became Dean. He founded the *St. Vladimir Seminary Quarterly* that has had great influence in Orthodox theological circles in the West. For several years he taught at Harvard as well as Princeton Universities. It can safely be said that from the beginning of ecumenical encounters Father Florovskii has been the leading Russian participant, playing an active, creative role in Amsterdam (1948), Evanston (1954) and New Delhi (1961) Conferences.

His most important works were written in the 1930's and include his monumental work, *Puti russkogo bogosloviia* [*The Ways of Russian Theology*], a widely ranging and penetrating study of not only the history of Russian theology but of Russian intellectual history giving a most thorough bibliography on this subject.[203] Florovskii's great contribution to Russian theology, especially in the context of modern Western life, has been to present the traditional Orthodox teachings on the basis of patristic traditions and in the spirit of the early Fathers. Resisting a blind fidelity to past traditions, he has defined tradition in these words: "Loyalty to tradition means not only concord with the past but in a certain sense freedom from the past. Tradition is not only a protecting, conservative principle, it is primarily the principle of growth and regeneration... Tradition is the constant abiding of the Spirit, and not only the memory of words. Tradition is a charismatic, not an historical principle."[204]

Like the formation of St. Sergius, St. Vladimir's Seminary in New York soon attracted not only Orthodox seminarians from Churches other than the Russian Orthodox, but also professors from other seminaries, especially those in Europe. Besides Georges Florovskii, Professors Nicholas Arseniev, Alexander Schmemann, John Meyendorff and Serge Verhovskoy moved from St. Sergius to St. Vladimir's Seminary.

As dean, Archpriest Schmemann did much to establish St. Vladimir's as a pan-Orthodox seminary for America. His energetic appearances before Roman Catholic and Protestant university groups, along with his direct involvement in the

World and National Council of Churches, as well as serving as an observer to Vatican Council II, have established him as one of the leading ecumenists in the New World. Besides his historical work, *The Historical Road of Eastern Orthodoxy*,[205] Father Schmemann has been mostly preoccupied with translating the spiritual riches of the Byzantine Liturgy and the Eastern sacraments into theological language relevant for modern Christians.[206]

One of the leading young Orthodox theologians in the West is Father John Meyendorff. Born of Russian parents in France, he completed his theological training at St. Sergius Institute and the Sorbonne. After teaching Church History and patristics at St. Sergius, he began his American career of teaching at St. Vladimir's Orthodox Seminary as well as at Columbia and Fordham Universities.

Although he has become a leading spokesman of the Orthodox position in both national and international ecumenical groups, Father Meyendorff still must be rated as one of the scholars who effected in the West a renaissance in the study of Gregory Palamas (d. 1359). His doctoral dissertation, *An Introduction to the Study of Gregory Palamas*[207] was the first full length treatment of the historical Palamine controversy and an attempt to interpret the theological teaching of Palamas to contemporary readers. He also edited in two volumes and translated the important work of Palamas on the defense of the hesychast saints.[208]

Other Russian scholars in Europe also contributed to this renewal in interest of the theology of St. Gregory Palamas. Even before the Russian Revolution, a shortlived doctrinal controversy in 1912-1913 developed on Mount Athos and spread finally to Russia itself. Certain Russian monks of the Athonite monastery of St. Panteleimon insisted that in the traditional hesychastic invocation of the Jesus Prayer, the invoked name became Jesus Himself. This controversy continued in Russia until it was condemned by the Holy Synod in 1913 and disappeared.

But the key ideas of Palamas' ascetical and theological doctrine were propagated in a more positive way in the West by such Russian scholars as Vasilii Krivoshein, Archbishop of the Moscow Patriarchate for Western Europe,[209] Kiprian Kern,[210] Vladimir Losskii,[211] as well as John Meyendorff.

Losskii, belonging to the Moscow Patriarchate, taught in Paris at the Institute of St. Denis. His famous work, *Essai sur la Théologie mystique de l'Église d'Orient,*[212] exposed the West to the central theological themes of the Eastern apophatic mysticism of Gregory of Nyssa, Pseudo-Dionysios and Gregory Palamas on the image and likeness doctrine of the Greek Fathers and on the Trinitarian and pneumatological emphasis in classical Orthodox theology. Losskii writes in his essay: "There is, therefore, no Christian mysticism without theology; but, above all, there is no theology without mysticism."[213] He lays great stress on the *Filioque* controversy as indicating a true dichotomy between Eastern and Western theology in their different approaches to God. "If we consider the dogmatic question of the procession of the Holy Spirit, which divided East and West, we cannot treat it as a fortuitous phenomenon in the history of the Church. From the religious point of view it is the sole issue of importance in the chain of events which terminated in the separation. Conditioned, as it may well have been, by various factors, this dogmatic choice was—for the one party as for the other—a spiritual commitment, a conscious taking of sides in a matter of faith."[214] He also rather strongly claims, contrary to the whole history of Orthodox piety, that the East never knew any devotion to the humanity of Christ.[215]

Losskii, Archbishop Vasilii and S. Troitskii, noted canonist and theologian even before the Russian Revolution, have contributed many creative articles in the Moscow Patriarchal journals for Western Europe and East Germany, namely, *Messager de l'Exarchat du Patriarche Russe en*

Europe Occidentale and *Stimme der Orthodoxie* of Berlin, both of which are printed also in Russian.

THE SITUATION IN THE SOVIET UNION

To make a comparison between the modern status of theology in Soviet Russia and pre-Revolutionary Russia would have little meaning. The level of theological development in contemporary Russia must be judged by the circumstances and dire limitations placed upon it.

The theologian most responsible for salvaging theological studies in Russia and for laying the groundwork for a new development that is now beginning to bear fruit was Father Nikolai Chukov, later Metropolitan Gregorii. After the Revolution, his task was almost one of beginning *ex nihilo*.

Before the Revolution, there were the four outstanding theological academies of Moscow, St. Petersburg, Kiev and Kazan' along with 58 seminaries, 20,000 theological students and 200 minor seminaries. Even after the decree of September 6, 1918, which separated all schools from the Church's influence, Chukov in 1919 assembled together an outstanding faculty of former St. Petersburg Academy, Professors Glubokovskii, Brilliantov, Karavinov, Sokolov, as well as the philosophers, L. Karsavin, N. Losskii, the historian, M. Priselkov and S. Bezobrazov (later Bishop Kassian of St. Sergius in Paris). This institute lasted only three years. By 1928 all formal theological courses had been terminated. For over a quarter of a century, therefore, theology in Russia, with no vital seminaries and academies to feed its development, came to a complete halt. In those years of the catacomb Church, it was the survival of the martyrs that took precedence over theological speculation. The results of bitter persecution against the Church left it with a depleted clergy, no seminaries and few professors capable even of teaching theology if there had been schools.

Archbishop Gregorii was given by Patriarch Sergii in 1944 the task to revive theology in Soviet Russia.[216] He proposed an ambitious program of an Orthodox Theological Institute in Moscow of three years studies that would correspond to the pre-Revolution academies, as well as theological pastoral schools of two years preparation on a secondary level of education. The brevity of the course was dictated by the great need of priests but it was felt that this would be compensated in turn by the seriousness and maturity of the students. A. V. Vedernikov, in an article on life in the theological schools,[217] points out why the plan was unfeasible. Students were unequipped especially intellectually and morally for the study of theology. Many of these had recently turned away from atheism to Christianity. Chukov revised his plan. A preparatory course of one year led then to theological courses of four years. The first two years were conceived as secondary theological-pastoral education while the last two functioned as higher academic training. In 1946 the Moscow Theological Institute was divided into the Moscow Theological Academy and the Seminary. This also took place in Leningrad.[218] A similar project to open the Kiev Academy remained only on paper.

The greatest difficulty at this period of transition was that of finding competent theology teachers. The old scholars of pre-Revolution times had either died or had fled to the West while no new ones had been permitted for 25 years to study theology. In 1945 there were established two academies at Leningrad and Moscow, along with eight seminaries in Leningrad, Kiev, Odessa, Moscow, Lutsk, Minsk, Saratov and Stavropol'.

The scarce information about theological life that appeared at this time in the *Journal of the Moscow Patriarchate* showed theology taught more in a pastoral, liturgical emphasis, "not study for study's sake, but study for the Christian life, for living pastoral work."[219]

New courses were introduced into the theological curriculum, unknown before the Revolution, such as the "Christian Study of Society" with emphasis on social phenomena and the pastoral training to cope with such problems, "Christian Pedagogics" which treated the psychological development of the human mind and spiritual influences upon it; and the "History of Russian Religious Consciousness" with particular stress on the impact of Russian society in the religious and moral field.

Heavy strictures upon printing were imposed upon theologians so that from 1943 onwards, one can say that no substantial theological writing had been published. The Soviet government from 1943 has allowed the publication of the *Moscow Patriarchal Journal,* which from time to time has printed articles, mostly touching upon liturgy, history of the Russian Church and, for a given period, several anti-Roman Catholic articles. Three numbers of an aborted theological journal entitled *Theological Studies* appeared in 1959-60 with mediocre articles by Professors Uspenskii, Ivanov and Borovoi but further publication was suspended by the Soviets.[220]

In 1960 the seminaries of Kiev, Stavropol and Saratov were closed and in 1964 those in Minsk and Lutsk, leaving only the two academies and seminaries of Leningrad and Moscow as well as the seminary at Odessa.

A few European scholars have been allowed to study the theological dissertations produced in the two academies in this modern period.[221] These works are typewritten copies that have been submitted to the faculties of the Moscow and Leningrad Academies in requirement for the master's degree in theology. The pressure from the government to discourage theological studies along with the lack of any consistent contact with theological developments in the West is evident in both the topics treated and the quality of research produced. The excellent library of 200,000 volumes in the Leningrad Academy as well as the superiority of the professors, as typified by the specialists, N. Uspenskii in liturgy and A. Ivanov in New Testament studies, place the Leningrad theological center above that of Moscow which is now housed on the grounds of the Holy Trinity Monastery of Zagorsk, outside of Moscow.

The theses show a preponderance of traditional and conservative theology, with very little done in systematic, speculative elaboration of Orthodox dogma. A lack of philosophical studies as a basis for dogmatic speculation plus the ignorance of theological development accomplished in the West explain the weakness manifested in dogmatic and fundamental theology and an evident preference for historical and patristic studies.

Of the 250 dissertations written since 1944 that Professor Johansen examined in the Leningrad Academy Library, 37 dealt with patristic themes, 25 with the Old Testament, 24 with the New, 6 with the history of the ancient Church, 46 with the history of the Russian Church, 9 with the history of the Slav Churches, 36 with dogmatic topics, 15 with Canon Law and 14 with the history of Western confessions.[222]

Under the influence of Professor Vitalii Borovoi, who served also in Geneva at the World Council of Churches and as an observer at the 2nd Vatican Council, ecumenism has entered, not only the theological investigations of the Leningrad Academy,[223] but also into the mainstream of the Russian Orthodox Church. In August, 1958, the Moscow Patriarchate began conversations with the World Council of Churches in Utrecht. In 1960 polemics against the other Christian Churches ceased and in November, 1961, at the World Council of Churches gathering in New Delhi, the Russian Orthodox Church, led by Metropolitan Nikodim, became an official member.

A limited contact with Western theological scholars is beginning to develop. In 1955 Professors L. Pariiskii and K.

Sbovoskii were sent as Russian delegates to the Second Patristic Congress in Oxford. In 1956 Russian theologians exchanged views with Anglican divines and since then there have also been exchanges with Protestants in Germany and Roman Catholic theologians in various encounters. Such meetings can only stimulate greater theological development within Russia.

In conclusion it can be safely affirmed that Soviets, insofar as they continue their campaign against religion in Russia, will also seek to prevent any free inquiry into theological problems. In such an environment of oppression, Russian theologians are trying valiantly not only to be faithful to their traditional Orthodox heritage but also, as far as possible, to create a meaningful theology for 20th century Russia. Some day the West will read the theological works that Russian theologians now fear to write but, however, which they have tried to incorporate into a lived-theology. Perhaps then the tired, rationalistic West will again turn to Russia as to the East for the light towards a new and more vibrant Christian theology.

PART TWO

The History of Orthodox Theology Among Greek-Speaking Churches

ON MAY 29, 1453, the Turks captured Constantinople. The New Rome and the Byzantine Empire came to an end. Yet Mohammed II and his Turks were hardened, even cruel soldiers and not thinkers, administrators or lawyers. The Sultan wisely did not attempt to convert the Christian Greeks to Islam. He needed administrators to run his vast new sprawling empire whose institutions were deeply saturated in the Byzantine Christian heritage. Mohammed promised his Christian subjects freedom to practice their religion and to hold property, even though, as long as they continued in their Christian faith, they could not hold public office. He was interested in the taxes that his Christian subjects paid him; other than this obligation he allowed them to live as though they were foreigners, the Roummilletti, under his Turkish administration.

By the terms of the *firman* given to Gennadios Scholarios by Mohammed II, all Greek Christians were under the religious and civil authority of the ecumenical patriarch.[1] Thus a totally new situation of far-reaching importance developed under the Turks. The patriarch, formerly the spiritual leader in a political empire in which his ecclesiastical jurisdiction was more or less separated from the civil jurisdiction, now combined in himself the civil as well as the spiritual power over his Christians. The ecumenical patriarch from this time on acquires for the Greek Orthodox Church greater influence and hence greater centralization. The power of the other three Oriental patriarchs of Antioch, Alexandria and Jerusalem yield to the ecumenical patriarch much more than a *primus inter pares*. The democratic equality exercised by a collegiality now disappears and yields much more to a monarchical form of administration with the largest part of jurisdictional authority in the hands of the patriarch of Constantinople.

Without a doubt it can be affirmed that the degree of general education and culture of the Greeks under the Turks fell to a very low level during the period from 1453 until 1821. Although Mattaeos Kamariotas continued to operate the patriarchal school under Mohammed II, other theological centers of learning were suppressed. Greek letters in general and Byzantine theology in particular suffered a blow that would force the Greeks to yield to the Slavs in the field of creative theology. Those thinkers who did continue to produce theological works in the Byzantine tradition were forced to study abroad in Germany, Italy and England or took up residence in Crete, which escaped the Turkish yoke, and met Western culture in their Venetian masters.

Byzantine theology became in this period mainly a defense and struggle for survival against external factors which the leading Byzantine theologians were constantly meeting in the form of Latin and Protestant theological influences. Lebedev asserts that the Greeks fought the Latins as though they were fighting a papacy of the 9th and 10th centuries that yielded nothing by way of creative theology.[2] The conservative theologians conceived theology as a holding of the insights acquired in a more fertile, creative period against any influence from the West. Still there were also those in the second class of Byzantine theologians of this period who definitely allowed themselves to be influenced by theological developments in the West, both from Latin Catholic as well as Protestant thought. Gennadios Scholarios, perhaps most responsible for setting the course of Greek theology as largely polemical against Western influences, proved to be an example of both tendencies: the conservative polemicist as well as the Byzantine theologian open to Western advancement.

GENNADIOS SCHOLARIOS

Gennadios Scholarios must be called the last of the theologians of the Byzantine Empire, not only because literally he was the last leading theologian at the time of the fall of Constantinople, but also because he was the most outstanding Greek theologian of the 15th century.[3] Leo Allatios and John Caryophyllos characterized Scholarios as two or three distinct persons.[4] Refusal of such scholars to accept one person stemmed both from the many names that Scholarios used as well as the contradictory positions proposed in his writings. He was born as George Courtesis in Constantinople about 1405. Educated by Mark Eugenicos in the elementaries of learning and the humanities, Scholarios taught himself rhetoric, philosophy and theology. Meriting the name Scholarios as an epithet, he opened a school of grammar and philosophy in the Imperial City that attracted Italians as well as Greeks. Gennadios was the monastic name he assumed upon becoming a monk in the monastery of Kharsianites in 1450. However, since the monumental critical edition of the complete works of Scholarios, launched by L. Petit (d. 1927), the then Latin archbishop of Athens, no present-day scholar doubts that the *Oeuvres*[5] are to be attributed to the same person, George (Gennadios) Scholarios.

A careful examination of Petit's critical edition reveals Scholarios as a scholar of great talents and yet basically weak in character. Krumbacher calls him the "last of the great Byzantine polemical writers."[6] And yet Scholarios, whose major works focused on polemics against Latin Catholics, was of all Byzantine thinkers, the most highly influenced by Western scholastic philosophy and theology. He made special studies of Augustine, Gilbert of La Porrée, Peter of Spain, Duns Scotus and the medieval Franciscan theologians. But St. Thomas Aquinas had the greatest influence on Scholarios' theological thinking. Thomas, except for his doctrine on the *Filioque* and the distinction between God's essence and His operations, was the supreme interpreter of Christian theology for Scholarios. He translated St. Thomas' *De Ente et Essentia* and his commentary on Aristotle's *De Anima* as well as making rather literal resumés of the *Summa contra Gentiles* and the *"Prima"* and *"Prima Secundae"* of Thomas' *Summa Theologica*. In the introduction to his translation of *De Ente et Essentia* he writes: "I doubt whether Thomas has any more fervent disciple than me."

Scholarios' writings reveal a very sensitive nature, afraid of criticism and opposition, proud of his intellectual prowess and eager for praises and honors. In a letter to Mark Eugenicos, he writes, "I suppose that no one is unaware that for rhetoric, philosophy and the highest science of all, theology, I learned from none of our teachers ... and now how much am I not better than all others in learning?"[7] Elsewhere he simply states, "In respect to sacred theology, which all my life through has had the greatest interest and profit for me, no one of all the men now living anywhere knows as much as I do."[8]

A gifted orator and preacher, he loved the acclamations of the court where even as a layman he preached each Friday before the senate and whole city. Yet he continually longed for the retirement of the monastic life which became a reality when he finally, after two abortive tries, succeeded in fleeing from the office of patriarch to retire to Mount Athos and eventually to the monastery of St. John the Baptist in Seres Macedonia where he died about the year 1472.

Thus we are not surprised that Scholarios could perform

a complete *volteface* in his theological positions from time to time as circumstances warranted. Nowhere is this clearer than in his position on the ecumenicity of the Council of Florence and more specifically in his attitude towards the Western doctrine of the *Filioque*. In various writings in preparation for the Council of Florence and during the sessions, Scholarios affirmed without hesitation that the Council was truly ecumenical, that the position of the Latins was confirmed by both the Greek and Latin Fathers and that an *entente* could and should be concluded as soon as possible.[9]

Even after his return from Florence to Constantinople, he continued his thinking as we see in his work, *Refutation of the Syllogisms of Mark Eugenicos,* requested, probably in 1440, by the pro-Latin protosyncellos, Gregory Mammas.[10] But it was Mark Eugenicos who recognized the powerful intellect of Scholarios as well as his vanity and capitalized at the opportune moment, namely, on Mark's deathbed, to appeal to Scholarios as the only one capable of taking over the task started by Mark—to defend Orthodoxy. Scholarios accepted the trust shown in him by Mark and thereafter became a bitter opponent of the Union of Florence as well as the main anti-Latin polemical writer of his century.

His main works center in the field of philosophy and theology, even though he also wrote a grammar and other works on philology, history and poetry. His philosophical works were chiefly translations or resumés of works written by Aristotle or his Western commentators, such as St. Thomas, Gilbert of La Porrée and Peter of Spain.[11] The major portion of his prolific writings, however, deals with theology. These works consist of homilies, dogmatic treatises on providence and predestination, on eschatology, ascetism and morality, apologetics in defense of Christianity over Islam, scriptural topics and finally, polemical themes, against Latins chiefly, but also against the Barlaamites, Jews, Acyndynes' followers, Gemistos Plethon and those guilty of simony.

Although Scholarios must be considered as a product of

the Byzantine culture that preceded the fall of Constantinople and the Hellenic subjection to Islamic conquest, yet precisely because he is the transitional link to a new type of Byzantine theologian that grew up under the Turkish oppression, it would serve us well to look more closely at his main doctrine. We will find it repeated by the less creative Byzantine theologians who were to follow Scholarios.

During the Middle Ages the chief polemical issue between Greeks and Latins concerned the procession of the Holy Spirit. Scholarios in two long polemical treatises laid the theological basis for future polemics on this subject. The first treatise of 1444 was written as a result of conferences at the Imperial Palace in Constantinople between the Dominican, Barthelemy Lapacci, pontifical legate, and Scholarios.[12] The second main treatise on the procession of the Holy Spirit is a re-editing of the first with a greater attention given to exposition.[13] A third shorter work is merely a compendium of the first two.[14] In these works Scholarios seeks to show that if the Holy Spirit proceeds from both the Father and the Son, there would be introduced into the Holy Trinity two principles of origin. Basing his arguments mostly on both the Greek and the Latin Fathers (for the Latin position he uses almost exclusively that of St. Augustine),[15] and using few arguments from Holy Scripture and reason, he seeks to interpret the patristic word, διά (*per* in Latin, meaning through) not in a causal sense of origin, but in various nuanced meanings such as 1) an equivalent of σὺν Υἱῷ (namely, the Holy Spirit proceeds from the Father along with the Son); 2) an equivalent of μετὰ τοῦ Υἱοῦ (the Holy Spirit proceeds in the company of the Son); 3) οὐκ ἐκτὸς τοῦ Υἱοῦ (not without the Son); 4) μετὰ τὸν Υἱὸν (after the Son).[16]

The Fathers, according to Scholarios, were not concerned with attributing a causality of origin to the Son in the procession of the Holy Spirit, but simply were giving the order in which the Son and Holy Spirit in relation to each other

proceed from the Father. We note that throughout Scholarios'
polemical writings against the *Filioque,* he never cites Photius
directly and in regard to the Photian formula, *"a patre solo,"*
Scholarios is most suspicious. "We do not canonize it; we do
not proclaim it publicly, but only in private conversation, for
we cannot proclaim that which has not had the acceptance
of the universal Church."[17] The Latin position is never branded
as heretical but he speaks of the Latins as dissidents or
separated Christians. His final statement on the problem is:
"We must hold fast to the traditional doctrine accepted by all
and confess simply that the Holy Spirit proceeds from the
Father. To hold anything else is dangerous."[18]

Scholarios in his full theological maturity wrote five
treatises that touched principally the doctrine of the origin
of the human soul and its finality.[19] These were written in his
latter years and show him at his greatest theological maturity
in dealing with a subject that allows him to utilize his
Aristotelian philosophy to produce a creative speculative
theology. Drawing his arguments in these works from philosophy, Holy Scripture, and the Greek and Latin Fathers,
Scholarios holds, against any traducianism, that God creates
the human soul immediately by infusing it into the embryo
when it has become sufficiently organized; namely, for
Scholarios, this is the 40th day after conception. He holds
a progressive evolutive development from a vegetative soul
to a sentient soul, leading at last to a rational soul. In the
third treatise Scholarios utilizes an opinion of Symeon of
Thessalonika on eschatology and teaches three categories of
souls: 1) those perfectly purified while waiting for the
resurrection which will give to them the full supernatural
beatitude, with the complete glorification of the body and
the vision, face to face, of God; 2) those souls dying in
serious sin are punished immediately by the pains of hell
which continue and increase after the resurrection of the
body; 3) those souls dying in charity with venial faults who
have not yet atoned sufficiently for their defects. Their

entrance into complete happiness is retarded. The prayers of the Church can hasten their purification. We see little difference in substance with the Latin teaching of purgatory, although Scholarios decidedly teaches against any material fire but holds a purifying pain of the moral, interior order. Using Byzantine medieval legends, recorded by St. John Damascene and Symeon of Thessalonika, Scholarios calls this state of intermediate purification the place of Τελώνιοι or the keepers (demons) of the outer tomb.[20]

In describing, chiefly in the fourth treatise, the resurrected body, he shows that it will be a totally integrated body, with sexual differences, however, retained. Using an exegesis of St. John Chrysostom on St. Paul's passage from 1 Corinthians 3:12-15, Scholarius admits that the prayers of the Church can mitigate to some extent the pains of the damned and he even believes that in some exceptional cases, God could deliver certain damned souls from hell.

Scholarius seemed to have been particularly drawn to the topic of God's foreknowledge and predestination, again because he was able to combine his native ability as a philosopher with a flexible speculative sense of theology. We possess five small treatises on this subject.[21] All were composed at Seres and show Scholarios at his best in the use of precise terminology and a fixed doctrine expressed over and over in new varying forms. We see in these writings the evident influence of St. Thomas Aquinas, yet a consistent stress along this same line in found in the best tradition of Greek theology on the free will of human beings. He quotes approvingly the great teachers of the Eastern Church: Dionysios the Areopagite, St. Basil, St. Gregory Nazianzus, St. John Chrysostom, St. Cyril of Alexandria, St. Theodoret, St. Maximus the Confessor and St. John Damascene.

From all eternity, teaches Scholarios, God knows all things, not as they truly exist, for they do not have an eternal existence, but in Himself in a mysterious manner becoming God in His infinite knowledge and wisdom of Himself as first cause of all. God not only knows all in advance but He predetermines all. His foreknowledge precedes his predetermination or the predestination (προορισμὸς) by which all things are fixed in advance. Yet the foreknowledge of God does not destroy man's free will but it is based on God's knowledge of man's free choices. Only because of man's free initiative to do good or evil does God foreknow man's choice. The first initiative towards good or evil comes from man's created will.

Scholarios describes the delicate relation of συνεργεία—the cooperation of God and man in doing good—by offering the example of St. John the Baptist and Herod.[22] The grace of God is absolutely indispensable for man to do good. God gives man his faculty of the will and the ability to choose to do good. God does not force St. John to choose nor does He force Herod to his choice. An evil act is brought about by man's freely withdrawing himself from God's grace. If Herod does not receive grace sufficient to act righteously it is because of his own freely posited bad disposition of will, "because the light of grace cannot inhabit the darkness of an evil will."[23] The choices of St. John and Herod were foreseen by God from all eternity as well as God's attitude towards them, to give or not to give His grace. God gives His cooperation to do good only to those who are freely (they choose to be so) orientated towards good. God abandons the evil ones to their own will, to their own choices that refuse to be open to the good.

Scholarios insisted most strongly on God as efficient cause of the world in his bitter polemical attack against Gemistos Plethon who died in Mistra in 1452. Plethon had developed, especially in his treatise on the political utopia described in his *Laws,* an idealized paganism based on elements drawn from Neoplatonic philosophy. Sin for Plethon was an error and in death the human soul returns to a spiritual existence that is in no way supernatural. It will exist in its perfectly sinless state.[24] Scholarios attacks Plethon for his assertion that Aristotle held no idea of a personal God as efficient Creator of the world. Scholarios refutes Plethon by having recourse to the order found in the universe and by appealing to the argument found in the writings of St. Thomas that the human soul is an image of the Trinity in its immanent operations of knowledge and love.

Among the apologetical writings of Scholarios the most famous is that which has come down through history as *The Confession of Faith of Gennadios.* Also entitled *The Unique Way of Man's Salvation,* this is a brief exposition of the Christian faith sent to the Sultan, Mohammed II, in the form of a Christian confession of belief. When troops took over Constantinople and the Byzantine Empire in 1453, Scholarios was living in the monastery of Kharsianites. He was taken captive to Adrianople but Mohammed had already decided that Scholarios was the religious leader capable of organizing the Greek Orthodox believers into peaceful subjects. Scholarios was enthroned as ecumenical patriarch on January 6, 1454 with the Sultan bestowing upon him the insignia of his Christian office.

He visited the Sultan three times to explain to him the religion of his new subjects. In his written confession of faith in twenty chapters,[25] Scholarios presents the basic Christian beliefs, beginning with an outline of the chief properties of the divine essence, especially God's goodness. He then appeals to the principles of those properties which God has within Him by His very essence (οὐσία) and in common with all three Hypostases. Scholarios beautifully describes the Trinitarian Persons and their inter-related activities as νοῦς (intellect), σοφία (wisdom), and ἀγάπη (love). Then he outlines the uniqueness of Jesus Christ in His Incarnation, life, passion and resurrection along with His properties. The resurrection of human bodies is affirmed as well as a universal judgment. The last seven chapters give the reasons why the Incarnation was necessary and serve the non-Christian as motives of credibility. Many writers praise this confession of faith for its gravity, simplicity, fidelity to traditions, but writers such as the Greek Androutsos, and the Russians, Antonios, Malinovskii and Nikitskii, do not consider it as a symbol of faith.[26] Androutsos complains that this confession is lacking in the one distinguishing mark of a true symbol of the Orthodox Faith. It gives the main teachings held by most Christian groups, but it does not clearly distinguish those teachings whereby the Orthodox Church is uniquely the one, holy, catholic and apostolic Church from the teachings of the other Christian Churches.[27]

Gennadios Scholarios, discouraged by his efforts to elevate the Christian level of life among the Moslem conquerors and opposed by his own Christian clerics and laity who sought advancements from the Moslems even at the cost of embracing Islam, finally, after one year, at the most two, in the patriarchal office, was allowed to retire to Mount Athos and from there to Seres in Macedonia. He returned for two short periods to re-occupy the patriarchal throne by order of Mohammed II but succeeded finally to enjoy the quietude of monastic life in Macedonia. There he continued his scholarly work of translating St. Thomas and Aristotle and of writing polemics against the Jews and the Latins. The date of his death is unknown but he must have died after 1472. Thus Gennadios Scholarios, the first patriarch after the Turks had captured Constantinople, provides the bridge from the old Byzantine world of theology to the new world under Islamic domination. He was the last great Byzantine theologian. With his death the Greek Orthodox Church enters into a period of holding what tradition had bequeathed to it and of passing it on to future generations.

JEREMIAS II

After the death of Scholarios the 15th century produced no singularly great Greek theologian. Joseph Bryennios and

Gennadios Scholarios had received their theological training in the Byzantine patristic tradition. The 15th century ended that older period. The 16th century begins a new period for Greek thought. The ever-pressing hand of the Turkish conqueror gradually extinguished most of the basic freedoms from the lives of the Greeks. No longer an independent free people, what they learned now had to be acquired in foreign universities. The clergy was reduced to a piteous state of ignorance, most schools of religious formation, especially seminaries, were closed and teachers of theology became a rarity. Few among the priests and bishops of the first half of the 16th century had received any theological training.[28]

Gradually there was a stirring out of the theological morass into which the Byzantine Greek Church had fallen after the fall of Constantinople. From the middle of the 16th century until the appearance of Cyril Lucaris, we find Byzantine theology characterized by a heavily anti-Latin polemics, an openness towards Protestantism, the development of popular literature in the Greek vernacular that fed the spiritual hunger of the Orthodox faithful and, finally, by an arch conservatism that developed under persecution by the Turks and an indirect proselytism exercised by the Latin Catholics through the zealous tactics of the newly founded order of Jesuits and, to some extent, by German Protestants. In such turbulent times the leaders of the Orthodox Church clung tenaciously to the canons and conciliar decrees fixed in the first seven ecumenical councils. Theology would appear to be a repetition of "What the Fathers had decreed," as Meletios Pigas would express it in the Synod of Constantinople of 1593.

Urged towards an openness by the overtures made to their Orthodox Church and buffeted in self defense by the theological attacks of Latin theologians, the Byzantine theologians sought to formulate their beliefs in language and concepts that would both be meaningful to the Protestants and Catholics who made inquiries of the basic beliefs of the Orthodox, but also which would be meaningful to the Orthodox believers who eagerly sought a brief summation of their faith.

The first of these attempts that followed upon the Confession of Faith of Scholarios was the symbolic book of the three responses of Patriarch Jeremias II to the Lutheran theologians of Germany. Contact with the German Lutherans began during the reign of Patriarch Joasaph II (1555-1565) who had sent deacon Demetrios Mysos to Wittenberg to investigate the innovations of the Lutherans.[29] Melanchthon, a great humanist and classical Greek scholar, had eagerly sought more intimate relations with the Greek Church. Having translated the Augsburg Confession into classical Greek, he implored Mysos to present his version to the patriarch along with other letters explaining the Lutheran position and expressing the desire for an exchange of theological views. Nothing came of this first overture.[30] New attempts were tried by David Ungnad, legate to Constantinople, and by the Tübingen Lutheran theologians, Martin Crusius and Jacob Andreas, and Stephan Gerlach. Gerlach, a master of theology, had been sent to administer to the Lutherans in the legation to Constantinople. He carried letters from Crusius and Andreas to the patriarch in which the two Tübingen theologians asked the new patriarch, Jeremias (Tranos) II, to examine carefully the Augsburg Confession.

Patriarch Jeremias (d. 1595)[31] was born in Anchialos on the Black Sea. He was a pupil of Hierotheos of Monembasia, Arsenius of Tirnova and Damaskinos the Studite. He had never studied abroad but was privately taught in the spare moments that he could devote to studies as patriarch. He had a great thirst for learning. John Zygomalas taught him ethics, dialectics and rhetoric while Theodore Zygomalas taught him Hermogenes, Hesiod and Aristophanes. A Catholic, Leonardus Mindonius, taught him Aristotle.[32] Once elected patriarch, Jeremias zealously strove to protect Orthodoxy from the inroads of Catholicism and Protestantism. Ph. Meyer writes that Jeremias never thought union with the Protestants was ever possible.[33] He was not a particularly deep theologian and he probably only gave his name to these three responses that have been considered by Orthodox theologians as a symbolical book. The editing of the responses was done by the protonotary, Theodosios Zygomalas.[34] Zygomalas wrote to Martin Crusius in 1575 that the patriarch had too many things to do so that he gave him the task of answering the questions submitted in 1575 by the Tübingen theologians. Others who assisted in drawing up the responses were John Zygomalas, Mindonios and a few members of the synod, probably Arsenius of Tirnova, Damaskinos, bishop of Naupactos, and Hieromonk Matthaeos. Gabriel Severos was in Constantinople in 1577 and probably also took part in the dialogue.

In 1576 Jeremias II sent his first response back to the Tübingen Lutherans. He complains against the Protestant principle of basing faith only on Scripture, and against the Protestant loss of tradition. The Holy Spirit has spoken also through the ecumenical councils and the writings of the Holy Fathers so that their opinions, founded on the Lord's words in Scripture, have also an eternal value. Jeremias takes up the problem of the procession of the Holy Spirit from the Son also. This Western opinion, both Catholic and Protestant, he finds repugnant to Holy Scripture and tradition. He develops the principal articles of faith such as Original Sin and the means to destroy sin, especially the sacraments of Baptism, Unction and Holy Eucharist. In this section of the sacraments he polemically attacks the different usages among the Latins as abuses, such as no triple immersion in Baptism. He insists firmly that faith without good works is dead. He holds the seven sacraments and discourses upon their nature. The priesthood can be exercised even without a saintly minister. In Chapter 10 he laments among the Protestants the errors pertaining to the Eucharist. The consecration of bread and wine means for Jeremias that the bread and wine cease to exist. He goes into detail in explaining how a confessor ought to hear confessions and absolve sins.

Chapter 13 deals with the sacraments, the Divine Liturgy and the aids flowing from these means to salvation. The necessity of priestly ordination through apostolic succession in order that sacraments be validly administered is handled in Chapter 14. Chapter 17 insists on obedience to civil authorities and exalts monasticism against the objections raised by the Lutherans. Jeremias insists in Chapter 18 on the resurrection of the dead and on the last judgment, on the absolute need of grace but also the free will cooperation of man with God, and on sin which flows from a disorientated will. In the last two Chapters, 20 and 21, the Protestants are criticized because they reject feasts of saints, fasts and monasticism as useless.[35]

Jeremias throughout this document never loses sight of the fact that he is aware of the innovations that Protestants have introduced into the Orthodox Christian faith and thus boldly calls the Tübingen theologians to these discrepancies between the two Churches. He terminates his response with an exhortation that the Lutherans join themselves to the Orthodox Church by submitting to a strict observance of the apostolic and synodal decrees.[36]

In the following year the Tübingen theologians, Crusius, Andreas and Luke Osiander sent Jeremias a reply to which Jeremias answered in 1579. The latter centers his second response mainly on man's free will in doing good or evil, on justification through faith and good works, on the seven sacraments, monasticism, on the invocation of the Saints and on the procession of the Holy Spirit. Like the first response, he again exhorts the Lutherans to observe strictly the apostolic and ecclesiastical traditions. The Holy Fathers have placed limits and no one can violate these norms by introducing novelties. "To err is indeed human; however, to correct errors is angelic and salutary."[37]

The Lutheran theologians sent their third letter in which they tried to justify their right of interpreting Holy Scripture for themselves and of refusing any sacred inspiration to the interpretation of the early Fathers. Jeremias answers in his third and most vehement response in 1581 by regretting that he cannot agree with them. In the final answer he touches again on free will, sacraments and the invocation and veneration of the Saints. He concludes not only the third response but thereby concludes also the correspondence for the future, with the sharp words: "We beg you, not to bother us in the future with your labors, with your letters and your sending to us your writings. You treat theologians who were the lights of the Church in one way by your words; you even render them honor and extol them; but you ignore them when it comes down to the practical. You point out that our arms are useless, namely, holy and divine works, concerning which we have written you and exhorted you. Give us rest from such bother. You go your way and do not write us any more concerning dogmas but write only if moved by the motive of friendship."[38]

On the surface of these responses there seems to be a heavy polemic directed towards the Lutherans, but in the style there is present very little of polemical undertones. Jeremias is not concerned with polemics but merely with pointing out Orthodox beliefs and tradition. Most modern Greek theologians consider the responses of Jeremias as constituting an authoritative symbolic book, a synthesis of authentic Orthodox teaching.[39]

Systematic theology in the early part of the 16th century was practically non-existent in the shattered Byzantine world. Gradually through study abroad and Latin Catholic missionary activities in Constantinople and the Near and Middle East, especially by Franciscan, Dominican and Jesuit missionaries as well as Greek priests trained in the newly opened

St. Athanasios Greek College in Rome, there soon began to appear with increasing quantity as well as quality more treatises, following the anti-Latin polemical lines of medieval Byzantine theological literature.

MANUEL OF CORINTH

The first of this type of Byzantine theologian is Manuel of Corinth (d. 1551).[40] He was a pupil of Mattaeos Kamariotas who was allowed by Mohammed II to continue operating the patriarchal school of theology in Constantinople. Manuel became famed as a systematizer of anti-Latin theology and a writer of church hymns and canon law. In his main work, an answer and refutation of the ten theses put forth by Fra Francis of the Dominican Order, Manuel sets forth the main differences between the Greek and Roman Churches. The main difficulties center upon the question of the procession of the Holy Spirit from the Father and the Son, the use of *azyme* or unleavened bread, purgatory, the primacy of the pope, no triple immersion in Baptism and total opposition to divorce. He condemns rather severely the opposing view of Latin theologians as a result of bad will and ignorance.[41]

Manuel wrote another leading defense of Orthodoxy in his work: Περὶ Μάρκου 'Εφέσου καὶ κατὰ Γεμιστοῦ καὶ Βεσσαρίωνος [*On Mark of Ephesus and Against Gemistos and Bessarion*].[42] The title is misgiving for the work says nothing about Mark of Ephesus nor about the Council of Florence. It is an attack against the philosophical principles used by Bessarion and his teacher, Gemistos Plethon. Another work was also directed against Plethon who seemed to be the deadly enemy of Manuel. In this work Manuel attacks Plethon's doctrine of the procession of the Holy Spirit.[43]

Another work attributed to Manuel that is free of any polemical tone, earnest and piously impressive, concerns the death of Christ.⁴⁴ It is an answer to a friend who had asked whether the flesh of Christ was divinized and given the glory of God during His life time. Manuel answers that the flesh of Christ was divinized at His conception but the effects of a divinized body were put aside, as it were, in order that Christ might be able to suffer in His human body. The transfiguration of the flesh [σάρξ] of Christ was shown fully only in His resurrection. Other unedited works include a tract on purgatory and another on the error of the Latins concerning the procession of the Holy Spirit.

PACHOMIOS OF RHUS

A much more interesting and talented theologian is Pachomios of Rhus (Rhusanos).⁴⁵ He was a monk of St. George Monastery of Zante but spent time also in monasteries on Mount Athos and on the island of Lesbos, in the Holy Land and in Venice. He died in his monastery at Zante about 1553. He had received a good classical training in theology and proves himself to be the most trained mind up to the middle of the 16th century. He was skilled in the Bible and in the theology of the early Fathers. This he demonstrates in a style that shows a certainty of conviction. Throughout his works he shows his passionate love for Orthodoxy and for his Greek nationality. He possessed something of medieval chivalry in regard to the honor that he deemed it to be to do battle for his Church.

His main works therefore always contain a polemical and apologetic thrust. A typical work: Περὶ τῆς ἐκ τῶν Θείων Γραφῶν Ὠφελείας [*On the Usefulness of Holy Scripture*], shows us his far ranging style, demonstrating a vast knowledge yet harnessed to combat error and abuse in his beloved Orthodox Church. The root of the pitiful state of Greek religion, he insists, is ignorance, a lack of true knowledge [ἀληθὴς γνῶσις]. God had sent to mankind Moses and then His Son, our Redeemer; He gave us the preaching of the Apostles, the deeds of the martyrs and the acts of the synods of the Holy Fathers. This paralyzing ignorance must be combatted by profound study of Holy Scripture. Religion and theology will be as strong as monasticism is vibrant. But monasticism has fallen into a morass of torpor due to the introduction of the idiorrhythmic type of monasticism which abolished the coenobitic or communal life and allowed each monk to conduct himself according to his own whims. Such freedom has destroyed discipline which alone can be restored by a continued meditation on Scripture. In the second part of this work Pachomios shows great linguistic learning by discoursing at length on the importance of the *Koine* or Byzantine Greek as the source of, and in preference to, the many Greek dialects. He fights the tendency to use the dialects because such an innovation destroys unanimity, for not all Greek speaking people understand all the Greek dialects while, with serious study, all could understand the *Koine*. This language alone will allow the Greeks an adequate theological tool for a renaissance in theology.

The subject of the *Koine* versus Greek dialects was the implied reason of one of Pachomios' strongest attacks against an adversary, who in this case was Joannes Kartanos, the leader of the sect called after him the Kartanitae.[46] In these writings Pachomios attacks the apocryphal statements that Kartanos confuses with inspired Scripture as well as his Christology and his pantheistic theology in his work, Ἄνϑος. The work of Kartanos was the first theological work written in the vernacular and Pachomios saw such an attempt as a destruction of theology as a science with a highly disciplined language. In many places Pachomios misunderstands what Kartanos wants to say simply because the latter was an unlettered writer who failed miserably to convey his thoughts in theological language.

Another polemical writing against the idiorrhythmic monasticism of his day[47] provides us with a collection of

writings and ideas drawn from synodal canons, St. Basil the
Great, the Gerontikon, St. Gregory the Great, the typikon
of Athanasios of the Great Lavra of Mount Athos, from one
of the Emperor Michael Palaeologos, and from an unknown
typikon of Empress Irene. Pachomios strives to persuade
monks living the idiorrhythmic life to return to coenobitic
monasticism in all things. He rails against such an adultera-
tion of monasticism. A monk, he insists, has four duties: to
keep himself from women and meat, to be truly poor and
to obey. The idiorrhythmic life prevents at least the last two
duties from being fulfilled.

Pachomios has written a series of more directly theological
tracts or *logoi* that unfortunately have remained unedited.[48]
In the first two tracts he combats heretics in general and
probably has in mind Kartanos and his followers in particular,
who deny the existence of a personal God. That God exists
can be seen from the beauties and harmony of the world
that should teach man that there is a Creator behind such
creation. As a man knows that when someone builds a perfect
lyre or a beautiful house he must have had first an idea, so
also from the things in the world we can know that there
must have been a Creator who possessed the idea according
to which He created the beautiful world. He develops at
length the providence of God as working out His design
and plan for the whole world. This providence does not
take away the responsibility of man but rather presupposes
man's faithful cooperation.

In the second tract he deals with creation in general and
the essence of man in particular. Unlike the world which was
created from nothing, man was created from existing creation.
The human soul, however, is created or produced directly by
God. Not only is the human soul immortal; first man was
created immortal even in his body. A physical death came
after the fall.

Pachomios also produced many works of piety such as
a work on the holy icon of the Blessed Virgin of Kassiopaia or

Kassopitra, the name of the harbor of Corfu; on the martyr-
dom and the service that the monks rendered who were
killed by the Turks in the Strophades, two small islands
near Zante, along with various homilies and canons.[49]

During the 16th century greater contact with the Latin
West was made. This is explained strangely enough by the
fact that Crete, which had been under Venetian rule from
1204 to the fall of Constantinople, stagnated culturally and
intellectually. Now it suddenly became the intellectual bridge
from East to West. Under the Venetians the influence of
the Orthodox hierarchy had been destroyed by Venice's ap-
pointing of *protopapades* or priests as administrators of the
dioceses. Social and economic conditions were repressive
which tended to discourage intellectual activity. But when
the Turks took Constantinople, Crete remained free of
Turkish domination and hence soon became the haven for
intellectual leaders who fled Constantinople. The Renaissance in Italy created a demand for Greek manuscripts and
Crete became a center for copying and disseminating to the
West, especially through Venice, the ancient texts of Byzantine
learning.[50] Michael Apostolis, scholar and scribe, is an example
of the Greek émigré man of letters who established Crete
as a bridge from the earlier Byzantine world to the Western
centers of humanistic studies. The lack of schools in Crete,
except for the elementary one connected with the monastery
of St. Catherine of Sinai in Candia, Crete's capital, wherein
Meletios Pigas and Maximos Margounios were trained, made
it imperative that both scholars and students migrate to the
West, especially to Italy. Padua and Venice were the two
outstanding centers of attraction for these Greek students,
professors and scribes. Venice soon had the greatest con-
centration of Greeks in the Western world. Greeks from
Crete established Greek presses such as the two Cretans,
Laonikos and Alexander, and the more important Zacharias
Calliergis who produced some of the most important Greek

texts that the West possessed. Padua, Florence and Bologna all boasted of universities with chairs of Greek studies. To Padua in 1508 came the outstanding Cretan, Mark Musuros, who made Padua-famous over all of Europe. Many of the Hellenists of the 16th century who spread Greek letters to northern Europe had been his students, including the Dutchman, Erasmus.

MELETIOS PIGAS

The first of the outstanding 16th century Byzantine theologians who migrated from Crete to Italy was Meletios Pigas (d. 1601).[51] Born in Crete sometime between 1535 and 1540, he studied at St. Catherine monastery and migrated then to Padua, where his classmates were Maximos Margounios and Gabriel Severos. Returning to Crete, he entered the monastery of Aggarathos. In 1580 he was made protosyncellos to Patriarch Sophronios of Alexandria. At this period of his life he became established as a powerful preacher. In 1585 he worked in Constantinople until 1590 when he was elected patriarch to the see of Alexandria. He held the vacant patriarchal throne of Constantinople for three years and died in Alexandria as patriarch in 1603.

He must be ranked as one of the most important learned theologians and church leaders of the Greek Church of the second half of the 16th century. In Padua he had received a good classical and theological education even though it was somewhat along the scholastic line. He wrote ancient Greek and Latin and was well versed in the Holy Scriptures. His stay in Italy did not make him overly friendly to the Roman Church. His writings are mostly of a polemical nature, due to his ardent defense of Orthodox teaching against the Latins, Protestants and Jews. Alarmed by Catholic proselytism in the Ukraine among the Slav Orthodox which resulted in the Union of Brest in 1596, and the formation of the Catholic

Slav Uniate Church, Meletios broke from his earlier Catholic sympathies to begin an anti-Latin campaign among Orthodox. Nicodemos Metaxas has collected into one volume four letters of this genre, three of which Meletios wrote to King Sigismund III, ruler of Poland who at that time controlled the Ukraine, and to other Slav Orthodox living under the Latin Polish King; the fourth he addressed to the Orthodox on the island of Chios where a similar attempt was being made by Catholic missionaries to form a uniate body of Catholics.[52]

One of Meletios' most interesting works, although he always appears, in the words of Meyer, as a systematizer,[53] is his treatment of the Church.[54] In this work written by Meletios when he was still a monk, the Church is described in biblical figures which is reminiscent of St. Augustine's descriptions.[55] There follows a description of the essence of the Church. There are two Churches, one true and the other false. The true Church is "the gathering of men from all parts of the world, chosen in Christ at the same time being called to salvation but in various ways to give glory to God through their true faith and the life of these members."[56] The true Church is *one* through the one Head, Jesus Christ, and this is shown also in the Old Testament. It is one since it is for all men. "The Church is formed from every race of men."[57] All men belong to it in the sense that Christ died for all. Yet only the true Church is capable of forming true believers. To the true Church Christ has given His justice and eternal salvation. The call to the Church has been founded in history, first through means of the Law, then through the Son of God for the salvation of men. The Church will coincide with the last aim of God, namely, His glory. He first gave the call to His twelve apostles and then to His 70 disciples and thus the call has been passed on. But never was there given to any one person in the Church an over-all power. Christ alone is the Head of the Church and all partial Churches make up the one, catholic Church. The Pope is not the head but is only the bishop of the Roman Church.[58]

Christ is still present in the Church in His divine and human natures. He gives His Spirit to govern the Church and this Spirit is passed on by His priests who carry it as the servants of Christ. There follows an entire discourse on the primacy of the pope of Rome in seven parts which forms a special part of the larger work with a particular polemic instituted against Pope Sylvester as the epitome of an exaggerated sense of papal powers.

Another polemical work of Meletios takes up the attack against the Jews. Writings among the Orthodox theologians during the Middle Ages against the Jews were not rare. The Jews had a great influence with the Turkish Sultan and it was an implied supposition that many of the repressions imposed upon the Christians by the Turks came through the suggestions of the Jews. Of this we have no proof; still it did not prevent leading Byzantine theologians such as Joseph Bryennios, Gennadios Scholarios, Damaskinos the Studite, Patriarch Meletios Pigas, and later Cyril Lukaris to write treatises against the Jews.[59]

One final major theological work of Meletios was first published in Vilna in 1596 in the form of a dialogue between a stranger and a child.[60] Meletios goes into a lengthy discussion on the abuses of the Latin Church in regard to the procession of the Holy Spirit, penance and purgatory. He shows little originality as he passes on the same arguments already presented by Scholarios and similar polemicists.

MAXIMOS MARGOUNIOS[61]

One of the most unique intellectual figures that Greek-Byzantine culture produced in the 16th century is Maximos Margounios. Living only 53 years (d. 1602), he spent most of his intellectually creative life in Venice where he wrote prodigiously in all areas of not only theology but of classical humanism. Perhaps more relevant to our 20th century is the breadth of not only his intellectual interests but his open-mindedness as a Greek towards Latin culture and theology. Unfortunately his life and works are very little known to Western historians and theologians; but he could provide those interested in the modern ecumenical dialogue not only with a model of tolerance towards other theological traditions than one's own but he could perhaps also provide them, especially Catholic and Orthodox theologians, with a theological basis to bring about an *entente* concerning the thorny problems of the *Filioque* and the primacy of the pope.

He was born in Candia, Crete and named Emmanuel. He studied with Meletios Pigas and Gabriel Severos in Padua for eight years, during which time he developed a broad knowledge of literature, philosophy, theology and medicine. He was called to Constantinople by Patriarch Jeremias II who wanted to gather around him a corps of theologians to effect a reform of his clergy. Although he did not remain there long, he did continue through correspondence to be an adviser and defender of Jeremias. In 1579 he became a monk in the monastery of St. Catherine of Sinai in Crete. He was consecrated bishop of Cerigo in 1584 but because of intrigues by the Venetian government, which saw in him a potential and valuable citizen, he was not allowed to go to Cerigo. He was offered free residence and an annual pension by the Venetian government which Margounios readily accepted, since it provided him with the type of scholarly life in contact with the greatest theologians and humanists of his time which greatly appealed to him.

The jealousy of Gabriel Severos, metropolitan of Philadelphia, who resided with Margounios also in Venice, and his suspicions of Margounios' overly friendliness towards the Latins, especially in seemingly adopting many of their teachings concerning the procession of the Holy Spirit, caused Margounios to be denounced to the patriarch of Constantinople as a heretic, but each time he was cleared of the charges made against him.

He was a man with a passionate love for truth and a broad tolerance for the views of others acquired by his strong philosophical background and general education in nearly all areas of knowledge. Although he remained thoroughly Greek and also faithful to his Orthodox religious traditions, this did not prevent him from being both sympathetic to Latin theological discoveries and positions as well as to Western methodology in theological speculation.

The main preoccupation of Margounios in his major theological works and also in his voluminous correspondence was to effect a better understanding and even reconciliation between the Western understanding of the *Filioque* doctrine and the Eastern traditional expression of the procession of the Holy Spirit from the Father. Gabriel Severos debated his compatriot orally and in writing, insisting against Margounios that Orthodoxy cannot accept a procession of the Holy Spirit that proceeds also from the Son for this would imply two first principles [ἀρχαι] in the one Godhead. Margounios was keenly aware of Orthodox sensitivity towards the Latin position, yet he felt that both formulations were orthodox and a rapprochement could be reached which could lead to a union of the two Churches. Margounios sought to penetrate beyond the emotionalism of the theological issue to return to a basic distinction lost sight of by later theologians and held by the early Fathers. When the Fathers spoke of the Holy Spirit proceeding from the Father they were viewing the eternal process within the Godhead wherein the Father is the only source or origin of both the Son and the Holy Spirit. When they spoke of the Spirit as proceeding from the Father through the Son or even also from the Son, they were viewing the temporal procession from the Son whereby the Son sends the Holy Spirit into the world to sanctify all creatures.

Geanakoplos' statement has much truth to it and explains

Margounios' view in reconciling the Eastern and the Western formulas:

> In one important sense at least Margounios was right. As he realized, the question of the *filioque* had become encrusted with the prejudices of centuries, psychological and cultural as well as theological. And thus any Orthodox who exhibited, or even suggested, any tolerance of the Latin view was suspect, even though in earlier centuries Maximos the Confessor and Gregory of Cyprus seemed to have suggested a rather similar approach. Now that the Greek homeland was in the hands of the Turks, the Greeks had become so sensitive about their religious and cultural traditions that any deviation from the Orthodox interpretation of the *filioque* was tantamount to a betrayal of their entire heritage. More than ever the *filioque* issue had become not only a symbol of the religious schism but representative of the deep cultural abyss that had now crystallized between East and West.[62]

One of Margounios' first works on the procession of the Holy Spirit was written about 1583 while he was still in Crete, and it was dedicated to Jeremias II.[63] It consists of three books in which he seeks to unite the Greek and Latin positions. Beginning with the teaching of St. Augustine as representative of the Latin position, he tries to show that the Church Fathers conceived the procession of the Spirit in a double manner, as has been mentioned above; namely, the eternal procession from the Father and the temporal procession from the Father through the Son or a procession from the Father and the Son.

Another work, written in 1584 in Constantinople and dedicated to the prince of Valachia,[64] stresses that Holy Scripture witnesses to a simple relation of the Holy Spirit to the Father, and in this sense it could be true that the Spirit, as hypostasis, proceeds from the Father alone. In another sense of temporal mission, the Son does not give the hypostasis-existence to the Holy Spirit but is represented as the giver of the charismata whereby the Spirit sanctifies mankind.

Margounios, in the form of a letter written in 1587 and printed in Frankfort in 1591 by his humanist-friend David Hoeschel, shows that the Holy Spirit comes from the Father but that the world comes from the Father and the Son or from the Father through the Son. The Spirit proceeding from the Father is an eternal process, while the procession from the Father and the Son touches upon the *economic* process of salvation whereby the created world of men and things is brought to its completion.[65] It was several of these pages that led Gabriel Severos and even Meletios Pigas to suspect the orthodoxy of Margounios.

One final work that deals also with the procession of the Spirit is Margounios' answer in the form of *scholia* to the Trinitarian doctrine of the German Jesuit, Jacob Gretser, who in 1598 held a disputation on the mystery of the Holy Trinity in Ingolstadt in which he refers to Patriarch Jeremias II's answer to the Tübingen theologians. Margounios had read the works of Gretser and answered him with his *Scolia anasceuastica.*[66] In this work Margounios again distinguishes between the eternal and the temporal processions. The eternal is *ad intra* and looks to the origin in hypostases while the other, *ad extra,* is dispensatory and relative, in the order of sanctification of God's creatures.

A more fruitful speculative work edited by Hoeschel gives Margounios' thought on how God can permit evil to exist in creatures when He has originally created them good. This is a letter directed to Patriarch Jeremias II from Venice in 1591. The author shows a great dependence upon the scholastic theology of the West, especially upon Peter Lombard. He distinguishes between the preordained will of

God which will always be done and the consequential will, namely, God's commandment, prohibition and forgiveness. In the second part Margounios gives a discourse on the good and points out how God permits evil so that good can be drawn from it. All events, including evil happenings, must serve the good and somehow lead to salvation for those who love God.

Much of the voluminous correspondence of Maximos remains still unedited and could throw much light on his relationship with the leading German Protestant humanists of the 16th century and their attitude toward the Orthodox Church. One of his leading correspondents in Germany was David Hoeschel.[67] This well-known German scholar and publisher of Augsburg received many manuscripts from Margounios which dealt with Byzantine humanism, e.g. the 11th century Byzantine philosopher and historian, Michael Psellos. In return Margounios requested from Hoeschel that he send him Greek manuscripts which he could not find in Italy. He had correspondence also with the German philologist and Jesuit savant, Frederic Sylburg, and with Andreas Schott; with the Italians, Philip Siminello and Rinaldo Molinetti; the Venetians, Aloysio Lollino, Dardi Bembo; and the English Hellenist, Henry Savile with whom Margounios collaborated in editing the works of St. John Chrysostom which appeared after Margounios' death.[68]

When Margounios died at the age of 53, he specified that his Greek manuscripts, which he had collected in his valuable library in Venice, be sent to his monastery of St. Catherine in Crete while his Latin manuscripts and printed books, numbering some 114, be sent to the Athonite monastery of Iviron.[69] His collection of Latin manuscripts and books reflect in subject matter his overall interest in biblical exegesis and medieval Latin philosophy and theology, especially as expressed in the writings of Thomas Aquinas, Bonaventure and Alexander of Hales.

Maximos Margounios remains historically one of the few

Byzantine thinkers who sought, not only in desire but through scholarly research on the basis of theological and philosophical literature of both the East and the West, to prepare for an *entente* between the two separated Christian Churches by presenting both positions which he equally well understood in order to dissolve the prejudices built up over centuries of suspicion, fostered all too often by a canonization of only one theological approach or formulation.

GABRIEL SEVEROS[70]

Gabriel Severos, bishop of Philadelphia, proves in his writings to be a mediocre theologian, zealous to defend Orthodox doctrine against Latin positions, at times not expertly acquainted with that Orthodox doctrine and heavily under the influence of the Latin theology that he proposed to attack. Born in 1541 in Monembas, he studied with Margounios in Padua. After ordination he settled in Venice in 1572 to become the pastor of the Greek Orthodox Church of St. George. Jeremias II, upon entreaties from a wealthy Cretan, consecrated him metropolitan of Philadelphia in Lydia but, similar to Margounios, he never took possession of his diocese. Gabriel did not seem willing to go to Philadelphia in spite of the demands of the people that he take over the diocese. He secured from Jeremias II permission to reside in Venice and to become the exarch of the Ecumenical Patriarch for all Orthodox living in Venice and Dalmatia.

Except for occasional pastoral visitations to Dalmatia, where on such an occasion he died in 1616, Gabriel spent most of his life in Venice defending Orthodox doctrine with a passion against all opposition. His main opposition came from the irenic Maximos Margounios as was already stated, whom Gabriel in public disputations and innumerable letters and treatises attacked as heretical. His writings reveal a theologian more practical and pastoral than speculative and theoretical, possessing a limited number of ideas and showing not much tolerance for the views of others.

Severus' main work, a polemical treatise against the Latins,[71] was written, as he tells us in the introduction, in answer to the petitions of Greeks living in Italy who were perplexed by the statements of the Jesuit theologians, Possevine and Bellarmine who consistently called the Greek Orthodox αἱρετικοί. The Greeks in Italy asked Severos whether the Latins had a right to call the Orthodox heretics. He confesses that he is unworthy to do such a difficult task but, as there is no one better to do the work, he consents. The work is divided into three questions: 1) How many are the chief differences between the Orthodox and Catholics? 2) What is the true holy, catholic and apostolic Church? and 3) How can we be called orthodox and hold fast to the ancient traditions and still be schismatics or heretics? Only the first part, which appears as a complete work in itself, is extant.

In listing the differences between the two Churches, he finds that there are in the main five, even though he confesses that there are others, less important such as the new calendar, fasting on Saturday, kneeling on Sunday etc. The first great difference is the doctrine of the procession of the Holy Spirit. On this already worn out problem, Severos offers nothing new or creative. He pinpoints the Latin difficulty that allows the Holy Spirit to proceed also from the Son (*Filioque*) as springing from the identification by Latin theologians of the person or hypostasis of the Holy Spirit and the operation or energy that according to Orthodox doctrine is common to the Holy Trinity. For Severos, ἐνέργεια, or the divine energy, is of the same being as the Divine Essence; it is not spatial nor is it created. He seemingly cites from Palamas and other Fathers to show the distinction between the Divine Essence and the Divine Energy. He says in regard to the "processions" of both the Son and the Holy Spirit from the Father: "They are similar to the river and the water which flow equally from the same source, so the Son and Spirit come from the hypostasis of the Father."

The second difference concerns the power of the pope. He denies that Peter received from Christ anything other than a primacy of honor over the other Apostles. The successors of Peter, the popes of Rome, have received from the Church in the ancient ecumenical councils a primacy of honor due to the rank of its see, the city of Rome, as the capital of the Empire.

The third difference deals with *azyme* or unleavened bread which the Latins use. Severos argues that Jesus Christ celebrated the Passover on the legal day but anticipated by a few hours the moment fixed by law. On the evening of Holy Thursday, the night of the Last Supper, there was both fermented and *azyme* bread available. Jesus instituted the Eucharist with fermented bread.

Purgatory constitutes the fourth difference. Severos concedes that there is a period of temporal pain after death for sins pardoned and a category of the dead can be helped through the prayers of the living. But he rejects purgatory as a place distinct from Hell. There are different levels of Hell and its punishment of a spiritual fire is eternal or temporal depending upon the sins of the persons being punished. He rejects the teaching that the pope has jurisdiction over the souls of the dead and that he can open at will the doors of Hell and secure the release of suffering souls.

He ends with the last difference which concerns the happiness of the saints. They do not enjoy the fullness of beatitude but they will possess this only when Christ will come to judge all souls at the end of time.

Another work which deals with the sacraments made Severos well known among the Protestant and Catholic theologians of the 16th and 17th centuries since in their mutual disputes they referred to Severos' work in confirmation of their own positions.[72] In the introduction we find

the usual prolegomena on the sacraments, then the number
of sacraments, the definitions of each and the differences
among the seven. He insists on seven sacraments and appeals
to the seven gifts of the Holy Spirit, the seven trumpets
which were instrumental in the collapse of the walls of
Jericho and the seven lamps of the candelabra seen by
Zacharias. He affirms the indelible character of Baptism and
Holy Orders as well as of Confirmation. This latter affirma-
tion goes contrary to the consistent teaching and practice of
the Orthodox who allow for the re-chrismation of apostates.
Each sacrament is then discussed in detail. His presentation
is heavily dependent upon both scholastic doctrine and
terminology. Severos uses the Latin concepts of matter and
form [ὕλη; εἶδος] and of transubstantiation [μετουσίω-
σις]. In dealing with the sacrament of Penance he gives
the Latin doctrine of the three constitutive parts of con-
trition, confession and satisfaction. He holds that there can
be temporal pain due to sins even after sacramental absolu-
tion. Contrary to the Orthodox custom and evidently borrowed from the Latin usage, he insists on five minor orders.
The form of marriage consists in the mutual consent of the
two spouses.

Three minor works deal with liturgical matters. One
deals with the defense of the Orthodox custom of kneeling
and venerating the gifts at the Grand Entrance before the
consecration during the Byzantine Liturgy.[73] In the Middle
Ages Symeon of Thessalonika defended the Orthodox faithful against the attacks of Latins who claimed the Orthodox
were worshipping idols, by worshipping simple bread, as
though it were God. Severos now comes to the defense of
this custom against the attacks of the Protestants of the 16th
century who hold up this custom as an example of the Orthodox denial of the Real Presence. Gabriel insists upon the
Real Presence by his doctrine of transubstantiation but
defends the practice of venerating the Holy Gifts because
of a participated honor rendered to them in lieu of the

following consecration. The second work deals with the particles placed on the paten during the Byzantine Liturgy which are not consecrated and hence are not distributed as the Eucharist. The third work touches on the *kolybes* or cakes distributed to be eaten at the services for the dead or in honor of the saints.

These writings, along with his many letters, show us a theologian of limited vision and power of speculation with a certain degree of dependence upon Latin theology, especially in his sacramentology. He is consistently defensive and not too well informed about the doctrine of the Greek Fathers and Orthodox teachings.

K. N. Sathas, in his authoritative work on medieval Byzantine literature,[74] shows the development of an important genre of religious literature, that of the popular devotional literature printed in the vernacular. Through the lack of education after the conquest by the Turks, the Greeks soon felt a complete rift between the classical, Byzantine Greek, which was spoken and written by the fortunate intellectuals who studied abroad and busied themselves in writing a literature that was the same as the Byzantine theological literature of the century before, and the vernacular spoken by the populace but hitherto never written. With the advent of printing and also the ever-developing polemical nature of theological literature, the ordinary Orthodox believers thirsted for a religious literature that would be relevant for their daily needs. Writers such as Emmanuel Georgillas Limenites of Rhodes, Manuel Sklavos, Joannes Koronaeos, Iakovos Trivolis, Justus Glykys, Bergades, Joannes Pikatoros, Mark Depharanas, Joannes Ventramos and Nikander Nukios provided popular stories in verse and prose that presented to the ordinary simple people their religious beliefs in settings familiar to their daily lives.[75]

JOANNES KARTANOS

Joannes Kartanos, however, proved to be the most popular with his singular work entitled "Ανθος.[76] He was born at the beginning of the 16th century at Corfu and later became a hieromonk and protosyncellos to Bishop Athanasios of Naupactos. He wanted to open up to the people the Holy Scripture which in the original *Koine* Greek language was no longer intelligible to the masses of the faithful. His *Anthos* is divided into short chapters arranged into four divisions: 1) In Chapters 1-24 he gives a popular presentation of the main dogmas of the Christian faith. 2) In Chapters 25-191 the historical part of the Scriptures is presented as a popular bible history. 3) In Chapters 192-211 he presents the ethical teachings of the Bible, stressing especially New Testament ethics and making them applicable to everyday life. 4) He concludes with a series of liturgical explanations and a meditative exegesis of the *Our Father*. Although, as we have already seen, Pachomios of Rhus opposed him as almost a heretic, it was due more to Kartanos' attempt to open up the Bible to the illiterate in their vernacular language plus his own lack of theological sophistication that embittered Pachomios rather than true heresies. His work had a great influence on the piety of the masses.

The printing presses allowed also in the 16th century a printing of more liturgical texts with accompanying explanations. The best printers of these works resided in Rome and Venice where there was money to subsidize such works. Editions of the *Triodion, Typikon, Psalterion, Horologion, Oktoechos, Paraklitikon,* the Liturgies, the *Menaeia, Pentecostarion* and the *Euchologion* were produced in editions easy to read and use, a great contrast compared to the handwritten copies that were few and generally poorly done.

Bible exegesis was mostly a repetition of that done by the early Church Fathers and the Byzantine commentators

of the early Middle Ages. This soon exalted the principle
that the Fathers have rightly given an inspired interpretation,
as Patriarch Jeremias II formulated it in answer to the
Tübingen theologians.[77]

Church History was not well developed in this period
and consisted usually of a mere chronicle of church events.[78]
Canon Law, as Krumbacher points out,[79] was not much
developed in the 16th century. Manuel of Corinth composed
a compendium of canon law; Janos Laskaris and Manuel
Malaxos composed handbooks of church laws. Maximos
Margounios wrote *scholia* or explanations of the canons of
the ecumenical councils and the Fathers of the Church. But
in general little new development took place in this area due
undoubtedly to the turbulent times in which the Orthodox
Church was living under the Turks.

Three other theologians complete the 16th century writers
and follow much in the mediocre line of the polemicists who
preceded them. These are Zacharias Skordylios, Nathanael
Chychas and Maximos Peloponnesios. Zacharias studied in
Padua and spent most of his life in Venice as a priest and
calligrapher. His chief theological work consists of the twelve
answers that he gave to Cardinal Karl von Guise on Orthodox
beliefs and practices.[80] Chychas came from Athens to Rome
where he became a Catholic. He lived in Venice and returned
to Orthodoxy with the help of Gabriel Severos. He was
ordained a priest and died in Corfu after writing principally
polemical works against Rome and in the vernacular.[81] Little
is known of the life of Maximos other than that he was a
student of Meletios Pigas and lived about 1602 in Alexandria
and 1620 in Jerusalem. His two main works are *A Collection
against the Schism of the Papists* and *On the Eucharist.*[82]

The final writer of this period who puts the finishing
touch to a plethora of mediocre theologians is Damaskinos
the Studite. He is noted for his most famous work, Θησαυ-
ρός, which was his attempt to give the masses more of Holy
Scripture as did Kartanos.[83] He did not want to write theology

yet he succeeded admirably in combining the best of Orthodox thought. He stressed a return to the patristic tradition of an apophatic theology concerning the essence of God. He has much on Marian devotion, eschatology, the practices of asceticism and almsgiving.

THE PERIOD FROM 1612 TO 1723

During the 17th century the predominant theme again in Byzantine theology is controversy and polemics. Both Catholics and Protestants fought bitterly to draw the Orthodox, weakened financially and intellectually by Moslem domination, into their camps. The earliest trend that we notice in these chaotic times is the open reception given by certain Greek theologians to Protestant ideas. A strong reaction both in the Russian and Byzantine world followed, with a return back to more ancient Orthodox sources and traditions. The first radical break from these traditions was attempted by Cyril Lucaris.

CYRIL LUCARIS[54]

Lucaris was born in Candia on the island of Crete on November 13, 1572. As a boy of twelve he went to Venice where his compatriot and patron, Maximos Margounios, taught him classical Greek, Latin and Italian and introduced him to philosophy. After returning to Crete, his uncle, Meletios Pigas, then patriarch of Alexandria, sent him to Padua in 1589 to study philosophy and theology under such famous teachers as Mark Musuros, Francesco Piccolomini and Caesar Cremonini. Undoubtedly the spirit of Italian renaissance humanism with its elegant scepticism rubbed off onto his delicate character. Called by Meletios, who was occupying the vacant throne of Constantinople, he was tonsured monk and changed his name of Constantine to Cyril. He was ordained priest in 1594 and began his quick ascent up the hierarchical ladder. With Nicephoros Cantacuzinos, Cyril was sent by Meletios on an important mission to Brest, a border town between Lithuania and Poland. Sigismund III effected the treaty of Brest-Litovsk of 1596 which officially created the Uniate Church of the Ruthenians, those Ukrainian Orthodox who the year before had met in the Council of Brest and had opted to unite with Rome while retaining their Eastern hierarchy and customs. Cyril spent five years in Poland but was unable to avert the movement towards the *unia*. He acted as rector of the theological academy of Vilna and then taught in Lvov in an effort to form well educated Orthodox clergy to stop the losses of Orthodoxy to Rome. Meletios called Cyril home to Egypt where his uncle died in 1602. Cyril was chosen at the early age of 29 to be the patriarch of Alexandria. He served as patriarch of the see of Alexandria for 18 years.

During this time Cyril renewed contacts with Protestant theologians, especially Calvinists, whom he had met earlier and sought to obtain their theological works. A lasting friendship began with the Dutchman, Cornelius van Haga, who had been appointed envoy to the Porte Sublime. Through van Haga Cyril met the famous Dutch theologian, J. Uytenbogaert, and read continually all the Calvinist theological literature that he could obtain from his friends. In a letter to Uytenbogaert of 1613, Cyril already apparently has come under Calvinist influence in regard to the sacraments. He denies any effectual power in the sacraments themselves unless there is faith in the recipient. He holds the only true sacraments are those found in the Gospel accounts, namely, Baptism and the Eucharist.[85]

Cyril met another Calvinist Dutchman, David Le Leu de Wilhem, during the years 1617 to 1619 with whom Cyril kept up a steady correspondence. In letters to him, Lucaris shows his steady movement away from the traditional Orthodox beliefs and his open confession of Calvinist tenets. He confesses to de Wilhem that he agrees with him that Holy Scripture is the unique rule of Christian faith and states with confidence and even a certain amount of joy that in the essentials of faith he is in full agreement with the Calvinists. He is convinced that the Greek Church must be reformed, putting aside its many superstitions for a more evangelical simplicity.[86]

He writes to Mark Antonio de Domnis, an Italian Catholic archbishop who became Protestant, of his new found theological vision:

> ... Having obtained through the goodness of some friends certain writings of evangelical theology which have not only remained unseen in the East but due to Roman censures have not even been heard of, I then begged earnestly the assistance of the Holy Spirit and for three years studied the doctrines of the Greek and Latin Churches with those of the Reformed Church. ... I left the Fathers and took as the sole guide Holy Scripture and the analogy of faith. Finally I was convinced with the help of God that the cause of the Reformers was more correct and more in keeping with the doctrine of Christ; I too embraced it. I can no longer endure hearing men speak of commentaries on human tradition as being equal with Holy Scripture. ... As for icon worship, I cannot say how ruinous it is under existing circumstances ... not that I can say, absolutely speaking, that images are to be condemned, because when they are not the object of worship they do no harm, but I despise the idolatry of which they are the cause to these blind worshippers ... As for the invocation of the Saints, there was a time when I too did not understand how it hid the glory due to our Lord Christ.[87]

Lucaris was elected ecumenical patriarch on November 4, 1620, after having furnished the Sultan with the humiliating *peshkesh* or tax necessary to be invested as patriarch. The Turks had recognized a means of added revenue and were easily moved by rumors to depose one patriarch in order to elevate another, provided that in the outstretched hand of the new incumbent were the necessary piastres. A vicious abuse had developed when the Turkish authorities invested not only spiritual power but also civil authority in the hands of the patriarch and his bishops. But to become a bishop one had to become a monk. The monasteries served as places of retreat and shelter for the members of the aristocracy who sought to escape Turkish oppression and at the same time who aspired to obtain wealth and power through ecclesiastical promotion. The wealth of the monasteries, along with the change from the coenobitic life of monasticism to the more lax idiorrhythmic type, made the lives of these noble monks easy, and they were quite free to devote their leisure to political intrigues to which the flagrant simony of ecclesiastical nominations opened an extensive field.

The character of Lucaris, as revealed through his letters, shows that he was not only capable of changing his theological beliefs through personal convictions, but he was capable of flattering and cajoling in complete *volte-face* in order to obtain his personal ambitious ends. In Poland Lucaris, in an attempt to escape political persecution, wrote to the Latin archbishop of Lvov, Demetrius Sulikowski, that he was against the Protestants:

> I know very well, and the patriarchs from whom I receive my powers also know, that not only the actions and the dogmas of these heretics [the Protestants] have caused the disorders and the ruin of the Catholic Church in the East as in the West, but they also have brought about a deplorable corruption of morals among Christians. They are

ever so far from us that a reunion is hardly possible.
On the contrary, if divisions seem to exist between
the Church of the East and that of the West, they
must be attributed only to illusions of certain
ignorant persons. In Greece as in Rome, all those
who have any knowledge profess the doctrines
that are absolutely similar or at least very close to
each other. Far from despising the chair of St.
Peter, we surround it with respect and the veneration that is due it and we recognize its primacy
and the title of mother.[88]

Later in a letter written in 1634 to Antoine Leger, the
Calvinist chaplain of the Dutch Embassy in Constantinople,
Lucaris insisted that he believes in the doctrine as he outlined in his *Confession* and which is the same as the Evangelical Churches and that he wishes to die in that belief.
"... I abominate the errors of the papists and the superstitions of the Greeks. I approve and embrace the doctrine
of the excellent doctor, John Calvin, and of all those who
are in agreement with him."[89]

In a sermon addressed as an *apologia* in the parish of
the Virgin at Leontopolis, Cyril insists that he is Orthodox
and abhors Protestant errors.

From my beginning, I imbibed the milk of piety and
was raised in the Orthodox teachings. We guard
always with tenacity the Orthodox teachings of the
Eastern Church, our mother . . . But enemies who
close their eyes to the light of truth, in their desire
to find blame with us, accuse us of Calvinism and
of heresy . . . they offend against God and against
the truth.[90]

These documents reveal to us a shifting character, an
opportunist, one who adapts to the situation and adjusts his

beliefs accordingly. His cleverness in adaptation, above all, his ever growing Calvinistic loyalties made him a cause célèbre and no little anxiety for the different countries that had invested interests in the Levant. The French, Austrian and Venetian embassies in Constantinople distrusted him and sought both from religious motives as well as for political interests to depose him, while the Dutch, English and German embassies supported him in his Protestant views. At times he was caught in the game of political intrigues, perhaps at times even unfairly. Such was the case when, after reigning as patriarch for three years, he was sent in exile to Rhodes. The Grand Vizir, Hussein Pasha, listened to rumors that Lucaris was in correspondence with the Tsar of Russia as well as inciting inhabitants of one of the Aegean islands to rebellion in order to facilitate a take-over by the Florentines. Cyril was removed and replaced by Gregory of Amassia. Cyril however was soon back with the necessary *peshkesh* and reinstated. Excluding the first occupancy of the patriarchal throne when it was vacant in 1612, Cyril ascended no less than six different times following always a new trip into exile.

In 1627 Cyril arranged that the Greek monk, Nicodemos Metaxas who had learned printing in England, set up a printing press in Constantinople in order to print Greek books that would provide the sources of education for a rather ignorant Greek clergy. In March of 1629 Lucaris finished writing his *Confession of Faith*. By that time the printing press of Metaxas had been destroyed by the Janissaries and Lucaris, according to the findings of Legrand, had his *Confession* printed in Geneva.[91]

Lucaris' *Confession,* first written in Latin and then in 1631 in Greek, followed by a French translation, is divided into eighteen chapters and four questions and answers. To round out each article a series of Holy Scripture references is added as corroboration of his position. In the first article an exposition of the mystery of the Trinity is given and his doctrine of the procession of the Holy Spirit is given as from the Father through the Son. What he means by the procession of the Spirit from the Son as well as from the Father, Cyril explains in a long letter written from Valachia in 1613 to Uytenbogaert. Admitting that he has taken much on this question from Jacob Arminius who had preceded Uytenbogaert as leader of the Remonstrant School of Theology in Holland, Cyril explains by making the distinction between internal procession whereby the Spirit as an *hypostasis* or person proceeds only from the Father and external procession whereby the Spirit proceeds also from the Son ["Quando vero de externa, et a Filio asserit"].[92]

In Article II, Lucaris develops his doctrine on Holy Scripture as the supreme authority in matters of faith. He is silent about the common Orthodox teaching that maintains tradition as an equal font of inspiration. But he does show without any equivocation that ecclesiastical authority is subject to error.

> We believe . . . the testimony of the Holy Scriptures to excel that of the authority of the Church. It is not the same to be instructed by the Holy Spirit and by men. A human may sin or be deceived through ignorance. Holy Scriptures cannot deceive nor be deceived; they are not liable to err for they are infallible and have an eternal authority.[93]

Article III shows how thoroughly influenced by Calvinist doctrine Cyril had become at the time of writing his *Confession*. He confesses his belief that "before the beginning of the world, the all-good God has predestined His chosen ones to glory and this without any regard to their works. The only cause is the good pleasure and mercy of God, and likewise, before the beginning of the world, He has rejected others and the cause of this reprobation is found in the very will of God . . . still God is merciful and just."[94]

In Articles IV and V he treats the difficult topic of the relationship of evil to the Creatorship of God and the mysterious inscrutable designs of God's providence. Many events are beyond our comprehension and it is in such circumstances that faith must assert itself in believing in God's goodness and wisdom. "In all humility we should rather be silent than indulge in superfluous speculation that is not constructive."

In Articles VI and IX Lucaris deals with his doctrine of soteriology. He posits the universality of Original Sin in all men through the fall of the first man and shows how the Son of God through His *kenosis* as Jesus Christ not only assumes humanity but above all empties Himself through His death and "grants salvation and glory to all who believe in Him" through His resurrection. He poses the question of salvation as an either/or alternative: does justification come by faith or by man's own good works? His answer is that no one is saved without faith in Jesus Christ. It is this faith that justifies. Connected with Article IX is that of XIII where Lucaris states emphatically that "man is justified by faith and not by works." Only faith can bring us into contact with the justice of Christ and be salutary for us. Human works are not sufficient to allow man, the doer, to stand boldly before Christ's tribune and claim his just reward. Do human works have any meaning for Lucaris? They are necessary means [μέσα ἀναγκαῖα], not to save us, but to manifest our faith and confirm us in our vocation.

In the following article (XIV) he describes the effects of sin on man's free will. Free will in the unregenerated is dead; man is absolutely incapable of doing good; in fact, all that man can do in such a state is sin. The regenerated, however, come alive through the Holy Spirit. Man can now do good, but a prevenient grace is necessary to heal the wounded free will.

The subject of the Church is dealt with in Articles X, XI and XII. He distinguishes between two Churches: the invisible and true Church to which belong the regenerated, the elect, those predestined eternally for beatific happiness and the visible Church in which "wheat and chaff are mixed together." Jesus Christ alone is the sole head of the Church; no human being or group of humans can ever take upon themselves this prerogative. The Church therefore, made up of human beings, has no infallibility. "It is true and certain that it is possible for the Church to err on its way and to choose falsehood instead of truth. From this error and deceit only the teaching and illumination of the Holy Spirit can deliver and not that of any human being."

Lucaris presents his sacramentology in Articles XV, XVI and XVII. "We believe the Gospel sacraments in the Church to be those which the Lord has delivered in the Gospels and these are two. Two have been given to us. And the Law-maker has given no more." He rejects, as bordering on superstition, the teaching of the efficacy of the sacraments "ex opere operato," merely through the proper performance of the sacraments. Only when the participator in these sacraments possesses a genuine faith do the sacraments become complete. Cyril's teaching about the Eucharist tries to maintain a balance between the belief in the true presence of traditional Orthodoxy and the "faith presence" of the Protestant tradition. He explicitly rejects the doctrine of transsubstantiation and insists that the believer does not partake of the body of the Lord with his teeth by chewing but spiritually and by faith. The presence of the Lord is secured "only if we believe; if we do not believe we are deprived of all profit from the sacrament."

In the final article Lucaris dismisses the teaching of purgatory as a fable and maintains only two classes of citizens entering into eternity: either those who have been justified in this life and those who before they died were not justified. He concludes: ". . . we declare that each one must repent now and seek the forgiveness of his sins through the Lord Jesus Christ in order to be saved."

Lucaris appended four questions and answers to his *Confession*. The first deals with the right of every Christian to read the Holy Scripture. This would follow from his insistence on Scripture as the only divine source of revelation. In the second question he faces up to the difficulty in interpreting Holy Scripture since there are many obscure passages whose meaning is not evident upon first reading. Cyril consoles the reader: for those who have been born again and enlightened by the Holy Spirit all things are gradually made clear. The third question deals with the canonical books and appeals to the canon from the Synod of Laodicea as the establishing norm. The fourth gives Cyril another opportunity to criticize the superstition that he thought he found rampant among the simple Greek believers in regard to icon veneration. After quoting, in the fashion of the best 8th and 9th century iconoclasts, the biblical command not to make graven images, he rejects any worship or adoration tied to them. Only God, the Creator of colors and art and all created things, is to be worshipped, but not the artistic expression of God and the Saints.

Not needing to claim any special charismatic gifts of prophecy, Lucaris ends his *Confession* with the statement: "This Confession of ours will be a sign which is spoken against"; and so it has become down through the centuries. Three months after Lucaris' death (on June 27, 1638, at the age of 66), Cyril Contari, bishop of Beroea, a great enemy of Lucaris and a friend of the Jesuits of Constantinople and Rudolph Schmidt, the Austrian ambassador in Constantinople, became patriarch. In the synod that gathered in 1638 in Constantinople, Cyril Contari, Theophanes, patriarch of Jerusalem, Metrophanes Critopoulos, protégé of Lucaris and patriarch of Alexandria, 21 bishops and 23 other clerical dignitaries, including Meletios Syrigos, signed the decree of thirteen anathemas against Lucaris' teachings and the condemnation of the man "who, intoxicated by a death-dealing poison and corrupted by an incurable sickness, propagated by wiles and deceits false doctrines concerning the principal points of faith."[95] Explicitly condemned were his teachings that the Holy Church can err, that God, before any merit on man's part, predestines some to glory, others to eternal punishments, that Saints are not mediators before God; that man has no free will to do good, that there are only two sacraments, that transubstantiation is a fabricated lie, that the prayers of the Church do not help the dead, that veneration of images must be done away with.

Still the influence of Lucaris' Protestant ideas and an incipient martyr's cult began to spread not only throughout the Greek world but even into Moldavia and as far as Kiev. Metropolitan Peter Mogila, who had participated in the 1638 synod of Constantinople, summoned a synod of the Kievan Church in 1640 in order to condemn the doctrines of Lucaris.

After Cyril Contari was deposed in 1642 and strangled on his way to exile, Parthenios I, the new patriarch, noticed that Lucaris' influence was still very much alive. Nicephoros Corydalleos, a friend of Lucaris, preached publicly a eulogy in which he praised Lucaris for his Orthodox teachings. Meletios Syrigos, who had participated in the 1638 synod and was instrumental in condemning the unorthodox doctrines of Lucaris, preached publicly against Lucaris. Parthenios sent out a letter summoning all Greek and Slav metropolitans to send their representatives to Jassy, Moldavia. His letter of 18 chapters opposed in detail the 18 chapters of Lucaris and served as the nucleus for the decree drawn up at Jassy in 1642. This synod lasted from May until September and in 20 sessions each item found in the Confession of Lucaris was subjected to criticism. The Confession of Faith drawn up by Peter Mogila, translated and amended by Meletios Syrigos, was accepted as an accurate confession of true Orthodoxy.

Mesoloras considers the Synod of Jassy as a great historical event which brought a unanimous rejection by the Greek and Russian Churches of all Western innovations and offered in answer the positive exposition of the true and authentic Orthodox doctrine as expressed in the Confession of Faith of Peter Mogila.[96]

One final reaction against the *Confession* of Lucaris was the condemnation in six decrees against the Calvinist doctrines by the Synod of Jerusalem that was summoned in March, 1672, some thirty years after the death of Cyril. Besides the unanimous decision to condemn the doctrine found in the *Confession,* there seemed to be an evident division among the participants as to whether Cyril Lucaris was really the author of this document that bears his name. Some insisted, by citing his sermons, that Cyril could not have been the author of such an heretical document; others wanted to condemn him as a heretic. The final decrees show the compromise as to the personal condemnation of Cyril.[97] In the first decree it is stated that Lucaris was not the author of the *Confession* while in the second, a more cautious assertion in the manner of a hypothesis, it is stated that if he really wrote the *Confession,* then Patriarch Cyril has insulted the Christians of the East. In the third and fourth decrees the Calvinistic doctrine put forth in the *Confession* is rejected as un-Orthodox and all association with Calvinistic teachings is rejected. The fifth decree concludes that if Lucaris was truly a Calvinist heretic, then "we are all of one accord in hurling against him and his heretical associates a perpetual sentence of anathema and excommunication."

The 6th decree introduces Dositheos' Confession of faith "for those who desire to learn what is the faith and profession of the Orthodox Church." Mesoloras has compared each chapter of the Confession of Dositheos with the corresponding chapters of Lucaris' *Confession* to show that Dositheos had in mind not only a refutation but a reestablishment through an "orthodox" confession of faith of the fundamental doctrines questioned by Lucaris.[98] This Confession will be analyzed later on. It suffices to say here in relation to Cyril Lucaris that the Confession of Dositheos, couched in strongly scholastic terminology, asserts the need of both faith and works, holds a state of purgation after death and even teaches the Latin concept of transubstantiation.

The whole problem of whether Lucaris was the true author of the *Confession* bearing his name is too involved to solve here.[99] One can certainly sympathize with the many Orthodox scholars who wish to clear away the taint of heresy from the name of one of the greatest patriarchs that occupied the throne of the patriarchate of Constantinople. The major proof seems to indicate, however, that he was the author. The *Confession* appeared nine years before his death and Lucaris never once denied that he authored the document; rather to the contrary, we possess many of his letters to Protestant theologians such as Uytenbogaert, Le Leu de Wilhem, Leger, Mark Antonio de Dominis and others wherein he clearly speaks about his *Confession* and his similar teachings that mirror exactly the teaching found in the *Confession.* The Roman Catholics, especially the Jesuits of Constantinople, used it against Cyril and still no protest came from Cyril denying authorship. We also have the strong condemnation of the person of Lucaris as the author of the heretical Confession in the Synod of 1638 with Metrophanes Critopoulos, who owed so much to Cyril as one of the signers. If there had been the slightest doubt that Cyril was the author, Critopoulos, Cyril's protégé, would have protested.

METROPHANES CRITOPOULOS[100]

Critopoulos, as recorded in his writings or in those of historians, is presented as a little-known personality. The facts of his life are told quickly and clearly. But what sort of a person he was, how he affected other persons, little of this shines through any account of this man. He was born in Beroea in Macedonia in 1589. As a very young man he embraced monasticism on Mount Athos where he met Cyril

Lucaris who seemed to be impressed by his talents. He accompanied Lucaris, at that time patriarch of Alexandria, back to Egypt where he was ordained priest and made protosyncellos. Lucaris arranged with George Abbot, archbishop of Canterbury, that Metrophanes be allowed to study in England. He studied at Oxford for about seven years and then traveled extensively throughout Germany and Switzerland. He returned to Egypt where he was made bishop and finally patriarch of Alexandria (1633-1639). He participated in the synod of Constantinople in 1638 which anathematized Lucaris; and he died suddenly, probably through an assassination, in Vallachia in 1639 at the age of 50 years.

While in Germany and Switzerland he was eagerly asked by the Protestant Lutherans and Calvinists to explain to them the Orthodox faith, since there was great interest among the Protestants towards the East. On such an occasion, encouraged by Protestant theologians of Helmstadt such as George Callixtus and Conrad Horneius, Critopoulos composed his major work, his *Confession of the Eastern Catholic Church.*[101]

The *Confession* of Critopoulos contains 23 chapters which purport to set out for the Protestants the whole compass of the Orthodox Faith. In outline form he treats of the following topics:[102]

1. Doctrine of the Church (1—51). The first Church begins within the bosom of the Holy Trinity. A long dissertation on the procession of the Holy Spirit follows with a detailed refutation of the Latin arguments concerning the *Filioque.* The patristic formulas: διὰ τοῦ Υἱοῦ, ἐξ ἀμφοῖν which speak of a procession through the Son or from both the Father and the Son refer to the temporal procession *ad extra.*

2. Creation (52-64). God created the angels in ten

ranks or orders. Lucifer and his followers were in the last order. God created man to fill the gap left in creation by the defection of the fallen angels. A discourse on the fall of man.

3. On the Incarnation (65-78).

4. On predestination (79-88). God predestines those whom He knows by foreknowledge to be worthy of His grace. The goodness and wisdom of God solely move God to bestow His gifts upon the elect. Seeing man's poverty and inability to rise from his fallen state, God is moved by pity. His wisdom allows God to give His gifts to those who will not misuse them.

5. Sacraments (89-93). There are three sacraments: Baptism and the Eucharist which are the sacraments of promises made to the elect; Penance is needed for further salvation. The other sacraments are considered as "mystical rites" but are not found in the Gospel, hence are not absolutely necessary.

6. On Justification (94-99). There are two aspects in justification. The first process frees man from Original Sin, and the sole cause of this is the goodness of the Father through the blood of Jesus Christ. The second phase of justification frees us from our own sins; its antecedent cause is again the goodness of the Father; its consequent cause is our own care and diligence.

7. On the Church (100-109). There is a general meaning of Church: it embraces all who answer to the Gospel, whether they be Orthodox or not. Specifically the Church applies to only those Orthodox who have been healed perfectly in

Christ. This they do by adhering to the true teaching as outlined in the Nicene-Constantino-politan Symbol. The true Church can be recognized by its teaching of the unanimous doctrine of her teachers wherein she neither adds nor subtracts but transmits faithfully that which she receives from the holy Fathers. The Church does not persecute but often will be persecuted. She, amidst persecution, will be faithful to observe the word of God as given by the Prophets and the Apostles. This revealed word is either written or unwritten. The Deuterocanonical books, Tobias, Judith, Wisdom, Baruch and Maccabees, are not inspired but apocryphal; hence there are only 33 books of true inspiration. The unwritten revelation of God touches the traditions of the Church such as the manner of administration of the sacraments and in other areas that lend to the benefit and honor of the Church.

8. On Chrismation (110-114). Chrismation and Baptism are complementary actions with Chrismation perfecting what is symbolized in Baptism. Most of this chapter deals with the effects of Baptism in destroying Original Sin.

9. On the Last Supper (115-132). The Real Presence is affirmed as permanent but the manner of the change is something that cannot be investigated.

10-13. On Penance, Holy Orders, Marriage, Anointing of the Sick (133-156).

14-22. On Other Rites of the Church: Icons, Relics, Invocation of Saints, Fasting, Monasticism, Prayers for the Dead, on Facing the East in Prayer, on not Kneeling on Sundays (157-202).

23. On the Situation of the Oriental Church (203-213). A somber picture of the imperfect state of the Eastern Orthodox Church but hope that comes from the unanimity among the four leading Eastern Patriarchs under Jesus Christ, the only Head of the Church.

There have been various schools of thought among the Orthodox theologians as to the value to be assigned to Critopoulos' *Confession*. Some such as Mesoloras maintain that it is pure, authentic Orthodox teaching and constitutes a symbolic confession.[103] Others hold that it has no universal symbolic value obligatory on all Orthodox but it constitutes a private confession, the doctrine of one theologian who thus sought to explain Orthodox doctrines to the Protestants without, as Androutsos insists, becoming tainted by any Calvinistic heresies.[104] Some think that he was influenced by Protestant literature and theology and although he does not swerve from the important, essential truths as taught by Orthodoxy, he does mingle Protestant terminology and viewpoints in lesser matters.[105] A final group calls him a Calvinist and accuses him of having taught heresies concerning his doctrine of the sacraments, definition of the Church, the inspired books of the Old Testament and his anthropology.[106] A synod was held in 1925 on Mount Athos which vindicated Critopoulos and his *Confession* as freed from Protestant errors. The Russians almost universally have ignored it as anything other than a private confession of faith of a Greek theologian trying to interpret his Orthodox faith in language that would be understood by German Protestants. Michalcescu's view, however, seems to be the predominant one among Orthodox thinkers today; namely, that this *Confession* was definitely under an influence from Protestant theology, especially in Critopoulos' treatment of the sacraments (admitting only three), in his concept of the Church and in his rejection of the Deutero-canonical Books.[107]

MELETIOS SYRIGOS[108]

Syrigos stands out uniquely during his lifetime as a theologian of the old Byzantine school. Fighting to preserve Orthodoxy from both Roman Latinism and Protestantism, he seemed singularly preserved in his manner of thinking from any Western scholastic categories or concepts.

Born in Candia, Crete about 1585, he studied as a young man rhetoric, mathematics and physics in Padua in preparation for a career in medicine. The unexpected death of his parents forced him to return to Crete where he entered a monastery and changed his name of Mark to Meletios. He soon distinguished himself as a preacher and by his zeal to defend Orthodoxy against Catholicism. This embittered him to the Venetian government which ruled Crete and so, to escape a death penalty, he fled to Egypt. After spending four years there, he was summoned by Cyril Lucaris to Constantinople. To counteract the disturbing Jesuits who had centered their activities outside of Constantinople in Galata, Cyril placed Meletios in the church of Chrysopeghe, opposite the Jesuits, where Meletios delivered weekly homilies covering the entire liturgical cycle.

Cyril sent Meletios on a series of important diplomatic missions into Rumania in order to see at first hand the proselytizing efforts of the Catholics among the Orthodox. Upon the death of Lucaris, Meletios became the theologian to refute Cyril's theological errors. No doubt he was the theological hand that Cyril Contari wielded in the Synod of Constantinople in 1638 to condemn both the memory and the *Confession* of Lucaris. Meletios began this same year to formulate his answers to Lucaris' *Confession* in a more detailed work that was finished in 1640 and entitled: Ὀρθόδοξος ἀντίρρησις κατὰ τῶν κεφαλαίων καὶ ἐρωτήσεων τοῦ Κυρίλλου.[109] First written in classical Greek, Meletios himself translated it into the vernacular Greek and Dositheos published it in 1690. Meletios follows rather

closely the subject matter treated in the 18 chapters of
Lucaris' *Confession*. The work is characterized by a lack of
speculation, especially in scholastic terms, a relatively serene
polemical spirit with an abundance of citations from Holy
Scripture and the Greek Fathers. His defense of the doctrine
of transubstantiation against the nebulous, speculation on
the Real Presence of Lucaris made this work, or at least
the section on transubstantiation, well known among Western
Catholics who reproduced it regularly.[110] The fact that Syrigos
had studied in Italy and knew Latin well opened up to
him Latin sources that he could use; still he remained free
from using their concepts, something which Dositheos did
not always succeed in doing, as will be pointed out shortly.

Patriarch Parthenios I, in answer to the summons of the
Metropolitan of Kiev, Peter Mogila, to send representatives
to meet in Jassy in order to draw up a refutation of Cyril
Lucaris' *Confession*, sent Meletios and a companion to
Moldavia. Mogila sent three delegates: Isiia Trofimovich
Koslovskii, hegoumen of the monastery of St. Nicholas of
Kiev, Ignatii Oksenovich Starusich, a famed preacher, and
Iosif Kononovich, the rector of the Kievan Academy. These
five constituted what Orthodox history has euphemously
called the Synod of Jassy of 1642. It consisted of a series
of theological discussions which did not always yield unanimity. The three Russians had brought with them Peter
Mogila's *Confession* in the hopes that it would also be
accepted by the Greeks as the true statement of Orthodox
confession to offset the Calvinistic version of Lucaris. The
problem of an intermediate state of purgatory and the
epiclesis proved to be two points of variance between the
more Occidental indoctrinated Kievan theologians and
Meletios, representing the more ancient Byzantine tradition.
Meletios was commissioned to translate the *Confession* of
Mogila into Greek and obtain approbation from Parthenios I.

Syrigos spent all of 1643 in southern Russia where he
met Peter Mogila and submitted to him his proposed changes.

Mogila would not change his *Confession* and later composed his *Small Catechism* as his answer to Meletios.[111] Syrigos' Greek translation of the *Confession* was probably done in 1643 or 1644; however the official text, approved in 1662 by the four Oriental patriarchs, was probably printed in Greek only in 1667 after Mogila's death and contained Meletios' emendations.[112] His corrections which received the approbation of the four patriarchs in 1643 and finally in 1662 touched on the rejection of a purgatory as an intermediate stage after death and the epiclesis.

When Syrigos had returned from his trip to Russia he found that Parthenios II, a friend to Lucaris and his Calvinistic ideas, had taken over the see of Constantinople and so Syrigos went into a series of voluntary exiles until Patriarch Parthenios II finally died in 1650. Syrigos returned to Constantinople where for the remainder of his 14 years he wrote and preached until his death in 1664 at the age of 78. Most of his writings have not yet been edited; chief among these are his many sermons and homilies. He also wrote several liturgical compositions and hagiographies which centered around the lives of the Greek martyrs of the 16th and 17th centuries under the fanatical persecutions of the Moslems.[113] One of his liturgical compositions had lasting effects upon the Russian Orthodox Church. In 1654, the Synod of Moscow, under Patriarch Nikon, sent to the Ecumenical Patriarch, Paisios I, a list of questions as a preparation for the reform of the Russian Byzantine Liturgy and the liturgical texts. Paisios responded to the 27 questions with a document signed by 25 metropolitans representing the Greek Church and translated into vernacular Greek by Syrigos. I. Troitskii published in 1881 the original document sent to Nikon which states that it was Syrigos "who composed this document on order of Patriarch Paisios and his synod."[114] This important document served as the basis for Nikon's liturgical reforms and hence triggered the schism between the official Russian Orthodox Church and the Old Believers.

PAISIOS LIGARIDES[115]

Ligarides, according to the details that Legrand has gathered together concerning his life and his character,[116] appears as a tragic character, caught in church politics and the theological problems of his times but yet completely victimized by his own greed and personal ambition. He strikes one as a cunning opportunist, clever, even at times intelligent, yet fickle in his readiness to betray his own principles for personal advancement and financial remuneration.

He was born in 1609 or 1610 on the island of Chios of parents who belonged to a very small segment of Catholics of the Greek rite. At thirteen years of age he was sent to the Greek College (St. Athanasios) of Rome where he obtained a thorough grounding in the humanities, philosophy and theology. Ordained a priest, he was sent in 1641 by the Propagation of Faith to the Near East to work there for reunion. He typifies the Roman policy that had despaired over long centuries of any corporate reunion between the Orthodox Churches and Rome. With the establishment of the Greek College and in rapid succession other similar Eastern rite colleges in Rome, the strategy of Rome, as incorporated into the working policy of the Propagation of Faith, was to prepare a cadre of intelligent native priests and even foreign missionaries to proselytize among the Orthodox faithful in an effort to form Eastern Catholic groups of the various Orthodox rites. Ligarides was one of the great hopes of the Propagation of Faith due to his intelligence and zeal. The history of this Greek proved totally otherwise. Receiving an annual subsidy to carry on his work among the Orthodox, Paisios managed not only to win the confidence of the Greek Orthodox but even of those who held high offices in the Orthodox Church. Patriarch Parthenios I gave him permission to preach, celebrate and to hear confessions in Constantinople, while later in Moldavia the prince of Vallachia

designated him his preacher, confessor and theologian. Here
he met Patriarch Paisios of Jerusalem who brought Ligarides
back with him to the Holy City. In Jerusalem Ligarides
became tonsured and changed his name of Panteleimon to
Paisios in honor of the patriarch. In 1652 the patriarch consecrated Paisios metropolitan of Gaza; still Ligarides insisted
before the Franciscans in the Holy Lands that he was still
Catholic. His duplicity both before the Catholic and Orthodox world reached its climax when he wrote Rome under
his new title, asking that his allowance be brought up to
date.

Returning to Rumania, Paisios received from Nikon, the
Moscow patriarch, an invitation to come to Moscow and
assist him in his liturgical reforms. Nikon needed someone
like Ligarides to carry out the needed corrections of the
Slavonic liturgical texts. He waited four years to go to
Moscow, perhaps waiting for a more opportune and more
remunerative time. Tsar Aleksei received him with great honor,
respect and even regarded him somewhat as a prophet, one
ready at least to prophesize great and pleasant things for
the tsar. Kapterev lists many of the underhanded intrigues
of Ligarides in his greed to exploit the Muscovites.[117] Ligarides
is characterized as: "... a metropolitan, a fairly talented ad-
venturist, sufficiently cultivated, capable of rendering in any
fashion whatsoever any service for which he hoped to be
richly reimbursed."[118]

Ligarides found himself the oracle to whom not only
Nikon and the clergy had recourse but also to whom Tsar
Aleksei appealed to straighten out the affairs in the Russian
Church caused by the condemnation of Nikon by the Synod
of 1660. Ligarides justified the action of the tsar and the
synod and personally sent out invitations in the name of the
tsar to all the other four Oriental patriarchs to come to
Moscow for a synod to re-examine the affair. Patriarchs
Macarius of Antioch and Paisios of Alexandria arrived in
Moscow in 1666 and assisted at the synod which Ligarides

inspired and carried through with amazing adroitness, even
to absolving his own character of accusations made by his
many enemies. Nikon was condemned and deposed through
the main efforts of Ligarides. Whether through naiveté
or the mere fact that he needed Ligarides, Tsar Aleksei began
to depend more and more upon Paisios to run the Moscow
patriarchate. Casimir, king of Poland, showed deference to
his influence by writing to Paisios, inviting him to work for
the reunion of the Russian Church and Rome.

But Ligarides was not to enjoy his role of influence upon
the Russian Church for long. Dositheos, patriarch of Jerusalem, following upon a war that his predecessor Nectarios
had waged against Paisios, sent the latter a letter in which
he excommunicated him and suspended him from not only
his office but also his rank. Paisios is called a "λατινό-
φρονα" because of his sympathies towards the Latins and
is considered not worthy to be further numbered among
Orthodox.[119] Tsar Aleksei refused him any further favor.
Upon the tsar's death, a strong reaction against Greeks and
Byzantine influence swept over Russia during the reign of
the new tsar, Feodor. Paisios Ligarides was forbidden to leave
Kiev where he died in 1678.

The writings of Ligarides have principally remained unedited or lost. Legrand gives a partial listing[120] which includes
an explanation of the Liturgy, four exhortations written to
Protestants in Vallachia to give up their errors; a collection
of oracles made of Constantinople, the new Rome, in the
past, present and future; and the history of the condemnation
of Patriarch Nikon, a work translated into English by William
Palmer.[121] Other works that we know he wrote include answers
to 61 questions that Tsar Aleksei addressed to him on various
religious problems, fourteen instructions on the feasts of Our
Lord and Lady and a famous history of the patriarchs of
Jerusalem, probably written in 1651-1652 when he lived in
Jerusalem. Dositheos used this in the writing of his own larger
work on the same topic even though he claims that Paisios

wrote it to defend the Roman primacy and Methodios III, patriarch of Constantinople (1668-1671), had condemned the work.

One work has been preserved for us in accessible form which treats Ligarides' doctrine of the Real Presence in the Holy Eucharist.[122] This is a treatise written in answer to the request of Count de Lilienthal, a Swede living in Moscow who wanted to know whether the Eucharist contains in a real manner, after the Consecration, or only virtually by way of symbolism, the Body and Blood of Christ. Ligarides in his answer depends completely upon Latin theology and philosophy to explain his doctrine of transubstantiation [μεταποίησις]. He strongly denies any impanation theory as preached by the Protestants. All of the substance of bread, is changed after the Consecration into the Body of the Lord; all of the wine is changed into His Blood.

Ligarides is not important for his theological writings as much as he stands as an example of many others of his epoch during which Greeks were educated in Italy, especially at the papal Greek College, only to return to Orthodox lands and there to live partly as Orthodox, partly as Catholics, at least in their theological thinking. He also lived in a period when the Russian Church was seeking under Nikon to make its last overture to Constantinople and Byzantine theological influence before it cut itself off conclusively from its maternal Church. The Likhoudes brothers are also part of that epoch.

LIKHOUDES BROTHERS[123]

Joannikos and Sophronios Likhoudes were born of an ancient Byzantine aristocratic family on the island of Cephalonia. Both studied in Venice and Padua for nine years and then returned to their native land in 1670 with their doctorate in theology. After receiving monastic tonsure and ordination to the priesthood, they met Dositheos, patriarch of Jerusalem, who sent the brothers in answer to Ioakim, patriarch of Moscow, who requested Greek professors to teach the Russians Hellenic culture. They accepted this arduous undertaking and set about in 1687 to develop an academy of learning in Moscow plus setting up a printing press. Theological disputes, not only with Latin Jesuits but with Kievan professors heavily imbued with Latin theology, occupied much of their activity. The main controversy in these beginning years in Moscow centered upon the question of the *epiclesis* and the exact moment of the consecration during the Liturgy. The Likhoudes maintained against the Kievan position, as proposed by Professor Medvedskii, the Byzantine position of Nicolas Cabasilas and Mark of Ephesus who taught the absolute necessity of the *epiclesis* to effect the transubstantiation.

Enemies soon began to focus attacks upon the brothers. One that caused them particular grief was Patriarch Dositheos who originally had sent them to Moscow. Hurt pride that the Likhoudes Brothers were not grateful enough to Dositheos and unwilling to follow his advice on how to administer the Academy of Moscow turned into bitter hatred and even accusations of heresy on the part of Dositheos towards the brothers. Certain Muscovites disliked their sense of superiority in advancing Byzantinism over Russian culture and Slavic theology and soon grew to suspect their orthodoxy. The brothers were deprived of their teaching posts in the Academy and allowed to operate only the printing press. During this time both brothers wrote many polemical works, especially against the Lutherans, Calvinists, Latins, and aided their disciple, Feodor Polikarpov, in editing his tri-lingual dictionary in Slavonic, Greek and Latin. In 1704 they were accused in true Byzantine-intrigue-fashion of having passed on valuable information in letters to the Sultan in Constantinople concerning the affairs of Russian politics and they were exiled to the monastery of Hypatiev in Kostroma.

They were sent to a monastery of Novgorod in 1706 where Metropolitan Job utilized their services in setting up a school and in correcting the Slavonic translation of the Bible. Joannikos died in 1717 while Sophronios was recalled as professor in the Moscow Academy until 1722. He died in the monastery of Novospasskii near Moscow in 1730.

The Likhoudes Brothers were primarily concerned with polemical writing. Roman Catholics, Protestants of Lutheran and Calvinist beliefs and Old Believers were the targets of their theological writings. Most of these works have remained unedited and contain no great theological originality. Against the Protestants, the Likhoudes composed three main polemical works: a work against the Lutheran heresy, giving 19 dogmatic or ritual differences between Lutheran beliefs and Orthodoxy; a discourse on predestination and a letter to Peter the Great on the heresies of Luther and Calvin.[124] In a work published a century ago with the title of *Mechets Dukhovnyi* [Spiritual Sword], the differences between the Orthodox and the Catholic Churches are presented in the form of 21 dialogues between a professor of the Greek language and a Jesuit.[125] The principal differences are listed as the primacy of the pope, the new calendar, *Filioque,* changes in the administration of Baptism, fasting, dropping of the *epiclesis* in the Divine Liturgy, prohibiting the chalice to the laity, refusing infants Holy Communion, insisting on fire in purgatory, teaching that the blessed enjoy immediately the beatific vision and the doctrine of the Immaculate Conception. A lengthy work on the sacraments in general and the *epiclesis* in particular takes the form of a dialogue between a teacher and a disciple and is their answer to the Kiev-Moscow disputes on the *epiclesis* doctrine.

Joannikos and Sophronios Likhoudes rendered valuable service to the Russian Orthodox Church through their many years of teaching and administering in the Moscow Academy and in other schools in Russia, in their correction of liturgical texts, and in the translation of the Slavonic Bible and in the

Slavonic edition of Mogila's Confession. They also brought into Russian theology from times past the Byzantine polemics as a genre of theological writing. They widened the gulf between the two leading theological schools of Russia, Kiev and Moscow, and in one sense, perhaps, they hastened exactly what they wanted to avoid, namely, an openness to the West that Peter the Great would inaugurate in spite of the efforts of the Likhoudes.

DOSITHEOS OF JERUSALEM[126]

Patriarch of Jerusalem for 38 years, Dositheos achieved outstanding results throughout the whole Orthodox Church by his unflagging zeal to combat Protestant and Roman Catholic influences that had begun to infiltrate into Orthodox teaching with the advent of Cyril Lucaris in the early part of the 17th century. Dositheos was born May 31, 1641 in the Peloponnesos. Orphaned at a very early age, he was placed in the monastery of the Holy Apostles by the metropolitan of Corinth, Gregory Galanos, where he did his studies. He met Patriarch Paisios of Jerusalem in Constantinople and accompanied him to Jerusalem. His talents and energies made him rise rapidly in episcopal honors. In 1666 he was made metropolitan of Caesarea and the following year was sent to Rumania as exarch. He was elevated in 1669 to the patriarchal see of Jerusalem when he was a mere 28 years old.

Eager to place his patriarchate on a sounder financial basis, he traveled extensively throughout Rumania, Bulgaria, Russia and Asia Minor to collect money. He waged a constant battle against the Franciscans for the possession of the holy places of Jerusalem and Bethlehem. After securing in 1675 a guarantee from Mohammed IV to rightly possess these sanctuaries, the intrigues of Marquis de Nointel, ambassador of France in Constantinople, regained the rights for the

Franciscans. From that time Dositheos, in his anger, refused to stay in Jerusalem.

Not possessing a deeply penetrating intellect, Dositheos, nonetheless, was filled with a dream that spurred him on to become a great defender of Orthodox doctrine, not merely within his own patriarchate but throughout all of the Greek and Slav Orthodox world. He took seriously his role as defender of the faith, not only in spreading what he conceived to be the true Orthodox doctrine in opposition to the errors of the Roman Catholics and the Protestants by means of the printing establishment that he financed in Jassy, Rumania, but also through his ecclesiastical and political intervention in practically all affairs that were of any magnitude during his life time in the Orthodox Church.

Patriarch Ioakim of Moscow (1674-1690) asked him to send to Russia some Greeks to help in spreading Byzantine learning. Dositheos sent the two brothers, Joannikios and Sophronios Likhoudes who opened in Moscow an academy of Greek, Slavonic and Latin learning. Dositheos was responsible for turning the Muscovites against the two brothers when the latter disagreed with Dositheos in regard to their unbending opposition to Occidental theology and the use of Latin. Dositheos did all he could to malign their reputation and they were eventually expelled from Moscow.

Dositheos also sought to rid Russia of Stefan Iavorskii who held the patriarchal see when it became vacant during Peter the Great's rule. Dositheos did not like Iavorskii's evident Latin theology on certain doctrines, but he did not succeed in having Iavorskii discharged. This was the great defeat in Dositheos' life as he saw Russian Orthodoxy move farther and farther away from his dream of a united Byzantine Empire based upon the religious and literary influence of Byzantine Hellenism.

When Patriarch Nikon had been expelled from his see and anathematized by the Synod of Moscow in 1666, it was Dositheos who interceded upon the request of Tsar Feodor

(1676-1682) with the Ecumenical Patriarch Iakovos (1679-1683) to absolve Nikon of all anathemas incurred from the 1666 synod.

Dositheos' greatest accomplishment that established his erudition before the whole Orthodox world for centuries to come came through the printing press that he set up in Jassy, Rumania, and entrusted to the monk Metrophanes. He demonstrated to the Christian world his ability as a compiler and indefatigable editor in the innumerable works that were published through his editorship. One of his main objectives in publishing Orthodox books was to provide the Orthodox faithful, living in countries that were exposed to Latin Catholic influences, with works of approved Orthodox theologians that not only refuted Latin doctrine and practices but above all presented the Orthodox position. The first work printed was a treatise of Nectarios, patriarch of Jerusalem (d. 1676), against the primacy of the pope.[127] This work, along with many others, Dositheos hoped would combat the progress of the Uniate movement in the Ukraine and overcome the apologetics of Allatios, Bellarmine and Richard.

In 1672 Dositheos called together in Jerusalem a synod of 71 members of his clergy, bishops and priests which furnished him the occasion to produce his most well known work. This synod was decisive not only in the history of his patriarchate but throughout all the Orthodox world as the summoning of forces to combat within Orthodox theology and piety any Protestant influences. The six decrees of the *Acta,* as has been already mentioned, dealt primarily with refuting the *Confession* of Lucaris. This section Dositheos called in his edition of the *Acta,* 'Ασπὶς or the *Shield.* The second half of the *Acta* contains his *Confession,* his most famous work that has been generally accepted by all Orthodox as a symbolical book setting forth the traditional teaching of the Orthodox faith.[128] Dositheos' *Confession* is divided into eight chapters, which present a systematic exposition of the Orthodox doctrine on God, the Trinity, Holy Scripture and its interpretation, God's foreknowledge, human liberty, the creation of the world, the goodness of God, Original Sin and evil, the Incarnation, redemption, the mediation of the Saints, faith and good works, the Church and the hierarchy, infallibility in the Church, the sacraments, especially the Eucharist, and eschatology. In four questions and answers appended to the Confession Dositheos takes up similar questions asked by Cyril Lucaris in his own *Confession:* Can everyone read Holy Scripture? What are the rules to avoid false interpretation of Scripture? What books are canonically inspired? Can we legitimately venerate Saints?

Michalcescu points out the evident dependence upon Latin theology in Dositheos' refutation of Protestant doctrine on the sacraments, transubstantiation and the life hereafter.[129] The patriarch clearly teaches the Latin explanation of transubstantiation [μετουσίωσις], and an intermediate stage of purification after death. Protestants have accused Dositheos of having depended excessively upon Roman Catholic doctrine. Greek theologians, as Archimandrite Chrysostom Papadopoulos, excuse him since he borrows from Latin doctrines which do not intrinsically contradict the Orthodox faith.[130] In spite of the Latinisms in the Confession of Dositheos, it was considered to represent, as far as any confessional symbol of faith could, an authoritative statement which the four patriarchs of Constantinople, Alexandria, Antioch and Jerusalem signed and sent to the Synod of St. Petersburg in 1723. But the Russians, as Makarii points out, accepted it only after the evident Latinisms were excised.[131] Dositheos himself later recognized that he had borrowed from Latin sources. It was probably due to a necessity. Faced as one of the early Orthodox theologians with the task of combatting Protestant influence within Orthodox theological circles and rather unprepared as far as having available an Orthodox apologetic methodology and terminology, Dositheos did rely upon Latin theology. In 1690 Dositheos himself rejected at least his teaching in the Confession on the inter-mediate stage of purgation.[132]

Again, as in the case of the other symbolic confessions of faith, there has not been universal acceptance of the exact degree of authority to be given to the Confession of Dositheos. The synod of Constantinople, called to anathematize Joannes Cariophyllos in 1691, declared that this confession was completely without blame and that it taught the full Ortho-dox faith.[133] Still modern Orthodox writers assign it various degrees of authority. Mesoloras ranks it equally with the *Confession* of Peter Mogila.[134] Michalcescu confirms this opinion.[135] Androutsos assigns to it the value of a symbol of faith[136] while Makarii, Sil'vestr and Malinovskii give the commonly accepted Russian opinion that ranks this con-fession as a private confession of faith.[137]

That so many works are attributed to Dositheos is a credit to his ability to compile from other sources to produce not so much individual books but compendia of writings on given topics. Dositheos usually wrote the preface intro-ducing the theme and generally stating the purpose for the work. This we see in his three other works: Τόμος Καταλ-λαγῆς [*Book of Reconciliation*]; Τόμος 'Αγάπης [*Book of Love*]; and Τόμος Χαρᾶς [*Book of Joy*].[138] The first work was aimed against Leo Allatios whose writings were directed towards the Orthodox to encourage the *Unia*. The *Book of Reconciliation* contains treatises written against the Latins by Macarios, metropolitan of Ancyra, George Cores-sios, Nicolaos Kerameos, Joannes Eugenicos, brother of Mark of Ephesus, and Mattaeos Blastares. The *Book of Love* aimed to draw the Latins by the bonds of Christian charity back to their traditions shared once with the Orthodox. In the preface of his posthumous work on the history of the patriarchs of Jerusalem, Dositheos admits that he had in mind in writing the *Book of Love* a rebuttal of the work of François Richard, S. J.: Τὰ ἔργα τῆς πίστεως published in the Greek vernacular.[139] The *Book of Love* is composed from 23 anti-Latin works that Dositheos brought together from various sources. His *Book of Joy* is composed from anti-Latin works written by Photios, Nicolaos Kerameos, Meletios Pigas, Theodore Agallien and Dositheos himself.

Dositheos' most outstanding intellectual work, which demonstrated his great synthetic mind as well as his deep hatred for the papacy, was his history of the Jerusalem patriarchs. It was edited and published in 1715 by Chrysanthos Notaras, Dositheos' nephew and successor to the see of Jerusalem, eight years after Dositheos died (d. February 7, 1707). Notaras divided the 1247 pages into twelve chapters, hence the title by which it is known today.[140] This is a sweeping history of the patriarchate of Jerusalem beginning from the time of James, the first bishop of Jerusalem, down to the end of the 17th century. It is a treasure of information touching on ecumenical councils as well as particular synods, emperors, heresies, Crusades, the struggles for the Holy Places and, ever present, the dominance of the primacy of the pope in church affairs of Jerusalem. Dositheos used many sources and acknowledges his special indebtedness to Paisios Ligarides, metropolitan of Gaza (d. 1678) who had published an earlier history of the Jerusalem patriarchs.[141]

Besides editing many other works which defended Orthodoxy against Protestantism and Roman Catholicism, Dositheos edited the refutation made by Meletios Syrigos (d. 1664) against the theological errors of Cyril Lucaris[142] and the Confession of Peter Mogila, as translated and emended by Meletios.[143] Dositheos of Jerusalem probably did more than anyone to stave off Protestantism and Latinism from infiltrating into Orthodoxy at a time when no original theology was being created by the Orthodox theologians. He also is more responsible than any other theologian for passing on to Orthodox theological history hatreds and distrusts bred in earlier times against Roman Catholics and Protestants. Through his editions of earlier polemical writings he perpetuated a negative theology that after his time would dominate Byzantine Greek theology until the 20th century.

In this period of the middle seventeenth until the middle of the following century there appeared a group of very mediocre theologians, most of them educated in Europe, usually in Italy, who, upon returning to their Greek homeland, wrote polemical anti-Latin works that had often taken many Protestant doctrines to counteract the Roman Latin teachings which they intended to combat. It is quite easy to understand how, removed in training from their own Byzantine patristic sources and educated according to scholastic categories which they learned in the West, they reacted violently against Latin training by employing Protestant insights.

GEORGE CORESSIOS[144]

Coressios represents this type of 17th century Byzantine theologian. Born in Chios in 1554, he studied medicine and philosophy in Pisa and Padua and then practiced medicine for a time in Livorno before returning to Chios. As an avocation, he edited polemical works against Latins. The synod of Constantinople in 1635 called him to defend Orthodoxy against Antoine Leger, the Calvinist chaplain of the Dutch embassy at the Sublime Porte.

Legrand gives 63 titles of his theological works, many of them editions of other polemical works. Patriarch Dositheos praised Coressios for his orthodoxy in defending the faith against Protestant innovations as well as against Latin errors. His most serious theological work on the procession of the Holy Spirit was incorporated by Dositheos into his Τόμος Καταλλαγῆς.[145] Coressios' long stay in Italy allowed him to become expertly acquainted with the Latin theologians who wrote against the Greeks and thus his anti-Latin writings abound in citations from the Western theologians.

ZACHARIAS GERGANOS[146]

Gerganos received his theological education in Wittenberg, Germany where in 1622 he published his Catechism.[147] Sathas believes that Gerganos was a favorite of Cyril Lucaris and it was through the latter's influence that Gerganos was elevated to the see of Artos and Naupactos.[148] Surely the Catechism shows Protestant theological influences that repeat many of the doctrines enunciated by Lucaris in his own *Confession* and that were so strongly condemned in various Greek synods, especially that of Constantinople in 1638.

Gerganos explains in his foreword why he writes his Catechism in the vernacular. No longer is there a Greek empire, no longer is there the Hellenistic wisdom and learning that in former times reached the highest peak of excellence. Now, he confesses, the Greeks have no secondary schools nor universities, only elementary schools. He writes for the simple people that they may understand their true faith.[149] The whole work is dedicated to the Prince of Saxony, Johannes George, and from the contents we can judge the main source of his doctrinal inspiration to be his Protestant professors in the University of Wittenberg. His Lutheran doctrines were strongly attacked and refuted by Joannes Mattaeos Caryophyllos, bishop of Iconium,[150] from whose works we judge that Gerganos, in a similar vein to the doctrine of Lucaris, taught in his Catechism that Holy Scripture alone sufficed, the Book of Maccabees was apocryphal, there was no intermediate stage of purification after death and the Holy Eucharist performed by a sinful priest was really not "valid." He employs much of the emotionally charged polemics of the Protestants against the "idolatry" of papal-worship [αἱρετικοσχισματοπαπαλάτρια].

THEOPHILOS CORYDALLEUS[151]

Another follower of the Protestant ideas of Lucaris was Corydalleus, mostly known for his liberal philosophical ideas that provided a basis for a Protestant view of the Eucharist. Theophilos was born in Athens in 1563 and studied at the Greek College in Rome and at Padua where he imbibed the philosophical liberalism of the famous Professor Tomaso Cremoni. Returning to Athens, he established a school of philosophy and soon enjoyed a reputation as the leading philosopher in Greece. He showed his sympathy towards the person and the ideas of Cyril Lucaris who appointed him to teach Aristotelian philosophy in the Patriarchal Academy in Constantinople. Theophilos became tonsured but practiced monasticism in his own peculiar style. After the death of his protector, Lucaris, Theophilos left the capitol and returned in 1639 when Parthenios I was crowned patriarch. It was on the day of Parthenios' enthronization that Theophilos, noted for his great oratory, delivered his famous defense of Cyril Lucaris. He claimed that Cyril's *Confession* was the pillar of Orthodox piety and an exact expression of the faith of the Eastern Church.[152] Shortly after, Parthenios I asked Meletios Syrigos to respond. The latter attacked Theophilos, comparing him to the great enemies of early Christianity as the philosopher Porphyry and Origen. Syrigos ended by calling him a "hater of God" [μισόθεος] instead of being what an Orthodox should be, a "lover of God" [θεόφιλος]. Theophilos was attacked for his denial of the Real Presence, his Calvinistic theology and his atheistic philosophy.[153]

Theophilos had left monasticism but soon embraced it again, only to be elevated to the episcopacy and the see of Artos and Naupactos, due perhaps to the sympathy of Parthenios towards Lucaris' teachings. Due to his heterodoxy, he was expelled from his see. He was reduced to extreme poverty and died in 1645.

MAXIMOS CALLIPOLITA

Maximos must also be numbered among the Protestantizers who approached in doctrine that of Cyril Lucaris. Sathas characterizes Maximos as "full of the poison of heresy [Protestantism] and made himself a profitable tool in its service."[154] That which we know of him is that he belonged to the group of Orthodox theologians who brought Protestant ideas into the Greek Church.

Although Maximos did not leave to posterity many writings, he is known for having been the first to have attempted to translate the New Testament into vernacular Greek.[155] The project was supported by Cornelius von Haga, the Dutch ambassador in Constantinople, Antoine Leger, the Calvinist chaplain at the Dutch embassy, and Patriarch Cyril Lucaris. In 1632 Haga wrote to the Dutch government in Holland that Callipolita's translation was already finished. He proposed that, after the translation was checked with the original *Koine* Greek, preferably by Lucaris, the manuscript be sent to Geneva to be printed. The book was to be printed in two columns with parallel texts in ancient Greek and in the vernacular. It was proposed that 1,500 copies were to be printed in Geneva, but the printing was delayed due to the unexpected death of Maximos, on September 24, 1633, in Constantinople. He was buried in Halki.

The translation which Maximos had made was finally printed in 1645 through funds given by the Dutch government. Cornelius von Haga received the printed copies in order to distribute them to circles that could best profit by the use of such a translation, but still in 1666 the books had not yet been distributed.[156] Meletios Syrigos rose up in indignant protest when the book had reached the faithful. In public sermons he would argue directly from the two volumes (one of the Gospels and the other the remaining books of the New Testament) against the Protestant doctrine implied in the translation and the exegetical explanations given. Patriarch Parthenios II, who was sympathetic towards Lucaris and Callipolita, exiled Syrigos to the island of Chios and the translation thereafter was no longer the object of any attack by any synod or theologian.[157] Alexander Helladios, writing in 1714, criticized Maximos' translation for inaccuracies and even errors, certainly for his Protestant ideas. He exhorts any Greek finding such a copy to throw it to the flames.[158]

There can be little doubt that the influential Dutch Calvinists in Constantinople had conceived the project and had financed the printing in order to reach the faithful with basic Protestant ideas. We find further proof that their hopes were carried out when we read the introductions made by both Maximos and Cyril Lucaris. Maximos declares in the introduction to his translation that there is an absolute necessity on the part of the faithful to read the Holy Scriptures. He cites from St. Paul that everything which does not flow from faith is sin; but faith flows from the word of God. Every human action that it not founded on Holy Scripture is not from faith but from sin. For Maximos we find that Holy Scripture is the sole authority in the Church, even higher than the authority of the teaching hierarchy empowered to properly interpret Scripture. Maximos cites many passages from St. Basil the Great, St. John Chrysostom and St. Athanasios the Great in support of his thesis that readers of Scriptures do not need the interpretation of the clergy. Unclear passages are rendered clearer by a comparison with more certain passages. The exegesis of the Fathers leads only to darkness and confusion.[159]

It is difficult to judge the influence of this translation of the New Testament in the vernacular upon the faithful of that epoch. It seems clear, however, that some of Maximos' own contemporaries seemed very much disturbed with this new method of Protestant proselytism and tried to combat Maximos' translation since they were aware of the success it was having in the 17th century to draw the Greek faithful towards Protestant ideas.

JOANNES CARYOPHYLLOS[160]

Born in the village of Caryes near Constantinople in the beginning of the 17th century, Caryophyllos studied at the patriarchal school under the Protestantizer, Theophilos Corydalleus, from whom he received certain unorthodox views concerning the doctrine of the Holy Eucharist and transubstantiation. Patriarch Parthenios II heard of his writings and threatened to excommunicate Caryophyllos unless he recanted his errors. This he did and was allowed to teach in the patriarchal school from 1646 until 1665. He was appointed the great logothete of Constantinople until 1691.

Although he made public avowal that he had changed his views on the Eucharist in order to embrace the more traditional Orthodox teaching, he nevertheless, hiddenly, began to spread his former ideas. Patriarch Dositheos, ever vigilant to defend Orthodoxy in any part of the world, heard about his teachings and insisted that he stop spreading his errors. Caryophyllos answered with a treatise in which he explained his position. He was not against the doctrine of the Eucharist, but only against such expressions as *transubstantiation* since it came from Roman Catholicism. Still, according to Dositheos in his Ἐγχειρίδιον, Caryophyllos denied even the existence of the Real Presence in the Eucharist, insisting on a rather Protestant sense of a spiritual presence of Christ through faith.[161] Dositheos claims that should one ask Caryophyllos what a pious Orthodox layman would receive in going to Holy Communion, he would answer that he would be receiving the real body and blood of the Lord; but should a sinner receive the same sacrament, he would receive only bread.

Dositheos sees in such teaching a return to the Protestant errors of Berengarius and Calvin.[162]

In 1691 Patriarch Callinicos II called a synod in Constantinople to judge the doctrine of Caryophyllos concerning the Eucharist. Again, as before, the latter denied any unorthodox teaching; still from Caryophyllos' own writings the synod anathematized his teaching and ordered his works to be burned.[163] The synod, no doubt influenced by Dositheos who relied heavily upon the teaching of the Council of Trent in regard to the doctrine of transubstantiation, taught against Caryophyllos that "in each particle of the Eucharistic bread and wine there is no individual part of the body and blood of Christ but the whole Christ, the Lord in His essence, with soul and divinity, in a word, perfect man and perfect God. The same body of Christ is found in heaven that is present in the sacrament but it does not descend from heaven but bread and wine essentially are changed into the body and blood of Christ. Therefore the body and blood of the Lord are truly and actually left, however unseen to the human eye in the sacrament. And even though through the world there are offered many Eucharistic sacrifices, nevertheless, Christ remains one."[164]

Caryophyllos was forced to leave Constantinople in 1693 and journeyed to Bulgaria where he labored as a priest and continued to hold and teach his own doctrine of the Eucharist.

OTHER POLEMICISTS
SEVASTOS KYMENITES, ELIAS MENIATES, NICOLAOS KERAMEOS

Three final theologians who entered into the lists to combat Roman Catholicism must be mentioned: Sevastos Kymenites (d. 1702), Elias Meniates (d. 1714) and Nicolaos Kerameos (d. 1672). Their works were not very creative or original but they did succeed in adding to the ever-growing polemical literature produced in the 17th century, particularly against the Romans who had stepped up their missionary activities in the Greek world.

Kymenites was born about 1625 near Trebizond and studied at Constantinople in the patriarchal school. He began to teach there in 1671 and directed the school, but apparently his over-bearing manner did not make him acceptable to the students who revolted in 1682 and forced him to leave. After founding a school in Trebizond in 1683, he was called to be rector in Bucharest in 1690 of the theological school of the Greek monastery of St. Sabbas. He died there in 1702.

A most diligent worker, Kymenites, according to Papadopoulos-Kerameus, produced 106 works that, although they are mostly unedited, cover a wide area of interest in literature, philosophy, theology, liturgy, patristics and sacred eloquence.[165] Although he remained a simple lay man, he preached eloquently as well as wrote with a great zeal to defend Orthodoxy.[166] His two most important works concern certain liturgical questions[167] and an anti-Latin polemical work against three basic Latin positions which were also being advocated by the Kievan Orthodox theologians under Catholic influence. These questions concerned the transubstantiation of the Holy Eucharist, whether the Mother of God was born in Original Sin, and whether the small particles on the paten besides the main host are consecrated by the priest in the Byzantine rite.[168]

Kymenites also produced a variety of other theological works, especially one in favor of Palamite theology entitled: Σύντομος θεωρία περὶ διαφορᾶς θείας οὐσίας καὶ ἐνεργείας, numerous paraphrases of the poems and homilies of St. Gregory Nazianzos along with a life of this Father who held for Kymenites a special interest.

Elias Meniates (1662-1714) came from the island of Cephalonia and studied in Venice. He returned to his native country where he preached throughout the Ionian Islands.

In 1711 he was made bishop. Two of his main works have had great influence even down to our present day. The first is his popular collection of sermons, called Διδαχαί,[169] which attests to his eloquence and great zeal to spread the Word of God to the masses. His most influential polemical work, translated into Latin, German and Russian as well as modern Greek editions, is called Πέτρα Σκανδάλου [*The Rock of Scandal*].[170] He divides this work into two parts. In the first he presents an historical view of the origin of the schism between the Eastern and Western Churches. He deals chiefly wih the Photian Schism but also presents information about the main attempts to re-establish union. The second part is devoted to the dogmatic differences between the Orthodox and the Catholic beliefs which he considers to be five. The primacy of the pope constituted the main "rock of scandal." This work is a mere assemblage of the arguments presented against Roman Catholicism beginning with Mark of Ephesus and Gennadios Scholarios.

Nicolaos Kerameos was born in Jannina but educated at the Greek College of St. Athanasius in Rome. Dositheos has preserved for us his main work, a polemical refutation of those who attack the Church.[171]

IRENIC THEOLOGIANS

Besides those educated in the patriarchal school of Constantinople and those who returned from studies in Italy who, as we have already seen, wrote polemics against both Roman Catholicism and Protestantism, there were also Greeks who studied abroad, especially in Padua and in the Greek College of St. Athanasius in Rome, who retained a certain amount of sympathy for the Roman Latin theology.

Nicolaos Bulgaris of Corfu, born in 1634, studied in Padua. He is noted chiefly for his popular catechism Κατήχησις ἱερά that is still well used among Greek Orthodox.

He presents the main dogmatic and liturgical beliefs and practices, however, not entirely free from a certain Romanizing influence. In the 1852 edition of this work by Andreas Mavromatis the doctrines manifesting a Western influence have been purified in the light of the Orthodox tradition.[172]

Although Gregory of Chios cannot be strictly called a Latinophile, hardly a compliment to his teacher of Chios, George Coressios, who was noted for his anti-Latin polemical writings, Gregory does approach in several dogmatic statements of the Orthodox faith a Roman Catholic position which has made his main work, a synopsis of the Church's dogmas,[173] a favorite source of citations by Roman theologians in their polemic literature against the Protestants.

Nicolaos Kursulas is perhaps more typical of this class of irenic theologians who borrowed heavily from Latin theology.[174] Palmieri credits him with the first theological compendium or synthesis after the fall of Constantinople,[175] even though his work was not published until 1862. Kursulas studied in the Greek College of St. Athanasios in Rome receiving his degree in both philosophy and theology. Returning to his native country, he became a monk and distinguished himself by his zealous preaching. He moved to Alexandria where again he proved himself outstanding in preaching. The Dutch proposed to name him patriarch of Alexandria on condition that he would embrace Calvinism which he refused to do. He returned to Corfu and then retired to Mount Athos where he died in 1652.

Chiotes has tried in his biography to defend Kursulas for his Latinisms, as lapses on theological points of no great dogmatic importance. It seems certain that Kursulas advocated both the Western and Eastern position in regard to the *Filioque* controversy, admitted the Western doctrine that the Holy Virgin was conceived without Original Sin and that the consecration of the Eucharist is effected not by the *epiclesis* but by the sole words of Our Lord. He also advocated the Latin doctrine on indulgences.

THE GREEK COLLEGE OF ROME[176]

To aid the Greeks who were deprived of public schools, Pope Gregory XIII founded at Rome in 1576 the Greek College of St. Athanasios. However, from 1622 the college took on exclusively a seminary aspect, mostly to prepare Greeks of the Byzantine rite to work in their native lands as Orthodox or Catholics. It soon became almost exclusively a seminary to prepare Uniate Greek priests to work among the Orthodox and the very small, almost insignificant group of Greek Catholics of the Byzantine rite. Later on, in 1829, after a fierce persecution against the Catholic Armenians in the Ottoman Empire, Sultan Mahmud II (1808-1839) conceded to Catholic non-Latin subjects of his Empire the emancipation from the authority of the Orthodox Ecumenical Patriarch. This opened the door for the establishment in greater numbers of a Greek Catholic community of the Byzantine rite.

However, in the 17th century, several Greeks, both Orthodox and Catholic, studied in Rome. It suffices to mention only some of the Greek Catholic scholars who only indirectly enter into the history of Orthodox theology. Joannes Matteos Caryophyllis (1556-1633), titulary archbishop of Iconium, who taught many years in the Greek College and worked also in the Vatican Library, is known for his refutation of the catechism of Zacharias Gerganos and a condemnation of the *Confession* of Cyril Lucaris.[177] Peter Arcudios (d. 1633) entered the Greek College and there made his profession to Rome as a Catholic. He was the first pupil to receive a doctorate in theology from the Greek College. More than any other theologian he was responsible for bringing about the Ruthenian Union of Brest.[178] He edited and commented on the works of John Beccos and Cardinal Bessarion on the procession of the Holy Spirit as well as the editing of the Greek menology.

Leo Allatios (d. 1669) was one of the outstanding Greek intellectuals who worked in the West during the 17th century.[179] After completing doctorates in theology and philosophy in Rome, he completed doctoral studies also in medicine. Most of his life was employed in scholarly work at the Vatican Library, editing a great many works, both of ancient as well as later Byzantine writers. His own original output was phenomenal. He had a great longing to bring both East and West together and devoted many treatises to this topic. His best work on this subject is entitled: *De Ecclesiae occidentalis atque orientalis perpetua consensione.*[180] Orthodox scholars throughout the world owe Allatios a special debt of gratitude for his scholarly work in editing works which would perhaps have remained hidden or even lost to later scholarship.

Other Greeks who studied at the Greek College in Rome and returned to their native lands to work as theologians or remained in the West include Nicolaos Alemannos (d. 1626)[181] Demetrios Pepanos (d. after 1696)[182] George Moschetti (date of death unknown, after 1629).[183] Neophyte Roodinos, (d. 1655) a disciple of Maximos Margounios, upon finishing at the Greek College, taught theology and Greek literature at the University of Salamanca. His main work is entitled Πανοπλία Πνευματική and is known also for having translated the *Imitation of Christ* into modern Greek.[184]

One final Greek writer who strove in an irenic spirit to create better understanding between the East and West was Agapios Landos. Born in Crete, he became a priest and monk on Mount Athos in the middle of the 17th century. He translated many spiritual classics into vernacular Greek, thus making available to the faithful a living theology, drawn from the fonts of Byzantine spirituality of a richer age. His most famous works were the translations of the lives of the Saints taken from Symeon Metaphrastes and entitled by Agapios Νέος Παράδεισος.[185] Other collections of the lives of the Saints include his *Eklogion* and *New Eklogion*, selected lives of the Saints.[186] His Σωτηρία 'Αμαρτωλῶν [*The Salvation of Sinners*] has always enjoyed great success in the Orthodox world of piety[187] as well as his Γεωπονικόν, a Poor Richard's Almanac of various suggestions from farming techniques to cures for all diseases.[188]

EIGHTEENTH CENTURY THEOLOGIANS

The 18th century proved to be the nadir in theological development among Greek theologians. The fact that it became the age of the compendia of theology proved that there were very few creative thinkers. Latin Catholic and Protestant missionaries in the Greek speaking world stepped up their proselytizing efforts and forced the Orthodox to formulate in clear, almost scholastic, statements their fundamental positions in opposition to those of the Western thinkers. The formation in this century of the Melchite Catholic Church put the other Greek Orthodox Churches even more on the defensive. Also the pressure of three centuries under the Turks without their own Christian schools produced eventually a class of poorly educated priests and a paucity of scholars. Hence the need again for compendia which could present in outline form Orthodox theology to candidates for the priesthood who probably never would live a day in a seminary.

Typical of the Greek theologians of this period who composed compendia were Vincent Damodos (d. 1752), Antonios Moschopoulos (d. 1788), Joannes Kontones (d. 1761), Theophilos Papaphilos and the famous theologian of this century, Eugenios Bulgaris (d. 1806).

Damodos composed in 1730 his compendium of dogmatic theology which he draws together from Sacred Scripture, the apostolic traditions, the ecumenical councils and better known particular synods as well as from the authoritative

writings of the Holy Fathers. It consists of five tomes which
deal with God and His divine attributes, the Trinity, the
Incarnation, grace, the sacraments, and a polemical attack
against the primacy of the pope, the *Filioque* and the dropping of *epiclesis*.[189] Damodos exhibits a vast knowledge not
only of his Orthodox teachings but also of the 17th and
18th century theological disputes.

Moschopoulos, a disciple of Damodos, also wrote a compendium which treats together both dogmatic and moral
theology.[190]

EUGENIOS BULGARIS (d. 1806)[191]

Considered by many scholars both of the East and West
to be the outstanding Orthodox theologian of the 18th
century, Eugenios Bulgaris does present a picture of a versatile
and many talented thinker. Born in Corfu in 1716, he showed
an early aptitude for a life of learning. After finishing his
studies in Corfu and Jannina he was sent by wealthy Greeks
to Padua to further his theological studies. There he learned
also Italian, French, Latin and Hebrew besides developing
a strong foundation in philosophy and theology. He set up
schools in Jannina and Kozani in Macedonia, but it was
chiefly his sermons that attracted the attention of Patriarch
Cyril V who entrusted Bulgaris to direct the newly found
academy on Mount Athos.

Bulgaris accepted this challenge in 1753, the first time
that this holy mountain had an intellectual academy. Soon
Mount Athos became as famous for its academy, which soon
had some 200 pupils, as for its ancient monasteries that
generally despised human learning as a deceit of the devil.
A change soon took place when Patriarch Cyril V lost his
throne and took up residence on Mount Athos in 1757. Cyril
caused great dissension and forced Bulgaris to resign. The
main reason was that Bulgaris used too much of the Ratio-

nalistic school of philosophy as typified by the French Encyclopedists. He began to teach philosophy and mathematics in
the patriarchal academy of Constantinople but Patriarch
Samuel soon suspected Bulgaris' new methods of teaching
and Bulgaris again resigned to travel to Leipzig. He met
there the Russian Marshall Theodore Orlov who recommended him to Tsarina Catherine II. She brought him to St.
Petersburg and encharged to him her library in 1771. He
was ordained a priest in 1775 and was named archbishop of
Cherson in 1776. He continued his writing but soon found
no taste or talent for running a Russian diocese so he submitted his resignation and returned to St. Petersburg where
he engaged again in writing polemical and exegetical works.
He retired in 1802 to the monastery of St. Petersburg, St.
Aleksandr Nevskii, and died in 1806 at the advanced age
of 89.

Bulgaris appeared so much superior to any other theologian in his 18th century more because of the poverty of the
other thinkers than because of his own native genius. Gifted
as a polyglot with a talent for organization and great literary
output, he did produce a prodigious amount of witing in
addition to forming students in Jannina, Mount Athos, Constantinople and Russia. He possessed encyclopedic knowledge
in many fields other than philosophy and theology. But in
his theological writings he shows little creativity and originality. Although he was formed as a thinker in the categories
of scholastic philosophy and made no pretense to hide his
dislike for it, he nevertheless did present Orthodox theology
to the East in a scholastic garb. He wrote in an affected
archaic Greek style, trying to imitate classical Greek writers
and through such a medium brought a popular version to the
Greek reading world of Western philosophies.

His main theological work, a compendium known as
Θεολογικόν, was published by Archimandrite Agathangelos
Lontopoulos in Venice, 1872 and has since enjoyed great fame
as a standard Orthodox manual of dogmatic theology. As

in most compendia, popular in Russia at the time of this printing, Bulgaris deals with the nature of theology, its various divisions, the nature of God, the Trinity, the creation, Incarnation, and a detailed exposition of the procession of the Holy Spirit with a refutation of the Western doctrine on the *Filioque*. As the Russian manuals written by Makarii, Malinovskii and others of the 19th century, so Bulgaris uses principally the scholastic method of presenting theology according to various tracts. He obviously was under the influence of Western theology and relied greatly upon the dogmatic theology text-book of Tournely.

Bulgaris also is noted for his translations of philosophical and theological books from European languages into Greek and editing of Greek works. Among these must be listed his three volumes of the works of Joseph Bryennios.[192] The third volume contains a translation of Feofan Prokopovich's Latin work *Historia controversiae de processione Spiritus Sancti* and a commentary on the Greek text of Nicephoros Blemmydes on the same question.[193] In the same anti-Catholic spirit Bulgaris translated Voltaire's bitter attack against Catholics and aimed it at the Orthodox Church in Poland which had suffered persecution for their faith in a forced proselytism to become Catholic Uniates. Yet strangely enough Bulgaris appends a small treatise against religious tolerance in which he favors the State control even with violence of those who do not practice the official religion of the State.[194] Another polemical work is his translation from the Latin of the work *De processione Spiritus Sancti a solo Patre,* written by Adam of Tsernikau in the Ukraine who had passed from Protestantism to Orthodoxy.[195] However, Bulgaris never gave a mere translation but appended, as in this case, much of his own creation by way of scriptural and patristic texts and arguments from reason against the Latin doctrine of the *Filioque*. The second volume contains the treatise of Mark of Ephesus on the procession of the Holy Spirit along with the dogmatic letter of Theophilos Corydalleus to Sofronii Pokzanskii, rector of the Kievan Academy.[196]

An interesting confession of faith that Bulgaris directs to the Jesuit theologian, Peter Leclerc, allows him to present what he holds to be essential to the Orthodox faith along with his refutation of the beliefs of Protestants and Catholics.[197]

Although his sermons show a great knowledge of biblical exegesis, the one major work that we have of Bulgaris' serious exegesis demonstrates a conservative and cautious spirit, perhaps because he felt less secure and expert in the area of biblical studies. This work is a series of theological meditations on the Pentateuch, and its conservatism encouraged Patriarch Gregorios VI (1835-1840; 1867-1871) to translate this work into Turkish.[198]

Two disciples of Bulgaris followed in his footsteps and also produced theological compendia. Athanasios of Paros (d. 1813) wrote his Ἐπιτομή, using much of his teacher's writings.[199] Theophilos Papaphilos, bishop of Campania, gathered together a variety of theological problems in the form of a dialogue. His Ταμεῖον Ὀρθοδοξίας[200] [*Treasure of Orthodoxy*] has proved most popular even to the present time.

EIGHTEENTH CENTURY POLEMICISTS

Before we treat of the 18th century polemicists and in a particular way of Eustratios Argenti who definitely summarizes the typical polemicist who consistently appeared in Byzantine theology from the 15th through the 19th centuries, we must understand how in the 18th century hostilities between the Orthodox and Catholics in many parts of the Near and Middle East had intensified.[201]

We have already pointed out how the stepped-up missionary activities of Catholic Orders such as the Franciscans,

Dominicans, Capuchins and Jesuits in the Near East in the 16th and 17th centuries had laid the foundation for suspicions and misgivings on the part of the Orthodox towards the Roman Catholics. These Catholic priests were in general better educated than the ordinary Orthodox clergy and hence they easily attracted by their better sermons and greater aggressiveness many of the Orthodox faithful. These missionaries with their small flock of Catholics, even though they constituted a very small minority over the majority of Orthodox Christians living under the Ottoman Turks, nonetheless, did enjoy the patronage of the powerful European embassies, such as the French and Austrian, represented at the Sublime Porte.

In the 17th century these factors were not sufficiently strong to precipitate any arresting of the pastoral friendliness and cooperation, even in *communicatio in sacris*, that existed at this time between the Orthodox and the Roman Catholics. Latin missionaries were gladly welcomed by the Orthodox bishops who availed themselves of their services to provide their faithful with preachers and confessors superior to the Orthodox clergy who were generally quite uneducated and even apathetic in zealous promotion of the faith among their people. Even though Rome tightened regulations for the Catholics living in the Orthodox countries, *"communicatio in sacris"* continued to be an actuality as Orthodox and Catholic priests gave Holy Communion to each other's faithful without any scruples. Mixed marriages were common occurrences and children were brought up in both faiths as though there existed no schism.

But matters changed at the turn of the century. Greater distrust on the part of the Orthodox towards the proselytism of the Roman Catholics developed rather strongly because of a variety of factors. No doubt the Turks and the Protestant embassies in Constantinople were ever eager to dampen such a growing rapprochement between Orthodox and Catholics. But primarily it was the Venetian occupation of the Peloponnese from 1685 to 1718 that spread the alarm among the Orthodox. The Venetians openly discriminated and promoted the Roman Catholic cause over that of the Orthodox. Many of the re-converted mosques were made into Latin churches instead of being given back to their original owners, the Orthodox. Latin bishoprics were increased while the existing Orthodox bishops felt their own influence over their flock diminishing as the Venetian government supported the Roman Catholics. If Notaras could say in the 15th century: "Better the Moslem turban than the Latin mitre,"[202] the Greeks of the 18th century living under Venetian control were justified in their mounting suspicion of the Latin masters. The same process of growing hostility developed in the island of Chios under Venetian conquest (1694-1695).

Perhaps the greatest factor, as Ware points out,[203] in creating a religious "cold war" environment was the policy of concealment used by the Latin missionaries. Openly aggressive proselytism and intercommunion were frowned upon by the Propagation of Faith that sent out its directives to the Latin missionaries working among the Orthodox. The policy was to make out of certain influential Orthodox church leaders crypto-Romans who would remain in office as Orthodox while exercising a Roman influence on the other Orthodox faithful. The list of patriarchs and bishops who in the 17th and 18th centuries either had made a formal submission to Rome or at least were exceedingly friendly to and cooperative with Rome constantly grew to include Patriarchs Neophytos II, Timothy II, Gregory IV, Athanasios III, Cyril II (Contaris), Parthenios II.

It was, however, the sad history of the patriarchate of Antioch from 1724 onwards that put most Orthodox on a newly stirred vigilance towards Roman Catholicism. Seraphim Tanas, educated in Rome, was elected patriarch of Antioch, taking the name of Cyril VI while an anti-Roman faction of Antioch elected Sylvester to represent their patriarchate. Thus, as the Byzantine Greeks saw these two Antiochene factions reduce their patriarchate to an enemic skeleton of what it was formerly, they realized the dangers of taking any position with Roman Catholicism other than a complete separation insured by constant polemical attack.

Diamantes Rhysios, a married layman, who had studied at the patriarchal school of Constantinople and had taught and directed that institution, is known for his polemical anti-Latin poem in iambic trimeter in which he lists 33 dogmatic points of controversy between the Latins and the Greeks along with three others separating the Armenians from the Orthodox. He rails against the Latin usage of statues, the Gregorian calendar, shaven priests, denial of the Taboric light and the teaching of the Immaculate Conception of the Blessed Virgin Mary.[204]

EUSTRATIOS ARGENTI[205]

Argenti was born on the island of Chios about 1687. He studied medicine at Halle in Saxony and lived for periods in Germany, Italy, and Egypt, practicing medicine and devoting as much time as he could to the defense of the Orthodox faith by his polemical writing and disputations.

A married layman, Eustratios was a controversialist who strove by polemical attacks to give clear answers to his Orthodox brethren against the theological positions held by the Latins. His writings manifest a great clarity and coherence that undoubtedly came from his disciplined training in medicine. He did not strive to be original, but rather to give his arguments in the context of his basic principle: the true Church was the Orthodox Catholic Church precisely because it remained faithful to the ancient traditions. He attempted in all his polemical treatises against the Latins to show that they had fallen into heresy because they introduced changes into Roman Catholicism contrary to the traditions of the early Church.

These changes are, according to Eustratios, the basic five singled out by the participants of the Council of Florence in its *Decretum pro Graecis*: the procession of the Holy Spirit, unleavened bread, purgatory, the blessedness of the saints, and the primacy of the pope. His principal treatises focus upon the question of unleavened bread (*Treatise against Unleavened Bread*),[206] on purgatory (*Short Treatise against the Purgatorial Fire of the Papists*),[207] and on the primacy of the pope (*Concerning the False Infallibility of the Pope of Rome*).[208]

Perhaps his most important polemical work was the one he entitled *Manual Concerning Baptism*.[209] Patriarch Cyril V had requested the aid of Argenti in the baptismal controversy that had broken out in Constantinople in 1750.[210] Cyril, seeing the rapid inroads made among the Orthodox by Roman Catholicism, sought to delineate more clearly the doctrinal differences separating Orthodox and Catholics. He insisted that Latin Baptism was invalid and that the Catholics in Galata who desired to become Orthodox had to be re-baptized. Not only did the influential Catholics of Constantinople protest loudly and seek his dismissal as patriarch, but also his own Orthodox metropolitans of the Holy Synod of Constantinople sought to remove him. Although Cyril was most popular among the faithful and his gesture against Rome endeared him all the more to them, nevertheless his stronger opponents succeeded in sending him into exile and having Paisios II enthroned as patriarch.

Auxentios,[211] a monk, reputed by the populace to be a saint and miracle worker, began to preach openly against Latin Baptism until the Turks removed him as well as Paisios and restored Cyril as patriarch. The metropolitans met in session without Cyril and condemned the work of Christophoros the Aetolian who had also written against Latin Baptism. This brought Cyril's fight to a climax, when he issued his anathema of June, 1755, against his own metropolitans, and the next month he issued his decree, "A Definition of the Holy Church of Christ defending the Holy Baptism given from God and spitting upon the baptisms of the heretics which are otherwise administered."[212] In his *Definition* Cyril holds that since the Orthodox Church is the only one true Church, she alone possesses the only true divine sacraments. Hence all other baptisms are to be rejected as coming from heretical groups who have separated from the true, holy, apostolic, and Catholic Church of Christ.

Cyril appealed to Eustratios for help, and the latter responded with his *Manual Concerning Baptism*. In this work Eustratios was not concerned with the problem of "economy" [οἰκονομία][213] and "rigorism" [ἀκρίβεια], since he feels that in the case of Roman Baptism there is question of aspersion [ῥαντισμός] and not immersion [κατάδυσις]; hence economy could not be applied, since for Eustratios Roman Baptism violates completely the validity of a Christian Baptism which must be performed by immersion. This he proves by an analysis of the word *baptisma,* which comes from the word meaning to dip [βάπτειν], by the theological symbolism of an inward and outward meaning of washing and renewal, and finally by the historical practice of the Church which has always, even in the West, insisted upon immersion in Baptism. His conclusion is that all Roman Catholic baptisms are invalid and must be redone:

> From what has been said throughout this short treatise, we conclude correctly that Westerners who come to Orthodoxy require to be baptized. This practice is not called 'rebaptism' for we do not baptize them because we think that they have been badly baptized, but because they are entirely unbaptized. For what they call 'baptism' is falsely so named, and is a false baptism.[214]

Although Eustratios does not produce anything new in his treatises on the questions of unleavened bread, purgatory, or the papacy, and his polemical style, although more moderate and balanced than most polemicists of this period, is fundamentally a negative one, still he succeeded in filling those who read his works with a love for the ancient traditions of the Church. Fundamentally he fought for the truth which he saw as unchangeably tied to the traditions of the early Church. He prepared the way for another traditionalist, Nicodemus of Mount Athos, who went back to the roots of Orthodoxy as found in the Eastern monastic tradition, especially of the Hesychast school.

ADAMANTIOS KORAES

One of the great influences on Greek theology in the 18th and early 19th centuries came from the Rationalism of the West which had first entered the Orthodox world through the eclectic use that Eugenios Bulgaris made of the writings of Locke, Leibniz, Wolf, and Voltaire. It was more a spirit and a mentality than any special doctrines borrowed from the West. The Greek who most typified this Western mentality was Adamantios Koraes.[215] Koraes was born in Smyrna in 1748 and died in Paris in 1833. In an ideological way he proved to be one of the most important figures in Greek literature of the 18th century. In Smyrna he learned Latin from the Dutch Calvinist, Bernhard Keun. After a journey to Holland he studied medicine at Montpellier, where he dreamed of plans to liberate Greece from the yoke of the Turks. In order to prepare the Greek people for liberty, there was need for a whole cultural renaissance. Schools for him became more important than churches. Not only did he plan to translate the ancient classics into modern Greek, but he wanted to start with the Bible in the vernacular.

In 1808 he sought help from the English Bible Society to furnish a complete translation of the Bible for Greece, and he provided the first translation of the epistle of Paul to Titus. The monk Hilarion of Mount Athos also attempted in 1818 a vernacular translation of the New Testament. At first Patriarch Gregory V in 1820 was in favor of such a translation, in which he was supported by Constantine Economos, the leading preacher of Constantinople. But when the latter had a change of mind, the Holy Synod in 1824 reverted back to the traditional use of the *Koine* Greek for the Scriptures. Hilarion's translation was finally printed in 1828 along with the ancient Greek. Koraes published his translations of Paul's epistle to Titus and the two epistles to Timothy in his Συνέκδημος ἱερατικός.[216]

Despite the strong opposition of the Holy Synod in Constantinople against the Bible in the vernacular, through the efforts of Koraes, Hilarion and finally Neophytos Vamvas, the Old and New Testaments appeared in 1845 in the vernacular.[217] The main reasons given for opposing the vernacular translation of the Bible stemmed from the fear that the people, having the Bible in the vernacular, would follow the basic tenet of Cyril Lucaris that Scripture alone sufficed. There was also mistrust of the foreign missionaries and the proselytism that could follow from a foreign-financed Bible project. There were also mounting fears of linguistic and national dangers, the rejection of the Septuagint for a translation based solely on the Hebrew in the case of the Old Testament, and the fear that such a vernacular translation would hasten the desire on the part of the people for the liturgy in the vernacular.

Koraes strongly criticized the hierarchical structure of the Greek Church as well as the clergy, who in his eyes constituted a separate class more tyrannical than the Turks. He proposed to overthrow the antiquated ritualism by a new Christian education of youth in new catechetical centers similar to those he had seen in Holland. One indispensable condition of reform was the establishment of the autocephalous Church of Greece, freed from the strictures of the ecumenical patriarch and his synod.

Spending most of his adult life in France, Koraes was the first Greek who seriously anticipated the mounting conflict that would soon break upon the spiritual and theological life of the Church of Greece. Unfortunately, although Koraes insisted upon his loyalty to Orthodoxy, he nevertheless unknowingly had lost contact with its traditional spiritual sources.

THEOPHILOS KAIRIS

Theophilos Kairis (1784-1853) was another example of a Greek coming under the influence of French rationalism. As a monk, he traveled in 1801 to Pisa to study for six years before moving to Paris. There he met Auguste Comte and brought back to Greece not only a love for national freedom, but also a positivistic philosophy that soon led him to found his own type of religion which he called Θεοσέβεια or Θεοσεβασμός [God's worship].[218] Kairis denied the Trinity, all defined dogma and tradition, the divinity of Christ, the inspiration of Holy Scripture and the efficacy of the sacraments. He developed a deistic cult and a humanistic philanthropy drawn from Comte's teachings. Condemned by the Greek Church, he escaped to France and England but returned in 1844 and demanded freedom of conscience according to the new legislation made in that year. He died in prison.[219]

A RETURN TO TRADITIONALISM

A conservative reaction and a desire to return to the ancient fonts of Orthodox spirituality and theology bound together in friendship three leaders of a renaissance of Byzantine spirituality in Greece: Athanasios of Paros, Macarios of Corinth and Nicodemos the Hagiorite.

Athanasios (1723-1813), born on the island of Paros,

was a student of Eugenios Bulgaris in the academy on Mount Athos.[220] He succeeded Bulgaris but was forced to resign because of his opposition to the innovators of St. Anne's monastery of Mount Athos in regard to the controversy of the *kolybes*. For this he was excommunicated in 1776 by Patriarch Sophronios, but after a humiliating public retraction the sentence was lifted in 1781. He preached in Salonika and finally directed a school in Chios where he died.

Next to Bulgaris, Athanasios was one of the outstanding theologians of the 18th century. Of a passionate nature, he fought by preaching and writing to defend Orthodoxy against the innovations of the West, whether these appeared under the guise of Latin scholasticism, Protestantism, or the Voltairian philosophy of the Encyclopedists. His knowledge extended to all areas of theology: dogmatics, liturgy, homiletics, and hagiography. He is perhaps best known for his compendium of theology, ἐπιτομὴ εἴτε συλλογή.[221] It was composed principally for his students in Chios and contains five parts: the first three, which deal with God, creation, and redemption, are substantially what he had taken from the lectures of Eugenios Bulgaris; the fourth and most original part deals with the sacraments. For the final part he borrows heavily from Gregory Palamas in his explanations of the commandments.[222] Athanasios also published works dealing with the life of Palamas, Mark of Ephesus, an attack on modern progress, and lives of the saints.[223]

Macarios of Corinth was born in 1731 of the illustrious Notaras family.[224] As bishop of Corinth he strove to reform his clergy and elevate the education of the youth. Desirous to offset the inroads made into Orthodoxy by Western rationalism and positivistic philosophies, he planned an ambitious program of translations into modern Greek of the Orthodox classics. Although more retiring than Athanasios and Nicodemos, Macarios seems to have been the inspiring force that gave purpose and content to the group of traditionalists. Besides making the selections and translations into modern Greek of the *Philokalia,* to which Nicodemos added the introduction and biographical sketches of the Fathers, and composing the main part of the Νέον Λειμω-νάριον, lives of the Greek saints and martyrs down through the ages, he was responsible for the publishing and transla-tion into modern Greek of the collection of the sayings of the early Fathers, the so-called Εὐεργετικός. To him must be attributed the anonymous work on frequent Communion which touched off a heated controversy throughout the Greek Church. He was strongly supported by the monks of Mount Athos, and Nicodemos composed a similar work using his main arguments.[225]

NICODEMOS THE HAGIORITE[226]

Nicodemos was born on the island of Naxos in 1748. On his way to Mount Athos he met Macarios of Corinth, who proposed to him his plan of editing some of the ancient classics of Orthodox theology, canon law, liturgy, hagio-graphy, and asceticism. He entered the Athonite monastery of Dionysios, and in 1777 Macarios interested him in editing the *Philokalia,* the collection of ascetical and mystical writings of the hesychast Fathers. He collaborated again with Maca-rios to publish in 1783 the famous *Evergetikos,* the 11th century collection of sayings of the early Fathers of the desert. He added much to Macarios' *Encheiridion,* particularly by his encouragement of frequent Communion. This second edition appeared not under Macarios' name, but anonymously, and was printed in Venice in 1783 only to be condemned in 1785 by the bishop of Smyrna, Procopios, as being against the Orthodox traditions. However, Patriarch Neophytos (1789) annulled this after the monks of Mount Athos pro-tested. He collaborated again with Macarios to produce edi-tions of the works of Symeon the New Theologian and several other works on prayer and the ascetical life.

One of his most important works was the editing with Agapios Leonardos of the *Pedalion,* which attempted to assemble all the important canons of the Greek Church with commentaries and notes.[227] The full title of this noted work reads: "The Rudder of the Metaphorical Ship of the One Holy Catholic and Apostolic Church of the Orthodox Christians or All the Sacred and Divine Canons of the Holy and Renowned Apostles, of the Holy Councils, Ecumenical as well as Regional, and of Individual Divine Fathers as embodied in the original Greek text for the sake of authenticity and explained in the vernacular by way of rendering them more intelligible to the less educated."[228] Since its first publication in 1800, the *Pedalion* constitutes the most famous of all Byzantine collections of ancient canons, not only because it brought together in one book all the sacred canons of the Apostles, ecumenical councils, and regional synods, and the approved Holy Fathers, but above all because of the clear and precise commentary appended to each canon by Nicodemos and Agapios.

One sad feature marring a most productive life was the controversy that embroiled Nicodemos and the monks of Mount Athos on the problem of the *kolybes,* the blessed wheat, which was boiled and distributed as cakes in remembrance of the dead.[229] He also had to defend unjust attacks against his quite orthodox teaching on frequent Communion.

Without doubt Nicodemos proved to be one of the most productive authors and editors of Greek works in recent times. A catalogue of all the books that were printed under his editorship or composed originally by him would be too long to append here.[230] In the area of hagiography his translation of Maurice the Deacon's classical work on the lives of Greek Saints, entitled Συναξαριστές, and his many ἀκολουθίας or liturgical services in honor of individual saints have established Nicodemos' reputation among Orthodox monks. He was also preoccupied with editing liturgical compositions such as the Εὐχολόγιον and the canons of the

Ὀκτόηχος, along with explanations of the canons.

Perhaps no one single work has opened up to Western readers an understanding of the riches of Byzantine asceticism and mysticism as his edition, together with Macarios, of the *Philokalia.*[231] These ascetical writings are drawn from the early Fathers of the desert, the Syrian Fathers, those of Mount Sinai and of Mount Athos, and touch principally on hesychast spirituality, centering particularly around the prayer of the heart (The Jesus Prayer) and the ascetical practices involved in purifying the Christian in order to "pray always." This work has seen several translations into Slavonic and Russian, of which the best known is that by Paisii Velichkovskii and Feofan the Recluse, entitled *Dobrotoliubie* [*Love of the Good*].[232]

Nicodemos is also noted for his translation and adaptation of two Western ascetical classics. His Ἀόρατος Πόλεμος [*Invisible Warfare*] is almost a literal translation of the work of the Italian Theatine, Lorenzo Scupoli, *The Spiritual Combat* and *The Guard of Paradise,* and it has become a handbook of asceticism for Greek and Russian monks.[233] His Πνευματικὰ Γυμνάσματα [*Spiritual Exercises*] is a rather literal translation of the Italian work of G. P. Pinamonti: *Esercizi spirituali di S. Ignazio di Loyola distinti e divisi nelle meditationi, negli esami e nelle lezioni.* The first part consists of 34 meditations developed in the manner of Ignatius according to three considerations, and in the second part there are given 30 short meditations for a month's retreat with eight examens and eight conferences. His main ascetical work is his own synthesis of the doctrine of the hesychast Fathers on guarding the senses, imagination, intellect, and heart to develop a discipline necessary for continued prayer.[234]

Besides his canonical works he also translated exegetical works of authors such as Theophylakt the Bulgar[235] on the epistles of St. Paul, of Euthymios Zigabene and his commentaries on the Psalms[236] and on the catholic epistles.[237]

Another prolific writer of the 18th century was Caesarios Dapontes (d. 1784).[238] Before he settled down as a monk on Mount Athos and devoted himself to writing, he led a hectic life of political intrigue in Rumania and the Crimea which brought him imprisonment and a loss of his fortune. After an unfortunate marriage he became a monk on the island of Piperi, but went to Athos after quarrelling with his superior.

Besides works on church history, he wrote lives of the saints, ascetical treatises, panegyrical works such as the Ἐγκόλπιον λογικόν, in honor of the Mother of God, and translations of the main discourses of Saints Basil, Gregory of Nazianzos, and John Chrysostom[239] as well as the *Dialogues* of St. Gregory the Great.

THE AUTOCEPHALOUS GREEK CHURCH

Tension mounted in this century between the two main currents of theological thought: the Occidentalists influenced by the French Revolution and positivistic philosophy and the Conservatives who sought to restore both a theology and spirituality which stemmed directly from the golden age of the Byzantine Empire. This tension exploded as theologians turned politicians or nationalists and began to use theology as a means to work out a new Church-State relationship. The two opposing movements, one that sought to break away from the traditional Hellenism and its close association with the patriarchal see of Constantinople, and the other that clung in the midst of an ever-growing nationalism and the development of an independent Greek nation to the ecclesiastical bosom of Constantinople, may be typified by their two chief representatives: Theoclitos Pharmakidis (d. 1860) and Constantine Economos (d. 1857).

Pharmakidis exemplified in his character and his activities the whole new current of theological thought and political nationalism: unrest, a violent breaking from past traditions, and a spirit of autonomy and initiative.[240] Born in 1785 near Larissa, he studied theology in Bucharest and in Göttingen. He was thus exposed to other currents of thought than the traditional views presented by the patriarchal academy of Constantinople. Although he may, as he confessed often, have remained faithful to the doctrines, sacraments, and traditions of his Orthodox Church, he nevertheless developed a completely untraditional πολίτευμα or theory of the constitution of the Church in regard to the State. Imbued with ideas similar to those taught by Koraes, Pharmakidis led a very turbulent life, both as a theologian and as a politician, forming and actualizing the policy of the Bavarian regent Maurer. Both as a professor of theology in the Ionian Academy and the University of Athens, he based his teaching on ideas taken from Feofan Prokopovich, with a great deal of stress on the dissolution of the hierarchical structure, the importance of Scripture, and the use of human reason. The day King Otho arrived at Nauplion, February 6, 1833, to declare Greece an independent kingdom, Pharmakidis strove to make actual his own personal conviction. "That day when the nation received its independence, so also the Church became autonomous and autocephalous, because the State and the Church under their external form are not two bodies existing for themselves."[241]

In July, 1833, the Greek Parliament meeting at Nauplion declared the autonomy of the Greek Church as a *fait accompli* and set up a Holy Synod to govern it in imitation of the Church of Russia. Pharmakidis' principle of *phyletism* that each independent nation enjoyed the right to ecclesiastical independence had won, and the Greek Church severed all bonds with the patriarchate of Constantinople, a fact that was recognized officially only in 1850 by the patriarch. But the breaking away from Constantinople did not proceed without opposition, chiefly in the person of Constantine Economos.

Economos was self-taught but formed along the traditional lines of Byzantine patristic theology and spirituality.[242] After traveling throughout Europe, he returned to Greece in 1834 to wage a campaign against Maurer and Pharmakidis in the name of Orthodox tradition. Destroying the bonds that linked Greece with the mother church of Constantinople was, as Economis viewed it, destroying the true faith inherited from the Fathers and all the synods upon which Orthodoxy was founded. It meant setting up a synodal Church based upon ecclesiastical structures borrowed through the Russian Church from Protestantism.

Especially the translation of Vamvas of the Bible into the Greek vernacular constituted for Economos the beginning of further Protestant errors and a departure from the official interpretation of the hierarchy. Once private reading of the Bible in the vernacular was tolerated, he argued, the truths taught by the Holy Fathers and handed down in church councils would be doubted, discarded, and the way was open for subjectivism.

Economos failed to realize the complexity of the problems that modern society and especially a nascent nationalism were bringing to the Greek Church; above all, that not all of the canons written by the Holy Fathers could be applied in the same autocratic way by decrees from Constantinople. His greatest weakness was to consider Hellenism as essential to Christianity and to make the patriarch of Constantinople the official and only interpreter of what constituted that Hellenism. Hellenism was not, as Patriarch Jeremias II implied earlier in his answer to the Tübingen theologians, of divine institution.[243] Where Economos' Hellenism looked to ancient Byzantium, the Hellenism of Pharmakidis looked to the West.

Pharmakidis and his views triumphed when the national Constitution in 1844 voted to accept the decree of 1833 which declared the autocephaly of the Church of Greece and the sole governing organ to be the Holy Synod of Greek Bishops. The decree read: "The Orthodox Church of Hellas acknowledges our Lord Jesus Christ as its Head. It is inseparably joined in faith with the Church of Constantinople and with every other Christian Church of the same profession, but is autocephalous, exercises its sovereign rights independently of every other Church and is governed by the members of its Holy Synod."[244] It would remain principally for the University of Athens, founded in 1837, and its theological faculty to develop its own independent theology.

The Greek Church, now possessing its own theological academy, closely imitated the Russian Church under Count Protasov, the chief-prokurator of the Holy Synod of Moscow, in its attempt to stem the rising tide of Protestant thinking among the Orthodox. With pressure from the conservative theologians of Greece, led by Economos, Patriarch Gregory VI of Constantinople in 1836 issued his encyclical condemning the errors of Luther, Calvin, and Zwingli and their Protestant followers. At a time when the English Bible Society and other Protestant groups were flooding the Greek speaking world with the Bible printed in the vernacular, the encyclical forbade Greek Orthodox to read all Protestant books and, in particular, Protestant editions of the Holy Scripture.[245]

In order to arrest any possible bettering of relations with the Roman Catholics, an important theological statement, The *Encyclical of the Four Patriarchs of 1848,* was signed by the four principal Greek speaking patriarchs of Constantinople (Anthimos VI), Alexandria (Hierotheos II), Antioch (Methodios), and Jerusalem (Cyril II) along with 29 metropolitans. Popescu has shown that the real author of this polemical document was the patriarch of Constantinople, Constantios I (d. 1834), who had written it sometime previously.[246] It recapitulates the principal points of difference discussed in the anti-Latin polemical literature of previous centuries. Although Anthimos published it as an answer to Pope Pius IX's encyclical *In Suprema Petri Apostoli Sede* of January 6, 1848, in which the pope invited the Orthodox to reunite themselves with the Roman Church, it appears more as a diatribe against the assumed primacy of the Roman Pontiff. Papism is the chief error that has ruined the Roman Catholic Church, since it confuses religious authority with civil power which is then imposed upon the faithful under blind obedience. In this manner other heresies have infiltrated into the Roman Church such as the *Filioque,* baptism by aspersion, the lack of an *epiclesis,* communion under one species and the use of unleavened bread.[247]

APOSTOLOS MAKRAKIS

Apostolos Makrakis symbolized in his own passionate, contradictory personality the mixed-up times which the Greek Church itself was undergoing. The hierarchy, so closely dependent on the State not only for its creation but for its continuation, was unable to rectify the situation. It was infected with greedy, simoniacal, and often quite ignorant bishops. Priests had no seminary training and preaching of the Gospel was practically unheard of. Any ideas supported by a strong organization and backed by money coming from the West were sure of a hearing. Serious questioning had begun among the rising middle class of Greeks regarding basic Orthodox traditions, especially those that touched the hierarchical teaching authority. Masonry had begun to tear away at the monolithic structure of the Church, while atheism was becoming more common among educated Greeks. Zealous monks such as Cosmas Phlamatios, Christophoros Panagiotopoulos, or Papoulakos as he was popularly called, and Ignatios Lampropoulos followed in the footsteps of Cosmas the Aetolian to launch a serious religious renewal of the populace. Their efforts consisted primarily in negative attacks against Protestants and Masons or against the Bavarian Catholic king who was set over them. From the monastery of the Mega Spilaion in the Peloponnesos, Lampropoulos formed a nucleus of followers such as Eusebios Matthopoulos, the future founder of the *Zoe* Movement, Kallistos Eustaltion, Spiridon Gianouleas, Gabriel Papanikolas, Nil Nikolais and Elias Vlachopoulos. This group would become inspired by the fiery personality of Apostolos Makrakis.

Makrakis was born in 1831 in Siphnos, an island of the Cyclades.[248] Endowed with a fertile imagination and an ardent, even passionate spirit, he claimed at an early age to have been granted a vision of Christ who seemed to beckon him to become another Moses to lead the promised people of Orthodoxy into the Kingdom of God. In 1856 he proposed to offer himself as a final test of God's approbation of Orthodoxy over Islam. At a Congress held that year in Paris he offered to oppose any Moslem, in a test where each would carry his own Bible or the Koran and would enter into a blazing furnace. God was supposed to affirm in Old Testament style which religion was the true one by preserving the carrier of the Bible. His followers succeeded in dissuading him. While teaching boys, he sought to raise their spiritual level by daily study of the Bible and exhortations to frequent Communion. When he was reprimanded by the hierarchy as a "modernist," Makrakis in response began his long apostolate of the pen which has merited for him the honor of being the most prodigious Greek writer of the century. In 1858 he published *The Discovery of the Hidden Treasure.* This, along with his *City of Zion or the Church Built upon the Rock* or the *Human Community in Christ,*[249] presents his basic argument. There must be a complete reform of religious morals beginning with the lax bishops of Greece in order that there can be a proper listening to the saving word of Christ, who is the salvation of the nations, of the people, of the whole world. This salvation will be brought about only by the Kingdom of Christ on earth, which will be a renewed Byzantine theocracy.

He took his message to crowds who eagerly listened to him on the street corners. His frenetic physical appearance and burning zeal for the Gospel message inspired many to follow him. He carried his ideas further through means of his journal, Δικαιοσύνη [*Justice*] and later in his second periodical, Λόγος [*The Word*]. He railed incessantly against the professors of the University of Athens, especially against his chief opponent, Vimbos; he attacked the hierarchy for its simony and the ideas of the French positivists and Masons which were creeping into the school system. No one was safe from the scourge of Makrakis as he went about his self-appointed task of fighting abuses wherever they existed and establishing the Kingdom of Christ. He founded in 1874 his third journal Εἰρήνη [*Peace*], which was hardly true to its name, as he sought to bring about reform in the church life of Greece. The Holy Synod finally condemned him not only for his views on the trichotomy in the composition of man (body, soul and spirit), but also for the religious practices which he and his group of followers developed in the matter of frequent Communion and confession to one another. He was publicly accused of having opened a private school to rival the University of Athens without the necessary authorization, but he was never tried.

The literary output of Makrakis is staggering. (Petit gives the best listing of the main works.)[250] With charismatic insight Makrakis saw the centrality of Christ in history. Around His person and the Gospel he sought to build a whole system of philosophy and theology. The lack, however, of a solid philosophical and theological training prevented him from giving a systematic rebuttal to the enemies of Orthodoxy. He too often presented his own position in the light of an assembly of contradictory positions. He succeeded in writing some fifty books, dealing with theological, philosophical, exegetical, educational, historical and political topics, of varying importance and quality. His theological writings reveal a lack of solid foundation in the sources of Byzantine spirituality and theology. His approach was generally not an appeal to patristic sources, but an ardent apologetic against the pseudo-theologies, as he called them, "infected by the power of the Devil to lead all God-fearing men astray."

Makrakis saw the importance of contact with Christ through the Scriptures, and his greatest theological contribution was an exegesis of the entire New Testament, verse by verse totaling 2,470 pages, while his commentaries on the Psalms and on the nine odes (the scriptural texts used for Matins) total 1,250 pages.

One outstanding contribution, even beyond his literary achievements, was his missionary zeal, which left a strong impression on later generations. Unfortunately, this was tied too strongly to his messianic views of a re-establishment of the Byzantine Empire as the Kingdom of Christ on earth. Anyone who spiritually or politically presented a threat was classified as Anti-Christ. His ardent apostolate was carried on without the official benediction of the hierarchy and he was largely responsible for diminishing the respect for hierarchical authority among the faithful through his insistence on tying up the Greek Church with a Byzantinism that was dead and no longer had any relevance for a nascent country. He justly criticized the simony and the abuses of the hierarchy, but he weakened the position of the bishops by over-emphasizing the charismatic element in the Church to the detriment of any visible teaching body. The Church of Greece would never be the same after Makrakis; above all, he stirred the laity to realize their missionary call through Baptism and thus prepared for the beginnings of the lay groups that would become a distinctive feature of not only the Greek church in the 20th century, but also of the theological renaissance, that would be primarily the responsibility of the laity.

ORTHODOX-ANGLICAN RELATIONS

Before the 18th century, relations between the Church of

England and the Greek Orthodox Church consisted primarily
in correspondence between individual churchmen, such as that
between Patriarch Cyril Lucaris and Archbishop Abbot of
Canterbury (1611-1633). In the 18th century the Nonjurors,
a dissenting group, declared schismatic by the official Church
of England, made overtures to the Russian Church through
Peter the Great and to the Greek Church through the Eastern
Patriarchs. This correspondence (1716-1724), drawn up by
Archibald Campbell and Thomas Brett from among the
Nonjurors, was aimed from the English point of view at
effecting a union with the Orthodox.[251] The Anglican Divines
refused to break their oath of allegiance to the Stuarts, sent
three letters to the Patriarch of Constantinople stating their
conditions for reunion and received two letters in answer.
Nothing came of this early attempt at ecumenical dialogue,
but it revealed some interesting points of agreement and
disagreement. The Nonjurors feared that the Eastern Christians might be paying too much honor to the Mother of
God and the Saints, they preferred no icons, and held the
Real Presence to be only subjective in the soul of the communicant according to his faith. The English divines accepted Holy Scripture and Tradition, although the latter was
not conceived totally in the Orthodox sense. The Church was
infallible when it made a synodical pronouncement under
the Lordship of Christ. The Church was to be independent
of the State. They accepted all the sacraments as well as the
particular judgment but rejected the teaching on purgatory.
They proposed that the bishop of Jerusalem become the first
bishop of Christendom and that each Church draw up a
"primitive" liturgy in order to secure a uniformity of rites.

The Orthodox answer was quite traditional in tone. The
patriarch of Constantinople insisted that his church had kept
the catholic faith intact and can change nothing. The idea
of making the patriarch of Jerusalem first bishop goes
against all church tradition. The Byzantine liturgy is already
a "primitive" liturgy which the Anglicans could well enough

adopt. The Nonjurors were finally lectured by the Orthodox on their Lutheran and Calvinist errors and exhorted to be converted to the Orthodox faith.

In the 19th century, with the decrease of proselytism in the Near and Middle East, renewed contacts were made, both formal and informal. Bishops, theologians, and clergymen met at Lambeth and Bonn during this century; a greater immigration of the Orthodox to the West with the formation of Anglican communities within Orthodox jurisdiction increased contacts between the two Churches.

The Oxford Movement (1833-1845) inclined many Anglicans not only to re-examine their position towards Roman Catholics but also towards the Greek Orthodox. The first step towards anything that could be called inter-communion came as a result of correspondence in 1869 between Archbishop A. Campbell Tait and Ecumenical Patriarch Gregory VI. Permission was granted by the Orthodox for any Anglican dying in the East to be buried by the Greek priests in a special Orthodox service. The Bonn Conferences (1874-1875) brought the Anglicans closer to the Orthodox view of tradition as found in the symbols of faith and dogmatic decrees of the ecumenical councils. In the Third Lambeth Conference (1888) a commission was set up which studied the Anglican Church's relations to the Orthodox, which was reported in the fifth conference in 1908. Yet no substantial results in explaining the dogmatic differences between the two Churches were obtained.

ENCYCLICAL OF ANTHIMOS VII[252]

The most authoritative document of recent times which gives the key differences between the Orthodox and the Roman Catholic Churches is the Encyclical of Anthimos VII. It was intended as an answer to the encyclical of Pope Leo XIII, *Praeclara gratulationis,* of June 20, 1894, which the pope sent to the Orthodox hierarchs urging them to re-unite with Rome. The encyclical letter of Anthimos VII was signed by himself and his twelve metropolitans, but the text was composed by Germanos Karavangelis, then chorbishop of Pera.[253] Anthimos' answer has enjoyed since then the authority of being somewhat of an official summary of all the differences that the Orthodox find unacceptable in the Roman Catholic Church and which thus constitute the main impediments to union. The list repeats the essential points of difference as outlined in the *Encyclical of the Four Patriarchs* of 1848 with added arguments against the newly defined dogmas of the Immaculate Conception of the Virgin Mary (1854) and the infallibility of the pope (1870).

GREEK COMPENDIA OF THEOLOGY

While the University of Athens was developing its theological faculty, the Russian theologians of the 19th century, who had excelled in producing compendia along the lines of the classical scholastic textbooks in use in Western seminaries, enjoyed a popularity in Greece. These compendia were translated from Russian into Greek and used to instruct the Greek clergy; most widely used were those of Makarii Bulgakov[254] and Antonii Amfiteatrov.[255]

It was not long, however, before the professors of the University of Athens began to write their own compendia in Greek. Nicholas Damalas (d. 1892) wrote one which presented the chief differences between Protestants, Catholics and Orthodox[256] as well as a work on the relation of the Anglican Church to the Orthodox[257] and a standard work on biblical hermeneutics.[258] Zikos Rhosis, professor of dogmatic theology and Christian ethics in the University of Athens and in the Rizarion Seminary, was the first Greek to publish a complete compendium of dogmatic theology.[259] Rhosis felt that from the 8th century the Greek Orthodox Church had made no great development in theology; this was all the more true of the Church after the fall of Constantinople. An elaboration of systematic theology was needed and for this he fell back upon other than Orthodox sources. He believed that Orthodox theology could be greatly aided by Western, particularly Protestant, theology.[260] Theology, insists Rhosis, must not only treat of the history of dogmas, but must through philosophical and metaphysical speculation seek to gain deeper insights into the revelation handed down by the Church. In his introduction he investigates the relationship of dogmatic theology to other sciences and then treats of the existence of God, His essence, the Trinity, creation, providence, angels, demons, man, the human soul, religion and revelation, Sacred Scripture and tradition. Much is drawn from other sources, both Russian and Western, without proper citations.

Perhaps the classic compendium of this period is that of Chrestos Androutsos. He wrote his work as a protest against that of Rhosis in order to give theology a strong philosophical basis without at the same time borrowing from Protestant and Latin writings. He sought to balance the dogmas of the Orthodox Church as sources and norms for speculation while using human reason to strengthen the defined dogmas.[261] Androutsos recognized the difficulty of taking as normative the dogmatic statements found in the patristic traditions, ecumenical councils and later synods, especially those of the 17th century, and to elaborate these truths. Often there would be no authoritative declarations of the teaching Church. Then theologians would have to be guided according to the spirit of the Orthodox Church as manifested in practice.[262]

Androutsos divided his compendium into two parts, which would become the standard procedure for Greek compendia. The first section deals with God, creation, providence, the world, man and original sin. The second treats of the incarnational economy of salvation, the person of Jesus Christ, divine grace, the sacraments, universal judgment and the end of the world. The author has been severely judged by other Orthodox theologians, such as Constantine Dyovu-niotis,[263] for having taken much of his theology from Catholic and Protestant theologians.

D. S. Balanos produced some individual treatises which have been widely used in Greek seminaries, especially on justification and on the Holy Trinity.[264] I. Mesoloras saw the need of collecting all the documents enjoying any authority as expressions of the Orthodox faith. This he did in his famous and most helpful work entitled: Συμβολικὴ τῆς Ὀρθοδόξου Ἀνατολικῆς Ἐκκλησίας.[265] In the first two volumes the author has collected all the documents of the Greek and Russian Orthodox Churches which summarize in credal fashion the main tenets of the Orthodox Church. The third and fourth volumes deal with the dogmatic differences between Orthodox, Protestants, and Catholics. Nectarios Kephalos, Metropolitan of Pentapolis, and Nicholas Ambrazis[266] also composed compendia of note. The first wrote prolifically, not always concerned with a scholarly presentation but rather more for popular catechetical instruction.[267]

With the establishment of an independent state and an autonomous Church, canon law also began to be developed, and commentators came forth with collections of ancient canons and commentaries to fit the changing situation. One of the most influential works was the collection in six volumes by Rhalli and Potli giving the principal commentaries of previous Byzantine canonists together with many other documents relating to ecclesiastical discipline.[268] This work is divided into six parts. The first four consist of the *Nomo-canons* with the commentaries of Zonaras, Balsamon and Aritenis. The fifth part contains the decrees of the patriarchs of Constantinople, the imperial constitutions and responses; the final section is the *Syntagma* of Blastares. Finally, the decisions of the Holy Synod of Greece were collected and edited by S. Giannopoulos.[269]

THE THEOLOGIGAL ACADEMY OF ATHENS[270]

The center of modern Greek theology was founded as a faculty of theology of the University of Athens on April 14, 1837. The first professors were Michael Apostolides, who taught dogmatic and ethical theology, Theoklitos Pharmakidis and K. Kontogonis. The latter taught practically all the courses, owing to a lack of trained professors.[271] Gradually trained theologians such as Panayotis Robotes, Alexander Likourygos, Theoklitos Vimpos, Kyriakos and Nicholas Damalas, Nicephoros Kalogeras, Zikos Rhosis, I. Mesoloras, C. Rhallis, C. Androutsos, Chrysostom Papadopoulos, later to become the metropolitan of Athens, Philip Papadopoulos and Gregory Papamichael joined the faculty. The succeeding generation of theologians, practically all of whom studied in Germany, brought to Athens the critical techniques of the German universities of the latter part of the 19th century. Because of nationalism and the turmoil caused by the First World War and the Russian Revolution, they had little contact with the more relevant Orthodox theology developed at this same time among the Russian émigrés in Europe and America. In the main, the theology of the new generation of Greek professors at Athens was academic with little relevance to the spiritual needs of their own faithful or to the patristic traditions of the past.

Some of the leading professors of the faculty of Athens in the late 1920's to the present include C. Dyovuniotis, D. Balanos, V. Stephanides, G. Sotiriou, N. Louvaris, P. Bratsiotis, B. Vellas, E. Antoniadis, L. Philippides, D. Moraitis, P. Trembelas, C. Bonis, G. Konidaris, V. Ioannides, A. Phytrakis and C. Mouratides. The Academy was organized along the lines of a German university. It possesses two chairs of Old Testament, two of New, one chair of church history, patrology, hermeneutics of the Fathers of the Church, practical theology (which includes homiletics and catechetics), history of religion, hymnology, hagiology, palaeography, canon law and pastoral theology.

Having studied abroad, these professors were open to ecumenical contacts and not only wrote voluminously in the area of ecumenical theology[272] but also personally participated in sessions of the World Council of Churches, since the Greek Orthodox Church became an active member in 1947 at the first general meeting in Amsterdam. The faculty of the Academy played key roles in the organization and discussions of the First Theological Congress held in Athens in 1936 and the Pan-Orthodox Pro-Synods of Rhodes (1961, 1962, 1963, 1965), of Belgrade (1966) and of Geneva (1968), which were intended as preparatory for a Pan-Orthodox Synod to be held in the near future.

THE THEOLOGICAL ACADEMY OF THESSALONIKA[273]

The northern city of Thessalonika, open to more influences from Bulgaria, Macedonia, and the other Eastern European countries than Athens, even today breathes a freedom and a spirit of individualism not found in other parts of Greece. This is also reflected in its University and its theological academy. The university started on June 14, 1925, but the faculty of theology with 10 departments was inaugurated only in 1942. Today the Academy has 17 departments, similar to those found in the Academy of Athens. Students majoring in theology may register in one of five sections: systematic, history of theology, hermeneutics, pastoral and catechetics.

The members of the faculty have generally been much younger than the professors of Athens and are considered less conservative. A list of eminent professors who have taught in this academy would include P. Chrestou, I. Kotsonis (later Archbishop of Athens), G. Konidaris, V. Ioannides, A.

Papadopoulos, I. Trakas, A. Chastoupes, S. Agourides, E. Theodorou, A. Papageorgakopoulos and I. Anastasiou.

Scholarly theological journals began to appear in the early part of the 20th century. The quarterly, Θεολογία [*Theology*] is the principal theological review in modern Greece. It originated as the publication of the Patriarchate of Constantinople, Ἐκκλησιαστικὴ Ἀλήθεια [*Ecclesiastical Truth*], which was suppressed by the Turks in 1923. Ὀρθοδοξία [*Orthodoxy*] and Ἀπόστολος Ἀνδρέας [*Apostle Andrew*] became the official organs of the ecumenical patriarch but also printed learned theological articles; both were suppressed in 1964 by the Turkish government. Ἐκκλησία [*Church*] is the fortnightly organ of the Holy Synod of Greece, which also prints theological articles of high caliber. A Byzantine journal, which often contains patristic articles, is published under the title of Ἐπετηρὶς τῆς Ἑταιρείας Βυζαντινῶν Σπουδῶν [*Yearbook of the Society of Byzantine Studies*]. The metropolitan of Thessalonika publishes as his official organ the journal Γρηγόριος ὁ Παλαμᾶς [*Gregory Palamas*] while the metropolitan of Mytilene publishes Ποιμὴν [*Shepherd*]. Ἀκτῖνες [*Rays*] is an outstanding intellectual journal which prints theological articles of contemporary significance, written and operated by leading lay intellectuals of Greece. Holy Cross Seminary of Jerusalem publishes Νέα Σιὼν [*New Zion*], and the Alexandrian Patriarchate published Ἐκκλησιαστικὸς Φάρος [*Ecclesiastical Lighthouse*] replaced by Πανταῖος [*Panteos*]; Ἀνάπλασις [*Regeneration*] is another Alexandrian theological journal.

THE FIRST CONGRESS OF ORTHODOX THEOLOGIANS

In Athens (November 29th/December 6, 1936), under the presidency of Hamilcar Alivisatos, professor of canon law and pastoral theology of the University of Athens, the First Congress of Orthodox Theologians took place. The theological faculties of Athens, Bucharest, Kissinev [Jassy], Cernauti, Belgrade, Sofia, Paris, and Warsaw sent their outstanding theologians to discuss, as Alivisatos explained in his opening address, how to create "a unified conscience of the internal and external force which Orthodoxy represents."[274] Among the Orthodox theologians were Alivisatos, Mesoloras, Balanos, Bratsiotis, Vellas, Antoniadis, Moraitis, Dyovouniotis representing the Academy of Athens; Bulgakov, Zenkovskii, Kartashev, Kassian (Bezobrasov) and Florovsky of the Institute of Orthodox Theology of Paris; Stefanovich, Dimitrievich and Granich of the faculty of Belgrade; Ispir, Jonesco and Popescu of Bucharest; Savin of Kissinev, Cotos and Sesan of Cernauti; Zankov, Pashev and Gosheff of Sofia; and Arseniev, Basdekas and Zyzikine of Warsaw. There were also Roman Catholic, Anglican, and Protestant observers present.

One of the key problems, to which Alivisatos, Balanos, Zankov, Granich and Sesan devoted learned papers, dealt with the possibility of summoning the 8th ecumenical council. Most of the theologians agreed with Zankov[275] that a pan-Orthodox synod was the first important step to bring about an ecumenicity among Orthodox believers. To prepare for this the second congress of theologians was to meet in Bucharest in 1939 to discuss the following agenda: the sources of the Orthodox Faith, the Sacred Scripture, tradition, and the social mission of the Church. This meeting never took place because of the imminence of the Second World War.

Another need that was stressed was the revision of Eastern canon law. The Congress of theologians resolved to petition each Orthodox Church through the ecumenical patriarch to appoint a commission from the various faculties of theology to prepare for this gigantic undertaking.

Efforts were made to follow up the enthusiasm generated

by this exchange of views among the theological leaders of the free Orthodox world (the Russian theological schools were not represented) by establishing an Orthodox theological journal which would facilitate further scholarly exchange among the various academies.[276] Another project of mutual cooperation was suggested: a new, uniform revision of the "primitive" text of the liturgical books used in the Orthodox Churches.[277] Professors were also encouraged to organize conferences with visitors from other faculties as well as exchanges of students. The feast of the Three Hierarchs was established as the common feast to be celebrated among all faculties of Orthodox theology in order to reinforce their spiritual union.

Two related problems touched upon an area of Orthodox theology which had been neglected for centuries under the Turks; namely, the relationship of patristic theology to modern theological speculation and the relationship of modern biblical hermeneutics to ecclesiastical authority and traditional patristic exegesis. Orthodox theology of the 20th century had been stimulated by contact with the West. Nearly every theologian participating at the Congress of Athens had studied in Europe, especially in Germany. Many of them had engaged in ecumenical meetings since the early 1920's, when the ecumenical movement formed out of the gatherings in Lausanne, Stockholm and Copenhagen. The presence of so many Russian émigrés teaching theology in the West spurred an unparalleled creative theologizing that forced the Orthodox to answer the question continually asked of them in the West: What is the position of the Orthodox Church? This could not be answered by merely repeating patristic texts. Father Georges Florovsky in his speech to the Congress entitled, "Patristics and Modern Theology,"[278] disagreed with most Orthodox regarding patristic tradition: "Patristic writings are respected indeed, but more as historical documents than as books of authority. Numerous patristic references or even quotations are still usual in our theological essays and textbooks. But so often these old texts or quotations are simply interpolated into a scheme borrowed elsewhere. As a matter of fact, the conventional schemes of our theological textbooks came from the West, partly from Roman sources, partly from Reformed ones. Patristic texts are kept and repeated. The patristic mind is too often completely lost or forgotten."[279]

Professors Balanos[280] and Florovsky called for a return to the Fathers, not a return to the letter of the patristic texts in blind, servile imitation or repetition; but rather a further development of the patristic teaching, homogeneous with that corpus of teaching and yet creative enough to be meaningful for our modern age. But if so much Orthodox biblical exegesis is dependent upon patristic hermeneutics, what are Orthodox scholars to do about modern scriptural discoveries and research largely made by Western scholars? Professors Evanghelos Antoniadis and Basil Vellas of Athens sought to offer directional lines for a new Orthodox biblical hermeneutics that would be able to reconcile the patristic spirit of exegesis with the modern scientific research on the Bible as an historical document. Antoniadis insisted in his discourse,[281] as he had in his book printed in the same year as the Congress (1936),[282] that historical criticism is necessary if the Orthodox Church is to be relevant and effective in the 20th century. To ignore the findings of historical criticism is like a warrior setting out with bow and arrow to do battle with a foe bearing fire-arms. The Bible must be considered as an historical document, and in this regard there cannot be any conflict between the teaching authority of the Church and scientific research. The exegesis of the Holy Fathers cannot be regarded as absolute interpretations but as helpful guidelines.

Professor Vellas likewise insisted upon critical biblical work as imperative if the study of the Bible is to become a true science offered in Orthodox theological academies. Such critical study is a part of objective scientific research and as such cannot conflict with the teaching of the Orthodox Church.[283]

THE LAY MOVEMENTS

A feeling gradually grew up among the laity and the monks that theology in the 20th century was becoming a merely academic science, removed from both the praying community and the patristic fonts from which it originally developed. There began the formation of various lay groups intent upon preaching, writing and above all living a more effective theology. The lay organization responsible, at least in its early stages, for an Orthodox theology more in touch with modern problems was called *Zoe* [*Life*]. Although this brotherhood had been founded in 1911 by Archimandrite Eusebios Matthopoulos, it became genuinely effective only after the Second World War in the struggle against Communism. *Zoe* is a religious group whose members lead a common life under promises, a sort of semi-monastic order or secular institute. A quarter of the brothers are monks, the rest are laymen, most of whom possess a university degree in theology.

Both priests and laymen have become effective preachers and have been influential in raising the moral and intellectual level of life in Greece. To a large extent, their success in improving the religious life of the masses has been due to their publication of books and pamphlets. A weekly publication, called *Zoe,* with 200,000 subscribers, gives the people a sermon on the Sunday Gospel plus discussions of important, contemporary moral questions. Nearly 400 titles, totaling over 9 million books, for a population of 8.5 million people, have been printed and distributed at low cost and made easily available to all. *Zoe* operates 2,300 catechetical Sunday schools, influencing over 200,000 students. Since 1929 it has published the Bible in five editions of over 400,000 copies.

Bi-weekly and monthly magazines are printed to appeal to all classes of children, youths, and adults. Recently a conservative group within the *Zoe* Brotherhood, fearing the liberal tendencies of the younger theologians, broke away under the leadership of the noted theologian, Panayotis Trembelas, to form a similar brotherhood, *Sotir [Savior]*, and publish a periodical of the same name.

In 1936 the government established the *Apostoliki Diakonia* as the official instrument of the Holy Synod to accomplish what *Zoe* had set out to do. A vigorous program, launched after the Civil War against the Communists which ended in 1949, continues to train a corps of preachers, confessors and teachers for catechetical schools. Still, articulate laymen, well-informed theologically, have felt the need of smaller, more effective organizations to revitalize given areas of Christian living and have formed such associations which also produce their own publications. The Association of Lay Theologians, under the capable leadership of M. Keramidas, publishes the lay theologians' journal, *Enoria.*

The lay theologians who have graduated from the two academies of Athens and Thessalonika, especially those who continued their studies in Europe or America, have written a great deal in the various fields of theology, particularly in journals.[284] To a large extent, they have concerned themselves with editing and commenting on patristic texts and writing on some phase of the ecumenical movement.[285] Many Greek theologians seem to feel that, as representatives of the only free Orthodox nation, they have a mission to return to patristic sources and to defend the early traditions. As a result, modern Greek theology has been more conservative than original, more traditional than creative.

In 1968 Patriarch Athenagoras I established a patristic institute in the Monastery of Vlatadon overlooking the city of Thessalonika and placed it under the direction of Panayotis Chrestou, Professor of patristics at the University of Thessalonika. Manuscripts belonging to the patriarchate of Constantinople were transported from the Athonite monastery of Iviron where they had been stored for safe keeping during the Second World War, and it is hoped that this institute will be an international center of patristic studies. The Institute has a threefold purpose: 1) to prepare new editions of texts of the Fathers of the Church with translations in various languages; 2) to issue an international periodical devoted to patristic studies; and 3) to sponsor public lectures, symposia and conferences on patristic studies. It is supported by an annual grant from the Patriarchate of Constantinople and from other interested persons and institutions.

THE ECUMENICAL MOVEMENT

As far as the ecumenical movement is concerned, Greek theologians have taken an active part in meetings of the World Council of Churches at Amsterdam, Stockholm, Evanston, New Delhi, and Uppsala. Unfortunately, Archbishop Ieronimos Kotsonis of Athens withdrew the participation of the delegation of theologians from Greece at the international congress at Uppsala in 1968. In his work, *Okumenische Probleme in der Neugriechischen Theologie,* D. Savramis calls for a Pan-Orthodox Synod as a serious preparation for dialogue with other Christians, especially the Roman Catholics who, through Vatican Council II, have already effected much reform and adaptation. "Serious renovation, carefully planned intent and action, genuine love and real, lasting progress in knowing each other" are needed if the ecumenical movement is to produce solid results.[286]

SCHOLARLY ENDEAVORS

A noteworthy contribution to Greek theology was the

publication of the new encyclopedia: Θρησκευτικὴ καὶ Ἠθικὴ Ἐγκυκλοπαιδεία [*Religious and Ethical Encyclopaedia*].[287] In twelve volumes, leading Orthodox theologians from Greece and from other parts of Europe and America have contributed important articles that touch upon Orthodox theological life. Lay theologians who are not professors in the two leading universities have had an opportunity to write many of the key articles. Two such writers who have distinguished themselves not only in their capacity as editors of this encyclopedia but also by their creative articles are Basil Moustakis and Aristides Panotis.

The Theology School of Halki near Istanbul was founded in 1844 and since then has been the third leading Greek theological center in the world.[288] During the patriarchate of Germanos IV it was founded and organized by Archimandrite Constantine Tipaldos. Not enjoying the freedom and the prestige of being associated with a Greek university as the other two theological schools, Halki's school of theology has struggled under continued pressure from the Turkish government. This may explain why it has not rivaled Athens and Thessalonika in producing outstanding theologians.

GREEK THEOLOGY IN THE NEW WORLD

The Greek Orthodox Church had its beginnings in the New World in 1866 when Greek merchants living in New Orleans built a church of their own rite. In 1870 a great influx of Greek immigrants to the United States made it imperative that the Greek Orthodox Church establish itself permanently in America. At first the Greek Orthodox were under the jurisdiction of the American Russian Church, at that time a mission in Alaska and San Francisco of the Patriarchate of Moscow. In 1908, however, the ecumenical Patriarch Joachim III transferred jurisdiction to the Holy

Synod of the Church of Greece. Ten years later Meletios
Mataxakis, Metropolitan of Athens, organized the Greek
Orthodox Churches in America into a Synodical Conclave
with Bishop Alexander of Rodostolou as Synodical Super-
visor. On being elevated to the patriarchal see of Constantinople as Meletios IV, he placed the American Greek
Churches under the jurisdiction of the ecumenical patriarch.
In 1922 Bishop Alexander was appointed as archbishop of
the new Archdiocese of North and South America.

To form native American priests of Greek descent Holy
Cross Theological Seminary was founded in 1937 at Pomfret,
Connecticut and in 1946 transferred to Brookline, Massachusetts. In 1968 the seminary was incorporated into the
newly founded Hellenic University of America, under the
patronage of Archbishop Iakovos. The Seminary publishes
the *Greek Orthodox Theological Review* which contains
articles written primarily by professors of the Seminary and
by Greek theologians in Europe.

The Archdiocese with its 460 parishes, 400 afternoon
Greek schools, 17 parochial, 57 evening schools and 709
Sunday schools has been gradually raising the level of
religious education among the Greek Orthodox in America.
This has in turn challenged the leading theologians to develop
a Greek Orthodox theology relevant to the American situation
in which they live. Of the 10 bishops of the Archdiocese
and 460 priests, 265 are graduates of Holy Cross Seminary
or St. Vladimir's Russian Seminary, while the rest still come
from the theological schools of Halki, Athens or Thessalonika. Professor John S. Romanides, however, complains
that the orientation of Greek Orthodox theology in America
has been to produce priests, not theologians.[289] Graduates of
the Brookline Seminary, upon completing five or six years of
theological training after high school, received in the past
no accredited degree. If they pursue higher studies, they
usually do so in state universities or those of Protestant or
Roman Catholic orientation; thus there is danger, warns

Romanides, that Greek theology in America will lose more and more its contact with Orthodox theology in Greece and become a Western type of Orthodoxy, a form of Uniatism attached to Orthodoxy not by doctrine but only ritually.[290]

While Greek Orthodoxy in America has been busy building churches and schools and has not yet found the leisure to develop a creative theology of its own in the Western hemisphere, Greek theologians in the older parts of the Orthodox world have seen the slow penetration of technology into their countries. This has posed the major problem in Orthodoxy today: What must be changed in its theology to meet the pressing problems of the modern age and what of tradition must be strongly maintained? What organ of authority can effect such changes and, on the other hand, insist on retaining other traditional teachings? Thus most Greek theologians feel that a Pan-Orthodox ecumenical synod alone can open the doors not only to a more vibrant Orthodoxy among the faithful, but also prepare the way for a more creative theology to make Orthodoxy truly relevant for the 20th century.

PART THREE

The Bulgarian Church

NOWHERE is the intimate connection between the development of theology in a nation and its political, social,
and cultural evolution seen more clearly than in the case
of the Bulgarian Church. The history of Bulgaria is a sad
and glorious account of growth, golden eras, national freedom and high culture alongside rapid changes of abyssmal
ignorance, wars and slavery.[1]

Christianity had reached the present territory of Bulgaria
early, and its ecclesiastical life had been well established,
as may be seen in the Council of Sardica [Sofia] in 343. The
Slavic invasions, however, obliterated much of this earlier
Christianity, so that when the Bulgars, a Turkic tribe, came
to settle there in the 7th century, the country was virtually
pagan. The Bulgars soon adopted the Slavic language and,
under Byzantine influence, began to think of becoming
Christian. Prince Boris (or Bogoris, d. 907) was baptized
in 864 and wanted Christianity to be accepted also by his
people. Seeking to gain political advantages, he first courted
the favor of the Church of Constantinople, but seeing that
the patriarch would not grant him his own hierarchy and
independent church, he turned to Pope Nicholas I. Boris was
later dissatisfied with papal demands and again returned to
Constantinople. From 870 Bulgaria was attached, at times
rather loosely, to the Ecumenical Patriarchate.

In evangelizing his country, Boris was greatly assisted by the disciples of Sts. Cyril and Methodius who had been expelled from Moravia by the German bishops and who sought refuge with the Slavs in Bulgaria. Clement, Naum, and Angelar brought to Bulgaria the Byzantine Liturgy translated into Old Slavonic along with other liturgical books, the Bible, codes of canon law and lives of the Saints. Two great literary centers were established, one around Devol in southwest Macedonia under the leadership of Clement of Ochrid who established the monastery of the Archangel Michael (now called St. Naum) and the other in Preslav in north-east Bulgaria under the leadership of Naum. From 886 these disciples of Sts. Cyril and Methodius translated books from the Greek, corrected earlier translations and recopied others. It is estimated that thousands of priests, monks, catechists and calligraphers were involved in preparing this body of Christian literature and in giving it to the people through the churches, schools and monasteries that sprang up throughout Boris' kingdom. Christianity had produced such sudden results in transforming the land and the people, at least extrinsically, into a Christian country that in 893 a national assembly was called by Boris to declare Christianity as the state religion.

ST. CLEMENT OF OCHRID

Because of the ravages caused by five centuries of Turkish oppression and the ecclesiastical oppression of the Greek patriarchate of Constantinople, thousands of these early manuscripts had been destroyed by fire. The extant records are those that found their way to Russia, Mount Athos and other depositories of early Slavic literature. It would be impossible to estimate the extent of the books translated from the Byzantine treasury of liturgy, theology, scripture, canon law, hagiography and church history by these scholars.

A built-in handicap to such a literary boon would appear only much later, namely, that it encouraged a mere translation of literature and theology developed in different times under other cultural circumstances. The hieratic literature of Bulgaria in these early centuries was almost totally Byzantine, made available to the Slavic peoples of Bulgaria and eventually also to Serbia and Russia by means of the Cyrillic alphabet and the Old Slavonic language. The Bulgarian Church nourished itself on these readily accessible writings, but failed to develop a literature that reflected its own interior growth.

St. Clement (called, of Bulgaria, of Ochrid, or Slovenskii) carried on most of his literary activities in Ochrid, where he died in 916.[2] To him is attributed the Life [*Zhitiia*] of St. Methodius and a possible life of St. Constantine [Cyril], both of which are found along with a brief life of Clement himself in a collection called *The Bulgarian Legend* or *The Pannonian Legend*.[3] His own life and works are described in two *Lives* written by Bishop Theophylakt of Ochrid (1004-1107) and by Dimitrii Chomatian (1216-1234). Clement's more original works consist in the composition of liturgical services, explanations of the Gospels and panegyrics or *"Pochvali,"* probably preached and then written down for the feasts of the Saints. V. Vondrak counts 16 such compositions from his pen.[4] His great skill in translating the highly lyrical and poetical liturgical literature of the Byzantines is seen in his translation ordered by Tsar Simeon I of the *Triod* for the Pentecost season. Another composition attributed to him is on Confession, *Chin nad ispovedaoushimisoa.*

ST. NAUM

St. Naum worked in Plisk, the Bulgarian capital, from 886 to 893, and then moved to the monastery in Preslav:

finally he joined Clement in Ochrid where he died in 910. None of Naum's works has survived, but his own literary activity and organization of translations were appreciated by Boris and Simeon, who speak of him as the one primarily responsible for the great literary flourishing at the end of the ninth and the beginning of the tenth century.

KONSTANTIN THE PRESBYTER

More detailed information exists on the literary activity of Konstantin the Presbyter. He was bishop (906) of Solin and worked in Macedonia about the time of Clement and Naum.[5] Seeing the people's need for sermons that would explain the Gospels and the Christian life, Konstantin translated 51 sermons from John Chrysostom, Cyril of Alexandria, and Isidore of Pelicium for Sundays.[6] These seem to be literal translations from the original Greek, since Konstantin in his preface explains that a people with an undeveloped national culture would profit from works of the outstanding theologians and poets of Byzantium who excelled in their simplicity and clarity of presentation. Upon the request of Tsar Simeon in 906, Konstantin translated the Discourses of St. Athanasios against the Arians in an attempt to refute the errors concerning Christology that had arisen among the newly converted Bulgarians. His *Istorikiia* is the oldest work dealing with history in Bulgarian literature, and it is modeled on the Byzantine world chronicles which begin with Adam and trace human history through Scripture and the Roman and Byzantine Empires. As history this work has no value, but it is evidence of the powerful Byzantine influence of the 9th and 10th centuries in Bulgarian literature.[7]

TSAR SIMEON

Simeon, who succeeded Boris on the Bulgarian throne, had been educated in Constantinople and was very familiar with Byzantine civilization. During his reign Bulgaria reached its "Golden Age" in literature, centered chiefly around Preslav and Ochrid, and stressing primarily translations from Byzantine originals. Under Simeon Bulgaria attained a phenomenal political and economic growth that allowed for a high development in literature and the arts. He was well versed in Byzantine learning, especially in the encyclopedic collections which he found useful in trying to educate his hitherto illiterate nation. He ordered the building of schools, monasteries, and churches, which cooperated to turn out an ever-increasing number of literary works written in the Bulgarian-Slavonic language. The monastery of Patleina was transformed by Simeon into a national academy to train translators and calligraphers, artists, teachers, and writers. Very few of these writings were original works, and the majority of manuscripts forming the literary foundation of Bulgaria's national culture contained lives of the Saints, homilies, theological and philosophical *"catenae"* and popular histories along with the legends found in every national literature. The amount of written works produced during the reign of Boris and Simeon can be deduced only by the great impact they had in forming the basic literature, especially theological and liturgical, of Serbia, Rumania, and Russia.

Simeon, so eager to promote Byzantine learning, was nonetheless anti-Greek in his own desire to make Bulgaria replace the Byzantium that he saw falling to pieces in a slow but definite process even in the 9th century. He reorganized the hierarchy of the Bulgarian Church, replacing the Greek bishops with those of Slavic origin and set up the first Bulgarian Patriarchate of Preslav.[8]

Tradition has described Simeon himself as not only learned but also as an original author. In the prologue of a book that had great influence in the other Slavic countries, the *Zlatostrui,* a collection of discourses of John Chrysostom, Simeon is considered the author. The preface tells us that he selected some of his favorite sermons and assembled them together in this work.[9] Several scholars have investigated the authorship of the *Zlatostrui.* Malinin gives the predominant theory that the Slavonic translation was made from an already abbreviated Greek version. Such a *catena* or abbreviated discourse of Chrysostom on Matthew's Gospel was the source that Konstantin the Presbyter used for his *Teacher's Gospel,* mentioned above. The preface is an imitation of the poetic *"pochvali"* or praises sung to the reigning emperor, especially one who may have commissioned the work to be done, common in Byzantine dedications. Malinin insists that the preface is a panegyric to Simeon and it does not mean that he actually composed the work.[10]

Another work traditionally attributed to Simeon's authorship is *Sbor ot mnog otets,* a commentary on the Gospels and Epistles gathered from the writings of various early Greek Fathers. This work is known also as the *Collection of Sviatoslav [Izbornik Sviatoslava]* because in the extant manuscripts it is dedicated to Prince Sviatoslav (d. 1076).[11] The preface speaks of Simeon's great interest in Byzantine literature and of his compiling a selection of his favorite authors. Simeon probably had in hand a Greek collection of encyclopedic character and added some selections of his own choice.[12]

GRIGORI THE PRESBYTER

One of the scholars close to Simeon was Grigori the Presbyter who translated books from the Old Testament from Greek into Slavonic, and who assembled translations of the Pentateuch, the books of Joshua, Judges, and Ruth in a collection under the title of *Vosmiknizhie* (8 books).[13]

IOAN – EXARCH

From the writings of Ioan-Exarch one obtains a fairly good picture of the intellectual level of the Bulgarians of his day. He was probably a Bulgarian by birth, but he knew Greek and was very well educated, probably in Constantinople. He mastered the Old Slavonic language from the disciples of Cyril and Methodius, and gives some details about the two Slavic apostles in the preface that he wrote to his translation of St. John Damascene's *De Fide Orthodoxa* which he calls *Nebesa* [Heaven]. Cyril, according to Ioan's introduction, gave the Slavs their alphabet and translated selections from the Gospel and Epistles. Methodius is given credit for translating 60 books from Greek to Slavonic. His own humility shines through as he writes: "And I wanted to give in Slavonic the commentaries of the masters, but I feared to continue the work of Methodius, recognizing my own dullness and lack of culture...After some years, the monk Doks (brother of Boris) insisted that I should translate the works of the masters since this was a most priestly work. For this reason I do this work of Damascene."[14]

The Slavonic translation done by Ioan consists of only 48 chapters of the original 100. Ioan writes that he omitted the chapters that Damascene wrote against the Nestorians and the Eutychians.

Another of his Damascene translations is Ioan's *Liubo-mudrie* [Love of Wisdom], an exact Slavonic translation of Damascene's *Philosophia*. This is a philosophical commentary on Christian truths to prepare the reader for a more intelligent, conscious understanding of the Christian faith. A compilation of a philosophical-theological character Ioan named *Shestodnevom,* a translation of St. Basil's commentary on the six days of creation [*Hexaemeron*]. In his prologue Ioan explains that he took part from Basil and Damascene and the rest from other commentaries that he had read. He criticizes the theory of creation as presented by the pagan philosophers—Plato, Parmenides, Democritos and above all Aristotle—and seeks to show the personal creation by a spiritual deity as opposed to a purely materialistic explanation. His admiration for Tsar Simeon is shown in his dedicatory preface and also in the sixth discourse, in which he describes the luxury and riches of the Preslav castle, the personal bearing of Simeon, his wisdom and authority over his loving subjects.

One can see the great difficulties that the Bulgarian translators must have had on reading Ioan's caution in which he begs pardon of the reader if his translation is not faithful to the original, since the Greek language is not always capable of being translated exactly.[15] The written Slavonic language had not a large vocabulary, at least compared to the rich and highly nuanced language of Homer and John Chrysostom. But it appears that Ioan himself evidently made mistakes in his translations by not understanding very simple Greek words or their context.[16]

The fact that Bulgarian scholars were exerting so much influence upon the other Slavic countries with their liturgical and theological books written in Old Slavonic caused a great deal of tension between the Greek hierarchy in Bulgaria and the native Bulgarian clergy. The Greeks, supported by the patriarch of Constantinople, opposed the Bulgarian-Slavonic rite by maintaining the theory that only three languages were acceptable in Christian worship, Latin, Greek, and Hebrew. The Bulgarian monk Khrabar, in his strongly worded *O pismenekh,* writes a defense of Slavonic directed against the chauvinistic Greeks and claimed equal dignity for the Slavonic alphabet as for the Greek.

TSAR PETER

Tsar Peter (927-969), despite the growing anti-Byzantine sentiments of the Bulgarians, in his pious but impractical reign sought better relations with both Rome and Constantinople. Monasticism had its greatest flowering in this period, but Peter was responsible for opening the door to greater influences from Constantinople. The country became split into two opposing camps, those for and those against Constantinople. It was not long before the Byzantine armies invaded Bulgaria, occupying the eastern part in 972 and the western part in 1018. The patriarchal see, which had earlier been transferred to Dorostol, was replaced by the so-called "patriarchate" of Ochrid ruled by Greek prelates appointed by Constantinople. Ochrid then became a center for carrying out the Hellenization of the Bulgarian Church.

THE BOGOMILS[17]

In addition to combating Greek efforts to Hellenize Bulgaria, the Bulgarian Church was disturbed by heresies and sects. A Judaizing tendency, a forerunner of that which would occur in 15th century Russia, was a constant reality in Bulgaria. It is believed that the Bogomil movement, named after the priest, Bogomil (a Slavonic translation of the Greek name Theophilos), had received some Judaizing influence. At any rate, this heretical movement made itself strongly felt during Peter's reign and thereafter until the 17th century.

A contemporary document written by the Bulgarian priest, Cosmas, the *Sermon against the Heretics* [*Slovo sviatago Kozmi prezvitera na heretiki preprenie i pouchenie ot bozhestvennikh knig*],[18] casts light on the theology and beliefs of this group. "They hold that all things belong to the Devil: the heavens, sun, stars, air, man, churches, crosses; all things that have been created by God they ascribe to the Devil; in general they hold that everything on earth, animate and inanimate, belongs to the Devil."[19] Cosmas was concerned with exposing the aspects of the heresy which were more immediate and accessible to the ordinary people. Since the fundamental ethical teaching which flowed from cosmological dualism held all matter, even the body of Christ and all human flesh, in disdain, marriage, eating meat and drinking wine were to be avoided. This view of marriage as an obstacle to holiness presented a serious threat to the Bulgarian Church by the middle of the 10th century. Liturgically other consequences followed: the validity of Baptism and the Eucharist, as well as the Divine Liturgy and the Real Presence were denied. The ecclesiastical hierarchy was looked upon as an instrument of the Devil; icons and other material aids to religious devotion were ruled out by the heretics. In the political arena they preached civil disobedience and hatred for the tsar. Against such aberrations Cosmas strenuously defended orthodoxy, especially the sanctity of matter and the legitimacy of temporal power enjoyed by the ecclesiastical and civil authorities.

THEOPHYLAKT, METROPOLITAN OF OCHRID

Leo, primate of the "patriarchal" see of Ochrid and a Greek, was one of the tenacious supporters of Michael Cerularios in maintaining the condemnation of Roman abuses that grew out of the excommunications of 1054. But Theophylakt was the most famous of the Greek hierarchs to rule the Bulgarian Church. As his letters to his friends in Constantinople indicate, he considered his appointment to the Bulgarian Church as an exile.[20] But the distance from the distracting Byzantine capital allowed him time to study and write. A talented scriptural and patristic scholar, he must be ranked among the foremost Byzantine theologians and, even though he wrote in Greek, he certainly had some influence upon Bulgarian writers; his published works occupy four volumes in Migne's patrology (*PG* 123-126).[21]

Theophylakt wrote commentaries[22] on the five minor

prophets: Hosea, Habakhuk, Jonah, Nahum, and Micah, on the four Gospel narratives, the Acts, Paul's epistles, and the Catholic epistles. In Old Testament exegesis he depends chiefly upon Theodoret of Cyrus and for the New Testament he follows John Chrysostom, the three Cappadocians, Clement and Cyril of Alexandria and Pseudo-Dionysios, using their three traditional senses of the literal, moral and analogical meaning. His other writings include homilies on the Cross, the presentation of the Virgin Mary, a panegyric on the fifteen martyrs who were put to death at Tiberiopolis [Gumuldjina] by Julian the Apostate, and another one on Alexis Comnenos. Over 130 of his letters are extant, written mostly to high dignitaries in Constantinople or fellow bishops.

In his more polemical works, especially his famous treatise against the Latins,[23] Theophylakt is rather moderate in exposing the differences that exist between the Latins and the Greeks. He does believe in a primacy given by Christ to St. Peter, but he does not believe that Peter's successor in the person of the pope of Rome has also received such a primacy. On the problem of the *Filioque* he allows the Latins, due to their inadequacy in theological language, to use their formulation, provided that it is done privately and not in official theological language nor in the Liturgy. In discussing the azymes controversy, Theophylakt concedes that Our Lord used unleavened bread at the Last Supper, but he strongly insists that bread made without leaven is a symbol of the Old Testament era which has passed away with Christ's institution of the New Covenant.

Byzantine influence over Bulgarian political and religious life began to decline towards the end of the 11th century as contact with Western Europeans, Normans and Crusaders brought new ideas and new desires for freedom. From the newly established Norman principalities in Apulia and Calabria, Roman and Norman influences were extended into the Balkans. A general revolt against the Byzantines in 1186 freed eastern Bulgaria and not long thereafter Ioan Asen II (1219-1241) brought into being the Second Bulgarian Empire. The new capital was established at Trnovo, which also became the residence of the archbishop. An agreement in 1204 effected ecclesiastical union with the Church of Rome and, in return, Pope Innocent III granted Kaloian the title of king, and the archbishop Basil was honored with that of primate; as a matter of fact, both soon entitled themselves emperor (tsar) and patriarch respectively. Whatever good relations had been established with Rome soon deteriorated, largely because of the problems caused by the Latin occupation of Constantinople. Ecclesiastical relations were re-established again with the Greek patriarchate of Constantinople, which had moved to Nicaea, and Bulgaria again came under Byzantine influence.

THEODOSIOS OF TRNOVO

The short-lived literary and spiritual renaissance of the Second Bulgarian Empire also saw the introduction of hesychast spirituality into the Balkans, the result of the efforts of Theodosios of Trnovo. He had learned the secrets of contemplation from the initiator of the Athonite hesychast renaissance of the 14th century, St. Gregory of Sinai, whom he had met in Paraoria, north of Adrianople on the Byzantine border. At the death of his teacher, Theodosios succeeded him as spiritual director. After visiting the main centers of Byzantine spirituality, Mount Athos, Thessalonika, and Mesembria, he finally settled in Bulgaria. Tsar Ioan Alexander gave him and his 50 disciples land on the hill of Kiliphar near Trnovo to build a monastery.

From this monastery, which became the leading intellectual center of Bulgaria, Theodosios led the reform of monasticism which had lasting effects in planting Hesychasm strongly in the other Slavic countries. In a period when the

level of education of the Bulgarian clergy was extremely
low, he also became the leading defender of the Orthodox
faith against heresies. Bogomilism had reached a peak of
strength as a result of the constant wars at the close of the
14th century and the general ignorance of the Bulgarian
clergy and monks. People had little moral guidance and
tended easily to a scepticism that led to extreme asceticism
mingled at the same time with extreme immorality. It was
largely through the teaching and labors of Theodosios that
Bogomilism was defeated as a religious and cultural threat
to Bulgaria.

Our knowledge of the 14th century Bogomils comes from
the *Life of Theodosios,* the authorship of which has been
traditionally attributed to Patriarch Kallistos.[24] This *Life* is
the first source to associate sexual immorality with the
Bogomils. Lazaros and Cyril Bosota, two monks expelled
from Mount Athos for adhering to the Messalian heresy,
began to preach in Trnovo. Lazaros walked about naked,
insisting upon the necessity of castration as a necessary
condition for entering into the Kingdom of God, while
Cyril preached the dissolution of marriage. Theodosios, as
the most learned man of his time, was asked by the Bulgarian
patriarch to take action against their teaching. A council
was convened in 1350, during which Lazaros repented of his
errors, while Cyril and a disciple, Stephen, remained obdurate
and were branded on the face and sent into exile. In another
council held ten years later Theodosios dealt severely with
the growing Judaizing tendencies that were making themselves felt in Christian circles and also obtained a severe
condemnation of Bogomil doctrine. As a sect, Bogomilism
disintegrated rapidly after the Turkish conquest, although
some continued to exist isolated from the rest of society.
Many of these were converted to Roman Catholicism in the
17th century, but some trace of them can be found today
around Philippopolis.[25]

PATRIARCH EVFIMI

Among the many disciples of Theodosios were Dionysios, best known for his translation into Bulgarian of the *Margarit* of John Chrysostom, Kiprian Tsamvlak, Metropolitan of Kiev and Lithuania, and then of all Russia (1373-1406), who together with Grigori Tsamvlak, Metropolitan of Kiev, spread Bulgarian culture and letters throughout Russia.[26] But the most outstanding disciple of Theodosios and the leading intellectual of the 14th century was Evfimi.[27]

Evfimi, born about 1320 of a noble family, was initiated by Theodosios in the Hesychast writings of Gregory of Sinai and Gregory Palamas. He assisted Theodosios in the direction of the monastery of Kiliphar and in the preparation of synods against heretics. After the death of Theodosios he went to the Studite monastery in Constantinople and there engaged in writing, translating and copying. In 1365 he moved to Mount Athos, first in the Great Lavra of St. Athanasios and then in the Bulgarian monastery of Zographou. He returned to Bulgaria about 1370 and lived in the Holy Trinity Monastery, devoting himself to translating liturgical and theological books from Greek into Slavonic and correcting those already translated. He was elected patriarch of Trnovo shortly after his return to Bulgaria.

Evfimi is most important for his original works, especially those of a liturgical character, for his lives of the Saints, such as St. Ioan of Rila, St. Hilarion, St. Petka and Mother Philophea, and for his many letters concerned with solving liturgical and canonical problems of his day. Of lasting service to all who celebrate the Byzantine Liturgy in Slavonic was his *Ustav* of the Liturgy of John Chrysostom and his *Sluzhebnik,* which corrected and brought some uniformity to the texts and rituals then in use. Of his many letters those to Kiprian, monk of Mount Athos, to Metropolitan Anfimus of Valachia and to the priest-monk Nikodim of Valachia are typical of the liturgical, theological and canonical problems he was asked to solve. In all his writings, Evfimi shows a keen, critical sense, admitting only genuine facts backed up by concrete evidence. The ideal of sanctity which he held out to his readers was that of the best in the Byzantine Hesychast tradition.[28]

When the Turkish army marched on Trnovo to deal Bulgaria its *coup de grace* in 1393, Tsar Ioan Shishman had already fled to Nikopol, but Trnovo held out for three months under Evfimi's courageous leadership. The Second Empire of Bulgaria ended, and five centuries of Turkish oppression began, yet it had not been without its cultural brilliance. The Gospel of Tsar Ioan Alexander (1331-1371) with its 369 hand-painted miniatures of exquisite beauty is one indication of this. In his library were also to be found such books as the Psalter of 1337 with precious historical data concerning his reign, the *Sbornik* of 1345, an encyclopedic collection of fifteen works and the *Chronicle of Manasses,* a history of salvation beginning with Troy and continuing through Roman and Byzantine times.

The *Sbornik* of Vidin belonged to Ioan Alexander's son, Ioan Stratsimir, to whom Vidin was given by his father and which soon rivaled Trnovo as a leading cultural center of Bulgaria. Sirku claims that this *Sbornik* is one of the most important documents of the 14th century. Written for Stratsimir's wife, Anna, it contains various literary works, lives and praises of women. It also reflects the influence of Western Europe upon Bulgarian culture, which came by way of Hungary, Dubrovnik, and Venice.[29] The number of books written in Bulgaria during the reign of Ioan Alexander attests to a great theological productivity. These, however, were rarely original creations, at least as far as can be judged from the works which have been preserved. They consist mostly of translations from the Greek of such noted Fathers as John Chrysostom, Pseudo-Dionysios, Gregory of Sinai, Ephrem the Syrian, Gregory of Nazianzos, Basil the Great, Gregory of Rome, John Klimacos and John Damascene, which found their way to Russia and the other Slavic countries and thus escaped the looting and burning of the Turks and the Hellenizing Phanariots of later centuries. Sirku lists 30 names of Eastern and Western Fathers whose works came to form part of the theological patrimony of the Slavic countries through Bulgarian *sborniki* and *pateriki*. He also gives the names of 13 Bulgarian writers and translators.[30]

ROMAN CATHOLIC ACTIVITIES IN BULGARIA

As the darkness spread over Bulgaria and extinguished the light of learning which had burned so brilliantly during the Second Empire, a ray of light shone momentarily around the Roman Catholic center which had developed at Chiprovets near the Serbian border. Even under the Turks Roman Catholic merchants from Dubrovnik, Venice and Saxony had kept the Bulgarians in some contact with the West, but in 1595 the Franciscan friars from Bosnia and Croatia opened a mission headed by Peter Solinat. The predominantly Orthodox Bulgarians resisted conversion to Rome, and the Franciscans concentrated their efforts on the Bogomils and Paulicians. Bishop Solinat was concerned with raising the educational level of his clergy and people. His successor, who had the title of bishop of Sofia, Iliia Marinov, opened the first Roman Catholic school in Chiprovets in 1624 in which Latin was taught along with Slavonic. Filip Stanislavov, Roman Catholic bishop of Nikopol, strove also to elevate the level of education in Bulgaria and published the first modern Bulgarian book, the *Abagar* (1651), which was printed in Rome.

An outstanding and well-educated Roman Catholic and Bulgarian patriot was Peter Parchevich (1617-1674), a native of Chiprovets. He obtained a doctorate in theology and canon law in Rome and returned to Bulgaria to become the archbishop of Martsianopol. He spent most of his days seeking to influence the Roman Catholic rulers of Europe to liberate Bulgaria from the yoke of Islam.

The Roman Catholic mission, however, was not to last long. After the Turks razed Chiprovets in 1668 in retaliation for its revolt against them, the Franciscans were expelled and a mission that had sought to raise the level of Bulgarian cultural and theological life through sound schooling and greater contact with western Europe came to an end.

In 1767 the Greek patriarch of Constantinople obtained a *firman* from the Sublime Porte which brought the Bulgarian Church directly under his control. Added to the *Cheno Teglo,* the black weight, of almost unbearable Turkish oppression, of the denial of basic human rights and exhaustive taxes, was the new yoke of Greek oppression with its aim of suppressing anything reminiscent of the Bulgarian Church or even of Bulgarian culture. The Greek patriarch not only represented the Bulgarian Orthodox Church before the Turks, but he also became their civil representative. Not only could he sell bishoprics to the highest bidder, especially those of Greek descent, but at the same time Phanariot princes and wealthy merchants, doctors, and lawyers came into Bulgaria and monopolized the better part of the economy. The Bulgarian language, literature, books, schools, liturgy, songs, customs, all were stamped out and replaced by Greek equivalents. Any Bulgarian wishing to obtain an education had to do so in a Greek school. The Cyrillic alphabet was officially outlawed and those who still wrote Bulgarian were supposed to do so in Greek characters. The manuscripts and books written in Slavonic or Bulgarian were burned.

It was only in remote mountain regions and in monasteries that the Bulgarian language and culture were somehow perpetuated. The monasteries of Rila and Bachkovo and the two Athonite monasteries of Zographou and Hilander became the strongholds of this preservation. There monks copied the theological anthologies, lives of the saints and even non-religious, often patriotic literary classics, to feed a starving nation that had almost forgotten how to read its own language. Many of Bulgaria's most learned literary personalities left Bulgaria and went to Serbia, Russia, Rumania, and Mount Athos and there worked to transcribe manuscripts and to translate theological works into Bulgarian. Grigori Tsamvlak of Trnovo is an example, already mentioned, of one such scholar who went to Moldavia, Serbia and eventually to Kiev to become its metropolitan. He produced 25 literary works, often permeated with his great dislike for the Turks and his nostalgia for his native land, when it was a true intellectual force among the other Slavic nations.

PAISI OF HILANDAR[31]

Economic changes took place in the 18th century that allowed for the formation of a Bulgarian bourgeoisie. The *Chorbadzhii* or landed peasants who gradually assumed a certain degree of local political power due to their accumulated wealth began to make their voices heard with greater insistence, not only in cornering more of the markets for themselves but also in attempting to obtain more political freedom. The Bulgarian struggle for political and religious freedom which would climax in their liberation in 1878 began with the writing by Paisi of Hilandar of what can be considered the first classic in Bulgarian literature. His efforts to stir up a spirit of patriotism among the Bulgarian people had been prepared by other personages of lesser note. Iosif Bradati, a monk of the Rila Monastery, had traveled much about the country stirring up the people with his fiery sermons, which were aimed at raising the moral tone of the people and at creating a sense of national consciousness. Parteni Pavlovich of Silistra, also a great popular preacher and writer, wandered from monastery to monastery recalling to the mind of his listeners the glorious days of

Bulgarian intellectual prowess. Christofor Zhefarovich of Doiran (claimed also as a Serb) wrote the *Stematografia,* vignettes of Serbian and Bulgarian kings and saints, along with the 56 coats of arms of the various Slavic and non-Slavic countries.

Little is actually known of the personal life of Paisi. He was born about 1722 in Bansko in the eparchy of Samokov, in eastern Bulgaria. When he was 23 years old, he went to Mount Athos and joined the Hilandar Monastery of which his brother was the *hegumen* or abbot. Hilandar and Zographou, along with the Russian and Rumanian monasteries of Mount Athos, became the citadels of southern Slavic culture and learning. Precious manuscripts from the First and Second Bulgarian Empires were preserved. Although Paisi did not have much formal education, he did have an unquenchable thirst to learn. Hilandar at that time included among its monks Serbs, Greeks, Russians and Bulgarians. Taunted by the Greeks and Serbs that Bulgaria had neither its own language nor its own culture, Paisi determined to investigate the manuscripts which contained the story of his nation's past. In Hilandar and in Zographou, the Bulgarian monastery to which Paisi later transferred, he found the sources that gave him the background for his famous work, *Istoriia slavianobolgarskaia* (1762), the Bulgaro-Slavic History. The previous year Paisi had been sent on a mission to Karlovtsy for the monastery of Hilandar and there found the work of Mauro Orbini, *Il regno degli Slavi.* Paisi probably read it in the Russian translation that Peter the Great had ordered.[32] This was his main source for his own history.

Paisi began his history by stating his purpose:

> I have an ardent zeal for my race and my Bulgarian homeland, and I have taken great pains to study many books and histories in order to write the chronicles of the Bulgarian nation. It is for your good and your glory that I have written, you who

love your race and your Bulgarian homeland and
who long to know about your race and your language.

Defending his race against the chauvinism of the Greeks
and other Slavic races as the Russians and Serbs, he insists
that his nation had been responsible for the written language
of the other Slavic peoples:

> The Russians and Serbs pride themselves on having
> received before us the Slavonic alphabet and also
> Baptism, but it is not true. They cannot produce
> any proof of this. I have seen many Bulgarians
> adopt the language and customs of strangers and
> even hate their own language. It is for this reason
> that I have written against those who insult our
> ancestors and those who do not love their own
> language and their country as well as on your
> behalf, you who long to know your language and
> your race, so that you may know that our tsars, our
> patriarchs and our Bulgarian prelates have not been
> deprived of chronicles, books, tropars and to tell
> you their long history of glorious reign.

This work cannot be recommended as a flawless history,
since his two main sources, the histories written by Orbini
and Cardinal Cesare Baronius (1538-1607),[33] contained many
historical errors. Its chief value is the spirit of patriotism
and healthy national pride that it engendered in the readers.
Paisi was not a historian; he was more concerned with
stirring up a love for the Bulgarian language and nation.
The impact of this work upon Bulgaria and the history of
a national language, literature and a national Church must be
judged by the results it accomplished in the following
century.

SOFRONI VRACHANSKII (1739-1814)[34]

Numerous copies of Paisi's manuscript of his history of
the Slavic-Bulgarian people circulated throughout the Balkan
Peninsula. In 1764-1765 Paisi visited Kotel where he met
the young priest, Stoiko Vladislavov, later called Sofroni,
bishop of Vratsa. The reading of Paisi's work had a lasting
effect upon Sofroni, who in the early part of the 19th century
not only laid the foundations of modern Bulgarian literature,
but also launched an intellectual renaissance that produced a
network of native schools, teachers, the beginnings of a
national literature and culture that climaxed in the liberation
of the Bulgarian nation.

Sofroni was born in 1739 in Kotel, in southern Bulgaria.
This was a commercial city which had given outstanding
men to Bulgaria, to mention only Georgi Rakovskii (d. 1868),
famous politican and publicist, and the monk, Neofit
Bozvelli, who was the first to organize a national Bulgarian
Church (d. 1849). Sofroni's father sent him to a Greek
school, but after two years his father died and Sofroni had
to earn his living. Ordained a priest in 1762, he suffered
greatly from jealous fellow-priests, the Greeks and Moslems.
Made bishop of the frontier town of Vratsa, chiefly because
no Greek would have wanted the see, he again encountered
great difficulties in evangelizing his people, largely because
of the *Kirdjalis* (Turkish for the brigands of the desert).
He fled to Bucharest where he wrote his memoirs in which
he confesses:

> I have only one worry. I fear lest God judge me for
> having taken charge of this flock and then having
> abandoned it. But I hope in His grace, for I did
> not abandon it to give me repose but to give me
> distress. Now I work day and night writing some
> books in our Bulgarian language so that if I, a
> sinful man, can no longer speak to them so they

can learn from me, then they can read my writings and gain some use from them and pray to God for me, even though unworthy that I am, that He should overcome my ignorance.

With the help of fellow exiles in Bucharest and Vidin, he was able to engage in a most fertile literary apostolate. He produced a great number of works in a vivid, modern Bulgarian, a new creation from the older Bulgarian written language, a mélange of Russicisms, Serbianisms and Church Slavonic. He translated two anthologies from Greek and also re-translated into modern Bulgarian mediaeval Bulgarian literature of moral and theological value. His most famous work, printed in Rimnik (1806) was called *Kyriakodromon* or *Nedelnik,* a book of instructions on the Sunday Gospels together with sermons for the great feasts of the liturgical year. It was not an original work but a translation and resumé from various Slavonic and Greek texts. The importance of this work consisted in its simple style, which produced a modern language approximating the spoken language. So popular has been this work that it is still referred to by the ordinary people of Bulgaria as their *Sofronie.*

Another work that he compiled in 1805 was an anthology entitled: *A Confession of the Orthodox Faith,* which also includes his autobiography, written in realistic, popular language.[35] Highly influenced by the Renaissance and by the Age of Reason which launched the French Revolution, Sofroni translated the work of the Protestant, Wilhelm Stratemann, *Theatrum Historicum,* which he knew in Greek translation. Here again ideas that had been only embryonically present in Paisi's history were developed to increase the Bulgarian people's thirst for autonomy.

Sofroni had great influence in the field of education, at least as a pioneer of Bulgarian schools. He taught in the Bulgarian language and insisted on the necessity of opening national schools in which Bulgarian language and culture could be taught.

GROWTH IN EDUCATION

The only non-Greek schools that existed in the 18th and 19th centuries in Bulgaria were the so-called "cell" schools which taught Old Slavonic by reading from the Psalter, Holy Scripture and the liturgical services. The primary purpose was to train candidates for the priesthood. Gerlach, the German consul in Constantinople in the second half of the 16th century, claimed that in Sofia there were only two schools preparing seminarians for the whole of Bulgaria. In 1750 there were 21 of these "cell" schools; in 1843 they numbered 189.[36]

If during the five centuries that Bulgaria was maintained in ignorance by the Turks and the Phanariots no theology was produced, the reasons are understandable. Real theology could only be written in the framework of a living national language and a strong educational system. Sofroni first organized the Bulgarian popular schools and employed the Eastern Bulgarian dialect so that his people might advance in politics as well as in theology. Neofit Bozvelii (1784-1848), the last of the "warring" Bulgarian monks, did much to give the growing educational system textbooks that were freed of Greek influence.

But the person most responsible for developing the schools in Bulgaria in the 19th century was Vasil Evstatiev Aprilov. Well-educated in Vienna, Moscow, and Odessa, Aprilov was a Graecophile until he read the book of Iuri Ivanovich Venelin (d. 1839), a Carpatho-Russian, who in 1829 wrote his *History of the Ancient and Present-Day Bulgars*. As a result, Aprilov became anti-Greek and pro-Russian. He saw the future of Bulgarian education as tied to Russia, since it could aid in supplying teachers, textbooks, and even financial aid to effect a literary renaissance. In Gabrovo he set up the first modern Bulgarian school and placed it under the direction of the monk, Neofit Rilskii, in 1835. Neofit, besides being an outstanding pioneer in developing the free Bulgarian schools, also translated the New Testament from Slavonic into modern Bulgarian, published in Smyrna in 1840. Aprilov was instrumental in arranging with Russian institutes of higher learning for the education of future Bulgarian teachers who began to return home in the 1850's to launch secondary education in Bulgaria.[37]

One of the classics in Bulgarian literature produced in this time was the *Riben Bukver* (*The Fish ABC's,* so called because of a picture of a dolphin on the book cover). Its author, Beron, a layman, emigrated to Rumania, but completed his medical studies in Germany. He lived mostly in Europe constantly studying and exploring all fields of learning. He produced this work, a general encyclopedia printed in the Old Slavonic alphabet, but in the popular Eastern Bulgarian dialect. This is considered as the first book written in the spoken language and it became a literary milestone in the history of Bulgarian letters.

A Bulgarian printing press was set up in Thessalonika in 1838 by Haji Teodosy that allowed for publication of textbooks in the Bulgarian language. Periodicals such as the *Filologiia* of K. Fotoniv and Bogorov's Bulgarian newspaper, *Bulgarski Orel,* began to bring Bulgarian culture and religious thought into the homes of a reading public that was rapidly growing. A national language was being created. Theological thought would soon develop once schools of higher learning were established.

THE AUTOCEPHALOUS BULGARIAN CHURCH

From 1393, when the national Bulgarian Church lost its independence and became subject to the Greek Patriarch of Constantinople, until the 19th century the Bulgarian Church knew no freedom in government. Greater demands for ecclesiastical and political autonomy were heard until in 1860 the First Bulgarian Church in Constantinople was inaugurated among the Bulgarian émigrés living there under the leadership of Bishop Ilarion Makariopolsky. On Easter Day, 1860, he refused to commemorate the patriarch of Constantinople in the liturgy. Other pressures mounted, forcing the issue of an autocephalous church in Bulgaria. After the defeat of Russia in the Crimean War, union was proposed with Rome through French aid. Dragan Tsankov actually signed a bill of union with Rome setting up a uniate church in Bulgaria. Russia, eager to exert a leading influence in Bulgaria, felt that it should encourage a national church rather than one connected with Rome. The uniate movement made rapid progress after 1860 when Iosif Sokolsky, abbot of the monastery at Gabrovo, was appointed to head the re-union movement. Sokolsky, however, was kidnapped to Russia, where he renounced the union and it came to an end.

In 1870 the Turks wished to divorce Bulgaria from Russian influence and complied with the Bulgarian wishes for an independent church. The Bulgarian Exarchate was set up by a *firman* issued from the Porte, and Ilarion was chosen exarch. He declined, and Antim of Vidin became the first exarch of the newly established national Bulgarian Church. The Greek Church refused to recognize the autocephaly of the Bulgarian Church and considered it as schismatic until 1945, when the Patriarch of Constantinople, Benjamin I, waived the so-called Bulgarian heresy of *"phyletism"* and restored communion. The final stage in complete ecclesiastical autocephaly came in 1953 when the Synod of Bishops in Sofia proclaimed the "third" Bulgarian patriarchate. The

Ecumenical Patriarchate of Constantinople, however, refused to recognize the Bulgarian Patriarchal Church until 1961.

DEVELOPMENT OF SEMINARIES

One should not be surprised to find that there was practically no theological development in Bulgaria during the five centuries under the Turks, when that nation was not allowed to have its own schools and even its own Church. With both political and ecclesiastical independence recovered in the second half of the 19th century, there followed the beginning of seminaries as well as of scholarly theology in Bulgaria. The leaders of the national movement had hoped to establish seminaries in each diocese in addition to one superior theological academy. The Ecumenical Patriarch, Gregory VI, presented such a request to the sultan, Abdul Aziz, but without success. When the Turks recognized the Bulgarian exarchate in 1870, along with its ecclesiastical constitution, a plan for a higher school of theology was approved. This first major seminary was inaugurated in 1874 near Trnovo under the patronage of Sts. Peter and Paul and existed until 1886.[38] It was suppressed by the Bulgarian government for financial reasons, and a more modest theological school was established in the monastery of St. Ioan of Rila, which also had a very brief existence. Another seminary was opened at Samokov, closed during the Russo-Turkish War, and was reopened in 1878. From 1894 Samokov was the only seminary in all Bulgaria. In 1901 it had 188 seminarians, an indication both of the dearth of candidates for the priesthood as well as the poverty of theological development.

In 1902 Prince Ferdinand I and the dignitaries of the Bulgarian Church laid the cornerstone for the theological school of St. Clement of Ochrid at Sofia. Another seminary had been erected in 1884 for the Bulgarians living in European Turkey; at first located in Constantinople, it was transferred to Prilep in Macedonia, then to Adrianople, again to Constantinople, and finally in 1894 to the hills of Chichli above the capital. These two seminaries of Sofia and Chichli trained no more than 280 students in theology over a four year course. Since only half of these actually embraced the clerical state to serve a Church of four million faithful, one can imagine the inadequacies of the lower clergy.

Largely because of their lack of theological training and piety, the clergy did not present an attractive picture of a vibrant Bulgarian Orthodox Church. State officials were at least indifferent and often openly hostile towards the Church. State schools in which teachers openly sought to destroy religion[39] proliferated at a rapid pace. What theological works were printed were usually translations into Bulgarian of Russian compendia of the 19th century. Some of the more popular Russian works used as basic theological texts in Bulgaria at this time were those of Filaret Drozdov,[40] Antonii Amfiteatrov,[41] Makarii Bulgakov,[42] Metropolitan Platon of Moscow,[43] Silvestr Malevanskii,[44] Bishop Augustin,[45] Dimitrii Sokolov,[46] and A. N. Muraviev. The treatises on moral or pastoral theology written by M. Olenitskii, A. Pokrovskii, P. Soliarskii were also translated into Bulgarian. Nikodim Milash, the Serbian bishop of Zara, an outstanding Church canonist, had his famous two volume work on Orthodox Canon law [*Pravoslavno tsrkveno pravo*] translated into Bulgarian in 1903.

The few original Bulgarian works were evidently greatly dependent upon the classics of Russian theology. Such Bulgarian authors as Stephan Buntovnikov, Anfim Chivachev, Christo Pavlov, R. Popovich, and P. Cherniaev produced short theological tracts used as teaching aids, but which were mainly syntheses of Russian compendia.

THEOLOGICAL JOURNALS

Vesti became in 1890 the first official organ of the re-established exarchy, but was superceded in 1900 by *Tserkoven Vestnik,* which still functions as the official voice of the Holy Synod. Other journals appeared: *Svetnik* in 1888; *Pravoslaven Propovednik* (1893); *Zadrujen Trud* (1902). In 1901 the Holy Synod had translated and printed the whole Bible based on the Russian text of 1876 to replace the Bulgarian version made by the Protestant Bible Society.[47] The Holy Synod also publishes *Dukhovna Kultura,* which presents theological articles of a more general appeal.

The most scholarly theological journal is *Godishnik* [Yearbook], published by the professors of theology of the Academy of St. Clement of Ochrid in Sofia. This faculty had formed part of the University of Sofia until 1950, when the Communist government separated it from the University and made it an autonomous theological academy. The first volume of *Godishnik* was published in 1951, and each number since then contains scholarly articles on scripture, patrology, church history, dogmatics, symbolics, ethics, apologetics, canon law, liturgy, and ecumenism.

STEPHAN TSANKOV [Zankov]

One of the outstanding theologians of 20th century Bulgaria was Professor Stephan Tsankov (d. 1959). At any rate, he has been the best known Bulgarian theologian abroad, chiefly because of his active participation in ecumenical circles during the formative period of the World Council of Churches. A number of his articles, which appear in *Godishnik,* touch upon the unity and catholicity of the Church,[48] Christian unity as a problem to be faced in Orthodox theology,[49] the essence and function of the Church,[50] the unity of the Orthodox Church of the East,[51] and the aspirations towards unity within the Orthodox Churches.[52] Possessed of a broad theological and historical knowledge, he added to this a deeply irenic presentation. He lamented the lack of unity in ecclesiastical administration that came from the absence of any general jurisdictional authority in legislative and administrative matters within the Orthodox Churches. This he conceived as the primary problem in the Orthodox Churches to be faced and hopefully solved in a forthcoming ecumenical council.

THEOLOGICAL TEXTBOOKS

The Communist Revolution in Bulgaria took place in the autumn of 1947, and from this time to the present theological development has consisted almost exclusively of the textbooks produced for the Theological Academy of St. Clement of Ochrid in Sofia. A. Johansen, a Danish Lutheran professor of theology, visited Bulgaria three times between 1956 and 1960 with the expressed intention of investigating the theological textbooks printed since 1948. The following data have been taken mainly from his report.[53] All the textbooks published in this time, during which theologians have not been allowed to travel and study freely in the West, are characterized by a fairly conservative, mediocre type of theology, still highly dependent upon Russian sources. In 1948 Djulgerov and Zonevski published a text on Orthodox dogmatic theology for use in the fourth and fifth classes of the theological seminaries. Dogmatics is presented as a science based upon divine revelation. "We can only attain knowledge of God insofar as Revelation reveals Him... We cannot receive new dogmatic truths outside of divine Revelation."[54] The central doctrine of the relationship between justification and sanctification is dealt with in great detail but with little originality. The Protestant view of the invisible Church is condemned while the Roman Catholic view as formulated by Anselm of Canterbury is dismissed as one-sided and legalistic. "Faith and good works are not only in the same degree necessary for salvation, but unimaginable without their mutual connection."[55]

The textbooks on biblical studies show very little acquaintance with modern research done abroad by leading Protestant and Roman Catholic scholars. The two main works dealing with the Old Testament are an introduction to the Holy Writings of the Old Testament by Professor Ivan Markovsky, published in 1957, and a similar study done by Konstantin Sakhariev in 1955. New Testament studies seem weakest, with only two commentaries appearing during this period, one on the Epistle to the Galatians done by the priest-monk Sergius in 1961 and one on the Epistle to the Ephesians by Christo Giaurov in 1962.

The most prolific theologian has been Professor Ivan Panchovsky, whose main field is ethics. In 1955 he collaborated with Metropolitan Nikodim Christov to produce a textbook on Orthodox Christian Ethics. Panchovsky also wrote in 1958 an introduction to moral theology, which stands out among most of the Bulgarian theological textbooks because of the author's acquaintance with Western sources, especially concerning the nature of religion and the moral obligations flowing from the religious experience. His use of Western theological literature is evident also in his book on methodology used in ethics, published in 1962. Panchovsky also wrote two books dealing with apologetic matters. One on the personality of Jesus Christ (1959) seeks to refute Soviet atheistic polemicists by proving the historicity of Christ while at the same time pointing out the divine-human character of Christ as seen through His teaching, the impact He has had on the world, especially on the great, literary figures of the West, and His continuous presence in the world among the suffering. His other work on life and happiness (1957) seeks to answer the question posed by existentialists and nihilists as to whether life has any meaning especially in the light of modern evils.[56]

The area of immediate pragmatic use, that of pastoral theology, has been explored by Christo Dimitrov in a two volume work, which emphasizes the Church's role in facing problems of the contemporary world and demonstrates a broad knowledge of the approaches to pastoral problems among the European Protestants and Roman Catholics. The problems of the Bulgarian Church under the Communists are not much different from those faced by the Russian and Rumanian Orthodox, but Dimitrov seems to be quite concerned about solutions as he proposes means for remedying the modern problems facing his Church.

One final work by Todor Todorov on homiletics highlights the importance of making Orthodox theology relevant through the preached word. A two-volume work (printed in 1956 and 1959) of great comprehension, it covers the forms of sermons and content with particular emphasis on the social sermon, as well as a presentation of the history of the sermon in the Bible and throughout the history of the Church.

MONASTICISM

Monasticism in the 20th century has suffered the greatest setbacks of all areas of Orthodox religious life. This has been most regretable, especially since the Bulgarian monasteries had served so nobly throughout the long centuries under the Turks as the preserver of Bulgarian letters and of serious theological pursuit. In 1905 there were in Bulgaria 180 monks and 318 nuns living in 89 monasteries. In 1936 there were 105 monasteries, 79 of which were for only 99 monks, and 26 monasteries for 212 nuns. Many of the monasteries have since been closed because of a lack of monks and have been taken over by the government, generally for use as holiday resorts. The abbot of the famous St. Ioan of Rila Monastery died in prison in 1944, and the few remaining monks were moved to the Bashkovo Monastery. In 1961 the government gave permission for the Rila Monastery to be reopened, but it numbers only a few monks. The famous Athonite Bulgarian monastery of Zographou still functions, but it too has greatly declined in members and in intellectual activity. In 1966 the Greek government had finally allowed new monks from Bulgaria to take up residence in Zographou, but the paucity of Bulgarian monks has not allowed many to take advantage of this.

CONCLUSION

To understand Bulgarian Orthodox theology, one must, therefore, understand something of Bulgaria's long, stormy history, clouded by centuries of wars and oppression by foreign powers that sought to destroy everything uniquely Bulgarian, whether in language, culture, letters or theology. After a brilliant era under Boris and Simeon, theology fell into decadence, as popular education for over five centuries was practically reduced to a few Greek schools. In the second half of the 19th century with autonomy granted both to the Bulgarian nation and the Bulgarian Orthodox Church, the stirrings of a creative theology began to be felt. This took its first unsure steps, clinging tenaciously to the strong hand of Russia. Still trammelled by the Communist government in recent decades, the theologians in Bulgaria have been working heroically under adverse circumstances to develop a living theology that will answer the needs of the times. Perhaps their greatest contribution will be to give to the Christian world a theology, not highly speculative and scientific, but one of living the Gospel spirit of *kenosis,* the emptying of oneself, of one's Church and of one's nation of all self-complacency to rise through a theology lived in suffering to a much needed vision of optimistic transformation of all things in Christ.

PART FOUR

The Serbian Church*

PERHAPS of all the traditionally Orthodox countries, Serbia and its national Church have had the most uneven growth. Continual political upheavals caused by wars and mass migrations, coupled with four centuries under the Turkish yoke, can account in great part for the lack of a rich theological heritage. In viewing Serbian theology, therefore, it is imperative that one keep ever in mind the many non-theological factors that determined to a large extent the quality of theology produced over the centuries.

Christianity came to Serbia from two directions and from two diverse religious cultures: from the Latin West through Dalmatia and the areas of Serbia bordering on lands under the Roman Catholic patriarchate and from the East through the missionaries sent by the Byzantine emperor.

The Serbians descended from Slavs who inhabited the region between the Carpathian Mountains and the Dniester River. Encouraged by the Byzantine emperor, Heraclios, they migrated into what is today southern Dalmatia, Herzegovina, Serbia proper and neighboring areas. True evangelization was effected through the Byzantine and Bulgarian missionaries during the 9th and 10th centuries. The center of this ancient Serbia was much further south than the present

---

*The "c" used throughout is soft and is equivalent to the English "ch."

Serbia, in the central Balkan mountains in a region called
Ras or Rashka (Rascia).

Politically Byzantium and Bulgaria alternated in ruling
over this region until Stephen Nemanja (1114-1200) succeeded in establishing a strong Serbian state.

SERBIAN ARCHIEPISCOPATE[1]

After a reign of 36 years, which laid the foundation
for the Nemanja dynasty which would rule Serbia for two
centuries, Stephen left the administration to his son, Stephen
II, called *Prvovenchani,* the First Crowned, who received the
royal crown from the delegate of Pope Honorius III in a
ceremony presided over by Stephen's brother, Sava.

At an early age Sava went to Mount Athos where he
became a monk.[2] His father, upon resigning the throne,
joined him and together they founded the Athonite monastery of Hilandar, which in the following centuries would
play an important role in the history of Serbian Orthodoxy.
Stephen II arranged that Sava return to be made archbishop
of the Serbian National Church with its ten suffragan sees.
In 1219 Patriarch Manuel of Constantinople consecrated Sava
at Nicaea.

EARLY RELIGIOUS LITERATURE

Serbia received its first Christian literature in Old-
Slavonic translations, principally from Bulgaria. During the
period from the 12th to the latter part of the 18th century,
the religious literature of Serbia consisted primarily of
Slavonic translations from the Greek and Russian of liturgical, canonical, and hagiographical works.

An example of the earliest type of such literature is the
Marujunsko Jevanhele, (named for the ascetic, St. Deve

Marije) and written in Glagolithic.[3] Other Old Slavonic translations of the Gospels are those listed by Popovic[4] and Novakovic[5] with the title of *Miroslav'levo Jevanhele* (written from 1169 to 1197), *Vukanovo Jevanhele* (copied by the starets of Pec, Simeon), the *Svrlishko Jevanhele* (1279) and the *Nikolsko Jevanhele* (done in the monastery of St. Nicolai).

The first literary, original work in Serbia is the Slavonic *Letopis* of the anonymous priest of Dioclea, Pop Duklanin, a very arid chronicle interspersed with popular legends such as that of St. Jovan Vladimir.[6] But Serbian literature really begins with the writings of St. Sava.

His first two writings, the *Karejski Tipik*[7] and the *khilandarski Tipik,* written about 1199, were heavily monastic and liturgical in character as any monastic rule would be. His rule, which still governs the monastic life of Hilandar on Mount Athos, was greatly influenced by the *Tipik* or *Rule* of Evergetinos for the monastery of the Blessed Virgin of Constantinople.[8]

His major, more original work which became the model for the flood of hagiographies during the Serbian Middle Ages was his *Life of St. Simeon,* the life of his father, Stephen, who had changed his name to Simeon upon becoming a monk. This work in twelve chapters was intended to attract candidates to the monastic life that was beginning to take solid roots throughout all Serbia. Andrea Gabrilovic justly observes that for simplicity and beauty of style the *Zhivot Svetoga Simeona* deserves to be ranked among the classics of ancient Serbian literature.[9]

Sava supposedly collected together the *Kormchaia Kniga* or *Nomocanon.* The two ancient manuscripts have an introduction which, however, was not written by Sava himself.[10] It has been maintained by some scholars that Sava founded a center or school in which Bulgarian books were translated into *Srbiji* or the Serbian dialect.[11]

Stephen II also wrote a life of his father in 1216, which

testifies to his broad knowledge and relatively high degree of education.[12] But the outstanding hagiographer, next to Sava, was the priestmonk, Domentijan, who proved himself to be well versed in the Old and New Testaments, and was acquainted with Greek and Russian lives of saints. His *Life of St. Sava [Zhivot Svetoga Save]* demonstrates well his original style and his breadth of knowledge. He also wrote the *Life of St. Simeon* which, however, depends greatly upon that written by Stephen II and upon material found in his *Life of Sava.*[13]

The monk Teodocija also wrote a life of St. Sava as well as *Pochvale,* Praises of St. Simeon and St. Sava, but of him nothing else is known. He is usually identified as the pupil of Domentijan. His writings show him to be a modest writer, projecting little of his own personality or reflections; yet his style was that of the romantic bent of the 13th century that allowed the personalities of Sava and Simeon to come alive as individuals.[14]

Another writer of the early Middle Ages is Archbishop Danilo II, who is known for his lives of the Serbian kings and archbishops. These were probably written about 1375 while Ephrem directed the Serbian Church. Although very few details of his own life are known, he was probably of the noble class and wrote the lives of the rulers: Dragutin, Urosh, Radoslav, Vladislav, Helen and Milutin, along with the lives of the archbishops Arsenija, Sava II, Danilo I, and probably also of Jakov, Jevstatiji II, and Sava III. A very prolific writer, Danilo II had many and varied talents.[15] D. Pavlovic claims that he learned the art of writing from studying the translations made by Clement of Ochrid. His lives of the kings and archbishops of Serbia manifest a warmth of style and creativity that make his subjects come to life. He was an outstanding historian for his times and had great influence on succeeding ecclesiastical and theological writers.

Two remaining biographers who should be mentioned among the known medieval writers are Grigori Tsamvlak and Konstantin the Philosopher. Tsamvlak was born about 1364 in Trnovo, educated in Constantinople and Mount Athos, and then was made hegumen of the monastery of Visoki Dechani in Serbia. He is known for his biography of Prince Stephen of Dechani and a liturgical service in his honor. Konstantin was born in Trnovo and came to Serbia in 1402. In 1431 he wrote the life of the Serbian Prince, Stephen Lazarevic, an extremely useful historical source for the period.

MONASTICISM

Until the 17th century almost all Serbian writing was done by monks and centered primarily on translations of the necessary ecclesiastical books, with some original biographies of saints and rulers. Schools of any quality were nonexistent except for the private tutoring that went on in monasteries where a learned monk might be found who had been educated outside of Serbia, chiefly in Bulgaria or Mount Athos, or by some educated monk before him.

A great impetus to monasticism in Serbia was given in the two centuries between 1220 and 1420 when princes and nobles of the kingdom vied with each other to build monasteries and convents. In this period there were built the famous monasteries of Zhica, Mileshevo, Pec, Sopochani, Gradac, Banja on the Drina, Ljevishka, Grachanitsa, Dechani, St. Nikita of Banja, St. George of Nagorichino, Ravanica, Kalenic, Ljubostinja, and Manassia.

Although wars have destroyed many of these ancient monasteries, the modern state of Yugoslavia has set about to restore many of them to their pristine beauty, even though the number of monks has fallen off drastically in the 20th century.[16] Unfortunately, amidst the ruins have fallen also the libraries and the manuscripts which were so painstakingly copied out and passed on to succeeding generations by these early monks.

The Serbian monastery of Hilandar of Mount Athos continued to provide Serbia with monks trained in the best Byzantine spirituality, as well as hagiographies, liturgical books, and a few theological treatises, such as the *Expositio fidei* of St. John Damascene, which was translated in the 14th century into Serbian.[17]

SERBIAN PATRIARCHATE

Sava had set up his metropolitan residence in the monastery of Zica but his successor, Arsenije I, transferred the see to Pec (or Ipek), which remained for many centuries the ecclesiastical center of Serbia. In 1346 King Stephen III Dushan (1331-1355) had himself proclaimed as emperor. At the same time he announced that the Serbian Church was autocephalous and independent of the jurisdiction of Constantinople and was now a patriarchate. Joannikios was consecrated by the Bulgarian patriarch of Trnovo and the Greek-Bulgarian archbishop of Ochrid as patriarch of Pec with jurisdiction over Serbia, Bosnia, Herzegovina, Montenegro, the southern part of Dalmatia, and portions of Macedonia and Bulgaria.

This flash of glory soon faded with the Turkish victory at Kossovo Polje (1389). The Serbian empire was reduced to a vassal state of the Turks and in 1459 it ceased to exist. By order of Mohammed II the patriarchate was suppressed, and the Serbian episcopate was placed under the jurisdiction of the Bulgarian archbishop of Ochrid. Many of the Serbian nobility and the better educated went over to Islam. Although the Turks allowed the Serbs to continue to practice their Christian religion and to maintain their own language, the intellectual life encouraged by Sava and Stephen Dushan declined. The monasteries, which were in vital contact with those of Mount Athos and Bulgaria, were the only source of intellectual and artistic development. These monasteries, preserved to some extent today, bear witness to the high degree of perfection reached as models of Byzantine church art.[18]

Serbia's life under the Turks has been characterized by Isidore Sekilic in these words: "There was no bread, no schooling, no ruling power after Kossovo; but Kossovo was a grave, a grave that covered everything. But the resurrection passes through the grave."[19] Deprived of political independence and religious autonomy, the Serbs began a slow movement back to national greatness that would only be realized in the 19th century. The first step in this direction came with the help of the Grand Vizier, Mehmed Sokolovich, a Serb who had been forced to become a Moslem as a child. Sokolovich interceded with Sultan Suleiman II to re-establish the patriarchate of Pec, and Makerije, his brother, was chosen as patriarch (1557-1571). Suleiman hoped that by such a move the Serbian patriarch would function as a part of the Turkish political organization and unite all the Slavs up to the Carpathian Mountains, thus bringing them under peaceful submission to the Turks and away from the Anti-Turkish leagues of Austria, Venice, and the other Western European powers.

This period also saw the beginning of mass emigrations of Serbs towards the Danube regions. Turkish oppression, along with encouragement from Hungary and Austria, attracted the Serbs to the hope of a new awakening as a nation. A new life indeed opened to those who migrated into the southern provinces of Hungary, Slovenia, Croatia, and along the shores of Morlacca. Western influences in Serbian thought had come primarily through Dalmatia and the Venetian occupied cities along its coast. *The Codex* of Stephen Dushan, the first collection of Serbian laws [*Zakonik Tsara Dushana*, 1349] had been inspired by Latin codes that had reached the Dalmatian cities. With no real possibility of cultural development in their own country, the exiled Serbs came in touch with the Italian Renaissance in Dalmatia, and they read the counter-reform works of theologians such as Bellarmine, Canisius, Ledesma, and Christobal de Vega. The complete version of the Bible had at this time been translated in the region of Croatia.

SECOND SPRING

But it was in the regions of Southern Hungary, East Slovenia, and Austria that a new life opened to the Serbs. The Hungarian ruler, Mathias Corvinus (1458-1490), needed reinforcements to stave off the advancing Turks on his southern borders. He recognized the migrating Serbs as a unified national group under the "despot" Vuk Brankovic. The Austrian emperor, Leopold I, also promised the migrating Serbs national and religious independence within his kingdom. Mass movements of Serbs around their religious leaders took place in the 17th and 18th century, for example, the historical trek of 30,000 Serbs in 1690 under the Patriarch Arsenije III and that in 1739 under the Patriarch Arsenije IV.

Leopold recognized the spiritual leadership of the metropolitans with residence in the small town of Sremsky-Karlovtsy along the Danube. The patriarchate of Pec was abolished by the Turks in 1766, when the Phanar obtained from Sultan Mustapha III a firman bringing all eparchies in the Ottoman Empire under the direct control of the ecumenical patriarch.

Enjoying a new-found freedom and contact with Western culture and thought, the Serbian Church developed into an autocephalous Orthodox Church under the protection of the Roman Catholic emperors. The primate at Karlovtsy soon found himself directing a dynamic Serbian Church that had never before reached such heights of intellectual development. Eventually the metropolitan of this autocephalous

Church enjoyed the title of "patriarch," granted him by the emperor, Franz Joseph, in 1848.

The exiled Serbs found a nucleus of Serbian culture and intellectual life in the *Fruska Gora* in Sirmium, which had become a new Holy Mountain for Serbian monasticism. Such monasteries as Hopovo, Vrdnik (Ravanica), Beochin, Krushedol, Sisatovac, Kuvezhdin, Besenovo, Grgetek and Fenek became the spiritual and cultural centers of the new Church of Karlovtsy.

Patriarch Arsenije III was eager to promote learning on all levels. He sought from the Austrian emperor permission and the means to set up a Serbian press and to open Serbian schools. The first step towards alleviating the low level of education among the clergy was taken by Metropolitan Pavle Nenadovic who in 1763 opened the first clerical school in Karlovtsy called "Our Lady of Protection School."[20] In a popular assembly of Serbs in Karlovtsy it was decided that schools of all levels had to be established. To do this it was imperative to form teachers. Unfortunately, the monks near Karlovtsy Church had produced no scholars or books; in fact, of the 259 monasteries of men and women, few knew how to read or write. Some studied privately and traveled to Russia, Mount Athos, the Holy Land, Mount Sinai, and even to Venice on missions dealing with monastic affairs, sometimes even national affairs, but such cultured monks were few indeed.[21]

Even before the migrations into Hungary and Austria, the Serbs had become more dependent financially and intellectually upon Kievan Russia. Russian princes became the chief builders of Serbian monasteries and churches under the Turks.[22] In the 15th century, especially under Patriarch Paisy of Pec, Serbia and Russia enjoyed closer bonds. Paisy sent monks to Russia to obtain financial assistance, as well as liturgical and theological manuscripts. In the 17th century Russia provided the Serbian bishops in Karlovtsy and in Serbia itself with books and even teachers.[23] In 1724 the Holy

Synod of Russia sent Maksim Suvorov to open a school in Sremsky-Karlovtsy. In the 18th century there was a constant migration of Serbian youths from Karlovtsy to the Kievan seminary, and eventually the better students also remained to complete their studies at the Kievan Academy. Emanuel Kozachunsky established in Karlovtsy a Latin school and a school to form instructors of theology, which was most needed in Serbia at the time.

METROPOLITAN STEPHEN STRATIMIROVIC

One of the most learned of the hierarchs of Karlovtsy was Metropolitan Stephen Stratimirovic.[24] After studies in philosophy and Magyar law in Buda, he went to Pec where he met Adam Kolar, who convinced him to study the Slavonic language and Serbian history.[25] Encouraged by Kolar, Stephen went to Karlovtsy in 1783 with the intention of becoming a priest. Metropolitan Mojsije Putnik saw his native ability even though Stratimirovic was only 26 years old and still had not studied theology. One of the few theologians and historians of the Serbian Church at that time was Archimandrite Jovan Rojic, and it was under his private tutoring that Stratimirovic was formed as a theologian.[26] Rajic had been formed in the theology of the Russian, Feofan Prokopovich, and his rationalism was handed down to his young theology student. In 1784 Stratimirovic was ordained priest by Metropolitan Putnik, was consecrated bishop of Buda two years later, and in 1790, at 28 years of age, he was chosen as metropolitan.

Metropolitan Stephen (d. 1836) was dynamic and open to the problems of his people. He knew civil and ecclesiastical law well and he was especially convinced of the importance of training good theologians, who in turn could impart their knowledge of Scripture and tradition to students preparing for the priesthood. In 1794 he opened a seminary at Sremsky-

Karlovtsy under the direction of Sava Tekelija. Russian theological books provided the basis for study. Other seminaries
were opened at Plashki, Pakratz, Temesvar, and at Brshtsa.[27]
Stephen insisted that no one could be ordained unless he first
finished one of these seminaries.

From Russia he obtained theological books, liturgical
works, and texts of a non-religious nature. He had the most
common liturgical books as well as commentaries on the
Gospels and Bible history printed in Karlovtsy.[28] He saw to
the publication of the Slavonic Bible, which had appeared
earlier in Moscow and Kiev.[29]

SERBIAN INDEPENDENCE

While Karlovtsy developed into a Serbian intellectual
and cultural center, Serbia itself was feeling the stirrings
for greater political and religious freedom. Having sided
with the Austrian rulers, Joseph II and Catherine II, in
their war against the Turks (1788-1790), Serbia suffered
from the atrocities inflicted upon them in revenge by the
Janissaries. Rising up in rebellion, the Serbs, led by Karad-
jordje Petrovic, freed the country from the Turkish soldiers
and even in 1807 freed Belgrade. Russia, however, failed
to support them fully, and in the Treaty of Bucharest in 1812
the Serbs obtained complete amnesty and were granted a
limited degree of internal self-government but were largely
still under the power of the Turks. A new revolt broke out
under the leadership of Milosh Obrenovic in 1815 which
resulted, by means of cooperation with the Russians, in the
recognition by the Porte in the Treaty of Adrianople (1830)
of the right of the Serbs to self-administration with a pledge
to pay a fixed annual tax.

In 1832 the Serbian Church was also granted greater
autonomy when the patriarch of Constantinople recognized
the archbishop of Belgrade as the metropolitan of the Church

of Serbia, elected by the Serbians without interference from the Phanar. With the return of autonomy in governing the Church, the Serbs were powerfully supported by the higher clergy of Karlovtsy and its superior schools, especially of theology. The greatest need of the newly created Serbian principality under Milosh was that of schools and of books.

THE SEMINARY OF BELGRADE

The Phanariots who ruled the Serbian Church from 1766 until 1832 were not concerned with creating seminaries in Serbia. All too often these served as a means of fostering a sense of both national and religious independence, and Constantinople wanted to maintain its control over the Serbian Church as long as it could. Any cadre of well formed Serbian priests always posed a threat to Greek clerical control. Dositej Obradovic, the first so-called "minister" of instruction, sought to establish a seminary as early as 1810. In 1822 Milosh wrote to Archimandrite Lukijan Mushicki, known in Serbia for his erudition. Lukijan advised the ruler of the need for two distinct schools, one to form young priests in a proper seminary and the other to form intelligent teachers who would then staff the national schools. He concluded his appeal to Milosh with the words: "No country in all Europe enjoys a greater peace and tranquility than ours. It is in peace that sciences best prosper."[30]

In 1822 Milosh called a synod at his capital of Kragujevac, which approved various reforms including his proposal to found a seminary. The low level of education is indicated by the circular that Milosh sent to the local authorities on the problem of education in Serbia. He laments that there is hardly a man educated enough to be ordained a priest or become a monk, since few are the men who are educated enough to even understand what they might be able to write.[31]

METROPOLITAN PETAR

The outstanding intellectual leader of the Serbian Church under Milosh was Metropolitan Petar. He it was who persuaded Milosh to convene a reform synod [*sobor*] in 1834 in Kragujevac.[32] Petar's dream of a seminary at Belgrade was fulfilled when it opened its doors in 1836 to 46 students. At first it was a two year course of theology, but in 1844 it was changed to four years.[33] The subjects taught included the Slavonic language, dogmatic and pastoral theology, Biblical exegesis, moral theology and canon law. The rector was Pavle Popovic.

In 1850 two young Russian theologians were sent to teach in the Belgrade Seminary, Vasa Vardish and Dimitrii Rudinskii, and were paid by Russia. Petar was eager to keep contact with Russia in order to obtain books of theology, liturgy and of any other field of knowledge. It is difficult for us to appreciate the low level of learning in Serbia even at this period in the 19th century. In 1836 Milosh wrote Petar, regarded as one of the most learned men in Serbia at the time, to supply his race with its first Serbian grammar which was desperately needed in the national schools.

Petar was tireless in developing a Serbian press to print theological books and liturgical texts. He had the *Psalter* and *Trebnik* printed, books on sacred history and catechisms, histories of the Serbian Church, dogmatic theology and the *Menaea*.[34] Books principally came from Austria and Russia and provided Adolf Bermann, a Prussian who directed Milosh's printing press, with the models for Serbian texts. Up to Petar's time books were rare, and equally rare it was to find priests who could read them. One of Petar's predecessors, Metropolitan Cyril (d. 1827), left a library that contained three books.[35] The ordinary people was not cultivated and there existed, as always among illiterate people, a great deal of superstition, beliefs in false prophets and the practice of magic and vampirism.[36]

Petar drew heavily upon the better educated priests of Karlovtsy, while Russia offered scholarships to Serbian students. In 1846 Petar sent six young Serbs to study in Kiev, among whom was Miloje Jovanovic, the future Metropolitan Mihailo and successor of Petar. Miloje followed the celebrated theology courses of Professor Dumitrashkov. When Count Protasov opened the doors of the Academy of Kiev, Miloje and Vasilije Nikolajevic began their higher theological studies. The level of theology in Kiev was higher than that in Cernauti (Jassy) and offered in addition rich libraries, excellent professors and a deep religious spirit.

METROPOLITAN MIHAILO

Miloje was ordained in Kiev, taking the name of Mihailo, and returned to Serbia in 1854. He was the first ardent Russophile among Serbian churchleaders, and he used the favors that he received from the Russian Church and government to create a better relationship with his own country and the Serbian Church. Mihailo was elevated to metropolitan of Belgrade in 1859 at the early age of 33. A frail, small man with brilliant, burning eyes, Miloje was ambitious to awaken greatness in the Serbian nation. In Russia he saw a protector of the young Church of Serbia. Although he was more a diplomat than a grass-roots reformer as Petar was, Mihailo did effect great changes. He was convinved that people should read Holy Scripture in their own vernacular. At that time there were two Serbian versions produced and disseminated throughout the country by the British Bible Society. However, the two versions were quite different. Mihailo felt that time would reveal which version, that produced by Stojkovic (1834) or that by Vuk Karadzhic (2nd edition in 1857), was the more correct, but in the meantime the masses should be given the Scriptures and encouraged to read them.[37]

Metropolitan Mihailo could be rightly called the founder of Serbian theological literature. He furnished seminarians and priests with the best of Russian theological and apologetical works. Possessing a fiery nature that often became aggressive, Mihailo proved himself to be the first Serbian polemicist to defend both the Church of Serbia and its doctrine against attacks. He refuted the "Jesuitical attacks" made by a certain Tschorkljan in a book published in Vienna strongly attacking Orthodoxy and intended to undermine the faith of the Serbians.

A listing of his theological writings allows one to agree with Radoslav Grujic[38] that Metropolitan Mihailo was "the first outstanding theological writer of Serbia, who left about 50 printed works of which some dealt with most important matters." Having taught dogmatic theology and homiletics upon his return from Russia, Mihailo, even amidst his activities as metropolitan, never lost his interest in theology and in preaching. Eager to aid his priests in their pastoral and spiritual life, he published various works of a pastoral-instructional nature such as his *Archijerejskog puchena novo-rukipolozhenom sveshteniku* (1860), *Mudrog higumana* (1863), *Ruchne sveshtenike knige* (1876), *O monashtvu* (1863) and *Dukhovnika* (1872).

Primarily a pastor, Mihailo was an outstanding preacher who brought to his sermons a great deal of solid theology as well as poetry. Some of the collections of his sermons and conferences on pastoral and devotional themes are his *Pastirske puke pravoslavnim khrishtianima* (1860), *Pastirske becede vojnitsima* (1865), *Puchene matere o vaspitanu male detse* (1870), *Devojachko punoletstvo* (1871) and *Prijatel' mladezhi* (1874). More directly to furnish his priests with theological material for preaching, he wrote *Pravoslavni propovednik,* a work of four volumes containing the basic teachings of the Orthodox faith, *Tsrkveni uchitel'* (1861), *Dukhevni dnevnik* (1859), *Priroda i razum* (1870) and *Tsrkveno bogoslovje* (1860). It would be impossible to ap-

preciate the full impact that such books in Serbian had upon
the clergy, and hence upon the faithful of the Serbian Church
in a period when there existed much ignorance about the
Church's teachings.

Mihailo's literary interests were wide and deep. He edited
a third edition of *Srblaka* (1861), taking the editions of the
liturgical services of the saints of Serbia and bringing them
up to date.[39] He also corrected and added to the services in
honor of Sts. Cyril and Methodius from the original work
done by Archbishop Antonii of Kazan. He also composed
liturgical services in honor of the Serbian Saints Prochor of
Pult and Peter of Cetinje who rank as favorite Serbian
saints.[40]

The first history of the Serbian Church was composed
by Mihailo and entitled: *Pogled na istoriju srpske tsrkve*
(1856). He followed this with a more detailed and scholarly
work: *Pravoslavna tsrkva u knezhevini Srbiji* (1874). Other
historical works dealing with the history of the Serbian
Church are his: *Pravoslavna tsrkva u kralevini Srbiji* (1895),
Khrishtianske svetine na Istoku (1886) and *Sveta Gora
Atonska* (1886). Mihailo, who died in 1898, can be called
the greatest intellectual force in the Serbian Church up to
the 20th century. He was, as an intellectual, not an original
thinker. His force lay in his zeal to promote letters among
all levels of his people. To accomplish this he translated,
mainly from Russian, pastoral and theological works, re-
edited former Serbian classics and had them reprinted for
popular reading, and created original works that touched
the pastoral and devotional life of his priests and people.

He lived under the Princes Milosh, Milan I, Michael and
Milan, II, all of whom strove to gain for Serbia its complete
independence from the Turks. Milan II accomplished this
through help from Russia, and in 1878 Serbia gained its
complete independence from the Turks. Milan then obtained
for the Serbian Orthodox Church its full independence from
Constantinople, which Patriarch Joachim III recognized in

1879. Only with the formation of a united nation of the Kingdom of the Serbs, Croats and Slovenes, upon the collapse of the Austro-Hungarian Monarchy in 1918, were the sectional Churches able to unite into one strong Serbian Church. The Serbian Patriarchate was re-established for the third time in 1920, and comprised the formerly autonomous Serbian metropolias of Belgrade, Karlovtsy, Bosnia-Herzegovina, Montenegro and the diocese of Dalmatia.

Truly creative theological literature in the 19th century in Serbia was very sparse and of inferior quality. Modern Serbian literature can be considered to begin with Dositej Obradovic (1743-1811) who, before he was made minister of instruction, had lived as a monk in a monastery north of Belgrade. Exposed to the rationalism of the West, Dositej, both in his autobiography and in his *Sovieti zdravago razum* [*Counsels of Sound Reason*], sought to reconcile the monastic idealism of the spiritual world with a rationalism of the concrete world of the Enlightenment. He is the first author who attempted to move away from the Old Slavonic language canonized by the Church and who wrote in the Serbian language as it was spoken.

In Montenegro—the only Serbian province that was able to retain its independence against the Turks—the Bishop-Prince Peter Petrovicha Negosha (1813-1851) was famed for his heroic verses written in imitation of folk epics that exalted the deeds of the Serbian national heroes and saints. His *Luchi mikrokozma* [*Ray of Microcosm*] is a philosophical-religious epic in Dantesque style of the journey of a soul through the heavenly spheres. In sixteen stanzas he confesses his faith in Christ, the Son of God who destroys evil and brings victory through His resurrection. "By His resurrection, He conquered death; Heaven by His praise is attained and earth praises its Savior." Velimirovic says: "Upon such an elementary Christology one can begin to lay an ecclesiastical Christology."[41]

THEOLOGICAL TEXTBOOKS

In the 19th century when Russian theologians were writing their famous compendia, Serbia, which was just taking its first steps in higher theological educaton at the seminary in Sremsky-Karlovtsy, declared a theological academy only in 1900,[42] and at the seminary at Belgrade, had to rely almost exclusively upon the Russian theologians for textbook material. Metrophanes Chevits translated the *Pravoslavnoe dogmaticheskoe bogoslovie* of Makarii Bulgakov into Serbian[43] as well as Makarii's *Rukovodstvo k izucheniu khristianskago pravoslavno-dogmaticheskago bogosloviia.*[44] C. Vecelinovic translated and contracted the first two volumes (of five) of Silvestr Malevanskii's *Opit pravoslavnago dogmaticheskago bogosloviia.*[45] Archimandrite Firmilian, professor of dogmatic theology in the Karlovtsy Seminary, compiled in 1900 a short course of dogmatic theology entitled *Dogmatitchko Bogoslovie* in two volumes and a third on Biblical and pastoral theology published in 1901.

The most noted name among modern Serbian theologians is that of Nikodim Milash, bishop of Zara. A Serbian from Dalmatia, Milash was in the fortunate position of having grown up in an area grounded upon both Byzantine and Roman law. His *Pravoslavno tsrkveno pravo* has influenced modern Orthodox Canon Law through the translations made of this work into German, Russian, Bulgarian, Greek and Rumanian. He has written many other works touching on various parts of Canon Law, such as a collection of the canons of the African Church,[46] a collection of the principal canons of the Orthodox Church,[47] and one of penal law.[48] A work giving the history of the Serbian Church in Dalmatia is entitled *Pravoslavna Dalmatsija.*[49] Milash also wrote a polemical work concerning Sts. Cyril and Methodius, in the second part of which he takes up the theological problems separating Roman Catholics from the Orthodox such as the procession of the Holy Spirit and its addition to the symbol of faith, the problem of unleavened bread, purgatory, the Immaculate Conception of Mary and the primacy of the pope.[50] Other Serbians who have written on Canon Law include N. Buzichic with a collection of the Nomocanons on matrimony and the Nomocanons of the Serbian Church,[51] E. Radic on the causes of divorce in the Orthodox Churches,[52] E. C. Mitrovic on the jurisdictional limits of Church and State,[53] I. Bojovic on mutual relations of Church and State,[54] and N. Duchic on Christian matrimony.[55]

THEOLOGICAL PERIODICALS

The first ecclesiastical periodical, *Beseda,* was published in 1868 by Andrija Monashevic, a parish priest in Novi Sad, who wanted to provide a religious journal for school, church, and popular use. It is a valuable source for the history of Serbia's relations with the Austro-Hungarian monarchy. This grew into the *Dukhovni Zbornik,* which proposed to translate into Serbian homilies of the early Church Fathers.[56] *Glas istine,* edited by Arsa Pajevic, specialized in spiritual exhortations, together with articles on art and archaeology. *Srpski Sion* was the first serious attempt to publish an official metropolitan periodical from Sremsky-Karlovtsy under the editorship of Sava Petrovic, the leading Serbian theologian at that time. It lasted from 1891 to 1907 and was valuable as an aid to priests and later, under the editorship of D. Ruvarats, as an important source of material on the Karlovtsy metropolia.

The *Bogoslovski Glasnik,* published at Karlovtsy from 1902 to 1914, proved to be an extremely important element in forming priests of the Karlovtsy Metropolia, since it sought to present the teachings of the Serbian Church in a more scientific and objective manner.[57] Since 1920 when Belgrade and Karlovtsy were united in one patriarchate, *Glasnik Srpske Patriarkhi* (with a circulation of 200,000) publishes official news of the patriarchate as well as theological articles by professors of Belgrade and Karlovtsy. *Bogoslovje* is the leading theological journal of the St. Sava Theological Academy of Belgrade and has been published since 1925. The union of the clergy publishes the *Vestnik Srpske Crkve* in Belgrade, which has become the voice of the parish priests in their attempts to make known their needs to the Serbian hierarchs. *Khristianski Zhivot* is a monthly bulletin aimed at providing devotional as well as theological reading suited to the laity. Each diocese has its own official organ, which often provides a medium for theological articles of a more popular nature. The *Narodna Enciklopedija Srpsko-hrvatsko-slovenachka,* under the editorship of S. Stanojevic, is a four volume encyclopedia, which contains articles written by leading Serbian theologians.[58]

MODERN MONASTICISM

When the Serbian Church obtained its independence in the 19th century and began to renew itself, a restoration of monasticism was expected, but it was never achieved. Over 400 years of oppression had destroyed or ruined many monasteries, their libraries, archives, and treasures. The government began a century ago to repair these ancient monasteries only to be interrupted in its work by the two World Wars. Now the work is being carried on by the present "Popular Republic" of Yugoslavia.

Amidst the material insecurity of the 17th and 18th centuries under the Turks, the convents of women progressively emptied. From the 18th century to 1914 not one remained open. Since then, Russian émigrés have aided in repopulating the convents in Yugoslavia. With the monasteries of men, however, there has been a gradual decline starting in the 19th century. In 1830 there were about 20 functioning monasteries with about 800 monks. Under Metropolitan Mihailo in 1867 there were 41 monasteries but, strangely enough, only 121 monks; in 1913 there were 54 monasteries with 93 monks. After the reestablishment of the patriarchate of Pec in 1920, the Serbian Church acquired the Orthodox faithful in Croatia, Slovenia, Voivodina, Montenegro, and Macedonia. At the time of the Second World War there were 166 monasteries with 540 monks, while 25 feminine convents housed 416 nuns. Great damage was caused by this war and the civil disruptions that followed; twenty monasteries were destroyed and 17 badly damaged. In 1960 there was a total of only 50 religious houses, many of which were maintained by nuns, since the number of monks had fallen off seriously. There remain today very few cenobitic monks and, in general, their intellectual life is at a nadir, except among those monks who are destined for academic work, seminaries, or chanceries. No theological life flowing from a strong monastic life has been possible for over a century.

THE MODERN ERA

In the period from 1920 to the present under the patriarchs, Dimitrije (1920-1930), Varnava (1930-1937), Gavriel (1937-1950), Vikentije (1950-1958) and Gherman (1958-), the Serbian Church reached its fullest development as an organized patriarchate embracing, besides the archdiocese of Belgrade with five dioceses, the metropolia of Karlovtsy with seven dioceses, the metropolia of Montenegro with three, Dalmatia and Boka-Kotor dioceses, Bosnia-Herzegovina with four dioceses and Macedonia with six. During the patriarchate of Dimitrije, the Serbian Church in America was formed into a diocese in Chicago in 1923 and given its own bishop in 1926.

Theological schools were strengthened at Sremsky-Karlovtsy, Cetinje, Prizren, Sarajevo, and Bitola. The Theological Academy of Belgrade attained a university status which, however, was taken away on ideological grounds by the Socialistic Republic in 1952. After the second World War when the new government, inimical to religion, took over, only two seminaries of the six were allowed to exist: the seminary in the Monastery of Rakovic in Belgrade and the one in Prizren. After the publication of the decree on Church rights and religious freedom (May 27, 1953), the original five seminaries were again in operation with a five year program training about 400 seminarians for the priesthood. Belgrade's Academy has a four year program and trains about 100 candidates.

The Second World War and the civil strife which followed took its toll not only on the entire population of Yugoslavia, reaching a death total of 1,700,000, but also decimated the ranks of the clergy and teachers of theology. Four bishops and 549 priests were killed in the wars of the 1940's, while 300 churches were destroyed, 49 chapels, and 20 monasteries with an equal number seriously damaged.

The theological faculty of Belgrade, which had provided instructors for the other five seminaries, had to be rebuilt after the Second World War. Professors Dushan Glumac and Milosh Erdelyan have distinguished themselves by their works on the Psalms and the Qumran Scrolls respectively. The first translated and explained the Psalms in an attempt to put them into more intelligible Serbian, while at the same time bringing into his commentary the latest studies in linguistics and archaeology.[59] The latter spent ten months in 1957 in the lands of Jordan, Israel, Syria, and Lebanon and a few months again in 1959 to work directly upon the original scrolls.[60]

One of the outstanding canonists has been Professor Sergije Troiskii, a Russian teaching in Belgrade. He has edited and explained the *Kormchaia Kniga* of St. Sava and is well known for his writings concerning inter-church juridical relations, especially touching ecclesiastical autonomy.[61] Dr.

Blagot Gardasevic has also contributed to the field of canon law with his research on Church-State relations as found in the *Kormchaia* of St. Sava. He has also investigated the early Christian parishes and their role in the Church as it developed into a juridical institution.[62]

New Testament studies have been developed by Professor Emilijan Carnic, who has specialized in the works of St. Paul, especially on the *Letter to Hebrews*. He has written commentaries on most of the other epistles of Paul and has examined the influence of Philo or the pre-Christian Alexandrian school upon the thought of Paul.

Original work has been done by Dr. Stojan Gosevic in the area of dogmatic theology.[63] He has explored the meaning of dogma, not merely as revelation from God but also as it has become sanctioned by the Church and formulized through ecumenical councils. In general, dogmatic theology appears as the weakest of all areas of theology in Serbian thought. Perhaps this is due to lack of training abroad, other than in Russia, and hence little contact has been had with other theologians, Orthodox, Roman Catholic, or Protestant.

Professor Dimitrije Dimitrijevic has taught Christian moral theology and has written several historical studies on ethics according to Old Testament revelation and also a comparison of modern ethics with ethics as taught by St. Sava. He is one of the most prolific writers in Serbian theology today.[65]

There has been some attempt on the part of Professor Radinoj Josic to confront the difficulties of modern science and atheism with new applications of Christianity that will offer satisfying answers.[66] Dr. Lazar Milin[67] and V. D. Popovic[68] also have engaged in answering the problems of the modern world, the meaning of death, and the belief in the resurrection.

Byzantine studies have always attracted Serbian scholars because of the close connection between their own civilization and that of Byzantium. Archimandrite Filaret-Branko Granic, a member of the Serbian Academy of Science, has reflected glory upon his Church and country by his learned works on Byzantinism and patrology.[69]

Encouraged and even subsidized by the government, scholars have done much in the field of archaeology and ecclesiastical art to uncover the glories of the first patriarchate of Pec. Dr. Lazar Mirkovic has done several studies for the Archaeological Institute of the Serbian Academy of Science in an attempt to publish ancient documents of the Serbian Church. His edition of the *Miroslavlevo jevangele* (1951), as well as his edition of the *Skitsky ustav* of St. Sava and the *Tipik* of Archbishop Nikodim (1319), are examples of his scholarship.[70]

Dr. Jordan P. Ilic (d. 1950) has left his mark in the area of religious pedagogy, which has made his name and works famous throughout the Orthodox world. He has principally investigated the character of religious pedagogy as a science and the precise aims to be attained in such religious education.[71]

Finally mention should be made of Dr. Cedomir Draskovic, professor of pastoral theology and homiletics at the faculty of Belgrade. He has sought to investigate the form of preaching used by Jesus Christ and His Apostles, the type used in the golden patristic era, especially by the Cappadocian Fathers and St. John Chrysostom, and the types used in the Serbian Church from the 12th to the 15th centuries.[72]

The Academy of Belgrade, besides its theological journal *Bogoslovlje,* has published since 1950 the *Zbornik pravoslavnog bogoslovskog faculteta* with outstanding articles of theological worth, but unfortunately only three numbers have so far appeared (1950-1954).

From 1920 until 1960 the Belgrade Academy has granted 715 diplomas, 18 doctoral degrees and three honorary degrees. The latter were awarded to Stevan Dimitrijevits, professor of the Belgrade University, Archbishop Dorotheos of Athens (1956), and Moscow Patriarch Aleksei (1957).

The Serbian Church, led by its theologians, has in recent years been finding opportunities to make contact with other Orthodox Churches, especially the Churches of Russia and Greece. In January 1965, the Serbian Church became a full member of the World Council of Churches after having participated at New Delhi in 1961. Such contacts are expected to continue and thus enrich Serbian theology, which until the present has received little influence from other Churches. As yet, very few Serbian theologians have written on the ecumenical movement.

One of the unfortunate features of the history of Serbia, and this includes the Serbian Orthodox Church, is that over the many centuries of its existence it never could constitute a compact and united nationality. Almost continually under foreign domination, Serbia has only recently come to experience some peace and relative freedom. But even today under Communist rule the Serbian Church is not totally free. Hence the theology that has been produced in times past and that is presently being produced must be judged in the light of the political and social conditions that have so strongly inhibited the full flowering of theology.

The Yugoslavian government has not allowed theological works to be printed with the result that any independent theological work can be produced only by means of mimeographing or some other duplicating process. Theologians have written longer articles than the usual theological periodicals carry and have had these printed in collections commemorating various political or ecclesiastical anniversaries. Several of these collections containing excellent theological articles by the leading religious thinkers in Yugoslavia today bear the titles of *A Commemorative Volume on the Occasion of the 80th Anniversary of the Occupation of Bosnia and Herzegovina* (1878-1958), *The 50th Anniversary of its Annexation* (1908-1958), and *The 40th Anniversary of its Liberation and Union* (1918-1958),[73] *The 100th Anniversary of Gorski Vijenac,*[74] *The 600th Anniversary of the Serbian Patriarchate,*[75] *The 150th Anniversary of the Revolution in Serbia* (1804-1954),[76] *The 100th Anniversary of the Folks' Movement in Voivodina* (1848-1948).[77]

PART FIVE

The Rumanian Orthodox Church

ORTHODOX THEOLOGY in Rumania represents one of the most creative and promising theologies of all the traditionally Orthodox Churches. To appreciate its wealth one must understand the history that produced modern Rumania as a rich residue of many diverse cultures that met and melted together over the past 17 centuries.[1] Unlike most other Balkan countries that remained fairly monolithic in their evolution of one culture and one language, be that Greek or one of the many Slavic nationalities, Rumania was exposed strongly to Latin, Slavonic, and Hellenic cultures. This is seen today in the Rumanian language, which is basically Romance, stemming from the Latin colonists who settled around ancient Dacia in the early centuries of the Christian era; yet a language that has been molded through centuries of using not only the Cyrillic alphabet but also the Slavonic as well as the Greek languages.

Christianity first came to the area now designated as Rumania in the third century through the evangelization of Latin missionaries.[2] The ancient ecclesiastical province of Scythia on the shores of the Black Sea gives historical evidence of the spread and strength of Christianity from the third to the sixth centuries. On the western side of the Danube, the diocese of Remesiana boasted of the renowned Latin

271

writer, St. Nicetas, as its apostle. After the sixth century, the barbarian tribes which continually invaded this region made Christianity seem to have become almost totally extinct. Contact with the Bulgars after the 8th century opened this land again to the influence of Christianity. The Rumanians accepted the Byzantine form of Christianity from the Bulgars and were thus, like them, opened to receive the rich theological literature of the Byzantine Christian Empire. Old Slavonic, which had become the vehicle of evangelizing the Slavs throughout the Balkan Peninsula through the missionary efforts of Sts. Cyril and Methodius and their disciples, now became the accepted language of the educated Rumanians and would remain so until the 18th century.

MONASTIC CENTERS OF LEARNING

As in all Orthodox countries, monasticism developed rapidly in the early centuries of Christianization, especially in the two principalities of Valachia and Moldavia, which became independent in the 14th century. Through intimate contact with other monasteries in Bulgaria, Serbia, Greece, especially Mount Athos and even southern Russia, the monasteries of Valachia and Moldavia soon amassed rich libraries of Greek and Slavonic manuscripts. The art of transcribing, translating, and decorating manuscripts with artistic miniatures became centered in the Rumanian monasteries of Bistrita, Neamt, Putna, Voronet, Slatina, Sucevita, Tismana, Cozia, Bistrita of Oltenia, Deahul, and Govora.[3] Liturgical service books, Holy Scripture, lives of the saints and chronicles formed the first literature of the Rumanian people.

One of the earliest chronicles and hence earliest original Rumanian pieces of literature is the *Letopisetul dela Bistrita,* a chronicle modeled on that of Manasses in narrating the history of Moldavia from the time of Adam.[4]

The *Chronicle of the Monastery of Putna* is a typical collection or *sbornic* containing a mixture of ascetical writings, lives of the saints, apocryphal stories, extracts from Byzantine nomocanons, grammatical treatises and various historical accounts. The *Chronicle* is signed by the monk Isaias of Slatina who translated from Old Slavonic texts to Rumanian. The Moldavian chroniclers, Macarius (c. 1558), Eftimie (c. 1565) and Azarie (c. 1577), told the history of Moldavia, each continuing where the other left off.[5]

DEACON CORESI[6]

One of the pioneers of the Rumanian language who brought the first type (Cyrillic) to Rumania was Deacon Coresi in the 16th century. Using the Cyrillic letters, he substituted the Transylvanian dialect for that of Valachia, which then evolved into the standard Rumanian language. Slavonic was not even understood by the priests who used it in the liturgical services, and there was a growing thirst among the populace for religious literature in the vernacular. This was Coresi's great contribution—to provide a printed literature in the Rumanian language. He printed one of the oldest works written in Rumanian, the *Psaltirea Scheiana,* produced in the Transylvanian monastery of Scheia in the 15th century. Coresi printed this at Brasov in Transylvania along with the *Psaltirea of Voronet* and the *Acts of the Apostles,* also of Voronet.[7]

But his great mission, Coresi felt, was to offset Protestant proselytism which had become so effective through the printed word in the vernacular. Honterus was a leading Lutheran reformer who, as many other Rumanians at that time, had studied in Germany, at the University of Wittenberg. Returning to his native town of Brasov, Honterus published in 1542 his Protestant reforms.[8] To offset Protestant literature, especially the translations of the Holy Scripture,

Coresi undertook the pioneering task of providing the Ortho-
dox faithful with published works that reflected more the
Orthodox tradition. With Hanas Benkner, Coresi set up his
printing press at Brasov and produced works, mainly in
Old Slavonic, such as the *Octoich*,[9] the *Gospels*,[10] *Triod*,[11]
and the *Psalter*[12] that would supply the Rumanian Orthodox
Church with the proper liturgical service books in the Old
Slavonic language.

But to offset the Protestant missionaries, Coresi began
to publish works in Rumanian. His *Catechism* [*Catechismul*],
printed quite early in his career as a printer (1559), was
composed of seven parts and was an evident attempt to
offset the catechism published by Philip Melanchthon in
1521, which had been translated into Rumanian in 1559.[13]
Other works printed by Coresi include a translation of the
Gospels with an explanation,[14] a *Pravila* or book of the
Nomocanons, translated from the Greek work of John the
Faster, patriarch of Constantinople (580-610) and a book
of prayers used by the Byzantine priests in celebrating the
Liturgy. Coresi was the first to promote the vernacular in
the Liturgy; yet it would be several centuries before Rumanian
would be the accepted liturgical language.

The reigns of Matei Basarab (1632-1654) in Valachia
and Vasile Lupu (1631-1653) in Moldavia saw an un-
precedented flourishing of religious and intellectual life in
Rumania. After the Tatars had withdrawn in the 13th century,
Valachia was formed as an independent principality in 1330
and Moldavia in 1363. Thus these two Rumanian speaking
princedoms enjoyed a religious and intellectual freedom unknown in the Hellenic, Bulgarian, Serbian, and even Russian
worlds, where the Turks or Tatars trammeled the full
flowering of learning.

METROPOLITAN VARLAAM (d. 1657)

This explains why the Synod of Jassy was called by Metropolitan Varlaam in 1642 to pass judgment on the *Confession of Faith* written in Latin by Peter Mogila, Metropolitan of Kiev. It was hoped that the Greek, Rumanian, and Slavic Orthodox Churches would agree upon Mogila's *Confession* as an antidote to the Calvinistic formulation of faith as found in the *Confession* of Cyril Lucaris.

Mogila himself was born in Moldavia (1597), but was educated in Lvov. As hegumen of the Kievan Pecherskii Lavra, he had an influence on Rumanian theology by not only furnishing the type for printing books in Rumania but also generously sending printers such as Timotei Verbitki, who set up a printing press in 1635 at Cimpulung, and others who established printing presses at Govora, Dealu, and Tirgoviste. Mogila also sent innumerable Slavonic theological books printed in Kiev and Lvov to Rumania which were reprinted or translated and printed in Rumanian.[15] Three representatives of the Russian Church, Isiia Trofimovich, hegoumen of St. Nicholas in Kiev, Ignatios Oksenovich, preacher, and Iosif Kononovich, attended the Synod of Jassy. The delegates of the patriarch of Constantinople were Porfiry, Metropolitan of Nicaea, and the hieromonk, Meletios Syrigos. This Synod lasted from September 15 to October 27, 1642, during which time Syrigos had translated the Latin text of Mogila's *Confession* into Greek and had also amended many points of Mogila's teachings. It was Syrigos' version that was printed on the presses of the monastery of the Three Hierarchs in Jassy, December 20, 1642 and was approved by Patriarch Parthenios of Constantinople in March 1643.[16] Thus, one of the earliest Confessions of the Orthodox faith had been formulated at Jassy, which was not only a unanimous answer of Orthodoxy to Protestantism, but would also be considered by the Slavs, Rumanians, and Greeks as enjoying the highest authority among the Orthodox as a symbolic book of faith.

Greatly concerned with the inroads into Rumanian Orthodoxy made by the Calvinists, Metropolitan Varlaam used his literary ability and theological knowledge to defend the Orthodox faith. Two of his principal theological works were directed against the Calvinists. The first, his *Raspunsurile la Catehismul calvinesc,* published in 1645, was a refutation of the Calvinist Catechism that George Rakoczy had allowed to be printed and circulated among the Valachians.[17] The other work, of a more dogmatic nature, his *Cele Septe Taine* [*On the Seven Sacraments*], also printed in 1645, defended the theology of seven sacraments against the rejection of all but Baptism and the Eucharist by the Protestants.[18]

METROPOLITAN DOSOFTEI (1624-1693)[19]

Bishop, and later metropolitan, of Moldavia, Dosoftei was one of the most gifted churchmen in Rumania in the 17th century. Having received a solid classical education in Greek and Latin in Lvov, Dosoftei knew Latin, Greek, and Slavonic well. His greatest contribution to Rumanian theology consisted in his zeal for promoting the Rumanian language as a suitable medium for the Divine Liturgy and for printing books of theology and spirituality. At Ouniev in Poland, he published a large number of translations from the Greek and Slavonic into Rumanian. If we consider Dosoftei as perhaps the best theologian of his century in Rumania, we can formulate a fairly accurate notion of the level of theology at that time. Utilizing the printing presses at Ouniev and at Jassy, he prepared Rumanian translations of the Slavonic and Greek liturgical books, such as the *Liturgy* of St. John Chrysostom, the *Octoich* and a book of the *Parameia* readings.[20] He translated the *Psalter* in 1673 into Rumanian verse, the first printed work of Rumanian poetry, and published an outstanding complete *Lives of the Saints* in Rumanian, printed in Jassy (1682-1686) and later translated into Russian and printed in Moscow. Liturgical books and the *Lives of the Saints,* therefore, for the most part direct translations from Slavonic and Greek, constitute the major activity of Dosoftei's theology, as well as being typical of the theological production of others. However, Dosoftei, by his printing of such works in Rumanian, was raising the general level of education for the day when more creative theologizing would be possible through a well-developed native language.

NICOLAE MILESCU[21]

A contemporary of Dosoftei, Nicolae Milescu continued in the tradition of the chroniclers, such as Grigore Ureche who told the history of Moldavia. Milescu was one of the most colorful personages of 17th century Rumania, because of his excellent education and life of constant travel which allowed him to serve on diplomatic missions for his country in the France of Louis XIV, in Russia, China, and Scandinavia. He typified in his breadth of vision a mixture of Western and Eastern cultures. A polyglot of great talent, Milescu wrote chiefly in Rumanian and Slavonic, although he was equally well versed in Greek and Latin. His theological writings center more along the lines of Oriental traditions, as may be seen in his translation from the Greek of various writings of St. Athanasios of Alexandria dealing with the problems of dogma, the nature of God, Trinity, Mariology, angelology, eschatology, the devil, and the nature of sin.[22]

Perhaps Milescu's greatest contribution to theology was his excellent translation from Greek into Rumanian of the Old Testament [*Vechiul Testament*].[23] This undoubtedly formed the basis for the famous Rumanian Bible of 1688

commissioned by Prince Serban Cantacuzenus (1678-1688).
E. Picot maintains that Milescu was responsible for the entire
translation,[24] while C. Solomon[25] and N. Cartojan[26] insist that
the two brothers, Radu and Serban Greceanu, were the
translators. In any case, this translation of the Old Testament
and that of the New Testament by Simon-Stefan in 1648[27]
provided a model for the compilers of the 1688 Bible that
would become one of the greatest pieces of literature written
in the classical Rumanian language.

Another interesting theological work of Milescu is his
Enchiridion, written in Latin at the request of the French
ambassador to Sweden in order to understand the Orthodox
position towards transubstantiation in the light of the heated
French controversy between the Port-Royalists and the
Jesuits.[28]

Milescu served in Russia as a counsellor to Peter the
Great and there had occasion to become familiar with the
theological work being done in the academies of Kiev and
Moscow, and he translated many of these works.

The age of literature confining itself to historical
chronicles was rapidly coming to an end with the 17th
century writers, Grigore Ureche, Miron Costin, Ion Neculce,
and Stolnic Cantacuzenus, all influenced by the education
they had received in Poland and by Polish chroniclers. Also
before Rumanian theological thought could unfold, a strong
reaction against Hellenism in Rumanian religious life had
to set in. This followed upon Greek influences brought into
Rumanian ecclesiastical life during the reigns of Serban
Cantacuzenus (1678-1688) and Constantin Brancoveanu
(1688-1714) in Valachia. Brancoveanu reorganized the Greek
school in Bucharest and entrusted it to the Greek, Sevastos
Kimentes. Greek professors from Constantinople and elsewhere were brought to Valachia to spread Byzantine culture.
Brancoveanu established five printing presses for the Rumanian, Greek, Slavonic, Arabic, and Georgian languages at
Buzau, Snagov, Rimnic, and Tirgoviste, but next to the Ru-

manian books printed, Greek books easily took a second place in the number published.

Patriarch Dositheos of Jerusalem and his nephew, Chrysanthos Notaras, both came to Rumania to manage the publication of Greek apologetical and polemical works against Protestants and Roman Catholics, works they hoped would stave off the proselytizing efforts of these two Christian Churches among the Rumanian as well as the Greek Orthodox.[29]

From 1711 to 1821 the Turks sent Greek princes and wealthy merchants, called Phanariots, to rule in effect the political and economic life in Valachia and Moldavia. Their generous contributions to the Greek monasteries of Mount Athos, Jerusalem, Constantinople, and Mount Sinai brought about such an anomaly that by the 19th century one-fifth of Rumania belonged to Greek monks or the Patriarchate of Constantinople.[30]

The educated class in Rumania read and spoke Greek, and the principal theological works consisted of translations from Greek works such as that done by Metropolitan Antim Ivireanu (d. 1716), one of the most cultivated prelates of this period. Still, he strove to offset the strong influence of the Greek language by writing in the vernacular and building up a sense of national patriotism.[31] But the greatest impetus to nationalism and an intellectual renaissance was to come from Transylvania through a movement that was both unifying and dividing in its effects upon the Rumanian nation and the Church.

THE UNIATES OF TRANSYLVANIA

Once the Turks withdrew after bitter fighting against the Polish and Austrian armies, Transylvania in 1688 became a part of Catholic Austria. Social and economic conditions were very low due to the lengthy wars and the excessive taxes levied upon the Rumanians living in that region. The majority of these Rumanians were Orthodox who were not recognized among the four privileged religions under Emperor Leopold I, namely, Catholic, Lutheran, Calvinist, and Unitarian. Leopold in 1698 promised equal privileges to the Orthodox hierarchs and clergy, provided they would become one of the four recognized religions. In two general synods of the clergy under Bishop Theophilus (d. 1697) and Bishop Athanasius Angel (1697-1713), it was decided upon by the majority of the clergy to unite with Rome, while keeping their own liturgical rite and ecclesiastical discipline. On October 7, 1698, in the Synod of Alba Julia presided over by Bishop Athanasius, 2,270 Rumanian priests officially accepted union with Rome.

In 1700 the "Biserica Unita" [Uniate Church] of Transylvania numbered 200,000. With the financial aid from Catholic Austria and the influx of Western Catholic religious groups such as the Jesuits, Franciscans, Passionists, and many other religious orders of both men and women, a cultural renaissance was soon launched that would have lasting effects upon Rumanian theology. Under the powerful triumvirate of Bishop Ioan (Samuel) Innocent Micu-Klein (1728-1751), Gheorghe Sincai (d. 1816), and priest-monk and later bishop, Petru Maior (d. 1821), a network of outstanding Rumanian-Latin schools beginning in Blaj was set up throughout Transylvania. Teachers, especially the Jesuits in Cluj and Alba Julia, educated in the leading universities of Italy, France, and Germany, returned to Transylvania to organize free schools for the populace.

Micu-Klein had studied in Blaj and Vienna and returned to Blaj to teach mathematics and write books that were most needed in the first free Rumanian schools that hitherto had taught from Greek and Slavonic books. He produced some 40 works at a time when Rumanian literature was still in its infancy. These works dealt with theology, philosophy, history, and philology and brought much of the best of Western thought into Rumanian literature, especially concerning theology.[32]

Gheorghe Sincai had made his studies at Cluj, Targul-Mures, Blaj, Rome, and Vienna, where he studied canon law and pedagogy. From 1782 to 1794 he was director of the Rumanian schools in Transylvania, during which time he worked to increase and consolidate the school system. He composed a quantity of catechisms, grammars and text books.[33]

Petru Maior, a classmate of Sincai in studies made in Rome and Vienna, taught logic and natural law in Blaj, but left due to tensions with Bishop Ioan Bob who was not favorable towards intellectuals of Petru's caliber. Working in a small parish, he published many works that provided both the Catholic Uniates and the Orthodox with much needed works in philosophy and theology.[34]

Another intellectual leader who strove to elevate the level of education in Transylvania by erecting schools and writing theological works was Bishop Petru Pavel Aaron (1752-1764). He opened secondary schools, diocesan seminaries, established printing presses and published liturgical as well as theological and historical works.[35]

From these free schools and the abundant literature, both religious and profane, written in the popular dialect, there developed a burning spirit of nationalism. Blaj produced many literate patriots who sought to rid the Rumanian speaking parts of Transylvania, Valachia and Moldavia from both the Greeks and the Hungarians. Timothe Cipariu (d. 1887) was a pioneer in fostering a history of the Rumanian language which would be very influential in forming Rumanian civilization. His monumental work on Rumanian philology was entitled *Chrestomathie*.[36] Through him and others forces were building up in Transylvania towards an autonomous and united Rumania. The Cyrillic alphabet was replaced by the Latin. Slavonic and Greek words that had become assimilated into the spoken Rumanian language now were replaced by more ancient Latin words.

In 1859 the two assemblies of the independent principalities of Valachia and Moldavia elected Colonel Alexandur Ioan Cuza (d. 1866) as the first prince for the country that Turkey and the other leading European powers from 1861 recognized as Rumania. Although Cuza set about to organize the new country on a solid, disciplined basis, he also enacted some laws contrary to the Orthodox tradition, such as allowing divorce and secularizing large monastic estates. He did, however, organize the Rumanian Orthodox Church as autocephalous in 1864, a fact that would be recognized by Constantinople only in 1885.[37]

One last intellectual leader who greatly contributed to the building of a united Rumania and a more articulate theology was Bishop Andrei Saguna, Orthodox bishop of Blaj, who founded in 1849 the theological seminary at Sibiu, which is still one of the two outstanding centers of theological learning in modern Rumania. At Blaj he founded in 1855 a printing press that furnished the Orthodox Church with its own liturgical books. Saguna is most famous for his theological works such as *Teologia Morala, Marturisirea ortodoxa* and *Chiriacodromiomul,* along with an extensive church history.[38] He founded in 1853 one of the early Rumanian newspapers called *Telegraful Romin* along with the annual publication of *Dreptul Canonic Oriental* which was concerned with the publishing and commenting on Oriental canon law. He founded *Astra* in 1861 in Sibiu which was a cultural society for Rumanians who wished to foster those elements that were unique in Rumanian culture.

In spite of the openness to Western culture that the renaissance of the 18th and 19th centuries developed, there was, especially theologically, a great dependence upon Russia. One of the great links between Russia and Rumania was Paisii Velichkovskii.

PAISII VELICHKOVSKII

In a period of openness to Western theology, Paisii Velichkovskii (1722-1794) served to ground not only Rumanian theology but above all Rumanian spirituality upon the best traditions in Byzantine monasticism.[39] Born in Poltava, Ukraine, he was early attracted to the asceticism of the early Fathers of the desert. After theological studies in the Academy of Kiev, he lived as a monk in the monasteries of the Pecherskii Lavra in Kiev, St. Nicholas in Moldavia, St. Nicholas in Valachia, and finally on Mount Athos. He attracted so many Russian and Rumanian monks to his skete of St. Elias that he moved it eventually to Moldavia. His community soon divided into 300 monks at Sekoul and 700 at Neamt. He organized in both monasteries large groups of translators, copyists, and correctors whose task was to produce translations and scientific revisions of the leading theological and spiritual works of the Fathers of both East and West.

Paisii's famous work, *Dobrotoloubie* [*The Love of the Good*], was his translation into Slavonic from the Greek *Philokalia* of Nikodim of Mount Athos and Macarios of Corinth. Thus, this rich collection of Hesychast writings drawn from the most orthodox spiritual writers of early times was made available to Rumanian, Russian, and other Slavic Christians. This started a renaissance of Orthodox spirituality not only among monks but also among the laity living in Rumania and the Slavic countries, especially Russia, that centered around the Jesus Prayer. Through his other spiritual writings and translations of Byzantine classics, and even more through his formation of disciples who later became the spiritual guides and monastic superiors in Rumania and Russia, a spiritual revival took place that continued until the Russian Revolution in 1917.

A host of students was sent to Cernauti in Bukovina and to the academies of Moscow and St. Petersburg to study theology. Professors and writers, such as Melchisec Stefanescu, Hristofor Scriban, Ghenadie Enaceanu, Silvestru Balanescu, Constantin Nazarie, Nicolae Filip, Gerasim Miron, the brothers, V. P. and G. Samureanu, and Clement Bontea had studied in Russia and helped to form Rumanian theology in much the same way as they had been taught in the Russian theological schools.[40]

THEOLOGICAL EDUCATION

A continuance of Russian influence was the direct result of the Turko-Russian War of 1828-1829. The Treaty of Adrianople (September 14, 1829) gave Russia a virtual protectorate over the two Rumanian principalities of Valachia and Moldavia. Through the efforts of Count Paul Kiselev, who governed more according to the writings of Voltaire and Diderot than the Russian models with which he was familiar, an ordered government was secured that replaced the chaos and instability of former centuries. The *Reglement Organique* attempted to formulate a constitutional regime ruled conjointly by the prince and the special assembly [*Adunare*]. Education was vastly improved, especially under the rule of Voda Sturdza.

Theological seminaries, modeled on those in Russia, were established throughout many of the dioceses. In 1803 Metropolitan Veniamin founded a very simple type of seminary connected with the monastery of Socola, which was expanded in 1840 into an outstanding theological faculty. In 1835 the central seminary of Rumania was founded to serve the diocese of Rimnic, Buzau, and Arges, and the following year a seminary was established in Bucharest, which would evolve into a complete theological academy. Other seminaries were founded for the dioceses of Buzau and Arges in the same year and in 1837 for Rimnic. Besides teaching grammar, arithmetic, geography, and liturgical chant, more theological subjects such as dogmatic theology, pastoral, Biblical history, church history and canon law formed the bulk of the seminaries' curriculum. Some of the leading theologians in this early stage of Rumanian theology were Nicolae Balasescu, Zaharia Boerescu, Gavril Munteanu, Dionisie Romano, and Radu Tempea.[41]

With the formation of seminaries and a serious curriculum in theology the manuals that served both the lecturers and the students were translated generally from Russian and Greek with gradual adaptation until original textbooks by native Rumanian theologians were soon being written. One of the outstanding translators of classical theological works from Greek into Rumanian was the monk of Neamt, later metropolitan, Grigorie Dascalul (d. 1834).[42] He was one of two monks commissioned by Metropolitan Veniamin to translate the principal dogmatic works of St. John Damascene used in his seminary at Socola. In 1803 they translated Damascene's *Exposition of the Orthodox Faith* in question and answer form and in 1806 finished his *Dogmatica* or *Doctrine of the Fathers*. Grigorie continued to translate works, such as St. Augustine's commentary on the Psalms (1814), the *Apologia* of St. Dimitrii of Rostov (1816), and the Ἐπιστομὴ τῶν Θείων δογμάτων of Athanasios of Paros. Made metropolitan of Valachia, he continued his work of translating the works of Cassian, Basil the Great, and Gregory of Nazianzos.

THE AGE OF COMPENDIA

The middle of the 19th century witnessed, as did also Greece at the same time, the multiplication of theological compendia to serve the newly established seminaries. The priest-monk, Melchisedec, professor of Socola and then Husi, is a typical compiler of compendia of this period. In 1857 he translated the Catechism of Filaret of Moscow.[43] All areas of theology were upen to his synthetic mind. He produced compendia in basic theology,[44] dogmatic theology,[45] on the liturgical typikon,[46] an introduction to the Old and New Testaments,[47] an explanation of canon law,[48] on pastoral theology,[49] and on the liturgy.[50] Other writers of theological compendia during this period include Filaret Scriban,[51] Neofit Scriban,[52] and Teoctist Scriban.[53]

Others whose theological compendia circulated throughout the seminaries of Rumania at this time were Nifon Balasescu, Gavrill Munteanu, Zaharia Boerescu, Damaschin Bojinca, Radu Tempea, and Dionsie Romano.[54]

THEOLOGICAL PERIODICALS[55]

Perhaps no Orthodox country has enjoyed as great a productivity as Rumania in the apostolate of the printed word. This is seen clearly in the history of its theological periodicals that developed not only in great quantity but also in superior quality in the second half of the 19th century until the present.

The first attempt at any theological-religious journal was made by Archimandrite Dionisie Romano (later bishop of Buzau) and Professor Gavril Munteanu. In 1839 they launched the religious newspaper called *Vestitorul bisericesc.* It lasted only two years but Dionisie tried again in 1850 to print a new ecclesiastical review, *Eho eclisiastic,* featuring studies on the Old and New Testaments.

The oldest review still in existence is the *Telegraful Romin,* founded in 1853 in Sibiu by the Transylvanian Metropolitan Andrei Saguna. Most ecclesiastical and theological reviews and newspapers, however, did not have the longevity of Saguna's paper. From 1857 to 1859 in Bucharest Ilie Benescu edited the *Predicatorul* which attempted to present a more systematic presentation of the faith and answers to modern moral problems. In Moldavia (1861-

1864) Clement Nicolau and Deacon Inocentie printed a paper that was aimed at elevating the theological and spiritual formation of the clergy, called the *Preotul*. A more ambitious publication edited in 1864 by Archimandrite Isaia Teodorescu, the director of the Socola Seminary at Jassy, was entitled: *Predicatorul moralului evanghelic si al umanitatii*. In Bucharest, G. Musceleanu published in 1862 *Biserica* which was soon replaced in 1864 by *Anuntiatorul bisericesc*. After Cuza had established the autonomy of the Rumanian Church, Carol Scarlat Rosetti in 1866 edited *Ecclesia* which primarily fought for full recognition by Constantinople and the other Orthodox Churches of the autocephaly of the Rumanian Orthodox Church.

The most important official publication was founded in 1874 by the Holy Synod, *Biserica Orthodoxa Romina,* which is still printed today as the monthly official organ of the Rumanian Patriarchate. Of more theological content was the *Revista Teologica* founded in Jassy in 1883 by Constantin Erbiceanu and Dragomir Demetrescu. *Ortodoxul,* edited in 1880 by G. Zottu, professor of Greek and canon law at the Nifon Seminary, aimed to produce longer and more scientific articles dealing with modern theological problems as well as presenting translations from Greek and Latin writers such as St. John Chrysostom and Tertullian.

The clergy's continued education was fostered by such publications as *Desteptarea,* printed in Jassy in 1882, and the clergy review of Bucharest, *Amnonul. Vointa Bisericci Romine,* printed in Bucharest in 1894, was the first theological journal that sought to collaborate with professors and students studying in the European seminaries and universities, especially in Leipzig, Berlin, and Vienna.

At the present time, the Rumanian Patriarchate publishes through its official printing organ, *The Bible and Orthodox Missionary Institute,* the three most important reviews: *Biserica Orthodoxa Romina, Ortodoxia,* and *Studii Teologice.* The first, published monthly with a circulation of 60,000, issues the official church documents. *Ortodoxia* is a quarterly journal that deals with theological and ecclesiastical problems of interest to non-Orthodox Christians as well as to Orthodox. The authors demonstrate a fair knowledge of Western Christian literature, especially in the area of ecumenical theology.[56] Its chief aim is to formulate through learned articles a theology that is relevant and missionary to the contemporary world. *Studii Teologice* is also a monthly review published by the two theological institutes of Bucharest and Sibiu and contains outstanding theological articles written by professors of these institutes and students seeking the master or doctoral degree. A great emphasis on patristic theology is found in the articles, especially those authored by Professors Ioan Coman and D. Staniloae. In addition, this journal is concerned with non-Christian religions and archaeology, particularly the Western scholarship done on the Dead Sea Scrolls. The ecclesiastical reviews published by the various metropolias, with a total circulation of about 80,000, deal more specifically with the problems of priestly education, homiletics, pastoral problems, and spirituality of the laity.[57]

REFORM OF THEOLOGICAL SEMINARIES

Educational reforms on all levels, including theological education, were effected by the minister of public instruction, Mihail Kogalniceau in 1860. The faculties of the seminaries of Bucharest, Arges, Rimnic, and Buzau were reorganized with excellent professors and a more serious theological curriculum. Theologians such as Meletie Miclescu, Grigorie Ghica, and the two Scriban brothers sought to raise the standard of theology taught in these seminaries. In Moldavia Professors Melchisedec, Filaret Scriban, V. Suhopan, Ieronim Butureanu, and Ghenade Popescu contributed to a superior theology taught in the seminaries, especially on the faculty of theology in the University of Jassy.

In 1890 the State recognized the Bucharest Seminary as a faculty of the University and granted higher degrees largely because of the academic excellence of such professors as N. Nitulescu, Gherasim Timus, Ghendaie Enaceanu, C. Erbiceanu, Pimen Georgescu, Alexandru Mironescu, Barbu Constantinescu and Seimeon Popescu.[58] The outstanding professor at Sibiu, Nicolae Balan, was made metropolitan in 1920 and was influential in granting to Sibiu equal status with the theological faculty of Bucharest in 1923.

The greatest churchman that the Rumanian Orthodox Church has seen is Patriarch Justinian Marina, consecrated in 1948. During his pontificate he has striven to reform and develop both Rumanian monasticism and the theological quality of seminarians and professors of theology. Today his seminary reforms demand that all interested in becoming priests (the 9,400 priests provide one priest for 1,500 faithful) should finish some level of theological training. This basically consists of five years spent in such seminaries as Bucharest, Neamt, Cluj, Craiova, Caransebes and Buzau. The first two years of the cycle are spent in a school of liturgical chant and the other three in a seminary leading to ordination. From among the better students who qualify by passing the examinations, candidates are chosen for the two higher theological institutes at Bucharest and Sibiu. Here the students who will eventually form the higher clergy of Rumania spend five years in one of the four theological sections offered for specialization: biblical, historical, systematic and practical theology. Courses in the biblical section deal with the study and exegesis of the Old Testament, biblical archaeology and the study of the Hebrew language, study and exegesis of the New Testament, Biblical hermeneutics and the Greek language.

Students specializing in history study the history of the universal Church, patrology, and the Latin language, the history of the Rumanian Church and its literature, the Slavonic language and its literature. Systematic theology centers on the study of basic theology with the study of the Latin language and the history of religions, dogmatic theology and the Greek language, the Creed, Christian morality, and missionary guidance. In the practical section, preaching and catechetics are stressed; canon law and administration, liturgy, Christian art and pastoral theology are also studied, together with a modern language such as Russian, French, English, and German.

After passing the oral examinations, the candidates must present a written work of at least 80 pages in order to receive the licentiate degree. Those desiring a higher degree, the master's, can continue study only at Bucharest, which is the sole theological academy able to grant the higher degrees in theology. Each year for three years the student must submit a work of at least 150 pages that is usually printed in the two leading theological reviews: *Studii Teologice* and *Ortodoxia.* One seeking the doctorate studies three more years after having obtained the master's degree and again must continue each year to submit a work of 150 pages. At the end he must submit to a grueling examination before a commission appointed by the patriarch and defend a thesis as well.

Flaviu Popan attributes the very viable, contemporary theology that is being developed in the two Rumanian academies of theology today to the emphasis on a theology that is socially oriented and that finds an apt vehicle of expression in the many theological periodicals.[59] Refresher courses are given by correspondence and in seminars to aid the priests already graduated from the seminaries to keep informed of the development of theology and its application to the modern scene, especially in terms of the social apostolate.

To aid in this, Patriarch Justinian has authored seven volumes of a work dealing with the social apostolate:

Apostolat Social,[60] as well as a popular explanation of the Gospels and sermons[61] for the Sundays of the year, which follows an early work of Nikifor Theotokes, the *Kyriako-dromion.*

DOGMATIC THEOLOGY

Popan, one of the few modern authors who has written about modern Rumanian theology, criticizes somewhat negatively the "new" theology that is evident in many of the articles that appear in Rumanian theological reviews.[62] Whatever criticism may be brought to bear against these articles, it does not apply to the theological books, mostly textbooks, printed in Rumania during the 20th century. The earlier books represented to a great degree translations from the standard works, especially dogmatic treatises, of Russian theologians of the late 19th century such as Peter Ternovskoi, Antonii Amfiteatrov, Makarii Bulgakov, Filaret Gumilevskii, Silvestr Malevanskii, and Filaret Drozdov. Alexis Khomiakov was also very influential in formulating an ecclesiology within the Rumanian Church.[63] C. Androutsos' Δογματικὴ τῆς 'Ορθοδόξου 'Ανατολικῆς 'Εκκλησίας along with his Συμβολικὴ formed the basis both in content and format, first in translation and then in adaptation, for original Rumanain compendia.[64]

Original Rumanian dogmatic treatises were written at the end of the 19th century and the beginning of the 20th but represent the traditional dogmatic teachings of the standard Orthodox Russian and Greek textbooks of the 19th century. Protopriest Melchisedec is the first Rumanian to have composed a dogmatic textbook, entitled, *Teologia Dogmatica a Bisericii Ortodoxe.*[65] Metropolitan Silvestru Andrievici of Bukovina,[66] Alexiu Comorosan,[67] Iosif Olariu,[68] and Metropolitan Irineu Mihalcescu[69] all produced solid and traditional manuals of dogmatic theology.

A look at the latest dogmatic theological manual, *Teologia Dogmatica si Simbolica,* produced under the general editorship of Professors Nicolae Chitescu, Isidor Todoran and I. Petreuta, bears out the same impression of a solid and traditional theology in continuity with the best of Orthodox teaching in the past.[70] Following the general plan of Androutsos' work, a general history of dogmatics in the Orthodox, Roman Catholic and Protestant traditions is given. The authors seem well versed, even beyond the bibliography given by Androutsos, in the latest literature of Roman Catholic and Protestant writers. It might be added here that most of the professors at Bucharest and Sibiu had studied in the West and have been very familiar with the theological literature of Europe at least through the 1940's.[71]

In dealing, then, with the sources of dogmatic theology of the Orthodox Church, this textbook outlines the two sources of Holy Scripture and Tradition. It touches on the necessary static formulation of dogma but offsets it with the Orthodox Church's teaching on *economia.* The position of the Roman Catholic theologians on implicit and virtual revelation in tradition is rejected for a more dynamic view of collegiality or *Sobornost'* according to Khomiakov's teaching.[72]

The three leading Confessions forming the main symbolic books for Rumanian Orthodoxy are listed as: Mogila's *Confession,* that of Dositheos and the 1848 *Encyclical* of the Orthodox Patriarchs. The secondary confessions enjoying lesser authority include the *Confessions of Gennadios Scholarios* and *Mitrophanes Critopoulos,* the *Responses of Patriarch Jeremias II to the Tübingen Theologians* and the *Catechisms* of Platon Levshin, Filaret of Moscow and those of the Greek writers, C. Iconomos, I. Mesoloras and Diomedes Kyriakos.[73] Part II deals with the one nature of God, Trinity and God as Redeemer, Sanctifier and Judge. The work as a whole veers very little away from the treatise on dogmatics of Androutsos.

Patriarch Justinian, in an attempt to develop the theological formation of his priests, gathered, during the summers of 1949 to 1951, the leading professors of theology from the academies of Bucharest and Sibiu at his villa in Dragoslavele and commissioned them to produce standard textbooks to be used in the seminaries of Rumania. Not all of these have been printed as yet, since the Communist government seems somewhat reluctant to produce books in quantity that develop in argumentative form theological doctrines that would negate its own atheistic approach to Rumanian life. However, the Rumanian Orthodox Church, through the agency of *The Bible and Orthodox Missionary Institute,* seems to fare much better than in the other Communist dominated countries, including Yugoslavia, in printing theological works.

One of the weakest and less developed branches of Rumanian theology seems to be that of Old and New Testament studies. This area shows the evident lack of contact with Western scriptural scholarship. Western studies are cited from 1950 to the present only through book lists. In the standard textbook used today, *Studiul Vechiului Testament,* a rather negative approach to new scholarship is taken in denying the four traditions responsible for the Pentateuch accounts. Moses is defended as the author of the Pentateuch, while the Prophet Isaiah is credited as the author of chapters 40 to 66, written before the Babylonian captivity.[74]

Although a new textbook of exegesis on the Old Testament is being prepared, an outdated work by Professor Nicolae Neaga of Sibiu[75] is still being used. It is, however, quite inadequate since it treats the Old Testament only from the Messianic viewpoint.

The textbook printed in 1954 on the New Testament, *Studiul Noului Testament,* is quite conservative in its presentation of inspiration, canonicity and the history of the New Testament text. Verbal inspiration is maintained as well as the authenticity of Matthew's Gospel as written by him originally in Hebrew and then translated into Greek to form the basic first Gospel text from which Mark depended.[76]

In regard to the study of patrology, one could regret the cessation of the excellent series begun in the late 30's and 40's at Sibiu that provided not only patristic series in Rumanian but also critical texts of superior quality. The outstanding patrologist, Professor Dumitru Staniloae of Sibiu, was greatly responsible for these editions. His principal works include an authoritative life of St. Gregory Palamas,[77] and four out of the seven proposed books translated into Rumanian from the original Greek *Philokalia.*[78] This outstanding contribution to the sources of the *"pneumatic"* Fathers has insisted on creating a synthesis in the thought of the Fathers found in the *Philokalia.* Staniloae in Volume I deals with the great hermits, ascetics and contemplatives. Volumes II and III present mainly the theological synthesis of Maximos the Confessor, while Volumes IV and V were to give a new synthesis of both theory and practice through the writings of Symeon the New Theologian. The last two volumes yet to be printed are to give the Hesychast Fathers of the 11th through the 14th centuries, especially the writings of Gregory Palamas.

The leading patrologist of Bucharest is Ioan Coman who authored the textbook, *Patrologie,* used throughout Rumania in all the seminaries. This work, through an excellent synthesis of the theological thought of each Father presented, illustrates how the doctrine of the Greek Fathers forms the basis of Orthodox theology. Coman deals in great detail with the theological contribution of Gregory of Nyssa and shows how influential he has been in later Orthodox theology through his ideas on the Trinity, Christology and anthropology.[79]

The textbook used in the course on Ethics, *Curs de Teologie Morala,* is representative of a fairly conservative approach to morality, giving the traditional presentation of moral order, the natural and positive law, the evangelical counsels of the New Testament, duties and rights, free will, virtues and sin. In the special section dealing with social ethics, the stress is placed upon the individual and his spiritual powers to act in a morally right way. The state cannot be venerated or respected except as an agency representing the will and interests of the people, and hence individuals are obligated to give to society what it needs to perform its mission so that human beings can live in an atmosphere that guarantees free exercise of man's spiritual powers.[80]

ECUMENICAL THEOLOGY

Although Rumanian theologians were represented at the early international ecumenical conferences at Stockholm (1925), Lausanne (1927), Oxford (1937) and other gatherings, there was no true enthusiasm among Rumanian churchmen for ecumenical dialogue. This undoubtedly was due to many factors, chief among which should be counted the distrust of other Churches resulting from past political pressures placed upon the Rumanian Orthodox, especially those living in Transylvania under Austrian Catholic and Hungarian Protestant domination as well as the political submission to Soviet Russia. Representatives of the Rumanian Church participated in the Pan-Orthodox Synod of Moscow in 1948 and agreed to suspend any participation in inter-Church discussions. When the Russian Church made open overtures to join the World Council of Churches in 1961 and actually did so, the Rumanian Orthodox did likewise.[81]

A very special bond of sympathy has long existed between the Rumanian Orthodox Church and the Church of England.[82] In 1935 theologians from both Churches met in Bucharest and effected the closest agreement hitherto made by any Orthodox Church with a non-Orthodox body. Archbishop Ramsey of Canterbury visited Patriarch Justinian in June, 1965 and His Beatitude returned the visit to England in

1966. The leading ecumenical figure representing the Rumanian Church in most international meetings is Metropolitan Justin Moisescu of Jassy, who heads a special commission for dialogue with the Anglicans along with such other noted theologians as Bishop Antim, Professors Todoran, Liviu Stan, Chitescu, Rezus and Staniloae. Other commissions for dialogue with the Oriental (non-Chalcedonian) Churches and the Old-Catholics have been created. The first include as members Bishop Antim and Professor Tudor Popescu, while Professor Ioan Coman heads the latter commission.

Lack of contacts with theologians from abroad and, above all, with their literature, along with a constant surveillance by the regime, has hindered a fuller cooperation. Still, an evident change has taken place in the openness of the Rumanian theologians to the changes taking place among all Christian Churches, especially among the Protestant groups participating in the World Council of Churches, as well as post-Vatican II Roman Catholicism. Interest has been created, at least through written articles, in effecting greater understanding and union with the non-Chalcedonian Churches. Practically every issue of the review *Ortodoxia* contains an article on the theology or history of these ancient Oriental Churches or some phase of the ecumenical dialogue with the Protestant and Roman Catholic Churches.[83] In many ways Rumanian Orthodoxy, deeply rooted in the traditional Orthodox faith, is still the most Western of all Orthodox Churches in its thinking and openness to dialogue with non-Orthodox Christians, and is in a position to function as a true bridge between Western non-Orthodox Christians and the Eastern Orthodox themselves.

MONASTICISM

One of the great reforms of Patriarch Justinian has been to rejuvenate Orthodox monasticism in Rumania. Exact statistics are difficult to obtain on the number of monks in Rumania. In 1955 there were 199 monasteries opened with an estimated 8,500 monks and nuns, an exaggerated 400 persons for each monastery.[84] Jean Lecerf reports that in the women's monastery of Agapia there were 300 nuns living a very dynamic monastic life.[85]

Young students, dissatisfied with Marxism as an answer to life's problems, have been attracted to the monasteries that have had no dearth of vocations. Patriarch Justinian has insisted that monks and nuns be of service to the country by their works. Many monasteries have been formed into state cooperatives and produce in their workshops carpets, vestments, candles, church utensils as well as books. According to the *Regulations for Organizing Monastic Life* (1959), anyone entering a monastery under 50 years of age must have had seven years of elementary schooling plus two years in a chanter school. Thus, through elevating the intellectual preparation of the monks and nuns, the Rumanian Church has restored to its life a most valuable contribution by deeply spiritual and intellectual monks and nuns who continue the glories of earlier Rumanian monasticism when monasteries were the chief centers of Rumanian culture and theology.

SUPPRESSION OF THE UNIATE CHURCH

After the Second World War, the Communist regime in Rumania subjected the Catholic Uniate Church in Transylvania to destructive persecutions. On October 21, 1948, a law was passed officially suppressing this Church which possessed 1,560,000 faithful. A dynamic Church of five dioceses, three major seminaries, 1,800 parishes, 2,588 churches, 1,834 priests and members of nine religious orders who conducted schools, orphanages and hospitals, as well as operating 20 weekly or monthly periodicals and five printing presses, was suppressed and its property confiscated by the government or turned over to the Orthodox Church. The excellent school system set up by the Rumanian Uniates added a great deal of intellectual stimulus to the Orthodox Church, and its suppression constitutes a loss to the total intellectual and cultural life of Rumania.

In February, 1949 the Holy Synod promulgated a new constitution for the organization and functioning of the Rumanian Church. It includes five metropolias, each with its own suffragan dioceses numbering 12. At present there are an estimated 8,568 parishes with over 9,400 priests. The Rumanian Government does not apparently seek to eliminate the Orthodox Church from its social life and even pays the salaries of the clergy. Very little atheistic propaganda is in evidence, and whatever has been produced has come through translations of Russian publications. In a country with an atheistic government, most of the citizens are still believers and faithfully practice their religion.[86]

In the United States the Rumanian Orthodox are grouped under three jurisdictions. The Rumanian Orthodox Church and Canonical Episcopate of America directly under the Patriarch of Rumania number only 20,000 faithful. The second body is the Rumanian Orthodox Episcopate of the Western Hemisphere, which is under the ecclesiastical jurisdiction of the Russian Synodal Church in Exile. The third and most well established group of 60,000 members is the Rumanian Orthodox Episcopate of America under the protection of the Russian-American Orthodox Metropolia.

No one can predict the future of Rumanian theology. If, however, Patriarch Justinian can continue to develop monasticism, to raise the intellectual level of his priests, and to encourage his theologians to develop not only a scholarly theology based solidly upon the best of Orthodox traditions, but also a viable theology in constant dialogue with the modern world, then Rumanian theology will soon establish itself as the leading, authoritative voice among all other Orthodox.

PART SIX

In Retrospect

THIS rapid review of Orthodox theology has been seen through the prism of the historical development of each major Orthodox country from 1453 until the present. One of the characteristics of any theology is that it should grow out of the living context of the believers, as an expression of their lived faith. This is especially true of Orthodox theology, which has always looked upon itself as an expression of a Christian witness to the Gospel. Thus the political, economic, social, cultural, and religious factors of any given epoch will also color the theology developed in those concrete circumstances.

Therefore, by concentrating on these factors in the Orthodox countries of Russia, the Greek-speaking countries, Bulgaria, Serbia, and Rumania, one is able to see the interplay of theology with the milieu in which it developed. This method has the evident drawback of following the history of Orthodox theology country by country. The pieces have to be put together. If a certain nation's historical development can influence the development of theology within its boundaries, there must also be an influence of one Orthodox Church upon another. This has been pointed out but rather obliquely. The Russians, for example, did not begin their theologizing in a vacuum. They were intrinsically dependent upon the Byzantine theology that came to them through Greece, Bulgaria, and the other Balkan countries. Greek theology after the fall of the Byzantine Empire (1453) also grew out of the eleven centuries of Byzantine theological development. Bulgaria, Serbia, and Rumania also in their theological origins drew through Slavonic translations from this rich heritage and later depended greatly upon Russia for theological books, teachers, and models for seminary training.

To look in retrospect at the history of Orthodox theology from the 15th century to the present, one must attempt to synthesize the various individual points developed in a specific fashion in these earlier chapters.

BYZANTINE THEOLOGY AS AN INHERITANCE

Three factors which greatly influenced Byzantine theology and which influenced the succeeding centuries of Orthodox theology down to the present were: the emperors, the monks, and the faithful. In the Byzantine πολιτεία of symphony between the temporal and the eternal orders, the emperors considered themselves guardians of the Orthodox faith, and even some, such as Justinian I, had visions of being outstanding theologians. Monasteries in a society that saw great and almost constant political and social upheavals performed the task of being carriers of theological traditions. This was done through the manuscripts harbored in the monasteries throughout the Byzantine Empire, as well as by the educational process carried on in the monastic schools. Finally, the laity never felt that theology was an exclusive domain of clerics only, but saw it as doctrinal speculation of a lived experience that vitally concerned them also.

Thus one characteristic of Orthodox theology common to all predominantly Orthodox countries is that theology is intimately tied to the concrete lives of rulers, monks, and laity.

ORTHODOX SCHOLASTICISM

Another distinguishing characteristic of Orthodox theology is its unique type of scholasticism. If theology were to evolve into a system of articulated truths that flowed from an inner faith experience, it also had to be based on man's use of his human reason. But the Orthodox theologian also had to be in touch with the theological reflections and conclusions of the Christian past before he could weave his speculations into an ordered system. Von Campenhausen calls St. Cyril of Alexandria the "first of the Byzantine scholastics."[1] For St. Cyril the royal road of theology was to investigate the beliefs of the Holy Fathers of the early Church and to reflect upon their insights.

Hence, Orthodox theology's type of scholasticism is rooted in the writings of the Holy Fathers. Like Western scholasticism, it too uses human reason, but its use is not independent and original in depth and form from that of the early Fathers. Georges Florovskii, fifteen centuries after St. Cyril could write, "This call to 'go back' to the Fathers can be easily misunderstood. It does not mean a return to the letter of old patristic documents . . . What is really meant and required is not a blind or servile imitation and repetition, but rather a further development of this patristic teaching, both homogeneous and congenial. We have to kindle again the creative fire of the Fathers, to restore in ourselves the patristic spirit."[2]

Still this dependence upon the Holy Fathers did not lead to the formation of distinct schools of Orthodox theology. In the West certain theological schools were formed as disciples followed almost exclusively the writings of certain key theologians as Thomas Aquinas, Duns Scotus, Bonaventure,

Suarez, and others. Eastern Christian theologians felt free to use the writings of all Orthodox thinkers in the patristic tradition. Some of these early writers, such as St. Athanasios, St. Basil, St. Gregory of Nazianzos, St. Gregory of Nyssa, St. Cyril of Alexandria, St. John Chrysostom, Pseudo-Dionysios, St. Maximus the Confessor, St. John Damascene and St. Gregory Palamas never became heads of theological schools.

Another reason for this lack of schools of theological thought was perhaps related to what was said above; namely, Orthodox theology never developed as a speculative science, divorced from the Christian life. Heresies in the first eight centuries of Christianity had forced the early Fathers to develop a theology on the dogmatic teachings of the essentials of Christianity. After that time, much of the Byzantine and Slavo-Greek theology was engaged in anti-Latin polemics and a "retaining" of patristic theology against the Arabs and Turks, often amidst persecution.

St. John Damascene only in the eighth century became the first Eastern Christian theologian to give a complete and methodical exposition of Christian doctrine. And yet, as popular as his dogmatic work on the Orthodox faith was for succeeding Orthodox theologians, he never constituted a school of thought distinct from that of the other Fathers of the Church. This was probably due to his express desire, which later became an accepted principle among Orthodox theologians, never to go beyond the limits of doctrine set by the earlier Fathers.

This does not mean that Orthodox theology rejected philosophical systems as underpinning for its speculation. In the first part of his Πηγὴ γνώσεως St. John Damascene makes use of the philosophical notions of being, essence, and nature which he takes from Aristotle, Porphyry, and Leontios of Byzantium. Photios, the outstanding scholar of the 9th century, showed great originality by his use of Scripture, the Fathers and philosophical reasoning in developing a doctrine on the procession of the Holy Spirit. Michael Psellos in the 11th century strove to reconcile philosophy with the teachings of the Church. But philosophy never played the same role in Orthodox theological speculation as it did in Western theology, and this colored the development of theology during the period under study, giving it a distinct characteristic, different from the West, yet of one piece with the patristic tradition that preceded it.

Instead of contrasting Western and Eastern theologies, if one were to ask which theology had the greater influence upon the other during the modern era, one would have to admit that the West, until now, has had a greater influence on the East than vice versa.

With the domination by the Turks and the Tatars of most of the Orthodox countries of Byzantine Christian origin, theological education in the Greek speaking countries, in Bulgaria, Serbia, Rumania and Russia was generally not highly developed until fairly recent times. The major theological writings were of a "retaining" nature, to pass on the Orthodox doctrines to new generations deprived of freedom to create a more articulated theology, or they were of a strictly polemical nature intended to defend Orthodox teaching of the first eight centuries against Latin and Protestant teaching. Nationalism also fostered a lack of inter-communication among the Orthodox countries themselves which did not allow for more unified theological positions beyond those articulated before the 15th century.

THE 15th AND 16th CENTURY—A PERIOD OF THEOLOGICAL TRANSITION

Once the Byzantine double-headed eagle came to stand on Russian soil as a symbol to the rest of the Orthodox world that Moscow had replaced the Second Rome, and Russian theology was recognized as the leading force by the other Orthodox Churches, the shift of creative theology from Byzantine to Slavic scholars was an accepted fact by all. Yet it would be only well into the 17th century when Russia would prove herself as the center of Orthodox theology.

As theology searched among the Slavs for lands freed of the Turkish yoke in which to develop with new life and vigor, a corpus of theological literature had already been bequeathed to the Slavs centuries before. The Bulgars, under Clement of Ochrid, Naum and Konstantin, had inherited the beginnings of a Slavonic theological literature from St. Cyril and St. Methodius and had increased it through the many translations of classical Greek works. These at first consisted primarily in works of a didactic and moralistic character with the works of St. John Chrysostom and St. John Damascene the favorite sources satisfying the basic moral and dogmatic needs of the newly Christianized Slavic countries. In an age of great insecurity and mass migrations, theological libraries often consisted of collections of sayings of the Holy Fathers, often without citing their names. The *Pandectes* of the 7th century monk Antiochos and the *Pandectes* and *Taktikon* of the 11th century monk, Nikon of Montenegro, were favorites among the Slavic Churches. Innumerable *Catenae, Palaia,* and *Paterika* were translated and recopied, bringing into Bulgaria, Serbia, and Russia patristic sources that nourished the piety of the monks and laity.

Russian churchmen such as Illarion of Kiev, Clement of Smolensk, Kirill of Turov, and Avraam of Smolensk show the first promise of a new creativity among the Slavs. Still, through the monasteries, fed intellectually by the translations of Byzantine works, theology remained for centuries, not only in Russia, but also in Bulgaria, Serbia, and Rumania, a theology of translations. The common Slavonic language did not encourage anything but a passive reception of a Byzantine theology highly developed for former times and meaningful for a past culture quite different from the emerging Slavic world.

Bulgarian theologians, as Ioan Exarch, distinguished themselves as translators from Greek to Slavonic. Exceptions were the Greeks, Theophylakt of Ochrid and Theodosios of Trnovo, who continued creating theology in the Byzantine and Hesychast traditions. But Patriarch Evfimi marked the first attempt to produce a theology that answered the needs of his time. This is seen in his many theological letters, especially those that deal with liturgical problems.

Serbian theology in the 15th and 16th centuries continued along lines similar to those developed in Bulgaria. Most of its early literature came from Old Slavonic translations made in Bulgaria and was concerned mostly with liturgical, canonical, and hagiographical subjects. It was largely of the same literary genre as that set by Sava in his translations of various monastic rules and the *Kormchaia Kniga*. Chroniclers told the story of Serbian rulers in their emigrations towards the Danube regions, but serious, original theology had to await more stable times and the formation of a fixed nationality with its own language.

Rumania, after initially embracing Latin Christianity, made contact with Byzantine Christianity through the Bulgarians who opened to them the rich treasury of Slavonic translations. Monasticism played an important role in translating the Slavonic language into Rumanian which, however, used the Cyrillic alphabet for this basically Latin language. Original literature in this period consisted of *Chronicles* and *Shorniks* (or collections, mainly of ascetical writings, lives of the Saints, and canonical material).

The Greeks suffered greatly from a lack of institutions of higher learning. And still they became the objects of a special courting by Protestants and Roman Catholics in the 16th and 17th centuries. Patriarch Jeremias II cut off any further dialogue with the Lutheran professors of Tübingen University in his responses (1576-1581) to their requests for a possible rapprochement.

Greek theology during the 16th century may be divided

into three main tendencies: an acceptance of certain features of Roman Catholic theology; an orientation towards Protestant thought, at least an espousal of basic Protestant principles; and a conservative Byzantine emphasis with accompanying anti-Catholic or anti-Protestant polemics. The latter tendency grew as Roman Catholic missionary activities, especially by Jesuits, Dominicans, and Franciscans in the Near and Middle East increased. The first two tendencies grew also due to the education of many Orthodox theologians in Germany, Italy, France, and England; for many Orthodox this was the only opportunity to obtain a higher education.

Among the Greek theologians of this period several, such as Manuel of Corinth, Meletios Pigas, Gabriel Severos, and, to some extent, Pachomios of Rhus, engaged strongly in anti-Latin polemics that repeat fairly exactly the arguments of Photios and Cerularius of earlier centuries on the problems of the *filioque,* the primacy, unleavened bread, and purgatory. Maximos Margounios exemplified the influence of Latin theology upon the Greek, while the early part of the following century would witness to the influence of Protestant theology upon Patriarch Lucaris.

SEVENTEENTH CENTURY

The 17th century witnessed in all the Orthodox countries the miracle of the printing press. The transcription of manuscripts which had occupied the monks for years in remote monasteries now was done in a very short time in cities, and copies were able to be duplicated by the thousands. This discovery paved the way for a thirst for learning on the popular level. Instead of being restricted to isolated monasteries, schools were to become the common possession of even the simplest village.

Orthodox presses were first established in Kiev and Western Russia, which had by this period become a part of the

Polish-Lithuanian Empire. Artisans from the West brought the latest equipment and techniques to establish Kiev, L'vov, and Ouniev as three leading printing centers. From these presses, especially that of the Pecherskii Lavra under Peter Mogila, printing type and experts were sent to Rumania, a country that enjoyed more freedom from the Turks than Serbia and Bulgaria. Jassy, Bucharest, and Blaj became key centers of printing Orthodox theological works in Greek, Rumanian, Slavonic, Arabic and even Georgian.

But education in Western Russia became modeled upon the humanism of the West, especially as taught in the Polish Jesuit schools of the Polish-Lithuanian Empire. Soon not only was Kievan theology taught in Latin, but Latin textbooks formed the basis for lectures as well as the compendia written in Russian.

As a result of the Brest-Litovsk Synod of 1596, millions of these Russian Orthodox embraced Roman Catholicism to form the Ruthenian Uniate Church. The tightened bonds of cultural dependence upon the West would have a lasting effect upon Russian theology, which not only in the Academy of Kiev but also in Moscow was of a highly Latin scholastic nature.

Prince Konstantin Ostrozhskii in Western Russia, following the example of Prince Andrei Kurbskii, sought to publish classical Byzantine theological works, especially the works of the early Fathers, in an attempt to overcome Latin influence upon Russian theology by a return to Byzantine Orthodoxy. Ostrozhskii encouraged the development of brotherhoods in Western Russia to defend Orthodoxy against Western influences through schools, hospitals and printing presses. His greatest accomplishment, however, was the printing of the first complete Bible in Church Slavonic (1581), the Ostrog Bible.

In the Greek-speaking Orthodox countries theology also was influenced greatly by Roman Catholicism, both by the accepted Latin theological concepts and by the anti-Latin polemics dominating this century of Greek theology. But the two chief characteristics of Greek theology in the 17th century were those manifested by the pro-Calvinist theologians and the highly polemical writers.

Among the first group must be listed Patriarch Cyril Lucaris whose *Confessio Fidei,* first published in Latin, was censured for its Calvinist doctrine by the Synod of Constantinople (1638), the Synod of Jassy (1642), and the Synod of Jerusalem (1672). Still, the influence of Lucaris' Calvinism persisted in his disciples, Metrophanes Critopoulos, Zacharias Gerganos, Theophilos Corydalleus, Maximos Callipolita, and John Caryophyllos.

Strong reaction against Protestantizing influences in Greek thought came from Meletios Syrigos, who replaced the Latinisms of Peter Mogila's *Confessio Fidei* with a more traditional Byzantine presentation. His corrected version is the authoritative *Confession* of Peter Mogila, approved in the Synod of Jassy and later by all Orthodox Churches as one of the primary credal expressions of the Orthodox faith.

Dositheos, Patriarch of Jerusalem, became a self-styled defender of Orthodox teaching as he sought to extirpate from all Orthodox Churches any Latin and Protestant theological influence. Through his influence at the Synod of Jerusalem (1672) and through his writings, as well as his many editions of polemical anti-Catholic and anti-Protestant works, he did much to stem the growing Roman Catholic and Protestant proselytism in the various Orthodox countries.

Dositheos championed Orthodoxy against Roman Catholicism and Protestantism not only in the Greek-speaking countries, in Rumania, and the other Balkan countries but also in Russia. When Paisios Ligarides, in the words of Dositheos, a λατινόφρων, established himself in the court of Tsar Aleksei and in the eyes of the Russian Patriarch Nikon as the epitome of Byzantinism, Dositheos excommunicated him. A strong reaction in Russia against Byzantine influence set in, which had been caused largely by the activity of the

Likhoudes brothers in Moscow. Dositheos had originally sent these brothers to Moscow in answer to Ioakim, Patriarch of Moscow, who eagerly sought Greek professors to "re-educate" Russian theologians away from Latin scholasticism back to Byzantine theology. But the Russians resented their condescending attitude towards Russian culture and Slavic theology. Finally, these attempts to re-establish contact with Byzantine theology precipitated the *raskol* or schism of the Old Believers, who held tenaciously to their ancient Slavic liturgical customs and theological positions against any Greek changes brought into the Russian Church by Nikon's reforms.

In Serbia and Rumania the distant rumblings of an intellectual renaissance were beginning to be heard. Through the mass emigration of Serbs into Austria, southern Hungary and East Slavonia, contact was made with Western culture and thought. An autocephalous Church developed at Sremsky-Karlovtsy that became the theological center for a resurging Serbian Church. Textbooks from Russia and Rumania were imported, and Serbs were trained in Russia.

Rumania began its intellectual renaissance through the efforts of Deacon Coresi who obtained printing presses from the Kievan Pecherskii Lavra through the cooperation of Peter Mogila. Russian theological works as well as the more classical Byzantine works were now printed in Rumanian. Under the guidance of Metropolitans Varlaam and Dosoftei, the vernacular was developed as a literary language and became for the first time a vehicle for Rumanian theology. The printing presses of Rumania probably did more than any other agency to promote classical Orthodox theology and further general education in all Orthodox countries of that time.

Bulgaria, during its long five hundred years of servitude under the Turks, had to live without any possibility of its own schools, and hence its own theology. Of all the Orthodox countries, Bulgaria suffered the greatest darkness in the area of education and theology.

EIGHTEENTH CENTURY

The most powerful influence in Russian theology during this century was Feofan Prokopovich. As a youth he entered the Catholic Uniate Basilian Order and studied in Rome at the Greek College of St. Athanasius. He returned to Orthodoxy and began a life-time of teaching theology and of church administration. Two firm intentions motivated his approach to theology: he eagerly sought to cut out of Russian theology any Latin scholastic influence, and secondly, he wanted to replace Western innovations by a Protestant scholastic methodology as well as Protestant theological ideas. Complete submission of the Church to the state was accomplished through his cooperation with Tsar Peter the Great in the writing of the *Regulamentum ecclesiasticum.* He imported from Protestant Germany the model of the Holy Synod as the official organ of Church administration for Russia after Peter liquidated the post of patriarch.

Prokopovich left a large group of theologians who furthered his Protestant views, such as Koniskii, Mogilanskii, Mislavskii, Falkovskii, Florinskii, Volkhonskii, Platon Levshin, Petrov, Gorskii, Levedinskii, Karpinskii, and Medvedskii. Through their theological writings, Prokopovian theology moved into Serbia, Rumania, Bulgaria and the Greek world.

Yet there were those in the Orthodox world who fought these Protestantizing innovations. Chief among these were Stefan Iavorskii and later, Count Protasov. Iavorskii's *Kamen'very* (1712) formed the basis not only in Russia but in the other Orthodox countries for an apologetic against Protestantism.

A reaction in the 18th century against the prevalent

Latin and Protestant scholastic theologies quite divorced from true Christian pietism was felt in Russia with repercussions in other Orthodox countries. This took the shape of either a return to the Hesychast spirituality of the Fathers of the desert or an openness to Western pietism and even Masonry. The leaders of the first reaction were Paisii Velichkovskii and Tikhon Zadonskii. Both were deeply imbued with the spirit of Hesychast spirituality and brought to Rumania and Russia a renaissance of Hesychast literature, especially through the Slavonic translation of the *Philokalia.*

A second reaction came through a pragmatism inaugurated by Peter's reforms and encouraged by Catherine II that infected the money class of Russia and resulted in a Masonry of ritualism and earthly values, destructive both of theology and true Orthodox piety. Similar Western values influenced other Orthodox countries to foster not only a general thirst for national freedom but an hitherto unknown rationalism that clashed with the traditional faith-visioned theology of Orthodoxy.

Eugenios Bulgaris proved to be the outstanding Greek theologian and thinker of the 18th century. A polyglot, who had studied and traveled widely throughout Europe, he was a strange combination of Latin scholasticism and French rationalism. His theology was under the influence of Western theology in spite of his expressed desire to combat Latinisms in Greek theology. Other theologians open to Western rationalism, especially of the French vintage, were Adamantios Koraes and Theophilos Kairis, both of whom criticized the traditional binding of Greek thought to antiquated Byzantine models. Both lived in France for some time, and sought to create a new independent nation of Greece as well as an autocephalus Greek Church.

Other polemicists eager to offset the proselytism of Roman Catholicism and Protestantism in Greek speaking countries were Diamantes Rhysios and Eustratios Argenti. However, polemical theology produced nothing but a repetition of early polemical works that concentrated on the questions of the *Filioque,* primacy, *epiclesis,* unleavened bread, purgatory, and the administration of Baptism.

As in Russia, so in Greece of the 18th century, there followed a conservative reaction and a return to the earlier fonts of Orthodox theology and spirituality. Athanasios of Paros, Macarios of Corinth, and Nicodemos of Mount Athos were the leaders of this Byzantine renaissance. The publishing of the *Philokalia* and the *Pedalion* in Greek offered to the Greek Orthodox, both the faithful and the hierarchy, some balance amidst much hectic turmoil in unity and Church discipline.

The smoldering embers of nationalism began to ignite in Rumania, Serbia, and Bulgaria in the 18th century, but only the following century would see the day of full liberation from Greeks and Turks. An openness to the West resulted in Transylvania under the Austro-Hungarian Empire when the majority of Rumanian Orthodox united in 1700 with Rome to form the Rumanian Uniate Church [*Biserica Unita*]. Intellectual leaders such as Samuel Micu-Klein, Petru Maior, and Gheorghe Sincai developed an outstanding free school system, centered at Blaj, and promoted nationalism through a return to the Latin culture that was the foundation of the Rumanian language. The vernacular in Latin characters, purified of Slavonic and Greek influences, affected also the theological life of Rumania, although it still continued to be dependent upon Russia for theological books and teachers.

The greatest thirst for national freedom, because it had been so long repressed, was felt by the Bulgarians. The two writers, not strictly theologians, who were most important for the future of Bulgarian theology, were Paisi of Hilander and Sofroni Vrachanskii. Paisi's classical work on Bulgaro-Slavic history stirred his fellow men with a patriotic love for the Bulgarian language and nation and was the first step towards an independent Bulgarian Church. Sofroni promoted the vernacular and popular Bulgarian schools. Through his writings, especially his *Kyriakodromion,* a book of instructions on the Sunday Gospels, he produced a written Bulgarian vernacular language that approximated the spoken tongue.

The Serbian Church of Karlovtsy continued to flourish in the 18th century, especially under the enlightened direction of Metropolitan Stevan Startimirovic. The remaining part of the Serbian Church, centered at Belgrade, labored under the stifling control of the Greek Phanariots who ruled it from 1766 until 1832. Thus any independent Serbian seminary was ruled out which prevented in return any renaissance in theology.

NINETEENTH CENTURY

Except for Russia, which had enjoyed uninterrupted nationhood and freedom from foreign domination for over five centuries, the 19th century heralded into existence both national as well as intellectual freedom for Greece, Rumania, Bulgaria, and Serbia.

The revolt in Serbia under Milosh Obrenovic in 1815 brought freedom recognized in 1830 by the Porte. Under the dynamic intellectual leadership of Metropolitans Peter and Mihailo, seminaries were opened, with Belgrade the outstanding center for a theology that consisted mainly at first of Serbian translations from Austrian and Russian theological textbooks.

With the increase of general education in Bulgaria, especially through the efforts of Vasil Aprilov, who saw the intellectual future of Bulgaria as tied with Russia and not Greece, an independent Bulgarian Church was established in 1870 which, as in Serbia, resulted in the immediate erection of seminaries. The outstanding theological center became the Seminary of St. Clement of Sofia.

The two independent principalities of Moldavia and Valachia became united into one nation of Rumania in 1859 under Alexander Cuza, and in 1864 the Rumanian Orthodox Church was declared autocephalous. Seminaries were developed throughout Rumania, modeled upon the system of teaching theology then used in Russia. Compendia from Russian and Greek authors were translated into Rumanian. Rumania, known for its long history of printing, was quick to develop many theological periodicals that more than any other vehicle stimulated creative theological thinking in that country.

In Greece, also, theology in the early half of the 19th century developed abreast with the movement for the vernacular and great national freedom. Pharmakidis typifies the preoccupation of theologians with political freedom and the development of a Greek nation, while Constantine Economos exemplifies the theologians who sought at that time greater ties with Constantinople and a theology grounded more on the Byzantine past.

In 1833, the same year that Greece was declared an independent kingdom, the Greek Church was declared autonomous and its organization was modeled on that of the Holy Synod of the Russian Church. Soon the University of Athens, founded in 1837, had its faculty of theology, that paved the way for an independent Greek theology, although at first the textbooks used were principally translations of the 19th century Russian compendia.

With nationhood and more contact with European countries, the Greek Church had greater contact also with European, non-Orthodox Christian Churches. At times this relationship was a continuance of the polemics of earlier times as witnessed in the *Encyclical of the Four Patriarchs of 1848,* and in the *Encyclical of Anthimos VII* in 1894. Orthodox-Anglican relations resumed the Non-Jurors' attempts of the 18th century to seek a reconciliation in the 19th century Lambeth and Bonn Conferences; yet no substantial agreement in doctrine or Church structure was reached.

The 19th century in Russia began with the reign of Tsar Aleksander I (1801-1825), who greatly encouraged the mystical pietism found in the writings of Boehme, Swedenborg, Eckarthausen, Madame Guyon, and Jung-Stilling. Such stress on individual pietism lessened the teaching authority of the Orthodox Church and fostered an immediate experience of God without the mediation of a structured Church or even of a formulated theology.

Prince Golitsyn was charged with the development of an educational system that eventually tended towards open secularism. A reaction to this tendency led to the selection of Count Protasov as Head-Procurator of the Holy Synod whose chief aim from 1836 onwards was to excise all Protestant teaching from Russian theology. Theology again was grounded on the earlier theology of Mogila, Iavorskii, and the Kievan Academy. A feverish study of patristics ensued which reached a peak of excellence in the 19th century unsurpassed in any other century or by any other Orthodox Church for scholarship.

Protasov ordered Filaret Drozdov, Metropolitan of Moscow, to write his *Catechism* which followed the *Confession of Faith* of Mogila and became an authoritative symbol of faith for most of the Orthodox Churches, particularly the Slavic and the Rumanian.

This period was characterized by the use of Russian theological compendia as textbooks, not only in Russian seminaries, but also for those found in Rumania, the Slavic, and the Greek-speaking countries. The most well-known theologian of this compendium age was Makarii Bulgakov who wrote three works that became the standard theological textbooks in all Orthodox lands.[3] Among the great numbers of Russian theologians who composed theological compendia, the most noted were Filaret Gumilevskii, Nikolai Malinovskii, Sil'vestr Malevanskii, Antonii Amfiteatrov and Ivan Sokolov.

Imported Western rationalism and rugged individualism set up another reaction that was even deeper than a theological return to more Orthodox sources. This was the movement called Slavophilism, whose key idea consisted of a chauvinism that saw Russia's greatness lying not in an openness towards the West but rather in a return to the Messianic Muscovite dream of Slav domination as first envisioned by Ivan IV. The foremost theologian who formulated the Slavophile doctrine of the Church was Aleksei S. Khomiakov. Rejecting the ecclesiology of both the Roman Catholic and the Protestant Churches, he presented the Russian Orthodox Church as the synthesis of liberty and unity in love. *Sobornost'* was his doctrine of the special gift of the Holy Spirit that preserved unity and faith in the Church through the interior life shared by all members.

His ecclesiology caused great discussion and even dissent within the official teaching Church of Russia, and Khomiakov's works were heavily censored. Russian theologians such as Akvilonov and Svetlov sought to have his theological doctrines accepted in official Orthodox circles. Through the decades that followed, a moderate version of Khomiakov's basic teachings was held by theologians as Florenskii, Bulgakov, Florovskii, Berdiaev, Arseniev, Zankov and in the 20th century by most Greek theologians with the exception of Dyovuniotis and Trembelas.

German idealism also influenced V. Solov'ev, P. Florenskii and S. Bulgakov at the turn of the 19th and early part of the 20th century to formulate a mystical vision of reality called *Sophiology*. Solov'ev was also concerned with the unity of Orthodox, Catholics and Protestants into one universal Church by means of the principle of *vseedinstvo,* the "all unity" that is present and pervading all of creation. As in the other Orthodox countries, so in Russia of the 19th century, theological periodicals developed, especially as official organs of the four chief theological academies of St. Petersburg, Moscow, Kiev and Kazan'.

TWENTIETH CENTURY

For Russia the 20th century, until the Revolution of 1917, began as a most productive period of theologizing and systematizing into separated theological tracts, often using the Western scholastic or German scientific methodology of presenting revealed truths in an *a priori* demonstrative method which drew probative force from Scripture, the Fathers and human reason. The basic weakness, however, that same debilitating reason that haunted Latin scholasticism for centuries, was to over-systematize theology and remove it from living piety.

Another reaction, flowing out of the *kenosis* of Dostoevskii's writings and an earlier Russian type of monastic spirituality as typified by that of Antonii and Feodosii of the Pecherskii Lavra, Sergii and Nil Sorskii, sought to present theological truths as both speculative and as living experiences. Theologians as V. Ekzempliarskii,, A. Vvedenskii, V. Nikolskii and F. Golubinskii emphasized the living experience as the touchstone to true theology.

However, with the take-over of Russia by the Soviets, religious freedom down to the present was greatly lessened and almost at times totally extinguished. Theology no longer could develop creatively and for this reason many theologians either were exiled from their country by the Soviets or fled to Europe and America where in an ambient of freedom and fundamental good will among Western Christians, eager to share in the riches of Eastern Orthodoxy, these theologians found great stimulation to develop their insights. Such well-known theologians among the Russian émigrés were S. Bulgakov, N. Berdiaev, N. Arseniev, G. Florovskii, A. Khrapovitskii, A. Kartashev, Kiprian Kern, Kassian Bezobrazov, V. Losskii, V. Zenkovskii and N. Afanas'ev.

Serbia, Rumania and Bulgaria all developed in similar fashion: a movement away from mere translations of Russian and Greek compendia to the composition by their own national theologians of compendia. Academies took on greater seriousness as their respective theological journals developed into organs of creative theology.

With the two World Wars and the take-over by atheistic regimes, not favorable to Christianity, Orthodox theology in these countries developed into a conservative type of "repeating" theology worked out in earlier times. In a state of relative political peace, the Greek Church developed a theology of compendia that rivaled and in some respects excelled those produced in Russia during the latter part of the 19th century. Famous compendia were written by N. Damalas, Zikos Rhosis, Chrestos Androutsos, C. Dyovuniotis, D. Balanos, I. Mesoloras, Nectarios Kephalas, Nicolas Ambrazis, P. Trembelas and P. Bratsiotis.

The theological academies of Athens and Thessalonika possessed well-developed faculties, whose members had studied abroad, mostly in Germany. Travel abroad opened the Greek Church to contacts with other theologians. The growing involvement of Greek theologians in European ecumenical circles also encouraged greater contact with other non-Greek Orthodox theologians. The first Orthodox Congress of theologians was held in Athens in 1936 with representatives from the Orthodox theological faculties of Athens, Bucharest, Jassy, Cernauti, Belgrade, Sofia, Paris and Warsaw.

The expertise of Greek theologians in applying German scholarship to theology resulted in a flood of theological works but also precipitated a strong reaction. This came primarily through the *Zoe* Brotherhood whose aim was to make Greek theology more relevant to the needs of the Orthodox faithful. Through numerous publications, preaching and teaching, the members of *Zoe* and other similar apostolic groups sought to make theology more viable for the Orthodox of the 20th century.

THE NEW WORLD

The 20th century witnessed a new phenomenon. Greek, Russian, Rumanian, Bulgarian and Serbian Orthodox in large numbers emigrated from their native lands where the Orthodox faith had had a major role in forming the culture of those countries to take up residence in non-Orthodox countries in Western Europe, North and South America. In these countries in most cases, the mother language soon gave way to the new vernacular in which the Byzantine Liturgy was now celebrated. Theologians began not only to translate the classical Orthodox theological works into these modern languages but also began to write original works in these languages. New theological problems arose out of the Western cultures to challenge Orthodox thinkers. The Orthodox faith clashed with secularism and in many cases there was initially a lack of theologians capable of producing a more creative theology with viable and meaningful answers. The foundations of this theology rose in centers such as *St. Sergius Orthodox Theological Institute* in Paris, *St. Vladimir's Orthodox Seminary* in New York and *Holy Cross Greek Orthodox Seminary* in Brookline, Massachusetts. Through teaching, public lectures, and writing, theologians such as John Meyendorff, Alexander Schmemann, John Romanides, and a nucleus of other young Orthodox thinkers began to create a meaningful Orthodox theology for the 20th century. The greatest drawback in the New World for a strong Orthodox theology lies in the separation of various jurisdictional church groups that divide the theological strength of Orthodoxy within these countries. The movement towards greater cooperation among these groups offers some hope of greater theological development.

ECUMENISM

As the Orthodox Churches faced the modern world, they were also thrown into greater contact with non-Orthodox Christian Churches. An openness towards greater universalism and a sense of world mission began with the two encyclicals issued by the Patriarch of Constantinople in 1902 and 1920, calling for greater unity among the Orthodox Churches and for collaboration with non-Orthodox Christians in practical and moral areas.

Theologians, especially the Greeks and the Russian émigrés in Europe, engaged in the early ecumenical meetings in Lausanne, Stockholm, and Copenhagen, and in 1947 when the World Council of Churches was launched in Amsterdam the Greek Orthodox Church became a founding member. Only in 1961 did the Russian, Rumanian, Bulgarian, Serbian, and Czech Orthodox Churches become members. At the Fourth World Assembly in Uppsala in 1968 the Orthodox theologians took a leading part, except for the Greek delegates of the Holy Synod of Athens, who withdrew their participation.

In such meetings, Orthodox theologians not only articulated with great clarity their fundamental beliefs to a non-Orthodox world, but they also re-examined the polemical literature written in previous centuries against Protestants and Roman Catholics. Without falling into an indifference that ignored confessional lines or an attitude that fostered a pan-universal Church, these theologians began to see the progress made within these other Church groups; above all, they began to see the great many fundamental points of common agreement among Orthodox, Roman Catholics and Protestants.

Thus Orthodox theology at the present stands with one foot firmly planted in the old world while the other seeks a firm footing within the context of a new world culture. For the majority of Orthodox theologians in Russia, Rumania,

Serbia, Bulgaria, Poland, Czechoslovakia, Georgia and Albania, their freedom to develop is hampered by a state order that is professedly atheistic. These theologians heroically cling to a theology of the past, rooted in historical, liturgical and patristic studies. Those in the Greek-speaking world and the Western countries enjoy academic freedom to develop new insights that will allow the message of Orthodoxy to be spoken loudly and clearly over the din and confusion of secularism and an exaltation of subjectivism. These Orthodox theologians are learning that the Holy Spirit has also been working within the Churches of their separated brethren, especially the Roman Catholics and Protestants. Through the humility of a servant that has met God through centuries of suffering and persecution, the Orthodox Churches of the 20th century are developing a liturgical theology; but a theology of service to mankind through involvement in our world which is also God's world is needed. Their witness will be one not only of a transfigured world to come, but of a world that is being transfigured through their living for the other and loving him. Then they will teach the world the essence of Christianity: "No longer is there Jew or Greek; no longer is there slave or freeman; no longer is there male or female. You are all one in Christ Jesus. And if you are Christ's, then you are the offspring of Abraham, heirs according to the promise."[4]

Notes

NOTES ON PART ONE

[1]Cf. N. De Baumgarten, *Aux Origines de la Russie* (Rome, 1939), pp. 56-60. For possible Scandinavian influence, see R. Haugh, "St. Vladimir and Olaf Tryggvason: *The Russian Primary Chronicle* and Gunnlaug Leifsson's *Saga of Olaf Tryggvason*," in Volume VIII of *Transactions of the Association of Russian-American Scholars* (New York, 1974), 83-96.

[3]Cf. F. Dvornik, *Les Slaves, Byzance et Rome au IX Siècle* (Paris, 1926), 1904-22), pt. 1, ed. 6, pp. 80-98.

[3]Cf. F. Dvornik, *Les Slaves, Byzance et Rome au IX Siècle* (Paris, 1926) 318; G. Ilyinskii, *"Gde, kogda, kem i s kakoiu tsel'iu glagolitsa byla zamenena kirillitsei?"*

[4]*Byzantinoslavica* 3 (1931), p. 87.

[5]George Fedotov, *The Russian Religious Mind*, (Cambridge, Mass., 1946), vol. I, pp. 38-41. [Published in paperback as Volume III in *The Collected Works* of George P. Fedotov by Nordland Publishing Company].

[6]*Ibid.*, p. 40.

[7]Cf. Ikonnikov, *Opyt issledovaniia o kulturnom znachenii Vizantii v russkoi istorii* (Kiev, 1869), pp. 60-62.

[8]Cf. "Svedeniia o drevnikh perevodakh tvorenii sv. otsev na slaviano-russkii iazik," *Pravoslavnyi Sobesednik* III (1859), 254.

[9]E. Golubinskii, *Istoriia russkoi tserkvi*, vol. 2, 2.

[10]*Ibid.*, pp. 263-306. Cf. Gorskii and Nevostroev, *Opisanie slavianskikh rukopisei Moskovskoi Sinodalnoi biblioteki;* Metropolit Makarii, *Istoriia russkoi tserkvi*, 12 vols., V, pp. 247-8.

[11]*Op. cit.*, p. 292.

[12]Cf. M. Heppell, "Slavonic Translations of Early Byzantine Ascetical Literature," *Journal of Ecclesiastical History* (April, 1954), p. 86.

[13]Cf. E. Sreznevskii, *Svedeniia i zametki o maloizvestnykh i neizvestnykh pamiatnikakh*, pp. 96, 217, 218.

[14]S. Sol'skii, "Izuchenie i upotreblenie Biblii v Rossii," *Pravoslavnoe Obozrenie*, no. 11 (1896), pp. 268-9.

[15]*Nil Sorskii i Vassian Patrikeev, ikh literaturnye trudy i idei v drevei Rusi. Istoriko-literaturnyi ocherk.* I: *Prepodobnyi Nil Sorskii; (Pamiatniki drevnei pis'mennosti;* no. 25).

[16]Illarion's works can be found in: D. S. Likhachev, *Povest' vremennykh let,* vol. I., *Tekst i perevod;* vol. 2, *Stat'i i komentarii;* also A. I. Ponomarev, *Pamiatniki drevnerusskoi tserkovnouchitel'noi literatury,* I-III. See, for interesting comment, D. S. Likhachev, *Natsional'noe samosoznanie drevnei Rusi* (Moscow-Leningrad, 1945), pp. 24-33.

[17]The letter that is extant is not the original but a revision by Klimentii's pupil, Athanasius. It can be found in Loparev, "Poslanie Mitropolita k smolenskomy presvitery Fome," *Neizdanyi pamiatnik literatury XII v; Pamiatniki drevnei russkoi, pis'mennosti,* vol. 90 (1892). Cf. Nikol'skii: *O literaturnykh trudakh Mitropolita Klimenta Smoliatich pisatelia XII v.*

[18]Cf. N. Skabalanovich, "Vizantiniskaia nauka i shkoly v XI veke," *Khristianskoe Chtenie,* no. I (1884), pp. 344-369; 730-770.

[19]Nikol'skii, *op., cit.,* pp. 104-106.

[20]*Fedotov, op. cit.,* p. 64.

[21]His sermons are found in Ponamarev, Pamiatniki, *op. cit.,* pp. 126-198. Cf. I. Malishevskii, *Tvoreniia Kirilla episkopa Turovskogo;* Iaroslav Levitsky: *Pershi Ukrainski propovidniki* (Lvov, 1929). For an analysis of his works cf. Vinogradov: *O kharaktere propovednicheskogo tvorchestva Kirilla, episkopa Turovskogo,* 2.

[22]Cf. D. I. Abramovich, ed., *Zhitiia sviatykh muchenikov Borisa i Gleba* (St. Petersburg, 1916).

[23]Nestor, "Zhitie prepodobnogo Fedosiia," *Chteniia v Obshchestve Istorii* (Moscow, 1858, no. 3; 1879; no. 1; 1899, no. 2, Cf. V. A. Chagovets, *Prepodobnyi Feodosii Pecherskii, ego zhizn' i sochineniia* (Kiev, 1901); Bel'chenko, "Prepodobnyi Feodosii Pecherskii, ego zhizn' i sochineniia," *Zapiski Istoriko-filologicheskogo Obshchestva pri Novorossiiskom Universitete,* X (Odessa 1902).

[24]Cf. D. I. Abramovich, *Paterik Kievo-Pecherskogo monastyria* (St. Petersburg, 1911); N. Kubarev, "O Kievo-Pecherskom Paterike," *Chtenia v Obshchestve Istorii* (Moscow, 1947); N. S. Tikhonravov, ed., *Drevnie Zhitiia Sergiia Radonezhskogo* (Moscow, 1892); Arkhmandrit Leonid, *Pamiatniki drevnei pismennosti i iskusstva,* vol. 58 (Moscow, 1885); *Velikiia Chet'i Minei,* vol. I, Sept. (St. Petersburg, 1869), col. 1404-1578.

[25]Cf. N. Redkov, "Prepodobnyi Avraamii Smolenskii i ego zhitie," *Smolenskaia Starina,* vol. 1 (1900); G. Fedotov, "Zhitie i terpenie prepodobnogo Avraamiia Smolenskogo," *Pravoslavnaia Mysl',* vol. 2 (Paris, 1930); S. P. Rozanov, ed., *Zhitiia prepodobnogo Avraamiia Smolenskogo i sluzhby emu* (St. Petersburg, 1912).

[26]Cf. V. A. Sakharov, *Eskhatologicheskiia sochineniia i skazaniia v drevne-russkoi pis'mennosti* (Tula, 1879).

[27]Cf. Ikonnikov, *Opyt issledovaniia...*, *op. cit.*

[28]Cf. Kliuchevskii, *Kurs russkoi istorii...*, *op. cit.*, pp. 302-310.

[29]Cf. I. Smolitsch, "Das altrussische Mönchtumim-11-16 Jahrhundert," *Das östliche Christentum* (Würzburg, 1940); "Drevnie pustini i pustin-nozhiteli na severo-vostoke Rossii," *Prav. Sob.* III, (1960); V. P. Shevyrev, *Istoriia russkoi slovestnosti*, vol. 4 (Moscow, 1860); Kliuchevskii, *Kurs...*, *op. cit.*, vol. 2, 308-331; P. I. Kazanskii *Istoriia pravoslavnogo russkogo monashestva* (Moscow, 1855).

[30]Cf. Acta Patriarchat. Constantinop. II, 31; writings of Stephan, *Pamiatii Pavlova*, no. 25, col. 211, both of these works cited by Golubinskii, *Istoriia...*, *op. cit.*, vol. 2, 396-406. For writings of Stefan against the Strigolniki cf. *Russkaia istoricheskaia biblioteka* [RIB], Izd. Archiografi-cheskoi Kommissii (St. Petersburg, 1897), vol. 6, no. 25, col. 214, 220-221, 223.

[31]Cf. S. G. Vilinskii, *Poslaniia Startsa Artemiia* (Odessa, 1906), pp. 304-314; Makarii, *Istoriia...*, *op. cit.*, vol. 6, 82, 83, 85; Golubinskii, *Istoriia...*, *op. cit.*, vol. 3, 585; Ikonnikov, *Opyt...*, *op. cit.*, p. 146.

[32]The classical work on this heresy was written by I. Panov, "Eres' zhidovstvuiushchikh," *Zhurnal ministerstva narodnogo prosvesheniia*, 1877, no. 1, 1-40; no. 2, 253-295, no. 3, 1-59. S. Lur'e brings us up to date in his, *Ideologicheskaia bor'ba v russkoi publitsistike kontsa XV-nachala XVI veka* (Moscow-Leningrad, 1960), pp. 75-185. An adequate English summary is found in J. Fennell's, "The attitude of the Josephians and Trans-Volga Elders to the Heresy of the Judaisers," *The Slavonic and East European Review*, vol. XXIX, no. 73 (1951), 486-509.

[33]The best critical edition of Nil's *Predanie* and *Ustav* was done by M. A. Borovkova-Maikova, "Nila Sorskogo Predanie i Ustav s vstupitel'noi stat'ei," *PDP*, no. 179 (St. Petersburg, 1917). An English translation, although not quite complete, exists in Fedotov, *A Treasury of Russian Spirituality* (N. Y., 1965), pp. 90-133. Other leading works are: A. S. Arkhangelskii, "Prepodobnyi Nil Sorskii" (St. Petersburg, 1882), *PDP*, no. 25; F. von Lilienfeld, *Nil Sorskij und seine Schriften: Die Krise der Tradition im Russland Ivans III* (Berlin, 1963); G. Maloney, S. J., *The Spirituality of Nil Sorsky* (Westmalle, 1964).

[34]Kazan, ed. 1857, 1896, 1904.

[35]This is found in Makarii, *Velikiia Chet'i-Minei*, September volume, col. 499-615 (St. Petersburg, 1868). Cf. T. Spidlik, S. J., *Joseph de Volokolamsk. Un Chapitre de la spiritualite russe* (Rome, 1956); N. A. Bulgakov, *Prepodobnyi Iosif Volokolamskii* (St. Petersburg, 1865); I. Khrushchev, *Issledovanie o sochineniiakh Iosifa Sanina, prep. igumena Volotskogo* (St. Petersburg, 1868); P. Kazanskii, "Pisaniia prepodobnogo Iosifa Volokolamskago," *Pribavleniia k tvoreniiam sviatykh otets v russkom perevode*, vol. V (Moscow, 1858), 271-314.

[36]Cf. Makarii, *Istoriia...*, *op. cit.*, pp. 265-274, 300-307.

[37]Cf. E. Denisoff, "Maxime le Grec et l'Ocident," *Irenikon*, XVII (1940), 130-135.

[38]*Istoriia...*, *op. cit.*, vol. 4, pt. pp. 2, 233-263.

[39]Cf. his two works against the Latins, translated by A. Palmieri in *Bessarion*, series III (1912) vol. IX, 54-79; 379-384.

[40]On Maxim, cf. E. Denisoff, *Maxime le Grec et l'Occident, contribution a l'histoire de la pensée religieuse et philosophique de Michel Trivolis* (Paris-Louvain, 1943); V. Ikonnikov, *Maksim Grek i ego vremia* (Kiev, 1915), 2nd ed.; V. Rzhiga, "Opyt po istorii publitsistiki XVI veka, Maksim Grek kak publitsist," *Trudy otdela drevnerusskoi literatury* [TODRL], 1 (1934), 5-120; I. Budovnits, *Russkaia publitsistika XVI veka* (Moscow-Leningrad, 1947); R. Klostermann, "Legende und Wirklichkeit im Lebenswerk von Maxim Grek," *Orientalia Christiana Periodica* [OCP], no. 3-4 (1958), 353-370; B. Schultze, S. J., *Maksim Grek als Theologe, Orientalia Christiana Analecta* [OCA], vol. 167 (Rome, 1963).

[41]Cf. V. Zhbakin, *Mitropolit Daniil i ego sochineniia* (Moscow, 1881).

[43]Cf. *Velikiia Chet'i-Minei* (St. Petersburg, 1868-1915); St. Petersburg Academy of Sciences published the months of September to January, then January 1-11 and all of April.

[44]The best edition of Stoglav is that of Kazan, 2nd ed. 1887. E. Duchesne has a French translation: *Le Stoglav ou les Cent Chapitres* (Paris, 1920).

[45]*Istoriia...*, *op. cit.*, p. 789.

[46]*The Pilot's Book;* cf. F. Dvornik, "Byzantine Political Ideas in Kievan Russia," *Dumbarton Oaks Papers*, IX-X (Cambridge, Mass., 1956), 78.

[47]*Tserkovnyi Ustav;* cf. R. P. Dmitrieva, *Skazanie o kniaziakh vladimirskikh* (Moscow-Leningrad, 1955).

[48]Cf. I. Zuzek, S. J., *Kormchaia Kniga, OCA*, vol. 168 (Rome, 1963), 14.

[49]Cf. I. I. Sreznevskii, *Obozrenie drevnikh russkikh spiskov Kormchei Knigi* (St. Petersburg, 1897), p. 65 ff.

[50]Cf. Prosvetitel', *op. cit.*, p. 547; Spiridon's letter: cf. R. P. Dmitrieva, *Skazanie o kniaziakh vladimirskikh* (Moscow-Leningrad, 1955), pp. 159-170.

[51]Malinin, *op. cit.*, p. 55.

[52]Cf. W. K. Medlin, *Moscow and East Rome* (Neuchâtel, Switzerland 1952); H. Schaeder, *Moskau das Dritte Rom*, (Hamburg, 1929); O. Ohloblyn, *Moskovskaia Teoriia III Rimu V XVI-XVII Stol.* (Munich, 1951).

[53]M. A. D'iaknov has shown that it was primarily the Russian bishops who opposed and rejected the union of Florence. Cf. *Vlast' moskovskikh gosudarei* (St. Petersburg, 1889).

[54]Cf. A. I. Murav'ev, *Snosheniia Rossii s vostokom po delam tserkovnym;* vol. 1. (St. Petersburg, 1858), 265-279.

[55]Cf. *Deianiia moskovskikh soborov 1666-67 godov* (Moscow, 1893), vol. 83; W. Regel, *Analecta byzantino-slavica* (St. Petersburg, 1891), 85-89.

[56]Cf. "Poslaniia startsa Artemiia XVI veka," *Russkaia istoricheskaia Biblioteka;* vol. IV (St. Petersburg, 1878), col. 1201-1448. S. G. Vilenskii, *Poslaniia startsa Artemiia* (Odessa, 1906).

[57]Cf. S. Gorskii, *Zhizn' i istoricheskie znachenie kniaza Andreia M. Kurbskogo* (Kazan, 1958).

[58]Cf. Florovskii, *Puti...*, *op. cit.*, pp. 34-35.

[59]Text found in: *Russkaia istoricheskaia Biblioteka,* vol. VII (St. Petersburg, 1882), col. 223-256.

[60]Cf. O. Halecki, "Possevino's Last Statement on Polish-Russian Relations," *OCP* (Rome, 1954), pp. 261-302.

[61]Cf. Makarii, *Istoriia...*, *op. cit.*, vol. 9, 652-674. Khrushevskii, *Istoriia...*, *op. cit.*, vol. 5, 605-614. P. Skarga, *Synod Brzeski i iego obrona* (Craców, 1597). *RIB,* 19, col. 329-376.

[62]Cf. Malvy-Viller, "La Confession orthodoxe de P. Moghila," *Orientalia Christiana,* X, XII.

[63]Cf. Kimmel, *Monumenta fidei ecclesiae orientalis,* vol. 1 (Jena, 1850), 52-55. L. Hurmazki, *Documente privitoarela istoria Romanilor;* vol. 4, pt. 1 (Bucharest, 1882), p. 668.

[64]*Op. cit.*

[65]Cf. Malvy-Viller, *op. cit.*, LXII.

[66]Adrian's letter is found in *Khristianskoe Chtenie,* no. IV (1843), 376.

[67]Cf. Palmieri, *op. cit.*, pp. 560-562; Malvy-Viller, *op. cit.*, LXIV-LXV.

[68]Cf. Florovskii, *op. cit.*, p. 50.

[69]*Trebnik* (Kiev, 1646).

[70]For the Latin sources from which Mogila drew his "Catholic" doctrines, cf. Malvy-Viller, *op. cit.*, XCI-CV.

[71]Cf. E. Legrand, *Bibliographie, Hellenique ou description raisonnée des ouvrages publiés par les Grecs au XVII° siècle,* Vol. IV (Paris, 1896), 120-155.

[72]S. Golubev, *Arkhiv iugo-zapadnoi Rossii,* vol. IX, pt. 1, (Kiev, 1893), I-445.

[73]Cf. D. Vishnevskii, *Kievskaia Akademiia v pervoi polovine XVIII stol.* (Kiev, 1903); Makarii Bulgakov, *Istoriia Kievskoi akademii* (Kiev, 1843); A. Palmieri, *Theologia dogmatica orthodoxa,* vol. I, *op. cit.*, pp. 152-159.

[74]The writings of Avvakum are found in the work of Nikolai Subbotin, *Materialy dlia istorii raskola;* 9 vols. (Moscow, 1875-95). Vol. 5 contains his autobiography: *Zhitie protopopa Avvakuma* along with his other writings. Other works on the Old Believers' Schism: V. Kel'siev, *Sbornik pravitel'stvennykh svedenii o raskol'nikakh,* 4 vols. (London, 1860); *Pamiatniki istorii staroobriadchestva XVII veka,* col. 1, *Russkaia istoricheskaia biblioteka* (Leningrad, 1927); A. I. Zhuravlev, *Polnoe istoricheskoe izvestie o drevnikh strigol'nikakh i novykh raskol'nikakh* (St. Petersburg, 1795).

⁷⁵Cf. I. Tatarskii, *Simeon Polotskii, ego zhizn' i deiatel'nost'* (Moscow, 1886).

⁷⁶Cf. P. Popov, *Sv. Dimitrii Rostovskii i ego trudy* (St. Petersburg, 1910); A. Palmieri, "Dimitri Daniel, metropolite de Rostov," *DTC*, vol. IV, col. 1053-57; I. A. Shliapkin, *Sv. Dimitrii Rostovskii i ego vremia (1651-1709)* (St. Petersburg, 1891).

⁷⁷Cf. S. K. Smirnov, *Istoriia Moskovskoi slaviano-greko-latinskoi Akademii* (Moscow, 1895).

⁷⁸*Kamen' very mitropolita Stefana Iavorskogo, ego mesto sredi otechestven-nykh protivoprotestantskikh sochinenii* (St. Petersburg, 1904), esp. 188 ss. Cf. also: I. V. Morev, "Mitropolit Stefan Iavorskii v bor'be s protestantskimi ideami svoego vremeni," *Khristianskoe Chtenie,* no. 1, 1905, 254-265.

⁷⁹*Signa adventus antichristi et finis mundi* (Moscow, 1703).

⁸⁰Cf. F. Ternovskii, "Mitropolit Stefan Iavorskii," *Trudy* (Moscow, 1864) fasc. 1; Samarin, *Stefan Iavorskii i Feofan Prokopovich* (Moscow, 1880); P. Savluchinskii, "Russkaia dukhovnaia literatura pervoi poloviny XVIII veka i ee otnoshenie k sovremennosti (1700-1762 gg.)," *Trudy* vol. II (1878), 128-190; 280-326.

⁸¹Cf. G. Guriev, *Pravda voli monarshei Feofana Prokopovicha i ee zapadnoevropeiskie istochniki* (Dorpat, 1915); R. Stupperich, *Staatsgedanke und Religionspolitik Peters des Grossen* (Berlin, 1936); S. G. Runkevich, *Istoriia russkoi Tserkvi pod upravleniem Sviateishega Sinoda;* vol. I: *Uchrezhdenie i pervonachal'noe ustroistvo Sviateishego Pravitel'stvuiushchego Sinoda* (St. Petersburg, 1900).

⁸²Cf. for his life and writings: I. Chistovich, *Feofan Prokopovich i ego vremia* (St. Petersburg, 1868); p. Morozov, *Feofan Prokopovich kak pisatel': ocherk iz istorii russkoi literaturi v epochu preobrazovaniia* (St. Petersburg, 1880); P. Samarin, *Stefan Iavorskii i Feofan Prokopovich* (Moscow, 1880); P. V. Verkhovskoi, *Uchrezhdenie dukhovnoi Kollegii i Dukhovnyi Reglament,* 2 vol. (Rostov, 1916). His main theological writings include the following titles: *De Processione Spiritus Sancti* (Gotha, 1772); *Introductio in theologiam* (Königsberg, 1773); *De Deo (Ibid.,* 1775); *De Trinitate (ibid.,* 1775); *De Creatione et Providentia (ibid.,* 1775); *De Homine innocente* (Moscow, 1776); *De Homine lapso (ibid.,* 1776); *De Gratuite peccatoris per Christum justificatione* (Breslau, 1779); These were again published by Mislavskii in 3 vols. (Leipzig, 1782 and 1784). Some works were translated, as Palmieri notes (*Theol. dogmatica...*, *op. cit.,* vol. I footnote 3, 160) from Latin into Russian by the students, Matvei Sokolov and Iakov Evdokimov. The Russian titles, places and dates of publication are given by Palmieri, *ibid.*

⁸³Cf. P. Cherviakovskii, "Vvedenie v bogoslovie Feofana Prokopovicha," *Khristianskoe Chtenie;* 1878, no. 1, 18-32; *ibid.,* "O metode vvedeniia v bogoslovie Feofana Prokopovich," 1878, no. 1, 321-351. Also: F. Tikhomirov, "Ideia absoliutizma Boga i protestantskii skholastitsizm v bogoslovii Feofana Prokopovicha," *Khrist. Chtenie;* 1884, no. II, 315-326. A. Arkhangelskii, *Dukhovnoe obrazovanie i dukhovnaia literatura v Rossii pri Petre velikom*

(Kazan, 1883), pp. 67-74. H. Koch, *Die russische orthodoxie im petrinischen Zeitalter* (Breslau, 1929).

[84]P. Cherviakovskii, *op. cit., passim.*

[85]J. E. Gerhard, *Methodus studii theologici* (Jena, 1654). Cf. Cherviakovskii, "O methode..., *op. cit.,* 348-351.

[86]Cf. A. Arkhangelskii, *Dukhovnoe...,* *op. cit.,* 67-74.

[87]V. G. Kowalik, *Ecclesiologia Theophanis Prokopovicz, Influxus Protestantismii* (Rome, 1947).

[88]*Regulamentum Ecclesiasticum* (Mansi; vol. 37, 1-96).

[89]Cf. N. Pokrovskii, "Feofilakt Lopatinskii," *Pravoslavnoe Obozrenie,* vol. III, (1872), 684-710.

[90]A. Grigorovich, *Georgiia Konisskogo sochineniia* (St. Petersburg, 1835). Konisskii was professor of philosophy and theology in the Academy of Kiev 1751-1754. He greatly admired Prokopovich and continued to propagate his ideas on Sacred Scripture. He published a new edition of Prokopovich's *Catechism.* Cf. M. Pavlovich, "Georgii Konisskii-archiepiskop Mogilevskii," *Khristianskoe Chtenie,* no. 1 (1873), 3-46.

[91]His main dogmatic treatise is entitled: *Dogmata praecipua fidei orthodoxae catholicae et apostolicae Ecclesiae orientalis, nec non maxime necessaria creditu pro adipiscenda aeterna salute* (Kiev, 1760) in Russian and Latin. He not only sought to correct but also absolve Prokopovich of any taint of heresy, as Rozhdestvenskii points in his work: *Samuil Mislavskii Mitropolit Kievskii* (Kiev, 1877).

[92]Cf. Filaret: *Obzor...,* *op. cit.,* 309-311.

[93]S. K. Smirnov, *Istoriia Moskovskoi slavinano-greko-latiniskoi Akademii* (Moscow, 1895), 37.

[94]Smirnov, *op. cit.,* 242-245; gives a rather complete summary of this work. For his life and writings cf. *Dukhovnoe zaveshchanie Mitr. Platona. Zhizn' i deianiia Mitr. Moskovskii Platona* (Moscow, 1822); B. Novakovskii, *Biograficheskie ocherki: Platon, Mitr. Moskovskii* (St. Petersburg, 1882).

[95]G. Florovskii, *Puti...,* *op. cit.,* 111.

[96]St. Petersburg, 1765. Other subsequent editions were printed in St. Petersburg 1791: Moscow, 1780, 1880 etc.

[97]H. Gass, *Symbolik der griechischen Kirche* (Berlin, 1872), p. 89.

[98]Others of lesser note are: Makarii Petrovich who wrote: *Ecclesiae orientalis Doctrina Orthodoxa* (St. Petersburg, 1783 in Latin; 1790 in Russian) and Archimandrit Illarion (d. 1772) who founded the seminary of Holy Trinity Lavra.

[99]Cf. Mitropolit Makarii, *Skazanie o zhizni i trudakh preosv. Gavriila mitroplita Novgorodskogo i S. Petersburskogo* (St. Petersburg, 1857); I. Pikrovskii, "Gavriil, Mitr. Novgorodskii i Sankt-Peterburgskii kak tserkovno-obshchestvennyi deiatel'," *Khristianskoe Chtenie;* 1901, no. II. 482-510; 687-718.

[100]Gorskii relied greatly on Protestant sources, especially upon Buddeus. His two most well known works are: *Orthodoxa orientalis Ecclesiae doctrina de credendis et agendis usibus eorum qui studio theologiae sese consecrarunt addixeruntque adornata accommodataque* (Leipzig, 1784; St. Petersburg, 1818, 1827: Moscow, 1831) and *Dogmata Christiana fidei orthodoxae theologice proposita atque explicata* (Moscow, 1773, in Latin, Russian and German; St. Petersburg, 1792 in French).

[101]He wrote: *Compendium theologiae classicum didactico-polemicum, doctrinae orthodoxae Christianae maxime consonum* (St. Petersburg, 1799; Moscow, 1805).

[102]His work is entitled: *Bogoslovie Khristianskoe, dlia zhelaiushchikh v blagochestii vysshego uspekha* (Moscow, 1806).

[103]Cf. V. Kliuchevskii, *Kurs...*, *op. cit.*, part III, pp. 331-332.

[104]*Ibid.* p. 332.

[105]For biographical details see: A. Lebedev, *Sviatitel' Tikhon Zadonskii i vseia Rusi Chudotvorets* (St. Petersburg, 1865).

[106]His writings are found in: *Tvoreniia izhe vo sviatykh otsa nashego Tikhona Zadonskogo.* 4 vols., Moscow, 1898-99.

[107]Biographical material on Paisii's life can be found in: *Zhitie startsa Moldavskogo Paisiia Velichkovskogo,* Optina ed. (no date, no author).

[108]This was first published in Venice in 1782 and entitled: Φιλοκαλία τῶν πατέρων νηπτικῶν. The latest edition of five volumes was published in Athens in 1956.

[109]Cf. N. Subbotin, *Feofan, Igumen Kirillo-Novovezerskogo monastyria zhizneopisanie* (Moscow, 1862).

[110]N. Red'ko, "Protasov, graf Nikolai Aleksandrovich," *Russkii Biograficcheskii Slovar'* (St. Petersburg, 1910), 81-85.

[111]Biographical sketches of Filaret can be found in: I. Smirnov, & S. Dobronravin, "Vyssokopreosv. Filaret, mitropolit Moskovskii Kolemenskii," *Strannik* 2 (1868), 5-58, 65-86. D. Dmitrevskii, *Filaret mitropolit Moskovskii kak kanonist* (Moscow, 1893). M. Jugie, "Philarète Drozdov," *Dict. Théol. Cath.* v. XII, 1, c. 1376-1395. M. I. Zvezdinskii, "Dukhovno-prosvetitelnia deiatel'nost; Filareta mitr. Moskovskogo, v imp. Mosk. Universitete," *Vera i Tserkov'* (1907), 404-445.

[112]Cf. A. Smirnov, "Gody ucheniia i uchitel'stva F. M. Drozdova," *Vera i Razum.* 2 (1892), 359-402. I. Korsunskii, "Peterburgskii period propovednicheskoi deiatel'nosti Filareta," *ibid.* 2 (1886), 18 ss.

[113]Entitled: *Khristianskii Katikhisis Pravoslavnoi Katolicheskoi vostochnoi greko-rossiiskoi tserkvi* (Moscow, 1883).

[114]I. Korsunskii, *Sud'bi katikhizisov Filareta* (Moscow, 1883).

[115]*Dogmaticheskoe bogoslovie po sochineniiam Filareta mitr. Moskovskogo* (Kazan, 1883).

[116]*Uroki po Prostrannomu Khristianskomu Katikhizisu* (Moscow, 1904).

[117]*Uroki po Zakonu Bozhiiu Sposobstvuiushchie usvoeniu Prostr. Khrist. Katikh.* (Iur'ev, 1901).

[118]"Kritika sochinenii Filareta mitropolita Moskovskogo," *Khrist. Chtenie,* 1 (1887), 791.

[119]*Bogoslovie dogmaticheskoe ili prostrannoe izlozhenie ucheniia very pravoslavnoi katolicheskoi Tserkvi* (Moscow, 1838).

[120]He also published in Kiev, 1851, *Pastyrskoe bogoslovie;* (a treatise on pastoral theology). Cf. N. N. Glubokovskii, *Russkaia bogoslovskaia nauka v ee istoricheskom razvitii i noveishem sostoianii* (Warsaw, 1928), 71; also, Arkhimandrit Sergii, *Antonii Amfiteatrov-arkhiepiskop Kazanskii i Sviazskii* 2 vols., (Kazan, 1885-6).

[121]On Filaret see: I. Listrovskii, *Filaret arkhiepiskop Chernigovskii* (Chernigov, 1895); S. Smirnov, *Filaret Gumilevskii* (Tambov, 1880).

[122]*Istoriia russkoi tserkvi,* pp. 988-1826 (Moscow, 1848).

[123]*Istoricheskoe uchenie ob Otsakh tserkvi,* 3 v. (St. Petersburg, 1859). Cf. N. N. Glubokovskii, *Russkaia bogoslovskaia...,* *op. cit.,* pp. 40-41.

[124]In 2 parts (Chernigov, 1864).

[125]*Zhitiia sviatikh, chtimykh pravoslavnoi tserkov'iu,* 12 vols., (Chernigov, 1861).

[126]*Istoriia russkoi tserkvi,* 12 vols., (St. Petersburg, 1857-1883). Cf. M. D. Priselkov, "Mitr. Makarii i ego Istoriia russkoi Tserkvi, 1816-1916," *Russkii Istoricheskii Zhurnal,* 1918, nos., 177-196. For biographical data on Makarii, see: F. Titov, *Makarii Bulgakov, Mitr. Moskovskii i Kolomenskii. Istoriko-biograficheskii ocherk,* 1 (Kiev, 1895), 2 (Kiev, 1898); A. Vertelovskii, "Ocherk zhizni i deiatel'nosti Makariia mitr. Moskovskogo,"*Vera i Razum,* no. 1, 1917, 93-124; 232-249; 435-446; 718-731.

[127]St. Petersburg, 1847.

[128]*Ibid.,* 1849-1853.

[129]*Ibid.,* 1869.

[130]A French translation of the first two works quickly appeared: *Introduction à la Théologie orthodoxe* (Paris, 1857); *Théologie dogmatique orthodoxe* (Paris, 1859-60).

[131]G. Florovskii, *Puti...,* *op. cit.,* pp. 222-223.

[132]*Chteniia o dogmaticheskikh istinakh pravoslavno-Khristianskoi veri* (Kiev, 1882).

[133]*Vera pravoslavnoi vostochnoi greko-rossiiskoi tserkvi po ee simvolicheskimknigam,* 2 vols. (Moscow, 1889-90).

[134]*Uroki khristianskogo bogosloviia po novozavetnomu bogosloviiu* (Tver, 1889).

[135]*Kratkii kurs lektsii po pravoslavnomu bogosloviiu* (Moscow, 1889).

[136]*Ocherki khristianskogo pravoslavnogo veroucheniia* (St. Petersburg, 1893).

[137]*Pravoslavnoe dogmaticheskoe bogoslovie* (St. Petersburg, 1894).

[138]*Chteniia po pravoslavnomu khristianskomu bogosloviiu* (Iaroslavl', 1894-5).

[139]*Zapiski po pravoslavnomu dogmaticheskomu bogosloviiu* (Elizavetgrad, 1895).

[140]*Ocherki pravoslavno-khristianskogo veroucheniia* (Samara, 1896).

[141]*Pravoslavnoe dogmaticheskoe bogoslovie* (Sergiev-Posad, 1896).

[142]*Uchenie ob osnovnykh istinakh pravoslavnoi Tserkvi: kratkii kurs bogosloviia* (Moscow, 1906).

[143]I (Khar'kov, 1895); II (Stavropol', 1903); III & IV (Sergiev-Posad, 1909).

[144]Kamenets-Podol'sk, 1904.

[145]A. Kotovich, *Dukhovnaia tsenzura v Rossii (1799-1855 gg.)* (St. Petersburg, 1909). Also, A. M. Skabichevskii, *Ocherk istorii russkoi tsenzury (1700-1865)* (St. Petersburg, 1892).

[146]Cf. Ch. Quenet, *Tchaadaev et les lettres philosophiques* (Paris, 1931); *Sochineniia i pis'ma P. I. Chaadaeva*, M. Gershenzon ed., v. 2 (Moscow, 1913-14).

[147]For the influence of German idealism upon individual Russian philosophers see: A. Koyré, "La philosophie et le problème national en Russie au début du XIX siècle," *Bibliothèque de l'institut français de Leningrad*, 10 vols. (Paris, 1929) 37 ss.

[148]Cf. F. Nelidov, *Zapadniki 40-kh godov* (Moscow, 1910). M. Kovalevskii, "Shellingianstvo i gegelianstvo v Rossii," *Vestnik Evropy* (Nov. 1915) 133-170. Also D. Chizhevskii, *Gegel' v Rossii* (Paris, 1939).

[149]Cf. N. V. Riasanovskii, *Russia and the West in the Teaching of the Slavophiles* (Cambridge, Mass., 1952); F. Fadner, *Seventy Years of Pan-Slavism in Russia* (Washington, D.C., 1962); N. L. Brodskii, *Rannie slaviano-fily* (Moscow, 1910); P. K. Christoff, *An Introduction to Nineteenth Century Russian Slavophilism: A Study in Ideas*, V. 1 (The Hague, 1961). A. Gratieux, *Khomiakov et le Mouvement slavophile*, 2 v. (Paris, 1939).

[150]The literature on Khomiakov has been growing greatly in the last few decades. His complete works have been edited: *Polnoe sobranie sochinenii Alekseia Stepanovicha Khomiakova*, 8 vols. (Moscow, 1900-1914). His English letters to Palmer and other European dignitaries are found in W. Birkbeck, *Russia and the English Church during the Last Fifty Years*, v. 1. (London, 1895). A collection of various religious articles written on different occasions is entitled: *L'Église latine et le Protestantisme au point de vue de l'Église Orient* (Lausanne et Vevey, 1872). N. S. Arseniev, has edited other essays: *Izbrannye sochineniia* (N. Y., 1955). Secondary sources are: B. Baron, *Un Théologien laic orthodoxe russe au XIX siècle, Or. Chr. Anal.,* 27 (Rome, 1940); A. Gratieux, *op. cit.,* Suttner, F. C., *Offenbarung, Gnade und Kirche bei A. S. Chomjakov, Das östliche Christentum* (Würzburg, 1967); B. Zavitnevich, *Aleksei Stepanovich Khomiakov*, 2 vols. (Kiev,

1902); I. Barsov, "O bogoslovskikh sochineniiakh A. S. Khomiakova," *Prav. Obozr.* no. 1, (1880), 29-68.

[151]Cf. Solov'ev, *L'idée russe* (Paris, 1888), 35 note.

[152]Found in *Polnoe...*, *op. cit.*, v. 2 (1900), 3-26.

[153]Cf. *L'Église latine...*, *op. cit.*, p. 63.

[154]For a more complete examination of this term *Sobornost'* in relation to the Nicene term Καθολικὴ see: S. Bulgakov, *The Orthodox Church* (London, 1935), pp. 74-75; R. Barr, "The Changing Face of Sobornost," *Diakonia* v. 2, 3 (1967), 219-222. B. Plank, OESA, *Katholizität und Sobornost* (Würzburg, 1960).

[155]*L'Église latine...*, *op. cit.*, p. 61. The Encyclical text is found in Mansi, 40, col. 377-418; 407-408.

[156]*L'Église latine...*, *op. cit.*, p. 62.

[157]Khomiakov's system shows a form of conciliarism that perhaps goes back in root to William Occam (1290-1350) who taught that tradition was infallible through an historical consent of the faithful rather than through a visible organ of ecclesiastical authority such as the pope or the united bishops in council. Edmund Richeri, a Gallican (1560-1631), also taught that bishops in council were only the legates of the faithful.

[158]Frontispiece in: *Polnoe sobranie...*, *op. cit.*, v. 2 (Moscow, 1900).

[159]Cf. S. L. Frank, *A Solovyov Anthology*, tr. by N. Duddington (London, 1950), 10. Solov'ev's complete works in Russian (9 vols.) were printed in St. Petersburg, 1901-1907; 2nd ed. (10 vols.) printed 1911-1914. Other works include: *La Russie et l'Église universelle* (Paris, 1889); collected letters in Russian, 4 vols. (St. Petersburg, 1908-23). Secondary works include: K. Mochul'skii, *Vladimir Solov'ev; Zhizn' i uchenie* (Paris, 1936); E. Munzer, *Solovyev, Prophet of Russian-Western Unity* (London, 1956); D. Stremooukhoff, *Vladimir Soloviev et son oeuvre messianique* (Paris, 1935); M. d'Herbigny, *Vladimir Soloviev, a Russian Newman;* tr. by A. Buchanan (London, 1918); N. Zernov, *Three Russian Prophets: Khomyakov, Dostoievski and Soloviev* (N. Y., 1944); K. V. Truhlar, *Teilhard und Solowjew: Dichtung und religiöse Erfahrung* (Munich, 1966).

[160]For an interpretation of Solov'ev's position on the papacy cf. "V. S. Solov'ev kak zashchitnik papstva po knige 'La Russie et l'Église universelle'," *Vera i razum* no. 1 (1904), 614-638; v. 2, 13-35; also, "Vozzrenie V. S. Solov'eva na Katolichestvo," *ibid.,* no. 2 (1914), 49-71; 193-217; 483-525; 571-590; 720-746.

[161]P. Florenskii, *Stolp i utverzdenie istiny* (Moscow, 1914).

[162]S. Bulgakov, *Svet nevechernii* (Moscow, 1917).

[163]Cf. footnote 200 of this work for a bibliography of Bulgakov.

[164]In 1927 the Russian Synodal Émigré Church in the Synod of Karlovtsy condemned Bulgakov's position as being tainted by "Modernism." In 1935, Metropolitan Sergii of Moscow, through Eleutherius, metropolitan of Lithuania, also condemned Bulgakov.

[165]*Svet...*, *op. cit.*, p. 228.

[166]An index of the material contained in the collection from 1821 to 1903 was published in 1905: *Sistematicheskii ukazatel' statei pomeshchennykh v zhurnale Khristianskoe Chtenie za 1821-1903 goda* (St. Petersburg, 1905).

[167]Indices [*Ukazateli*] have appeared in *Pravoslavnyi Sobesednik* for the intervals of 1855-1876 (Kazan, 1877) and 1877-1891 (Kazan, 1895).

[168]Its index covers 1860 to 1904: *Sistematicheskii ukazatel' statei pomeshchennykh v zhurnale 'Trudy Kievskoi Dukhovnoi Akademii za 1860-1904 gg'* (Kiev, 1905) and a second index edited by E. Korol'kov, for 1905 to 1914 (Kiev, 1915).

[169]A. P. Dobroklonskii, professor of church history at the University of Odessa, published his four volume work on the history of the Russian Church: *Rukovodstvo po istorii russkoi Tserkvi* (Moscow and Riazan', 1884-1893) which contains a very rich bibliography. He gives in vol. IV, 223, an incomplete list of the Fathers and church writers that had through the ages been translated into Russian. St. Petersburg Academy in this period had done 93 translations.

[170]Its index is entitled: *Alfavitno-predmetnyi ukazatel' Tserkovnykh Vedomostei za 1888-1897* (St. Petersburg, 1899).

[171]Published in Moscow, 1773-1776 and later in five vols. in St. Petersburg, 1818-1819.

[172]Cf. I. P. Sokolov, "Protopresviter I. L. Ianishev, kak deiatel' po starokatolicheskomu voprosu," *Khristianskoe Chtenie*, v. 1 (1911), 230-231.

[173]The shortened German edition of his work appeared in the Old Catholic journal under the title, "Thesen über das *Filioque*," *Internationale Theologische Zeitschrift*, 24 (1898) 681-714. In Russian, A. Brilliantov, *K voprosy o Filioque* (St. Petersburg, 1914).

[174]I have relied in this section on the works of N. N. Gubokovskii, *Russkaia bogoslovskaia nauka v ee istoricheskom razvitii i noveishem sostoianii* (Warsaw, 1928); A. Palmieri, *La Chiesa Russa* (Florence, 1908), esp. pp. 632-669 and the *Acta Academiae Velehradensis*, v. XI (1920-22; ed. A. Spaldak, Prague, 1922).

[175]His main works are: *Ocherk pravoslavnogo dogmaticheskogo bogosloviia* (Kamenets-Podol'sk, 1904); *Uchenie o Boge edinom v sushchestve i troichnom v litsakh* (Khar'kov, 1895); *Uchenie o Boge tvortse i promyslitele mira* (Stavropol', 1903); *O Boge iskupitele* (Kamenets-Podol'sk, 1906).

[176]*Dogmaticheskoe bogoslovie pravoslavnoi katolicheskoi vostochnoi Tserkvi*, 2 vols. (Moscow and Kazan, 1885).

[177]*Chteniia o dogmaticheskikh istinakh pravoslavno-khristianskoi very* (Kiev, 1890).

[178]*Zapiski po pravoslavnomu dogmaticheskomu bogosloviiu* (Elizavetgrad, 1895).

[179]*Pravoslavnoe dogmaticheskoe bogoslovie* (Sergiev-Posad, 1895).

[180]*Geneticheskoe vvedenie v pravoslavnoe bogoslovie* (St. Petersburg, 1877).

[181]*Bogoslovskie akademicheskie chteniia.* (St. Petersburg, 1897).

[182]P. Svetlov, *Znachenie Kresta v dele Khristovom: opyt iziasneniia dogmata iskupleniia* (Kiev, 1893).

[183]S. Stragorodskii, *Pravoslavnoe uchenie o spasenii: opyt raskrytiia nravstvenno-subektivnoi storony spaseniia na osnovanii Sv. Pisaniia i tvorenii sviatootecheskikh* (Sergiev-Posad, 1895; 4th ed. St. Petersburg, 1910).

[184]A. Khrapovitskii, "Dogmat iskupleniia," *Bogosl. Vestnik,* 8-9 (1917), 155-167, 285-315. Also in book form (Sergiev-Posad, 1917).

[185]V. Ekzempliarskii, *Bibleiskoe i sviatootecheskoe uchenie o sushchnosti sviashchenstva* (Kiev, 1904).

[186]A. Vvedenskii, "K voprosy o metodologicheskoi reforme pravoslavnoi dogmatiki," *Bogosl. Vestnik,* 4 (1904), 179-209.

[187]Vl. Nikolskii, *Vera v promysl Bozhii i ee osnovaniia* (Kazan, 1899).

[188]F. Golubinskii, *Umozritel'noe bogoslovie* (Moscow, 1868).

[189]Lebedev especially wrote against the Roman Catholic doctrines of the Immaculate Conception, the cult of the Sacred Heart and the primacy of the pope. Cf. his works: *Raznosti tserkvei vostotchnoi i zapadnoi v uchenii o preosv. Dievie Marii* (St. Petersburg, 1903); *O latinskom kultie serdtza Iisusova* (St. Petersburg, 1903); *O glavenstvie Papy* (St. Petersburg, 1903).

[190]An example of this is: P. Soliarskii, *Zapiski po nravstvennomu bogosloviu* (St. Petersburg, 1860-1863).

[191]I. Ianychev, *Pravoslavno-Khristianskoe uchenie o nravstvennosti* (Moscow, 1887).

[192]M. Olesnitskii, *Nravstvennoe bogoslovie ili khristianskoe uchenie o nravstvennosti* (Kiev, 1892).

[193]P. Ponomarev, *Dogmaticheskie osnovy khristianskogo asketizma po tvoreniiam vostochnykh pisatelei asketov IV veka* (Kazan, 1899). S. Zarine, *Asketizm po pravoslavno-khristianskomu ucheniiu* (St. Petersburg, 1907).

[194]Filaret Drozdov, *Zapiska o dogmaticheskom dostoinstve i okhranitel'nom upotreblenii grecheskogo i slavianskogo perevodov Sviat. Pisaniia* (Moscow, 1858).

[195]Filaret Gumilevskii, *Istoricheskoe uchenie ob ottsakh Tserkvi* (St. Petersburg, 1859, 2nd ed. 1882).

[196]His writings have been edited in Russian by Iu. Ivask, *Izbrannoe* (N. Y., 1956). His most remarkable work, *Uedinennoe,* was tr. by S. S. Kotelianskii as, *Solitaria* (London, 1927). For details of his life and his literary ideas cf. R. Poggioli, *Rozanov* (N. Y., 1962).

[197]The trilogy is individually entitled: *Smert' bogov: Iulian otstupnik* (St. Petersburg, 1895); *Voskresshie bogi: Leonardo da Vinchi* (St. Petersburg, 1901) and *Anti-Khrist: Piotr i Aleksei* (St. Petersburg, 1905).

His complete works are found in two editions: *Polnoe sobranie sochinenii,* 17 vols. (St. Petersburg, 1911-14); 24 vols. (Moscow, 1914-15). For details concerning his life cf. J. Chuzeville, *Dmitri Merejkowsky* (Paris, 1922) and Z. Gippius, *Dmitrii Merezhkovskii* (Paris, 1951, in Russian).

[198]Some of his main works are: *Dream and Reality: An Essay in Autobiography,* tr. K. Lampert (N. Y., 1951); *The Divine and the Human,* tr. R. M. French (London, 1952) *The Destiny of Man,* tr. N. Duddington (N. Y., 1960). For details on his life and an analysis of his thought, cf. E. Porret, *Berdiaeff: Prophète des temps nouveaux* (Neuchâtel, 1951); M. Spinka, *Nicolas Berdyaev: Captive of Freedom* (Philadelphia, 1950); D. A. Lowrie, *Rebellious Prophet* (N. Y., 1960).

[199]Donald A. Lowrie has written a history of this institute: *Saint Sergius in Paris. The Orthodox Theological Institute* (London, 1954).

[200]A partial biography of Bulgakov's main works: *Avtobiographicheskie Zametski,* ed. Lev Zander (Paris, 1956); *Agnets Bozhii* (Paris, 1933); *Apokalipsis Ioanna* (Paris, 1948); *Drug zhenikha* (Paris, 1927); *Karl Marx kak religioznyi tip* (Paris, 1929); *Kupina neopalimaia* (Paris, 1927); *Lestvitsa Iakovleva* (Paris, 1929); *Nevesta agntsa* (Paris, 1945); *O chudesakh evangelskikh* (Paris, 1932); *Radost' tserkovnaia* (Paris, 1938); *Uteshitel'* (Paris, 1936); *Filosofiia imeni* (Paris, 1953); *Le Paraclet: La Sagesse Divine et la Theanthropie;* v. II, tr. by Constantin Andronikof (Paris, 1947); *The Orthodox Church,* tr. by E. S. Cram (London, 1935); *The Wisdom of God: A Brief Summary of Sophiology* (N. Y. and London, 1937).

[201]The proceedings of this congress have been edited and published by H. A. Alivisatos, *Procès-Verbaux du Premier Congrés de Théologie Orthodoxe à Athenes (Nov. 29-Dec. 6, 1936)* (Athens, 1939).

[202]His ecclesiology has been developed in the following works: "Tainstva i tainodeistviia," *Pravoslavnaia Mysl'* (Paris, 1951) no. 8, 17-34; *Trapeza Gospodnia* (Paris, 1952); "La Doctrine de la primauté a la lumière de l'ecclesiologie," *Istina* 4 (1957), 401-420; "Le Concile dans le théologie orthodoxe russe," *Irénikon* 35 (1962), 316-339; "L'Infallibilité de l'Église de point de vue d'un théologien orthodoxe," *L'Infallibilité de l'Église* (Chevetogne, 1961), 183-201; "Una Sancta, En memoire de Jean XXIII, le Pape de l'Amour," *Irénikon,* 36 (1963), 436-475; "The Church That Presides in Love," *The Primacy of Peter in the Orthodox Church* (London, 1963), tr. by Asheleigh Moorhouse.

[203]His three main books written in this period are: *Vostochnye Otsy chetvertogo veka* (Paris, 1931); *Vizantiiskie Otsy V-VIII* (Paris, 1933); *Puti russkogo bogosloviia* (Paris, 1937). A rather complete bibliography of his writings from 1948-1965 was compiled by Thomas E. Bird, "Georges V. Florovsky, Russian Scholar and Theologian," *The American Benedictine Review,* vol. 16, n. 3 (1965), 444-454. His *Collected Works* are now being published in English by Nordland.

[204]"The Function of Tradition in the Ancient Church," *The Greek Orthodox Theological Review*, IX, no. 2 (1963), 181-200.

[205]New York, 1963.

[206]Two of his better known works on the liturgy are: *Sacraments and Orthodoxy* (N. Y., 1965) and *Introduction to Liturgical Theology*, tr. by A. Moorhouse (London, 1966).

[207]He wrote this originally in French: *Introduction à l'étude de Grégoire Palamas* (Paris, 1959).

[208]*Grégoire Palamas, Défense des saints hésychastes*, 2 vols. (Louvain, 1959). A shorter, more popular work in French is Meyendorff's *St. Grégoire Palamas et la mystique orthodoxe* (Paris, 1959). A popular historical view of the Orthodox Church is his *The Orthodox Church*, tr. from the French by John Chapin (N. Y., 1962); also *Christ in Eastern Christian Thought* (Washington, 1969).

[209]Krivoshein, "The Ascetical and Theological Teaching of Gregory of Palamas," *The Eastern Churches Quarterly*, III (1938-1939), 26-33; 71-84; 138-156; 193-214.

[210]Kern, "Les elements de la théologie de Grégoire Palamas," *Irénikon* XX (1947), 6-33; 164-193.

[211]Vladimir Lossky, *The Mystical Theology of the Eastern Church* (London, 1957), tr. by J. Clark, *The Vision of God* (London, 1963), tr. by A. Moorhouse.

[212]Paris 1944, tr. by J. Clark, *The Mystical Theology of the Eastern Church* (London, 1957).

[213]*Op. cit.,* 9.

[214]*Ibid.,* p. 13.

[215]*Ibid.,* p. 243.

[216]Important works that I have relied on for this information are: Vedernikov, A. V., *Patriarkh Sergii i ee dukhovnoe nasledstvo* (Moscow, 1947); Schmemann, "The Revival of Theological Studies in the U.S.S.R.," *Religion in the U.S.S.R.,* Series 1, no. 59 (July, 1960), a publication of the Institute for the Study of the U.S.S.R. in Munich, 29-43; N. Teodorovich, "Curricular Changes in Soviet Theological Schools," *Religion in the U.S.S.R. op. cit.,* 44-49; A. Johansen, "Ecumenism in the Leningrad Theological Academy," *Journal of Ecumenical Studies,* vol. 4, no. 1 (1967), 92-112; N. Struve, *Christians in Contemporary Russia* (N. Y., 1967).

[217]Vedernikov, *op. cit.,* pp. 383-410.

[218]Cf. *Zhurnal Moskovskoi Patriarkhii,* 1946, no. 10 3 & 6.

[219]*Zhurnal Moskovskoi Patriarkhii,* 1948, no. 11, 12.

[220]Church calenders and service instructions were allowed to be printed as well as a few books such as the sermons of Metropolitan Nikolai Krutitskii (2 vols.); *The Proceedings of the Conference of Heads and Representatives of the Autocephalous Orthodox Churches* (2 vols.); *The Truth about*

Religion in the U.S.S.R.; Patriarch Sergius and his Spiritual Heritage and the Speeches and Letters of Patriarch Aleksei. (All in Russian). Cf. Schmemann, "The Revival...," *op. cit.,* 39.

[221]Cf. especially A. Johansen, "Ecumenism in the Leningrad Theological Academy," *op. cit.*

[222]Johansen, *op. cit.,* 92.

[223]Evgenii Karmanov wrote two works on this theme under Borovoi's direction: *The History of the Ecumenical Movement* (1958) and *The Orthodox Church and the Ecumenical Movement in the 20th Century* (1959), in Russian.

NOTES ON PART TWO

[1]T. H. Papadopoullos, *Studies and Documents Relating to the History of the Greek Church and People under Turkish Domination* (Brussels, 1952) 1-122, outlines the constitutional, spiritual, administrative and geographical jurisdiction of the patriarch under the Turks.

[2]A. Lebedev, *Istoriia Greko-vostochnoi Tserkvi pod vlast'iu Turok* (St. Petersburg, 1903, 2nd ed.) p. 20.

[3]For some of the leading works on Gennadios Scholarios see: L. Petit, *et al, Oeuvres completes* (Paris, 1928-1936) 8 v.; M. Jugie, "Scholarios," *DTC,* 14.2: 1521-1570; "Georges Scholarios, professeur de philosophie," *Studi bizantini e neoellenici,* 5 (1939); "La publication des oeuvres de Georges Scholarios," *Échos d'Orient* 27, 300-325; "La forme de l'eucharistie d'après Georges Scholarios," *Échos de'Orient* 33, 289-297; "Les oeuvres pastorales de Georges Scholarios," *Échos d'Orient* 34, 151-159; "L'unionisme de Georges Scholarios," *Échos d'Orient* 36, 65-86; "Écrits apologetiques de Gennade à l'adresse des musulmans," *Byzantion* 5, 295-314; "La polemique de Georges Scholarios contra Plethon. Nouvelle edition de sa correspondance," *Byzantion* 10, 517-530; "Georges Scholarios, Questions scripturaires et théologiques," *Angelicum* 7, 303-313; J. Gill, *Personalities of the Council of Florence* (N.Y., 1964), 79-94; W. Gass, *Gennadius und Pletho: Aristotelismus und Platonismus in der griechischen Kirche* (Bratislav, 1844); K. Krumbacher, *Geschichte der byzantinischen Literatur* (Munich, 1897), 119-121; M. Crusius, *Turcograecia* (Basel, 1584), 15-17; 107-109; M. I. Gedeon, Πατριαρχικοὶ Πίνακες (Constantinople, 1890), 471-479; A. Lebedev, "Gennadii Scholarii, pervyi K. Patriarkh poslve padeniia vizantiskoi imperii," *Bogoslovnyi Vestnik* 3 (1894), 389-412; *Istoriya Greko-vostochnoi Tserkvi pod vlastiu Turok,* 199-221; K. N. Sathas, Νεοελληνικὴ Φιλολογία (Athens, 1868), 12-22; G. I. Zaviras Νέα Ἑλλάς (Athens, 1872), 19-33.

[4]Cf. Dräzek's investigations: "Zu Georgios Scholarios," *Byzantinische Zeitschrift,* 4 (1895), 564-580; "Zum Kircheneinigungsversuch des Jahres 1439," *Byzantinische Zeitschrift,* 5 (1896), 572-586; L. Allatius, *De Ecclesiae orientalis atque occidentalis perpetua consensione* (Cologne, 1648), col. 959-966; E. Renaudot, *Dissertatio de Gennadii vita et scriptis* (Paris, 1709).

[5]L. Petit.

[6]Krumbacher, v. 2, 119.

[7]Petit, IV, 446.

[8]*Ibid.*, 406, cited by Gill, *Personalities...* p. 92.

[9]Petit, I, 306-372.

[10]*Ibid.*, III, 476-538. Found also in Hergenröther's text: *PG* 161: 11 ss.

[11]Cf. Petit, VI, VII and VIII for resumes of Thomas' I^a-II^{ae}, his *De Ente et Essentia*, Thomas' translation of *De Anima* of Aristotle, Aristotle's *Categories* and *Interpretation*, Porphyry's *Isagoge*, smaller works of Aristotle, including his *Physica*, the *Summulae Logicae* of Peter of Spain and *De sex Principiis* of Gilbert.

[12]Petit, II, 1-268.

[13]*Ibid.*, 269-454.

[14]*Ibid.*, 458-495. Two dialogues complete the main sources of his teaching on the procession of the Holy Spirit. *Ibid.*, III, 1-204.

[15]St. Augustine's work, *De Trinitate*, was translated into Greek by the monk, Maximus Planudes, at the end of the 13th century.

[16]Cf. Jugie's treatment in "Scholarios," *DTC*, XIV^2, 1563-4.

[17]Petit, II, 256.

[18]*Ibid.*, 433.

[19]These are found in Petit, I. Of the five treatises on this subject, the second on the origin of the soul was previously edited by Eugenios Bulgaros (Leipzig, 1784). The third part, pp. 77-102, is found in the work of Nicephoros Blemmydes.

[20]Petit, I, 513.

[21]Petit, I. These are also found in *PG* 160.

[22]Petit, I, 403-440.

[23]*Ibid.*, 406.

[24]Cf. *PG* 160, 820-1020; E. Stephanou, *DTC*, 12.2: 2393-2404; F. Masai, *Plethon et le platonisme de Mistra* (Paris, 1956).

[25]Petit, III, XXXV-XLII, divides the Confession into 12 chapters with the last containing 7 motives of credibility. I have used the texts edited by Kimmel, *op. cit.* 1-10; I. Michalcescu, *Die Bekenntnisse und die wichtigsten Glaubens-Zeugnisse der griechisch-orientalischen Kirche* (Leipzig, 1904), 255-261; *PG* 160, 33-351; Mesoloras, Συμβολικὴ τῆς ὀρθοδόξου ἀνατολικῆς Ἐκκλησίας (Athens, 1883) v. I, 66-67. N. Ilminskii has reconstructed the original Turkish text: *Predvaritel'noe soobshchenie o turetskom perevode izlozheniia very patriarkha Gennadiia Skolariia* (Kazan, 1880).

[26]Cf. Palmieri, *op. cit.*, 439-440.

[27]Androutsos, Δογματικὴ τῆς ὀρθοδόξου ἀνατολικῆς Ἐκκλησίας (Athens, 1907), 32.

[28]Lebedev, *op. cit.*, 260-63.

[29]Crusius, *Turcograecia*, 484.

[30]Cf. Renaudin, P., "Les églises orientales orthodoxes et le protestantisme," *Revue de l'Orient Chrétien*, 5 (1900), 566-68.

[31]For literature on Jeremias, cf. Crusius, 485 ss; Sathas, 186; M. Gedeon, Πατριαρχικοί Πίνακες, 518 ss.

[32]Crusius, 208.

[33]Ph. Meyer, *Die theologische Literatur der griechischen Kirche im sechszehnten Jahrhundert* (Leipzig, 1899), 91.

[34]Crusius, 432.

[35]Cf. Mesoloras, *op. cit.*, 124-194. Also, Palmieri, *Theol. Dogm. Orth.*, *op. cit.*, 1, 455-6. The three responses are found in: *Acta et Scripta theologorum Wirtembergensium et Patriarchae Constantinopolitani D. Hieremiae*, (Würtemberg, 1633).

[36]Mesoloras, 194.

[37]*Ibid.*, 246-7.

[38]*Ibid.*, 264. The responses have been translated into Russian by Archimandrite Nilus, *Sviateishago patriarkha Konst. Ieremii otvety Luteranam: perevod s grecheskago*, (Moscow, 1866).

[39]Cf. Mesoloras, *op. cit.*, 123; Palmieri, *op. cit.*, 458; I. Karmires, t. I (Athens, 1960), 431.

[40]For literature on Manuel, cf. Crusius, 90, 146; Alatius, 983, 525; Sathas, Ν.Φ., *op. cit.*, 12; A. Moustoxydis, Ἑλληνομνήμων, (Athens, 1843-53), 313 ss; Zaviras, *op. cit.*, 437; Gedeon, Χρονικά, *op. cit.*, 36; E. Legrand, *Bibliographie hellenique* XVᵉet XVIᵉ, I, CVI.

[41]S. von Lemoyne edited this (1685) and it has been incorporated into Migne's collection, *PG* 140, 471-482.

[42]Archimandrite Arsenius edited this in *Khristianskoe Chtenie*, II (1866), 102-162 as did also L. Petit in *Patrologia Orientalis*, XVII, 491-522.

[43]Gedeon gives this title as: Κατὰ τὸν περὶ ἐκπορεύσεως τοῦ Ἁγίου Πνεύματος Πληθωνικοῦ συγγράμματος Meyer, *op. cit.*, 36, thinks this work could be that of a 15th century Manuel who became patriarch with the name of Maximos III and reigned about 1482.

[44]Arsenius edited this work also, cited in M. Jugie, *Theologia Dogmatica Christianorum Orientalium*, I (Paris, 1926), 494.

[45]For literature on Pachomius, cf. Sathas, Ν.Φ., 150; N. Katramis, Φιλολογικὰ Ἀνάλεκτα (Zante, 1880), 231 ss.; Legrand, I, 231 ss.; Krumbacher, I, 593; Moustoxydes, Ἑλληνομνήμων, 631-712, 442 ss.; Migne, *PG* 98, 1333-1360.

[46]Mingarelli has edited this with the title Περὶ Καρτανιτῶν Αἱρετικῶν —περὶ τῆς τῶν Καρτανιτῶν αἱρέσεως.

[47]*Graeci Codices manuscripti apud Nanios patricios Venetos asservati* (Bonn, 1704), 274 ss. Cf. also, Migne, *PG* 98, 1359-1363; Moustoxydes, *op. cit.*, 446-452; Legrand, I, 231 ss.

[48]These are found in *Cod. Berol. Philipp.* (1617) fol. 207-336, citation in Meyer, 47. Many other mss. are found in the Marciana Collection in Venice. Cf. Stathas, Ν.Φ., *op. cit.*, 150.

[49]Stathas, *ibid.*, 152.

[50]Cf. D. Geanakoplos, *Greek Scholars in Venice: Studies in the Dissemination of Greek Learning from Byzantium to Western Europe* (Cambridge,

Mass., 1962); *ibid., Byzantine East and Latin West* (Oxford, 1966); also, K. Setton, "The Byzantine Background to the Italian Renaissance," *Proceedings of the American Philosophical Society,* C, no. 1 (1956), 1-76.

[51]Concerning his life and writings, cf. Papadopulos, Comnenos, N., *Historia gymnasii patavini,* t. II (Venice, 1726), 279-280; Fabricius, *Bibliotheca graeca* (Harles, ed.) t. IX, 307-308; t. XI, 475-478; 521; 699-700; A. Demetracopoulos, Ὀρθόδοξος Ἑλλάς, 130-134; L. Allatius, *op. cit.,* col. 996; M. Le Quien, *Oriens Christianus* (Paris, 1740), t. 2, 503; Zaviras, *op. cit.,* 427 ss.; Sathas, *op. cit.,* 208.

[52]Metaxas, M., Περὶ τῆς ἀρχῆς τοῦ Πάπα ὡς ἐν εἴδει ἐπιστολῶν (Constantinople, 1627).

[53]Meyer, *op. cit.,* 55.

[54]The text is found in the Τόμος Χαρᾶς of Patriarch Dositheos, 553-604. Agathangelos Nikolakis published this again in Candia 1908: Ἡ πρὸς τοὺς Κρῆτας ἀλληλογραφία Μελετίου τοῦ Πηγᾶ, εἰς ἥν προσετέθη καὶ τὸ περισπούδαστον ἔργον αὐτοῦ κατὰ τῆς ἀρχῆς τοῦ Πάπα. Cf. Legrand, II, 119.

[55]*De Civitate Dei,* Bk. XI, ch. 1.

[56]Dositheos, *op. cit.,* 555. The division of the Church is reminiscent again of St. Augustine's description of the two cities of men found in his *De Civitate Dei;* Bk. XV, ch. 1.

[57]*Ibid.,* 559.

[58]*Ibid.,* 573-569.

[59]Legrand gives the title, II, 88 and claims that it was first written in Latin, but does not mention where it can be found.

[60]Legrand, II, 115. A. Demetracopoulos, Προσθῆκαι καὶ διορθώσεις εἰς τὴν νεοελληνικὴν φιλολογίαν Κ. Σάθα. (Leipzig, 1871), 20-32.

[61]Works treating his life and writings are: E. Legrand, *Bibliographie Hellenique des XVe et XVIe siècles,* II (Paris, 1885), xxiii ss.; L. Petit, "Margounios Maxime," *DTC,* IX[2], 2039-44; Meyer, *op. cit.,* 69-78; G. Fedalto, "Excursus storico sulla vita e sulla attivita di Massimo Margounios," *Studia Patavina,* VIII (1961), 213-44; (1963), 301-307; *ibid. Massimo Margounios e la sua opera per conciliare la sentenza degli orientali e dei Latini sulla Processione dello Spirito Santo* (Padua, 1961); Sathas, *op. cit.,* 212 ss. Zaviras, *op. cit.,* 111 ss. and 465 ss.; Lami, *Deliciae Eruditorum,* t. VII and IX; K. Dyobouniotes, in various numbers of *Gregorios Palamas* (1920-21) in Greek; P. Enepekides, "Der Briefwechsel des Maximos Margunios, Bischof von Kythera," *Jahrbuch der Österreichischen byzantinischen Gesellschaft* (Vienna, 1951), 13 ss.; *ibid.,* "Maximos Margunios an deutsche und italienische Humanisten," X (1961), 93-145; Ch. Astruc, "Maxime Margounios et les recueils Parisiens de sa correspondance," *Kretika Chronika* (1949), 211-61; D. Geanakoplos, *Greek Scholars in Venice: Studies in the Dissemination of Greek Learning from Byzantium to Western Europe* (Cambridge,

Mass., 1962); *ibid., Byzantine East and Latin West: Two Worlds of Christendom in Middle Ages and Renaissance* (Oxford, 1966).

[62]Geanakoplos, *Byzantine East, op. cit.,* 171.

[63]Demetracopoulos, *op. cit.,* Π. Δ., 22, gives the title of this work as: Περὶ τῆς ἐκπορεύσεως τοῦ Ἁγίου Πνεύματος βιβλία τρία. Cf. Petit, *op. cit., DTC,* 2040, who lists the mss. in which this work can be found.

[64]Demetracopoulos, *op. cit.,* 27-29; also, Legrand, *op. cit.,* t. I, XXXIII.

[65]This is entitled: Περὶ τῆς τοῦ Παναγίου Πνεύματος ἐκπορεύσεως ὡς ἐν εἴδει ἐπιστολῆς. Cf. Legrand, I, 237.

[66]Gretzer published both Margounios' *scholia* and his refutation in: *Jacobi Gretseni, S. J., Opera Omnia,* t. IX (Ratisbon, 1737), 48 ss.

[67]D. Hoeschel, Μαξίμου τοῦ Μαργουνίου Κυθήρων Ἐπισκόπου ἐπιστολαὶ δύο (Frankfurt, 1591), 1-24. Cf. P. Enepekides, "Maximos Marguinios an deutsche..." *op. cit.,* 101-131.

[68]D. Geanakoplos, *Byzantine East, op. cit.,* 174-176.

[69]Geanakoplos had visited Iviron and made a complete listing of his donation. The catalogue is given in his, *Byzantine East, op. cit.,* 183-190.

[70]For his life and works cf. Simon Richard, *Fides Ecclesiae orientalis seu Gabrielis metropolitae Philadelphiensis opuscula, nunc primam de graecis conversa, cum notis uberioribus, quibus nationum orientalium persuasion, maxime de rebus eucharisticis ex liberis praesertim manuscriptis vel nondum Latio donatis illustratur* (Paris, 1671); Fabricius, *Bibliotheca, op. cit.,* XI, 525; Zaviras, *N. E. op. cit.,* 216; Sathas, Ν. Φ., 218; Legrand, *op. cit.,...aux XVᵉ et XVIᵉ siècles,* t. II, XXVIII ss.; 142-144, 422; *ibid....du XVIIᵉ* t. I, 38-40, 239; t. II, 142-242; t. III, 2-3, 181; Crusius, *op. cit.,* 206-7; 220, 275, 522, 525, 533, 534; Demetrakopoulos, 32; Allatius, *op. cit.,* I, III, c. VII; M. Jugie, "Gabriel Severe," *DTC,* t. VI¹, 977-984; *ibid.,* "Un théologien grec du XVI siècle: Gabriel Savère et les divergences entre les deux Églises," *Échos d'Orient,* t. XVI (1913), 97-108. Some letters of Maximos Margounios dealing with the life and teaching of Gabriel are found in: J. Lami, *Deliciae eruditorum,* t. XIII, "Gabrielis Severi et aliorum graecorum recentiorum epistotlae" (Florence, 1744), 1-131; Meyer, *op. cit.,* 78-84.

[71]Ἔκθεσις κατὰ τῶν ἀμαθῶς λεγόντων καὶ παρανόμως διδασκόντων ὅτι ἡμεῖς οἱ τῆς ἀνατολικῆς ἐκκλησίας γνήσιοι καὶ ὀρθόδοξοι παῖδες ἐσμὲν σχισματικοὶ παρὰ τῆς ἁγίας καὶ καθόλου ἐκκλησίας. Cf. Legrand, *op. cit.,* t. I, 240-43. According to Sp. Lambros, *Catalogue of the Greek manuscripts on Mount Athos* (Cambridge, 1885), this work is found in *cod.* 1616, 2137, 2791 of Mt. Athos.

[72]Συνταγμάτιον περὶ τῶν Ἁγίων καὶ Ἱερῶν Μυστηρίων (Venice, 1600); Legrand,...*XVᵉ et XVIᵉ siècles, op. cit.,* t. II, 142;...*du XVIIᵉ* siècle, t. II, 2-3.

[73]Cf. Legrand, *op. cit.,...XVIIᵉ siècle,* 38-40.

[74]K. N. Sathas, Μεσαιωνική βιβλιοθήκη (Venice-Paris, 1872), t. VI, λή—μστ'.

[75]For descriptions of these authors and their works, cf. Krumbacher, *op. cit.*, II, 811-853.

[76]Cf. Sathas, *op. cit.*, N. Φ., 147; Zaviras, *op. cit.*, 100, 373; Legrand, *op. cit.*,...*XVᵉ et XVIᵉ siècles*, I, 226.

[77]*Acta et Scripta*, *op. cit.*, 263.

[78]Cf. Sathas, Μεσαιωνική...*op. cit.*, t. III.

[79]Krumbacher, *op. cit.*, I, 608.

[80]Cf. Lami, *op. cit.*, 72-118. On his life cf. Sathas, N. Φ., 181 and Legrand, *op. cit.*, I, 315 ss.

[81]Cf. Sathas, N. Φ., 231; Legrand, *op. cit.*, II, 348 ss.

[82]'Εγχειρίδιον κατὰ τοῦ σχίσματος τῶν Παπιστῶν καὶ περὶ τῆς Εὐχαριστίας. Cf. Legrand II, 475; also, Sathas, N. Φ., 224; Demetracopoulos, Π. Δ., 35.

[83]Cf. Legrand I, 444; II, 12 ss.; Sathas, N. Φ., 152 ss. and Zaviras, *op. cit.*, 250 ss.

[84]For sources of the life and writings of Cyril Lucaris, cf.: Legrand, *op. cit.*,...*au dixseptième Siècle* (Paris, 1896), 161-521; Thomas Smith, *Miscellanea* (London, 1686); *ibid.*, *Collectanea de Cyrillo Lucario, Patr. Const.* (London, 1707); Kimmel, *op. cit.*, t. I Secondary sources cf. G. A. Hadjiantoniou, *Protestant Patriarch* (Richmond, Va., 1967); J. Aymon, *Monuments Authentiques de la Religion de Grece* (Hagae Comitum, 1708), 1-200; A. Pichler, *Geschichte des Protestantismus in der orientalischen Kirche im 17 Jahrhundert oder der Patriarch Cyrillus Lukaris und seine Zeit* (Munich, 1862); V. Semno, "Les dernières années du patriarche Cyrille Lucar," *Échos d'Orient* (1903), t. VI, 97-107; C. Emereau, "Lucar, Cyrille," *DTC*, IX¹, 1003-1019; A. Brianzev, "Patriarkh Kirill Lukaris i ego zaslugi dlia pravoslavnoi Tserkvi," *Strannik*, t. I (1870), 3-37, 119-146, 195-238, 315-338; Lebedev, *op. cit.*, 633-673; Ph. Meyer, "Lukaris," *Realenzyklopädie für protestantische Theologie*, t. XI (Leipzig, 1902), 682-690; P. Trivier, *Un patriarche de Constantinople au XVIIᵉ siècle, Cyrille Lucar sa vie et son influence* (Paris, 1877); R. Schier, *Der Patriarch Kirill Lukaris von Konstantinopel* (Marburg, 1927); G. Hofmann, *Griechische Patriarchen und römische Päpste: Patriarch Kirillos Lukaris und die römische Kirche* (Rome, 1928); A. Demetracopoulos, "Βίος τοῦ Π. Κυρίλλου Λουκάρεως," 'Εθνικὸν 'Ημερολόγιον (Athens, 1870), 41-51; *ibid.*, Π. Δ., *op. cit.*, M. Gedeon, Κύριλλος Λούκαρις (Constantinople, 1876); A. Chrys. Papadopoulos, "'Απολογία Κυρίλλου τοῦ Λουκάρεως," Νέα Σιὼν (1905), t. II, 17-35; D. S. Balanos, 'Ομολογία Κυρίλλου τοῦ Λουκάρεως (Athens, 1906); E. Velanidiotis, 'Ο 'Εθνομάρτυς Π. Κύριλλος Λούκαρις (Athens, 1906); K. Sathas, N. Φ., 238 ss.; M. Rinieris, Κύριλλος Λούκαρις (Athens, 1859).

[85]Aymon, *op. cit.*, 142-3.

[86]*Ibid.,* 172-176.

[87]Legrand, *op. cit.,* IV, 329-340.

[88]Peter Skarga, S. J. in his: *Miscellanea de Synodo Brestensi,* cited by C. Emereau, art. cit. *DTC.,* 1014.

[89]J. H. Hottinger, *Analecta historica* (Zürich, 1652), 560, cited by Trivier, *op. cit.,* 78.

[90]Chr. A. Papadopoulos, "'Απολογία..." *op. cit.,* (1905), t. II, 33.

[91]Legrand, *op. cit.,* I, 270 ss.

[92]Legrand, *op. cit.,* IV, 298.

[93]Kimmel, *op. cit.,* I, 25-26.

[94]*Ibid.,* 26.

[95]Kimmel, 398-408; Mansi, 34, 1709-1720.

[96]Mesoloras, *op. cit.,* 36.

[97]Cf. also Aymon, *op. cit.,* 261-451; Lebedev, *op. cit.,* 58-62; A. Palmieri, *Dositeo, Patriarca greco di Gerusalemme* (Florence, 1909), 15-24. The *Acta* are found in Mesoloras, II, 55-86; 103-129; Mansi, 1651-1775; Kimmel, LXXV-XCII; 325-488.

[98]Mesoloras, *op. cit.,* 91-99.

[99]Palmieri, *Theologia...op. cit.,* I, 464-468 and 506-507 provides the fullest bibliography on this subject. Greek authors such as Mesolora, Sathas, Ch. Papadopoulos and E. Velanidiotes repudiate the charge of his authorship while other Greek authors such as D. Balanos and C. Androutsos maintain that he was its true author. An English version of the Confession is found in G. Hadjiantoniou, *Protestant Patriarch, op. cit.,* 141-145.

[100]For works dealing with his life and writings, cf., Kimmel, Appendix, 1-213; Mesoloras, *op. cit.,* I, 265-368; Michalcescu, *op. cit.,* 186-252; Legrand, I, 219; V, 192-218; Vretos, A. P., Ν. Φ., (Athens) I, 211-212; Sathas, Ν. Φ., 297-8; Zaviras, Ν. Ε., 449; W. Gass, *Symbolik der griechischen Kirche* (Berlin, 1872), 64-69; A. Palmieri, *Theologia...op. cit.,* I, 564-576; Jugie, *op. cit.,* I, 511-512, 580; V. Grumel, "Metrophane Critopoulos," *DTC,* X², 1622-27; A. Demetracopoulos, Δοκίμιον περὶ τοῦ βίου καὶ τῶν συγγραμμάτων Μητροφάνου τοῦ Κριτοπούλου Π. 'Αλεξ., (Leipzig, 1870); Aymon, *op. cit.,* 37, 327-8; Lebedev, *op. cit.,* 627-32.

[101]For the text of his Confession, cf. Kimmel, II, 1-213; Mesoloras, I, 279-361; Michalcescu, 186-252.

[102]We follow the pagination in Kimmel's text.

[103]Mesoloras, *op. cit.,* 277.

[104]Androutsos, Συμβολική..., *op. cit.,* 37.

[105]Cf. Trivier, *op. cit.,* 128-9.

[106]Papadopoulos, Comnenos, *Praenotiones mystagogicae* (Padua, 1697), 184, cited by Palmieri, I, 573. Critopoulos is called "a Greek Lutheran." Sathas and Porphyrios Uspenskii for this reason dispute the authenticity of the Confession, attributing it to Calvinist and Lutheran machinations.

[107]Michalcescu, *op. cit.*, 213-218.

[108]The most authoritative work on Syrigos has been written by P. Pargoire, in a series of articles in *Échos d'Orient*, t. XI, 264-280; 331-340; t. XII, 17-27; 167-175; 281-286; 336-342. Shorter notices are found in the following sources: Legrand,...*XVIIe siècle, op. cit.*, t. II, 458 ss.; Zaviras, *op. cit.*, 443-448; Sathas, *op. cit.*, 255-260.

[109]Edited and published by Dositheos under the title: Κατὰ τῶν Καλβινικῶν Κεφαλαίων καὶ ἐρωτήσεων Κυρίλλου τοῦ Λουκάρεως (Bucharest, 1690).

[110]Schelstrate, *Acta...op. cit.*, 396-401.

[111]Cf. "Moghila, La confession de Pierre," *DTC*, t. X, 2070, 2081.

[112]Cf. Legrand,...*XVIIe siècle*, t. IV, 114-119; 5. II, 264; Mesoloras, I, 362-9.

[113]Cf. P. Pargoire, *Échos d'Orient*, t. XII (1909), 337-42.

[114]Troitskii, I, in: *Khristianskoe Chtenie*, t. I (1881). The Greek title of the document is: Ἐξήγησις συνοπτικὴ τῆς Θείας καὶ Ἁγίας Λειτουργίας.

[115]The best biographical details about the life of Ligarides and his writings is found in Legrand,...*XVIIe siècle, op. cit.*, t. IV, 8-61. Other authors to be consulted: Vretos, Ν. Φ., t. I, 213-214; Sathas, Ν. Φ., 314-316; Demetracopoulos, *O.E.*, 161-162; *ibid.*, Π. Δ., 51; Zaviras, *N.E.*, 512-514; Wm. Palmer, *The Patriarch and the Tsar*, t. III, "History of the Condemnation of Patriarch Nicon" (London, 1873), XVII-LXIV, 1-14; Makarii, *Istoriia...op. cit.*, t. XII, *passim* in dealing with the history of Nikon.

[116]Legrand, *op. cit.*, t. IV, 8-61.

[117]Cited by Legrand, *ibid.*, 25-36.

[118]*Ibid.*, 25.

[119]*Ibid.*, 59.

[120]*Ibid.*, 49-56.

[121]This was published by Palmer in t. III of his work, *The Patriarch and the Tsar* (London, 1873), 15-311.

[122]Cf. Migne, ed., *La Perpetuité de la foi de l'Église catholique touchant l'eucharistie*, t. I, 1199-1223.

[123]The most complete life of the Likhoudes Brothers was written by Michael Smentsovskii; *Brat'ia Likudi* (St. Petersburg, 1899). Smentsovskii also has written a shorter account entitled: "Brat'ia Likudi i napravlenie teorii slovesnosti v ikh shkole," *Zhurnal ministerstva narodnago prosveshcheniia*, t. XLV (1845) 31-96; also, P. Obrasov, "Brat'ia Likudi. Epizody iz istorii russkago prosveshcheniia v kontse XVIII stoletiia," *ibid.*, t. CXXXV, section II, (1867) 736-753. Cf. also, Sathas, Ν. Φ., *op. cit.*, 358-371.

[124]Listed by Jugie, *Theologia...op. cit.*, t. I, 518.

[125]Printed in the theological review of the Academy of Kazan, *Pravoslavnyi Sobesednik* (1866-1867).

[126]The most detailed bibliography on the life and works of Dositheos is found in the article of A. Palmieri, "Dosithée," *DTC*, IV², 1788-1800.

[127]Περὶ τῆς ἀρχῆς τοῦ Πάπα—'Αντίρρησις (Jassy, 1682). This work is made up of several short treatises, done by other authors besides Nectarios. Dositheos introduces the work with a preface and a life of Nectarios. Other writings include the "Εκθεσις Πίστεως of Macarios, metropolitan of Nicomedia (1464); 'Απολογία of bishops and priests to John VIII in regard to Florence; the "Οροι of the patriarchs, Philotheos of Alexandria, Dorotheos of Antioch and Joachim of Jerusalem against the Council of Florence; the 'Ομολογία of Archbishop Joseph; Sermon of Nectarios on rebaptism; and finally, two short works against the Jesuits whom Dositheos all his life regarded as his greatest enemies.

[128]The Acts of the Synod of Jerusalem including the second part, the 'Ομολογία of the Confession of Dositheos can be found in Mesoloras, *op. cit.*, t. I, 55-129; Michaelescu, Θησαυρὸς τῆς 'Ορθοδοξίας (Leipzig, 1904), 123-182; Kimmel, *Libri symbolici, op. cit.*, 325-488.

[129]Michaelescu, *op. cit.*, 174-175.

[130]"Δοσίθεος Πατριάρχης 'Ιεροσολύμων," Νέα Σιών, t. V (1907), 104-108.

[131]Makarii, *Pravoslavnoe dogm. bogoslovie, op. cit.*, t. I, 63. Cf. the Russian edition of the Confession "Izlozhenie very sostavlennoe na sobore ierusalimskom," *Voskresnoe Chtenie* (Moscow, 1840), t. IV.

[132]'Εγχειρίδιον ἔλεγχον τὴν Καλβινικὴν φρενοβλάβειαν (Bucharest, 1690).

[133]Palmieri, *Dositeo...op. cit.*, 33-37.

[134]Mesoloras, *op. cit.*, 89-91.

[135]Michalcescu, *op. cit.*, 125.

[136]Androutsos, Δοκίμιον Συμβολικῆς, *op. cit.*, 35-36.

[137]Citation found in Palmieri, *Theologia...op. cit.*, t. I, 504-505.

[138]Published respectively, Jassy, 1692; Jassy, 1698; Rimnic, 1705.

[139]Cf. Δωδεκάβιβλος, 1177, edited by Dositheos' nephew and successor to the see of Jerusalem, Chrysanthos Notaras (Bucharest, 1715). Richard's work was published in Paris, 1658. Cf. Legrand,...XVII° siècle, op. cit., t. II, 104.

[140]It is listed at times under the title Δωδεκάβιβλος (Bucharest, 1715) or by Dositheos' original title: 'Ιστορία περὶ τῶν ἐν 'Ιεροσολύμοις Πατριαρχευσάντων.

[141]Δωδεκάβιβλος, 1180.

[142]This work is entitled: Κατὰ τῶν Καλβινικῶν κεφαλαίων καὶ ἐρωτήσεων Κυρίλλου τοῦ Λουκάρεως (Bucharest, 1690).

[143]'Ορθόδοξος ὁμολογία τῆς πίστεως τῆς Καθολικῆς καὶ 'Αποστολικῆς 'Εκκλησίας τῆς 'Ανατολῆς καὶ εἰσαγωγικὴ ἔκθεσις περὶ τῶν τριῶν μεγίστων ἀρετῶν πίστεως, ἐλπίδος καὶ ἀγάπης (Snagov, 1699).

144For details about the life and writings of Coressios, cf. Dositheos' Περὶ τῶν ἐν Ἱεροσολύμοις Πατριαρχευσάντων (Jassy, 1715), 1178-1179; Vretos, N. Φ., t. I, 209-210; Aymon, *Monuments...op. cit.,* 70-73; Sathas, N. Φ., 247-250; Zaviras, 321-325; Legrand,...*XVIIe siècle,* t. III, 255-272; A. Palmieri, "Coressios, Georges," *DTC,* t. III², 1847-1848.

145Τόμος καταλλαγῆς, (Jassy, 1694), 276-412.

146Lebedev, *Istoriia...op. cit.,* 674-678 and Legrand...*XVIIe,* t. I, 159-166 give the most details about this fairly unknown writer. Cf. also Jugie, *op. cit.,* t. I, 510-511; Sathas, N. Φ., *op. cit.,* 308.

147His Catechism, a collector's rare piece, is entitled: Χριστιανικὴ κατήχησις εἰς δόξαν τοῦ φιλανθρώπου Θεοῦ Πατρός, Ἰησοῦ Χριστοῦ καὶ Ἁγίου Πνεύματος τιμὴν βοήθειαν τε τῶν φιλοθέων Ρωμαίων (Wittenburg, 1622). Cf. Legrand, t. I, 159-170.

148Sathas, N. Φ., *op. cit.,* 108.

149Legrand, t. I, 159-166.

150Cf. his work: Ἔλεγχος τῆς ψευδοχριστιανικῆς κατηχήσεως Ζαχαρίου τοῦ Γεργάνου, (Rome, 1631; in Greek and Latin). Cf. Legrand, t. I, 159-170.

151Cf. Lebedev, *op. cit.,* 678-682; Jugie, *op. cit.,* I, 510; Meletios, Metropolitan of Athens, Ἐκκλησιαστικὴ Ἱστορία, t. III, 451 ss; Sathas, *op. cit.,* 251-253; Gedeon, Χρονικά, *op. cit.,* 74-75; Dositheos, Ἱστορία, *op. cit.,* Bk. XI, ch. 10, 2, 1172.

152For the account cf. Dositheos, Ἱστορία, *op. cit.,* 1172; also Sathas, 251-252.

153Sathas, N. Φ., 251-252; Gedeon, Χρονικά, *op. cit.,* 80; Dositheos, Ἱστορία, *op. cit.,* 1172.

154Sathas, 309.

155Cf. Th. Xanthopoulos, "Les traductions de l'Écriture sainte en neo-grec," *Échos d'Orient,* t. V (1902), 321 ss.

156On the history of this translation and the contents of the introduction, cf. Legrand, t. I, 363-388.

157Cf. Metropolitan Meletios of Athens, Ἐκκλησιαστική, *op. cit.,* t. III, ed. G. Vendotis (Vienna, 1784), 450; also Dositheos, Ἱστορία, *op. cit.,* Bk. II, ch. 10, 1173.

158A. Helladius, *Status praesens Ecclesiae Graecae* (place not given, 1714), 295.

159Legrand, t. I, 369.

160He is not to be confused with the Uniate bishop of Iconium, Joannes Mattaeos Caryophyllos (d. 1633).

161Legrand, III, 34-35. Dositheos entitles his work against Caryophyllos: Ἐγχειρίδιον κατὰ Ἰωάννου τοῦ Καρυοφύλλη. Cf. Legrand, III, 30-36.

162*Ibid.,* 34-35.

163Ἐγχειρίδιον, *op. cit.,* 35-36; also Zaviras, *op. cit.,* 363.

[164]J. Heineccius, *Eigentliche und wahrhaftige Abbildung der alten und neun griechischen Kirche,* vol. I (Leipzig, 1711), 41-46.

[165]Papadopoulos-Kerameos, in the collection ed. in Rumanian by E. Hurmuzaki *Documente privitore la istoria Romanilor, Texte grecesti,* XII-XXIII (Bucharest, 1909).

[166]Cf. the statement in Legrand, t. III, 47. Also, Émile Picot, *Nouveaux mélanges orientaux* (Paris, 1886), 539, 545; J. Bianu, and N. Horos, *Bibliografia romanesca veche,* t. I (Bucharest, 1903), 416-419; 450-451.

[167]Ἑορτολόγιον (Bucharest, 1701). The full title is found in the article by Jugie, "Kymenites, Sevastos"; t. VIII², *DTC,* 2381. The work deals more particularly with the dates of the feasts and their *raison d'être:* Easter, certain ecclesiastical canons, and the menology.

[168]Δογματικὴ διδασκαλία τῆς ἁγιωτάτης ἀνατολικῆς καὶ Καθολικῆς Ἐκκλησίας (Bucharest, 1703). For the full title cf. Jugie, *ibid.,* 2382.

[169]Published in various editions and languages but the main edition was published in Venice, 1720.

[170]Main edition published in Leipzig, 1718.

[171]This is found in Dositheos' Τόμος Χαρᾶς, *op. cit.,* 134-553 with the title Ἀντέγκλημα τῶν ἐγκαλούντων ἀδίκως κατὰ τῆς μιᾶς καὶ μόνης ἁγίας Καθολικῆς Θεονύμφου τῆς τοῦ Χριστοῦ Ἐκκλησίας.

[172]The main edition of his *Catechism* was published in Venice in 1681. An English was edited by Bromage.

[173]Σύνοψις τῶν Θείων καὶ ἱερῶν τῆς Ἐκκλησίας δογμάτων (Venice, 1635).

[174]Details of his life and writings are found in P. Chiotes, Βιογραφικὴ Ἀφήγησις t. I (Zante, 1862), 9-32; Zaviras, *N.E., op. cit.,* 494-495; Legrand, t. V, 261-268; Palmieri, *Theologia...op. cit.,* I, 144-145; Allatius, *op. cit.,* 990; Sathas, Ν. Φ., 254-255.

[175]Σύνοψις τῆς ἱερᾶς Θεολογίας, 2 Vol. (Zante, 1862).

[176]For a history of St. Athanasios Greek College in Rome, cf: C. Korolevsky, "Les premiers temps de l'histoire du college Grec de Rome (1576-1622)," *Stoudion* (1927-1930); Placide de Meester, OSB, *Le College Pontifical Grec de Rome* (Rome, 1910); "Historia dell'Erettione del Collegio Greco," *Archives of Greek College (AcGr),* I, 78-98; J. Krajcar, S.J., "The Greek College under the Jesuits for the First Time (1591-1604)," *Orientalis Christiana Periodica,* vol. XXXI (1965), 85-118.

[177]For a biographical sketch, cf. Legrand, III, 196-203.

[178]Cf. the article "Arcudius, Pierre," *DTC,* I², 1771-1773; also Legrand, III, 209-232.

[179]Biographical details and a list of Allatios' writings are found in: Legrand, III, 435-471; L. Petit, "Allatius, Leon," *DTC,* 830-833 and in the uncompleted biography of Stephen Gradi: *Leonis Allatii vita,* published by

Mai, *Nova Bibliotheca Patrum,* t. VI, 2nd part, V-XXVIII; also Sathas, N. Φ., *op. cit.,* 268-274.

[180]Published in three books (Cologne, 1645). Legrand gives the best description of Allatius' works, many of which are still unedited. Cf. Legrand, III, *passim,* 209-232 and Petit, art., *op. cit.,* 832-833.

[181]For a biographical sketch, cf. Legrand, III, 201-207.

[182]Legrand, III, 276-282.

[183]*Ibid.,* 238-251.

[184]*Ibid.,* 289-302.

[185]Printed in Venice, 1641; 2nd ed. 1853.

[186]Venice 1655 and 1679 respectively.

[187]Venice, 1641.

[188]Venice, 1647. Cf. Krumbacher, *op. cit.,* 184, 199, 202, 903.

[189]This work entitled: Θεία καὶ ἱερὰ διδασκαλία, has not yet been edited for publication. The ms. is found in the Greek Library in Vienna. Cf. Demetracopoulos, *O.E., op. cit.,* 179; Palmieri, *Theologia...op. cit.,* I, 145-146.

[190]This work was published in 1851 (Kephallenia) by G. Solomos entitled Ἐπιτομὴ τῆς δογματικῆς καὶ ἠθικῆς Θεολογίας.

[191]For biographical details about his life and writings, cf. E. Tantalides, Εὐγενίου τοῦ Βουλγάρεως ἐπιστολὴ περὶ φιλίας (Constantinople, 1850); G. Aenian, Βιογραφία τοῦ ἀοιδίμου Εὐγενίου ἐν ᾗ καὶ κατάλογος ἀκριβὴς τῶν συγγραμμάτων καὶ ἡ διαθήκη αὐτοῦ, (Athens, 1838), t. I, ἡ—μί; N. Katrami, Ἱστορικαὶ διασαφήσεις ἐπὶ τῆς πατρίδος, Εὐγενίου Βουλγάρεως, (Zante, 1854); A. P. Vretos, *Biographie de l'archévêque Eugene Bulgari redigée sur des documents authentiques* (Athens, 1860); Demetrakopoulos, *O.E., op. cit.,* 189-91 Chassiotis, *op. cit.,* 566-571; A. Palmieri, art. "Bulgaris, Eugene," *DTC,* t. II[1], 1236-1241; A. Soloviev, "Evgenii Bulgaris," *Strannik,* t. III, no. 7 (1867), 1-19 (this gives the most complete listing of his writings); A. Lebedev, "Evgenii Bulgaris," *Drevnaia i novaia Rossiia,* t. I, n. 111 (1876), 208-223; M. Jugie, *Theol. Dogm....op. cit.,* I, 526-527.

[192]Cf. Ph. Meyer, "Joseph Bryennios: Schriften, Leben und Bildung," *Byzantinische Zeitschrift* (Leipzig, 1896) T.V, 74-112; also, K. Heisenberg, *Nicephori Blemmydae curriculum vitae et carmina* (Leipzig, 1896), XXXIX.

[193]Leipzig, 1768, 1784. Cf. Krumbacher, *op. cit.,* 114.

[194]This point is discussed in G. Aenian, Βιογραφία, *op. cit.,* T. II, 172 ss.

[195]This work of Adam's was published in Latin in 1774 and 1776 at Königsberg. Bulgaris entiled his translation: Ἀδὰμ Ζαρνικαβίου Βορούσσου περὶ τῆς ἐκπορεύσεως τοῦ Ἁγίου Πνεύματος ἐκ μόνου τοῦ Πατρός, 2 vols. (St. Petersburg, 1797). A Russian translation was published later.

[196]Cf. Krumbacher, *op. cit.,* 116; Demetrakopoulos, *O.E., op. cit.,* 158.

[197]'Ορθόδοξος ὁμολογία σχεδιασθεῖσα παρὰ τοῦ σοφολογιω-τάτου ἱεροδιακόνου Κ. Εὐγενίου Βουλγάρεως (Amsterdam, 1767).

[198]'Αδολέσχια Φιλόθεος [God-pleasing Talkativeness]; 2 v. (Moscow, 1801).

[199]'Επιτομὴ εἴτε συλλογὴ τῶν Θείων τῆς Πίστεως δογμάτων, μετὰ πάσης ἐπιμελείας κατ' ἐπιτομὴν φιλοποιηθεῖσα, (Leipzig, 1806). Cf. Demetracopoulos, *O.E., op. cit.,* 197-198.

[200]Venice, 1780.

[201]I have used information gathered from the following sources: Paul Grigoriou, Σχέσεις Καθολικῶν καὶ 'Ορθοδόξων (Athens, 1958); J. Hajjar, *Les chrétiens uniates du Proche-Orient* (Paris, 1962); G. Hofmann, *Griechische Patriarchen und Römische Papste. Untersuchungen und Texte, in Orient. Christ.* vol. XIII, no. 47; vol. XV, no. 52; vol. XIX, no. 64; vol. XXV, no. 76; vol. XXX, no. 84; vol. XXXVI, no. 97 (Rome, 1928-1934); *ibid.,* "La Chiesa cattolica in Grecia (1600-1830)," *Orient. Christ. Periodica,* vol. II (Rome, 1936), 164-190; 395-436; W. De Vries, "Das Problem der 'communicatio in sacris' cum dissidentibus im Nahen Osten zur Zeit der Union (17. und 18. Jahrhundert)," *Ostkirchliche Studien,* vol. VI (Würzburg, 1957), 80-106; Timothy Ware, *Eustratios Argenti* (Oxford, 1964), 16-42.

[202]Ducas, *Historia Byzantina,* 38 (Bonn 1834) 264.

[203]*Op. cit.,* 25.

[204]For details of his life, cf. Sathas, Ν. Φ., 467; Gedeon, Χρονικά, 135; S. Petrides "Diamantes Rhysios," *DTC.,* vol. IV, 733-734. His work is entitled: Λατίνων Θρησκείας ἔλεγκοι 36 καὶ τίς ὁ ἑκάστου λόγος (Amsterdam, 1748).

[205]The best modern work on the life and theology of Argenti has recently been written by the Orthodox convert, Timothy Ware, entitled: *Eustratios Argenti; A Study of the Greek Church under Turkish Rule* (Oxford, 1964). Other works that are helpful include: A. K. Sarou, Βίος Εὐστρατίου 'Αργέντη τοῦ Χίου Θεολόγου (Athens, 1938); Sathas, Ν. Φ., *op. cit.,* 469-470; Demetrakopoulos, *O.E.,* 181-182; L. Petit, "Argentis Eustratios," *DTC.,* T. I², 1776-1777.

[206]Σύνταγμα κατὰ ἀφύμων (Leipzig, 1760). For the full title, cf. Ware, *op. cit.,* 176-177.

[207]Συνταγμάτιον κατὰ τοῦ Παπιστικοῦ Καθαρτηρίου Πυρός, ed. by M. Constantinides, (Athens, 1939).

[208]The original Greek, as Ware points out (*op. cit.,* 49), remains un-published and is preserved in ms. 32 at Budapest in the Zaviras Collection. This ms. contains two other short treatises against Roman popes, entitled: *The Acts and History of the Council of Constance* and *A Manual concerning the Latin Pope and Anti-Christ.* Cf. also p. 177 for the full Greek titles.

[209]'Εγχειρίδιον περὶ βαπτίσματος καλούμενον χειραγωγία πλα-νωμένων (Constantinople, 1756). A second edition was published in

Leipzig, 1757 under the title: "Άνθος τῆς εὐσεβείας, ἤτοι συνταγμά-
τιον περὶ ἀναβαπτισμοῦ. For the full titles, cf. Ware, *op. cit.*, 176.

[210]See Ware, *op. cit.*, 70 for a detailed bibliography on Cyril V.

[211]On Auxentius, cf. T. H. Papadopoullos, *Studies and Documents…*
op. cit., 203-216.

[212]Both the anathema decree and the definition are found in the Greek,
Papadopoullos, *op. cit.*, 440-447. Also in Mansi, vol. 38, 617-622. An
English translation in Wm. Palmer, *Dissertations on Subjects Relating to
the 'Orthodox' or 'Eastern-Catholic' Communion* (London, 1853), 199-202.

[213]On the doctrine of *economy* see the long discussion concerning it
and the problem of re-baptism in *The Rudder [Pedalion]*, tr. by D. Cummings
(Chicago, 1957), 68-91.

[214]Έγχειρίδιον, *op. cit.*, 86, cited by Ware, *op. cit.*, 97.

[215]For details of his life and writings cf. *Autobiographie de A. Korai*,
(Paris, 1833); Sathas, Ν. Φ., *op. cit.*, 662-672; D. Therianos, Ἀδαμάντιος
Κοραῆς, Τ. I (Trieste, 1889); T. II, III (1890).

[216]Printed in Paris, 1831.

[217]Cf. Th. Xanthopoulos, "Les dernières traductions de l'Écriture Sainte
en néo-grec," *E.O.* (1903), 230-240.

[218]For official documents dealing with his condemnation, cf. Mansi, *op.
cit.*, T. XI, 313-338. Also, I. Frankoula, Ὁ ἐν τῇ μονῇ τοῦ Εὐαγγελισμοῦ
τῆς Σκιάθου Περιορισμὸς τοῦ Θεοφ. Καῖρη (Athens, 1935).

[219]Cf. Jugie, *op. cit.*, T. I, 539 for the titles of his three best known works.

[220]For biographical details, cf. Sathas, Ν. Φ., 630-642; Ph. Meyer,
Realencyk für prot. Theologie und Kirche, 3rd ed. (Leipzig, 1897), T. II,
205-207; L. Petit "Athanase de Paros," *DTC.* I², 2189-2190.

[221]Συλλογὴ τῶν Θείων τῆς Πίστεως δογμάτων, (Leipzig, 1806).

[222]Cf. Meyer, *op. cit.*, 205.

[223]For a list of his works, cf. Petit, *art. cit.*

[224]For biographical details, cf. K. V. Skouteri, Μακάριος Νοταρᾶς,
(Athens, 1957); L. Petit, "Macaire de Corinthe," *DTC.* T. IX², 1449-1452;
Ph. Meyer, *Die Haupturkunden für die Geschichte der Athos-klöster* (Leipzig,
1894), 78-79.

[225]On the authenticity of this work, cf. Petit, *art. cit.*, 1450-1451.

[226]For biographical details, cf. Hieromonk Euthymius, "Βίος καὶ Πολιτεία καὶ ἀγῶνες Νικοδήμου μοναχοῦ" (ed. Lavriotes), Γρηγόριος ὁ
Παλαμᾶς Τ. IV (1920) 636-641; Τ. V (1921) 210-218; Monk Theoklitos
of Dionysiou, Ἅγιος Νικόδημος ὁ Ἁγιορείτης, ὁ βίος καὶ τὰ ἔργα
του (1748-1809), (Athens, 1959); Vretos, Ν. Φ., *op. cit.*, 233-234; Sathas,
Ν. Φ., 624; Zaviras, *N.E.* 469-470; 500-502; V. Grumel, art. "Nicodeme
l'Hagiorite," *DTC*, T. XI¹, 484-490.

[227]This was first published in Leipzig in 1800. Other editions: Athens,
1841; Zante, 1864; Athens, 1886. An English translation was done by

352   *A History of Orthodox Theology Since 1453*

David Cummings (Chicago, 1957) and entitled *The Rudder.*

[228]Cummings, *op. cit.,* frontispiece.

[229]On this controversy, cf. L. Petit, "La grande controverse des colybes," *E.O.* (1899), 321-331; M.-J. Le Guillou, "La renaissance spirituelle du XVIII° siècle," *Istina,* 7 (1960), 121-125.

[230]A fairly good picture can be had from the list of his works given by V. Grumel, art. "Nicodeme..." *op. cit.,* 487-490.

[231]This work is entitled in Greek: Φιλοκαλία τῶν ἱερῶν νηπτικῶν (Venice, 1782). The latest edition is in five vols. (Athens, 1957).

[232]Cf. Un Moine de l'Église Orthodoxe de Roumanie, "L'avenement philocaligue dans l'Orthodoxie roumaine," *Istina,* 3 (1958), 295-328; 4, 443-474. B. Krivochein, "Mount Athos in the Spiritual Life of the Orthodox Church," *The Christian East,* II, 2 (1952), 35-50.

[233]Ἀόρατος Πόλεμος, (Venice, 1796). On Nicodemos' dependence upon Western authors, cf. G. H. Viller, "Nicodeme l'Hagiorite et ses emprunts à la literature spirituelle occidentale," *Revue d'ascétique et de mystique,* T.V. (1924), 174-177, 416. An English translation, *The Unseen Warfare* (London, 1952) was done by E. Kadloubovsky and G. E. Palmer, from the Russian text of Feofan the Recluse with an introduction by A. H. Hodge. Cf. also L. Gillet, in his article in *Sobornost,* series 3, no. 12, 584-586 who says, "The book is a piece of literary and spiritual piracy" (586).

[234]Ἐγχειρίδιον Συμβουλευτικόν,...(no place given, 1801).

[235]Venice, 1819; 3 vols.

[236]Constantinople, 1819-1821; 2 vols.

[237]Venice, 1806.

[238]Cf. Sathas, Ν. Φ., 501-505; L. Petit, "Dapontes Constantin," *DTC,* IV¹, 140.

[239]Translated into modern Greek and published in Venice, 1779 with the title: Μαργαρῖται τῶν Τριῶν Ἱεραρχῶν.

[240]For the life of Pharmakidis, cf. Ch. A. Papadopoulos, Ἱστορία τῆς Ἐκκλησίας, *op. cit.,* (Athens, 1920), 55-56; Ph. Meyer, "Pharmacides Theoklitos," *Realenc.,* 15, 203 ss.

[241]Papadopoulos, *op. cit.,* 59.

[242]Cf. Papadopoulos, *op. cit.,* 145-164; Ph. Meyer, "Oekonomos," *Realenc.* 14, 299-304. His own work of course is the most important for his ideas: Τὰ σωφόμενα ἐκκλησιαστικὰ συγγράμματα Κωνσταντίου καὶ πρεσβυτέρου καὶ οἰκονόμου τοῦ ἐξ Οἰκονόμων (Athens, 1862).

[243]Michel D'Herbigny, "La vraie notion d'orthodoxie," *Orient. Christ.* (1923), T. II, 1, 6.

[244]A. D. Kyriakos, Ἐκκλησιαστικὴ Ἱστορία, T. III (Athens, 1898), 160.

245Cf. Mansi, *op. cit.*, T. XL, 245-264; also Gedeon, Χρονικά, *op. cit.*, 252.

246Cf. "Enciclica patriarhiler orthodosi del 1848," *Biserica Orthodoxa Romana*, 53 (Bucharest, 1935), 545-588.

247Mansi, T. XL, 377-418.

248For a lively account of his life, Cf. M.-J. Le Guillou, "Apostolos Makrakis: ses intuitions apostoliques et spirituelles," *Istina*, 7 (1960), 261-278; D. Balanos, "'Ο 'Απόστολος Μακράκης" (1831-1905), Γρηγόριος ὁ Παλαμᾶς T. IV (1920), 65-112; V. Grégoire, "Un reformateur laic dans l'Église grecque, Apostolos Makrakis, (1831-1905)," *E.O.* T. XIX (1920), 403-414; L. Petit, "Macrakès Apostolos," *DTC.*, T. IX², 1503-1507; Chr. Papadopoulos, 'Ο 'Απόστολος Μακράκης, (Athens, 1939).

249'Αποκάλυψις τοῦ θησαυροῦ τοῦ κεκρυμμένου, (Constantinople, 1858).

250L. Petit, *art. cit.*, *DTC.*, 1505-1507. A complete list of the works of Makrakis is given in English along with all the works that have so far been translated from Greek into English in the work: *Apostolos Makrakis; An Evaluation of Half a Century;* ed. by Constantine Andronis and published by the Orthodox Christian Educational Society (Chicago, 1966), 337-339.

251On this see: G. Williams, *The Orthodox Church of the East in the 18th century, being the correspondence between the Eastern Patriarchs and the Non-juring Bishops* (London, 1868). Also, V. T. Istavridis, "Orthodoxy and Anglicanism in the Twentieth Century," *Greek Orthodox Theological Review*, vol. V, no. 1 (1959), 9-26, and J. A. Douglas, *The Relations of the Anglican Churches with the Eastern-Orthodox* (London, 1921).

252For a detailed bibliography on this encyclical, cf. Palmieri, *Theologia... op. cit.*, 637-640.

253The text is found in 'Εκκλησιαστική 'Αλήθεια, Sept. 29, 1895. Also in Msgr. L. Duchesne, "L'Encyclique du Patriarche Anthime," *Église séparées* (Paris, 1896), 59-112.

254Macarii, *Vvedenie v pravoslavnoe bogoslovie* (St. Petersburg, 1847).

255*Dogmaticheskoe bogoslovie katholicheskoi vostochnoi tserkvi* (Kiev, 1848).

256Περὶ ἀρχῶν, (Leipzig, 1863).

257Περὶ τῆς σχέσεως τῆς ἀγγλικῆς ἐκκλησίας πρὸς τὴν 'Ορθόδοξον (London, 1867).

258'Ερμηνεία εἰς τὴν Καινὴν Διαθήκην (Athens, 1876) T. I, (1891); T. II, (1892), T. III.

259Σύστημα δογματικῆς τῆς 'Ορθοδόξου Καθολικῆς 'Εκκλησίας (Athens, 1903).

260*Ibid.*, δ'—ς'.

261C. Androutsos, Δογματική τῆς 'Ορθοδόξου 'Ανατολικῆς 'Εκκλησίας (Athens, 1907) θ'. See, Jugie, *op. cit.*, 534 for a list of his other theological writings.

262Δογματική...op. cit., ι'.

263C. Dyovuniotis, Ἡ δογματικὴ τοῦ Χρ. ᾿Ανδρούτσου κρινομένη (Athens, 1907).

264D. S. Balanos, Τὸ δόγμα τῆς ᾿Εκκλη. Ἑλλην. περὶ τῆς δικαιώσεως (Athens, 1904); Τὸ δόγμα τῆς ᾿Εκκλη. περὶ τῆς ῾Αγίας Τριάδος, (Athens, 1911).

265Athens, 1901-1904; 4 vols.

266N. Ambrazis, Ἡ ᾿Ορθόδοξος ᾿Εκκλησία ἐν σχέσει πρὸς τὰς ἄλλας Χριστιανικὰς ᾿Εκκλησίας ἐξεταζομένη (Athens, 1906).

267This is true of his popular work ᾿Ορθόδοξος ῾Ιερὰ Κατήχησις, (Athens, 1899). He produced other works on the importance of the seven councils, Christology, Penance, Orders the sacraments, ecclesiology, tradition and two volumes of sermons. Cf. Jugie, op. cit., t. I, 535-536 for titles.

268Σύνταγμα τῶν Θείων καὶ ῾Ιερῶν Κανόνων.

269S. Giannopoulos, Συλλογὴ τῶν ἐγκυκλίων τῆς ῾Ιερᾶς Συνόδου τῆς ᾿Εκκλησίας τῆς ῾Ελλάδος μετὰ τῶν οἰκείων νόμων, β' διαταγμάτων, ὑπουργικῶν ἐγγράφων κ.τ.λ., ἀπὸ τοῦ 1883 μέχρι σήμερον ἐκδιδομένη ἐντολῇ τῆς ῾Ιερᾶς Συνόδου (Athens, 1901).

270Cf. D. Moraitis, "Θεολογικὴ Σχολὴ Πανεπιστημίου ᾿Αθηνῶν," Θρησκευτικὴ καὶ ᾿Ηθικὴ ᾿Εγκυκλοπαιδεία (Athens, 1965), 267-269.

271Kontogonis had studied five years in the West and in his work on the critical history of the Fathers, Φιλολογικὴ καὶ κριτικὴ ἱστορία τῶν κατὰ τὰς τρεῖς πρώτας τῆς ᾿Εκκλησίας ἑκατονταετηρίδας ἀκμασάντων ῾Αγίων Πατέρων (Athens, 1846), he inaugurated scientific theological scholarship in modern Greece.

272For a detailed list of writings on the ecumenical movement, cf. B. Stavridis, "Die Griechish-orthodoxe Bibliographie zur Ökumenischen Bewegung," Aus der Neugriechischen Theologie; ed. Demosthenes Savramis (Würzburg, 1961); Das östliche Christentum; h. 15; 137-150.

273Chr. Evgenides, "Θεολογικὴ Σχολὴ Πανεπιστημίου Θεσσαλονίκης," Θ. Η. Ε., op. cit., 269-271.

274Procès-Verbaux du premier Congrès de Théologie orthodoxe; Athènes 29 novembre—6 décembre, 1936; ed. H. Alivisatos (Athens, 1939), 49.

275S. Zankov, "Die prinzipiellen Schwierigkeiten der Abhaltung eines ökumenischen Konzils," Procès...op. cit., 283.

276Procès...451-459; 463.

277Cf. Goscheff, I., "Die Revision der liturgischen Texte und die heutige liturgische Gesetzgebung der orthodoxen Kirche," Procès..., 324-328.

278Procès...238-242.

279Ibid., 239.

280D. Balanos, "Die neuere orthodoxe Theologie in ihren Verhältnis zur patristischen Theologie und zu den neueren theologischen Auffassungen und Methoden," Procès..., 232-237.

[281]E. Antoniadis, "Die orthodoxen hermeneutischen Grundprinzipien und Methoden der Auslegung des Neuen Testaments and ihre theologischen Voraussetzungen," *Procès...*, 143-174.

[282]Εἰσαγωγὴ εἰς τὰς ῾Αγίας Γραφάς (Athens, 1936).

[283]B. Vellas, "Bibelkritik und Kirchliche Autorität," *Procès...*, 135-143.

[284]For a detailed bibliography, cf. Demosthenes Savramis, "Zehn Jahre Neugriechische Theologie; Bibliographischer Bericht (1950-1960)," *Aus der Neugriechischen... op. cit.*, 151-208.

[285]Cf. D. Savramis, *Ökumenische Probleme in der Neugriechischen Theologie* (Leiden-Köln 1964); Stavridis Basilios, "Die Griechisch-orthodoxe Bibliographie zur ökumenischen Bewegung," *ibid., Ökumenische Probleme... op. cit.*, 137-150.

[286]*Ibid.*, 116.

[287]Athens, 1965.

[288]Cf. G. Strinopoulos, ῾Ι. Θεολογικὴ Σχολὴ τῆς Χάλκης—῾Ι. Μορ. καὶ Σύμβολα (1844-1944), (Thessalonika, 1962).

[289]John S. Romanides, "Orthodoxy in America," Θεολογικὸν Συμπόσιον, (Thessal., 1967), 509.

[290]*Ibid.*, 509-513.

NOTES ON PART THREE

[1]Some of the more important works dealing with the history of Bulgaria and its literature: N. S. Derzhavin, *Istoriia Bolgarii* (Moscow-Leningrad, 1945-1948) 4 vols.; *Istoriia Na Bulgariia, Bulgarska Akademiia na Naukite* (Sofia; Vol. I, 1954; Vol. II, 1955); *Istoriia Bolgarii, Akademiia Nauk, SSSR* (Moscow, Vol. I, 1954; Vol. II, 1955); K. E. Zacharia von Lingenthal, *Beiträge zur Geschichte der bulgarischen Kirche* (St. Petersburg, 1864); N. V. Mikhov, *Bibliographski istochnitsa za istoriiata na Turtsiia i Bulgariia;* 4 vols. (Sofia, 1914-1934); Marvin Pundeff, *Bulgaria; a bibliographic guide* (Washington, D.C. 1965); I. Duychev, "Slavyano-bolgarskiye drevnosti 9 vieka" *Byzantinoslavica* (Prague) 11, no. 1 (1950); Boyan Penev, *La renaissance bulgare* (Sofia, 1933); *idem, Bulgarska literatura; kratuk istoricheski ocherk* (Sofia, 1946); R. Stube, *Das älteste bulgarische Schrifttum und die altbulgarischen Alphabete* (Leipzig, 1916); S. S. Bobchev, *La lutte du peuple bulgare pour une église nationale independante* (Sofia, 1938); Zhak Natan, *Bulgarskoto Vuzrazhdane* (Sofia, 1949); N. Stanev, *Bulgariia pod Igo* (Sofia, 1935); S. Tsankov, *Die Verfassung der bulgarischen orthodoxen Kirche* (Zürich, 1918); *idem, Bulgarskata pravoslavna tsurkva ot osvobozhdenieto do nastoiashte vreme;* 6th series, *Godishnik na Sofiiskiia Universitet;* vol. 16 (1938-1939); G. Konstantinov, *Bulgarski pisateli biografii, bibliografiia* (Sofia, 1961); *idem, Stara bulgarska literatura ot sv. Kiril i*

Methodii do Paisii Khilendarski (Sofia, 1946); V. S. Kiselkov, *Prouki i ocherti po starobulgarska literatura* (Sofia, 1956); M. Arnaudov, *Bulgarski pisateli; zhivot, tvorchestvo-idei* (Sofia, 1929-1930), 6 vols.; *Opis na rukopisite i staropechatnite knigi na Narodnata Biblioteka v Sofiia* (Sofia, 1910); Mercia MacDermott, *A History of Bulgaria, 1393-1885* (New York, 1962); S. Runciman, *A History of the First Bulgarian Empire* (London, 1930); Alois Hajek, *Bulgarien unter der Türkenherrschaft* (Stuttgart, 1925).

[2]Cf. on the life and works of Clement: Iordan Ivanov, *Bulgarski Starini iz Makedoniia* (Sofia, 1931) and N. L. Tunitsky, Sv. Kliment *episkop slovenskii. Evo zhizn' i prosvetitel'naia deyatel' nost'* (Sergiev-Posad, 1913).

[3]Ivanov, *op. cit.*, 314-321.

[4]V. Vondrak, *Studie z oboru cirkevno slovanskeho pisemnictvi* (Prague, 1903). B. Angelov, counts 27 in his work, *Bolgarska literatura;* vol. 1 (Sofia, 1923), 43.

[5]Cf. A. I. Sobolevsky, "Gde zhil Konstantin bolgarskii?" *Materiali i issledovaniia, Sbornik,* T. LXXXVIII, no. 3 (1910), 127-131.

[6]This work is discussed thoroughly and a Russian translation is appended in the work of Archimandrite Antonii, *Iz istorii drevne-bolgarskoi tserkovnoi propovedi Konstantin episkop bolgarskii i evo "Uchitelnoe evangelie"* (Kazan, 1885). No. 42 seems to be original to Konstantin.

[7]Ivan Duichev, *Pregled na bolgarskata istoriographie* (Belgrade, 1938), 42.

[8]Cf. V. S. Kiselkov, "Volgarskata knizhnina prez Simeonoviia Vek" *Bolgariia 1000 godini (927-1927)* (Sofia, 1927).

[9]There are two mss. of this collection: one of the 12th century, the Chudov Ms. kept in the State Library in Leningrad, giving 73 discourses of Chrysostom and the other of the 16th century, the Uvarov Ms. with 135. The latter coincides with the Greek original and perhaps is more ancient. Cf. B. Angelov, and M. Genov, *Stara Bolgarska Literatura (IX-XVIII v.)* (Sofia, 1922) 322.

[10]V. Malinin, *Issledovanie Zlatostruia po rukopisi XII v* (Kiev, 1878), passim.

[11]This ms. was edited under the title: *Izbornik velikovo kniazia Sviatoslava Iaroslavicha 1073 g.* (St. Petersburg, 1880) ed. *Obschestvo liubitelei drevnei pismennosti.*

[12]This is the conclusion of L. Mazing, "Studien zur Kenntniss des Izbornik Svjatoslava vom Jahre 1073 nebst Bemerkungen zu den jüngeren Handschriften," *Archiv. für Slav. Philologie, VIII* (1885), IX (1886).

[13]Cf. I. Evseev, *Grigorii presviter, perevodchik vremeni bolgarskogo tsarvia Simeona,* II, *Akademia Nauka* (1902), VII, book 3.

[14]Cited by N. S. Derzhavin, *Istoriia Bolgarii,* t. II (Moscow-Leningrad, 1946), 77-78.

[15]*Ibid.*, 78.

[16]Cf. A. Leskin, "Die Übersetzungskunst des Exarchen Johannes," *Archiv.*

für Slav. Philosophie, T. XXV (1903) 48-66; also, *idem,* "Zum Sestodnev des Exarchen Johannes," *ibid.,* T. XXVI, (1904) 1-70; V. Yagich, "Rassuzhdenie Ioanna ekzarcha bolgarskogo o slavianskom iazike v predislovii k evo perevodu 'Bogosloviia' Ioanna Damaskina," *Rassuzhdeniia starini o tserkovno-slavianskom iazike, issledovaniia po russkomu iaziku,* T. I (St. Petersburg, 1885-1895) 320-325; V. Vondrak, *O mluve Iana Exarcha, bulgarskeno* (Prague, 1896).

[17]Three leading works on this heresy are: D. Obolensky, *The Bogomils: A Study in Balkan Neo-Manichaeism* (Cambridge, 1948); S. Runciman, *The Medieval Maniches: A Study of the Christian Dualist Heresy* (Cambridge, 1947), reprinted (1955); and I. Ivanov, *Bogomilski knigi i legendi* (Sofia, 1925).

[18]This was edited by M. G. Popruzhenko, and printed in his *Kozma Presbyter, bolgarski pisatel' X vieka* (Sofia, 1936), *Bolgarski Starini* series, vol. XII. A French translation exists: H.-C. Puech, and A. Vaillant, *Le traité contre les Bogomiles de Cosmas le prêtre* (Paris, 1945).

[19]Propruzhenko, *Kozma...op. cit.,* p. 26.

[20]*PG* 126, 334-507.

[21]Cf. for details on his life and ideas: K. Prächter, "Antike Quellen des Theophylaktos von Bulgarien," *Byzantinische Zeitschrift* (Leipzig, 1892), no. 1, 399-416; B. Leib, *Rome, Kiev, Byzance à la fin du XI la fin du XI siècle* (Paris, 1924), 41-50; N. N. "Dogmaticheskoe uchenie v. blagovestnike blazhennago Theofilakta," *Pravoslavni Sobesednik* (Kazan, 1908), II, 160-180; 383-410; 600-618; 653-668; A. Leroy-Molenghem, "Les lettres de Theophylacte de Bulgarie à Grégoire Taronite," *Byzantion,* T. XI (1936) 589-592; K. Krumbacher, *op. cit.,* 133-135; 463-464.

[22]F. Foscati, edited these works in Latin, four vols. (Venice, 1754-1763) which were incorporated by Migne into his collection.

[23]Περὶ ὧν ἐγκαλοῦνται Λατῖνοι, *PG* 126, 221-229.

[24]V. S. Kiselkov, in his work, *Zhitieto no sv. Teodocii Trnovski kato istoricheski pametnik* (Sofia, 1926) i-lii, shows that the life of Theodosios is not Callistos' work but of a later date, probably of the 15th century and based on a shorter Greek work by Callistos but now lost. *The Life of Theodosios* has been edited by O. Bodyanskii, *Zhitie i zhizn' prepodobnago otsa nashego Feodosiia izhe v Ternove nostnichestvovavshegosia, Chteniia v imperatorskom obshchestve istorii i drevnostei rossiskikh pri Moskovskom Universitate* (Moscow, 1860), vol. 1.

[25]Cf. K. Jirecek, *Cesty po Bulharskii* (Prague, 1888), 101-103; 278.

[26]Cf. P. A. Sirku, *K istorii ispravleniia knig v Bolgarii;* t. I (St. Petersburg, 1899), 461-465.

[27]For details of his life and works, cf. Sirku, *op. cit.,* 411-551; E. Kaluzhniacki, *Werke des Patriarchen von Bulgarien Euthymius (1375-1393)* (Vienna, 1901); Tsankov, *Patriarch Evtimii* (Sofia, 1906); V. S. Kiselkov, *Patriarch Evtimii* (Sofia, 1938).

[28]Cf. K. Radchenko, *Religioznoe i literaturnoe dvizhenie v Bolgarii v epochu pered turetskim zavoevaniem* (Kiev, 1898); N. Golubinskii, *Istoriia pravoslavnikh tserkvei bolgarskoi, serbskoi i ruminskoi* (Moscow, 1871).

[29]Sirku, *op. cit.*, 444.

[30]*Ibid.*, 493.

[31]For information on the life and writings of Paisi Hilandarsky cf: *Paisi Hilendarski i Negovate Epocha (1762-1962), Bulgarska Akademiia na naukite* (Sofia, 1962); this collection contains the best presentation of Paisi's background and ideas as presented in the individual articles: D. Kosev, "Za ideologiate na Paisi Hilendarski," 7-32; Chr. Christov, "Paisi Hilendarski i Bulgarskoto Vozrazhdane," 33-70; E. Georgiev, "Paisi Hilendarski mezhdu Renesansa i Prosveschenieto," 253-284; E. Georgieva, "Nabludeniia Verchuezika na Paisievata Slavianobulgarska istoriia," 345-378; Al. Milev, "Gritskite i latinskite dumi v istoriiata no Paisi Hilendarski," 401-412; Cf. also Louis Leger, *Serbes, Croates et Bulgares—Études historiques, politiques et litteraires* (Paris, 1913), 185-191.

[32]Leger, *op. cit.*, 187-188.

[33]Cardinal Cesare Baronius' history was entitled, *Annales Ecclesiastici a Christo nato ad annum 1198,* but was undoubtedly read by Paisi in Karlovtsy in a Russian translation.

[34]For details of his life and writings, cf. Leger, *op. cit.*, 173-184; N. S. Derzhavin, "Ocherki po istorii bolgarskoi literaturi epochi bozrozhdeniia (konets XVIII-nachalo XIX v.)," *Sbornik statei i issledovanii v oblasti slavianskoi philologii* (Moscow-Leningrad, 1941), 61-213.

[35]L. Leger, *La Bulgarie* (Paris, 1885), reproduces in French his memoirs, *Zhitie i stradaniia,* 81-141.

[36]M. Macdermott, *op. cit.*, 117.

[37]For a statistical report of the rapid growth in schools, cf. N. I. Vankov, *Istoriia na uchebnoto delo v Bolgariia ot krai vreme do osvoboszhdenieto* (Lovech, 1903), 18-21.

[38]For a history of this first theological school in Bulgaria, cf. "L'école théologique de Bulgarie," *Échos d'Orient,* t. VI (1903), 74-82.

[39]Cf. "L'atheisme des instituteurs bulgares," *Échos d'Orient,* T. VI (1903), 332-335.

[40]Various translations into Serbian and Bulgarian were made of Filaret's *Catechism,* such as: Christo Danov, *Prostranen pravoslaven Katikhizis* (Belgrade, 1858; Vienna, 1863; Philoppopoli, 1879) and that of A. Govanov, *Prostranii khristianski Katikhizis pravos-katol-vostotchna tserkva* (Belgrade, 1852).

[41]Meletius Zographski translated Antonii Amfiteatrov's *Dogmaticheskoe Bogoslovie* with the title: *Dogmatitchesco Bogoslovie na provoslavnata katolitcheska vostotchna Tserkva* (Kichenevi, 1869).

[42]Makarii's *Rukovodstvo k izucheniu khristianskago pravoslavno-dogmatiche-*

skago bogosloviia was translated with the title: *Osnovnite istini na verata* (1901; no author, no place given).

⁴³Platon's *Pravoslavnoe uchenie ili sokraschennaya khristianskaya bogosloviia* was translated with the title: *Pravoslavno Utchenie ili secrateno khristiansco bogoslovie* (Constantinople, 1844; no translation given).

⁴⁴The work of Silvestr Malevanskii, *Opit pravoslavnago dogmaticheskago bogosloviia* was translated by three authors, Makarii, Tsankov and Bacalov, with the title of *Pravoslavno dogmatitchno bogoslovie,* 3 vol. (Sofia, 1912).

⁴⁵Bacalov also translated Bishop Augustin's (Vinogradskii) compendium, (written in Latin: *Dogmatica Theologia*) with the title: *Rekovodstvo po osnovno bogoslovie* (Sofia, 1907).

⁴⁶Mantchev translated Sokolov's treatise on fundamental theology *(Pravoslavnaia vera)* with the title: *Natchalno nastavlenie na pravoslavnata vera* (Philippoli, 1882).

⁴⁷Cf. "Traduction bulgare de l'Écriture sainte," *Échos d'Orient,* T. IV (1901), 245-247.

⁴⁸*Godishnik na Dukhovnata Adademiia "Sv. Kliment Okhridski,"* T. II. This is an article that he delivered as two lectures in Switzerland in 1942.

⁴⁹*Idem,* T. IV.

⁵⁰*Idem,* T. V, which was a lecture delivered at the Oxford Conference of Faith and Order in 1937.

⁵¹*Idem,* T. VIII. Cf. *Istina,* T. IX (1963), 382.

⁵²*Idem,* T. IX. Cf. *Istina,* T. IX (1963), 383.

⁵³Johansen published his findings in a short work entitled, *Theological Study in the Russian and Bulgarian Orthodox Churches under Communist Rule* (London, 1963). S. Tsankov has published an article on Bulgarian theological study that appeared in *Verkündigung und Forschung* (1959) but his article goes only up to 1955 and I was not able to consult it.

⁵⁴Cited by Johansen, *op. cit.,* 41-42.

⁵⁵*Ibid.,* 42.

⁵⁶*Ibid.,* 43-46; 51-52.

NOTES ON PART FOUR

¹One of the leading works on the Serbian Church is that of D. Slijepchevic, *Istorija Srpske Pravoslavne Crkve* (Munich, 1962), 2 vols. Other works of standard reference are: Alois Hudal, *Die Serbisch-Orthodoxe Nationalkirche* (Graz-Leipzip, 1922); R. Grujic, *Pravoslavna srpska crkva* (Belgrade, 1920); Ch. Marjanovic, *Istorija srpske crkve* (Belgrade, 1920-1930) 2 vols.; F. Taranovski, *Istorija srpskog prava i Nemanjickoj drzhavi;* 3 vols. (Belgrade, 1931-1934); Nicifor Duchic, *Istorija Srpske Pravoslavne Crke* (Belgrade,

1884); L. Hadrovics, *Le peuple Serbe et son Église sous la domination turque* (Paris, 1947); N. Ruzhichic, *Istorija srpske Crkve* (Vol. I, Zagreb, 1893; Vol. II, Belgrade, 1895).

[2]Petar Stokic, *Sv. Sava i znachaj viere i srpskoj istoriji* (Kraguijevac, 1898); J. Mousset, *La Serbie et son Église* ([1830-1904] Paris, 1938).

[3]This work was edited by Vatroslav Jagic. Cf. Stojan Novakovic, *Istorija srpske knizhevnost* (Belgrade, 1871), 38.

[4]Pavle Popovic, *Pregled srpske knizhevnosti;* 4th edit. (Belgrade, 1921), 4-5.

[5]Stojan Novakovic, *Istorija . . . op. cit.,* 52-53.

[6]Cf. Ferdo Schischic, *Letopis popa Duklanina* (Belgrade, 1928).

[7]Cf. P. Popovic, *O knizhevnom delu sv. Save* (*Bratstvo drushtva sv. Save;* Bk. XXVIII, 1934), 36.

[8]Lazar Mirkovic, *Spisis Svetoga Save i Stevana Prvovenchanoga* (Belgrade), 18.

[9]A. Gabrilovic, *Istorija srpske i chrvatske knizhevnosti* (Belgrade), 23.

[10]Cf. Alex. Belic, *Ucheshche Sv. Save i negove schole u stvaronu nove redaktsije cyrilskich spomenika* (Belgrade, 1936), 258.

[11]Cf. Vatroslav Jagic, *Historija knjizhevnosti brvatske i srpske* (Zagreb), 151.

[12]Milivoje Bashic, *O starim srpskim biographijama u ovome izdanu,* cited by Slijepchevic, *op. cit.,* vol. I, 257.

[13]Cf. P. Popovic, *Pregled . . . op. cit.,* 33.

[14]M. Bashic, *O starim srpskim . . . op. cit.,* XXI. D. S. Radojichic, *Stari srpski knizhevnitsi ruske narodnosti; Godishnak phil. fakulteta u Novom Sadu;* Bk. V (1961), 15.

[15]Nikola Radojchic, *O archiepiskopu Danilu II i negovim nastavlachuma* (Belgrade, 1935), XXIV.

[16]For a recent report on the state of Serbian monasticism cf. D. S. De Vos, "Le monachisme orthodoxe en Yugoslavic. Quelque notes sur la situation actuelle" *Irenikon* T. XXXIV (1961), 217-231.

[17]Jugie, *Theologia . . . op. cit.,* vol. I, 635-636.

[18]On the flowering of Serbian monasticism during the Serbian Dark Ages, cf. Slijepchevic, *Istorija . . . op. cit.,* 303-310.

[19]Isidore Sekulic, *Hegorshu kniga duboke odanosti* (Belgrade, 1951), 285.

[20]Cf. Jovan Skerlic, *Srpska knizhevnost u XVIII veku* (Belgrade, 1923), 75.

[21]Cf. D. Ruvarats, *Opis srpskikh Frushkogorskikh manastira* (Sremsky-Karlovtsy, 1905) 74, 191; D. Popovic, *Srbi u Budinmu do kraja XVIII veka* (Belgrade, 1955), 45.

[22]*Starine Jygoslovenske akademije znanosti i umjetnosti,* Bk. XII (1830), 16-41.

[23]Cf. J. Skerlic, *Istorija nove srpske knizhevnosti* (Belgrade, 1953), 18.

[24]Cf. for details of his life and accomplishments, Dimitrije Ruvarats, *Mitroplit Stevan Statimirovic; Glasnik ist. drushtva u Novom Sadu* Bk. IV (1931), 374-392; B. Slijepchevic, *Stevan Stratimirovic, mitropolit karlovachki, kao poglavar crkve, prosvetni i natsionalni radnik* (Belgrade, 1936).

[25]Evg. Jovanovic, *Slovo nadgrobnoje* (Buda, 1837), 6.

[26]Cf. Nikola Radojchic, *Srpski istorichar Jovan Rajic* (Belgrade, 1952), 63.

[27]D. Ruvarats, *"Klerikalna schola u gorno-karlovachkoj eparkhiji od 1690 do 1829," Glasnik srpske pravoslavne patrijarschije (G1)* (1925), 26-28.

[28]Stojan Novakovic, *Srpska bibliographija za noviju knizhevnost 1744-1867* (Belgrade, 1869).

[29]*Ibid.*, 41.

[30]Aleksa Ilic, *Petar Jovanovic mitropolit beogradski* (Belgrade, 1911), 344.

[31]*Ibid.*, 346.

[32]R. Markovic, *"Stogodishnitsa bogloslovije Sv. Save," Glasnik Jyugoslovenskog profesorskog drushtva* (September, 1936), 6.

[33]*Ibid.*, 7.

[34]Ilic, *op. cit.*, 233; cf. also Milan Milichevic, *Pomenik znamenitik ludi u srpskom narodu novijega doba* (Belgrade, 1888), 211.

[35]M. S. Petrovic, *Beograd pre sto godina* (Belgrade, 1930), 195.

[36]T. R. Djordjevic, *Iz Srbije Kneza Milosha* (Belgrade, 1924), 210.

[37]Jean Mousset, *La Serbie et son Église (1830-1904)* (Paris, 1938), 238.

[38]R. Grujic, *Istorija srpske pravoslavne crkve* (Belgrade, 1920), 153.

[39]There existed already two editions printed in Jassy (1761) and Kiev (1765).

[40]Printed in 1879 and 1895 respectively. Cf. N. Duchic, *Knizhevni radovi,* Bk. V (Belgrade, 1898), 315-316.

[41]Nikolai Velimirovic, *Religija Negosheva* (Belgrade, 1911), 162.

[42]Cf. VI. Maksimovic, *"Karlovachka bogoslovija i bogoslovski seminar," Bogloslovski glasnik,* V, Bk. IX (1906), 295-296, 369.

[43]Novi-Sad, 3rd ed., 1895.

[44]Belgrade, 1898.

[45]Belgrade, 1903.

[46]Zara, 1881.

[47]Neusatz, 1886.

[48]Mostar, 1911.

[49]Novi-Sad, 1901.

[50]Jugie, *op. cit.*, I, 637.

[51]Belgrade, 1880, 1882, respectively.

[52]Neusatz, 1884.

[53]Belgrade, 1900.

[54]Belgrade, 1895.

362   *A History of Orthodox Theology Since 1453*

[55]Belgrade, 1898.

[56]Cf. D. Ruvarats, *Crkveno-bogoslovski listovi u karlovachkoj mitropoliji do 1915, Glasnik istoriskog drushtva u Novom Sadu,* III (1930), 68.

[57]See the stated purpose in the first number published, *Bogosl. Glas.* I, 1 (1902), 4.

[58]For a listing of the main works of the leading Serbian theologians during this period, cf. Ts. Drashkovits, "Bibliographie der Orthodoxen Theologie in Jugoslawien 1945-60," *Ostkirchliche Studien,* 10, no. 2-3 (Würzburg, 1961), 221-256. A substantial bibliography is given of the leading theological articles which have appeared in *Bogoslovle* (1926-1940 and 1957-1960). Cf. *Bogosl.* V (XX) no. 1 & 2 (1961), 127-146. In this same number there is a bibliography of the articles that have appeared in the three numbers (1952-1954) of the *Zbornik pravoslavnog bogoslovskog fakulteta, ibid.,* 125-127. I am indebted for the following material to the article of C. Draskovic, "Der Stand der theologischen Orthodoxen Wissenschaft in Jugoslawien," *Orthodoxie heute in Rumänien und Jugoslawien* (ed., F. Popan, and C. Draskovic, [Vienna, 1960]), 160-174.

[59]Cf. *Starozavetna arheologija* (Belgrade, 1954); "Stari jevrejski rukopisi sa obale Mrtvoga Mora," *Letopis Matice srpske* (Novi-Sad, August-September, 1958), 153-170. "Knjiga psalama. Psalam 2 i 3," *Zbornik Pravoslavnog bogoslovskog fakulteta univerziteta u Beogradu (ZBF)* (Belgrade) II, 49-88; "Knjiga psalama. Psalam 4," *ibid., ZBV.* III, 47-62.

[60]Examples of his writings are "Novopronadjeni svitci starozavetnih i drugih knjiga u blizini Jerihona," *ZBF,* I, 193-198; "Supstitucija imena Bozheg JHVHU St. Zavetu," *ZBF,* II, 393-414.

[61]Some of his writings are the following: "Crkvena jurisdikcija nad pravoslavnom diasporom," *Glasnik* (1932), 196-201; 212-216; 229-232; 248-250; 262-264; 276-279; 294-297; 313-314; 328-329; 358-362; 374-376; 389-391; 42-422. "Sustina i faktori avtokefaliji," (*Arhiv za pravne i drushtvene nauke;* Belgrade), T. 43 (1933), 186-200. "Uprava udovom eparhijom," *Arhiv.* T. 54 (1938), 32-37. "O granicach rasprostrannenija prava vlasti Konstantinopoljskoj patriarchii na Diasporu," *Zhurnal Moskovskoi Patriarchii,* no. 11 (1947), 34-35; "Gde i v cem glavna opasnost?" *Zh. Mosk. Patr.,* no. 12 (1947), 31-42; "O cerkovnoi avtokefalii," *Zh. Mosk. Patr.,* no. 7 (1948), 33-54. *Crkveno-politichka ideologija svetosavske Krmchije i Vlastareve Sintagme; Glas Srpske Academije Nauka,* CCXII, Bk. 2, 155-203.

[62]"Crkva kao pravna institucija," *ZBF,* II, 239-268; "Uloga prvih khrischanskih opshtina u organizaciji crkve," *ZBF,* I, 146-173; "Znachaj Svetosavske Krmchiji za nashe crkveno i drzhavno zakonodavstvo," *Bogosl.* II (XVII) no. 1 (1958), 3-15.

[63]Examples of his writings: "Uchenje poslanice Jevrejima o Starom Zavetu," *Gl.* (1955) 8-14; "Hipoteza o Apolosu kao piscu poslanice Jevrejima," *Bogosl.* I (XVI) 2 (1957), 68-82; *Sv. apostola Pavla poslanica Efescima* (Belgr. 1957); "Pitanje 'Philonizma' poslanice Jevrejima," *Bogosl.* II (XVII) 2 (1958), 9-26.

[64]Cf. "Pojam o dogmi u Pravoslavnoj crkvi," *Bogosl.* II (XVII), 2 (1958), 3-8. "The Teaching of John Crysostom on Grace" (in Greek), *Theologia*, no. 25 (Athens, 1956), 96 ss.

[65]To list even partially his writings would be tedious. Cf. *Ostkirchliche Studien*, 10, n 9. 2-3 (1961), 243-244.

[66]E.g. "Egzegeza 'Shestodneva'-bibliske kosmogonije i geogonije," *ZBF*, II, 21-34; *Chrishcanska apologetika* (Belgrade, 1954); "Bogatstvo u svetlosti chrishcanstva," *Vesnik*, III (1951), 48.

[67]"Dijalektika i sekpticizam," *Gl.* (1958), 204-210; "Pravoslavje u srpskim narodnim pesmama," *Gl.* (1956), 37-40.

[68]"Christos u savremenoj filosofiji istorije," *Gl.* (1952), 166-176; "Chrishchanstvo i egzistencijalizam," *Gl.* (1955), 40-43; "Alber Ajnshtajn o potrebi religije," *Gl.* (1956), 104-108.

[69]"Vizantiska restauracija u Carigradu 1261 i crkvena unija u Lionu 1274," *Sp. (Shesta stogodnishnjica u Srbiji 1804-1954)* (Belgrade 1948), 149-154; *Patrologija* (Belgrade, 1954).

[70]"Tipik archiepiskopa Nikodima od 1319," *Sp.* (1946), 188-189; *Bogosl.* I (XVI) 2 (1957), 12-19; 1 (1958), 69-88; *Skitski ustav Sv. Save, Bratstvo dr. Sv. Save*, XXVIII (1934); *Miroslavlevo jevangele* (Belgrade, 1950) Bk. CLVI, *Arheoloshki institut I.*

[71]"Vaspitni znachaj religiske nastave i njena neophodnost," *Gl.* (1945), no. 1-2-16; "Vaspitni ideali chrishchanske religije," *ZBF*, I, 75-85; *Religisha pedagogika* (ed. C. Drashkovic; Belgrade, 1951).

[72]*Prvobitni oblici chrishchanske propovedi* (Belgrade, 1945); "Oblici propovedi Gospoda Isusa Christa i apostola," *ZBF*, 1, 87-106; "Zlatni vek chrishchanske propovedi," *ZBF*, II, 201-238.

[73]*Spomenica povodom osamdesetogodishnjice okupacije Bosne i Hercegovine (1878-1958), pedesetogodishnjice aneksije (1908-1958) i chetrdesetogodishnjice oslovodjenja i ujedinjenja (1918-1958)* (Belgrade, 1959).

[74]*Stogodishnijica Gorskog vijenca 1847-1947* (Belgrade, 1947).

[75]*Shesta stogodishnjica Srpske patrijarshije* (Belgrade, 1946).

[76]*Stopedesetogodishnjica ustanka u Srbiji 1804-1954* (Belgrade, 1954).

[77]*Stogodishnjica Srpskog narodnog pokreta u Vojvodini* (1848-1948) (Belgrade, 1948).

NOTES ON PART FIVE

[1]It is impossible here to present a complete bibliography of books dealing with Rumanian history. I have found the following helpful in preparing this chapter: *Istoria Bisericii Romîne*, 2 vols. (Bucharest, 1957-1958); N. Iorga, *A History of Roumania*, tr. by J. McCabe (London, 1925);

Histoire des Roumains de Transylvanie et de Hongrie, 2 vols. (Bucharist, 1916); *Histoire des Roumains de Bucovine* (Jassy, 1917); *Histoire des Roumains et de la Romanité orientale* (Bucharist, 1916); R. W. Seton-Watson, *A History of the Roumanians* (Cambridge-England 1934); N. Cartojan, *Istoria Literaturii Romane Vechi,* 3 vols. (Bucharest, 1940); C. Kormos, *Rumania* (N. Y., 1945); G. I. Bratianu, *Un enigma e un miracolo: Il popolo romeno* (Bucharest, 1942); *Istoria Rominiei,* ed. C. Daicoviciu (Bucharest, 1960); D. Alexandru, *Histoire des Roumains de la Dacie trajane depuis les origines jusqu'à l'union des Principautés en 1859,* 2 vols. (Paris, 1896).

[2]For works dealing with early Christianity in Rumania cf. J. Zeiller, *Les origines chrétiennes dans les provinces danubiennes de l'Europe romaine* (Paris, 1918); N. Dobrescu, *Introducerea crestinismului la Romini* (Valeni, 1910); R. Vulpe, "Histoire ancienne dela Dobroudja," *La Dobroudja* (Bucharest, 1938), 35-454; E. Panaitescu, *Latinità e cristianesimo nell' evoluzione storica del popolo romeno* (Rome, 1923).

[3]Cf. N. Cartojan, *Istoria Lit., op. cit.,* vol. I, 18-21; also, *Istoria Bisericii Romine,* vol. I (Bucharest, 1957), 433-440.

[4]Cf. N. Cartojan, *op. cit.,* vol. I, 33.

[5]*Ibid.,* 34-35.

[6]For works dealing with the accomplishments of Coresi, cf. D. Mazilu, *Diaconul Coresi* (Ploesti, 1933); L. Predescu, *Diaconul Coresi* (Bucharest, 1933); D. Simonescu, *Diaconul Coresi* (Note pe marginea unei carti) (Bucharest, 1933); V. Grecu, *Izvorul principal bizantin pentru Cartea cu invatatura a diaconul Coresi din 1581* (Acad. Rom.), *Studii si Cercetari,* vol. 35 (Bucharest, 1939); Cartojan, *op. cit.,* vol. I, 55-64 I. Bianu, and N. Hodos, *Bibliografia Romaneasca veche,* vol. I, 1-43; 54-93, 516-529 (a description of his works is given).

[7]Bianu-Hodos, *op. cit.,* 63, 52-56, 49.

[8]Honterus published his work in Latin with the title: *Reformatio ecclesiae Coronensis ac totius Barcensis provinciae.* He also published it in German, printed in 1574 and 1575.

[9]A liturgical book used in Byzantine rite services and containing the eight tones of the canons or poetic compositions (many of which were composed by St. John Damascene in the 8th century) which are sung during Matins.

[10]Printed in Brasov in 1562 and in 1579. Cf. Bianu-Hodos, 46-49, 73.

[11]*Triod* published in 1578 (cf. Bianu-Hodos, 68, 73-75) and referring to the liturgical books containing the odes or poetic compositions sung proper to a given liturgical period, such as the Lenten and the Paschal Triods.

[12]Printed in 1577, Bianu-Hodos, 68.

[13]This work of Melanchthon was entitled, *Loci communes rerum theologicarum* and had 50 editions, including the 1559 edition in Rumanian.

[14]This was entitled, *Evanghelia cu invatatura sau Cazania,* published at Brasov in 1581.

[15]On Mogila's influences in Rumania see: P. P. Panaitescu, *L'influence de l'oeuvre de Pierre Mogila archevêque de Kiev dans les Principautés roumaines, Mélanges de l'École Roumaine en France,* V (Paris, 1926).

[16]Cf. L. Hurmazki, *Documente privitoarela istoria Românilor,* vol. IV, 1 (Bucharest, 1882) 668.

[17]Bianu-Hodos, 150-151; also, Cartojan, vol. II, 113.

[18]Bianu-Hodos, 147-150; Cartojan, vol. II, 112-113.

[19]On the life of Dosoftei, cf. Cartojan, vol. II, 115-125; D. Gazdaru, "Contributii privitoare la originea, limba si influenta Mitropolitului Dosoftei," *Arhiva,* XXXIV (Jassy, 1927), 122-149.

[20]A *Parameia* was a reading from the Old or New Testament read during the Vesper services of an important feast. For descriptions of these liturgical works, cf. Bianu-Hodos, 262-269.

[21]On his life, cf. P. P. Panaitescu, *Nicolas Spathar Milescu (1636-1708), Mélanges de l'École Roumaine en France,* I (Paris, 1925); E. Picot, *Notice biographique et bibliographique sur Nicolas Spathar Milescu* (Paris, 1883).

[22]This work he called *Intrebare si Raspunsuri [Questions and Answers].* Cf. Cartojan, vol. II, 131-132.

[23]Cartojan, vol. II, 32.

[24]Cf. E. Picot, *Notice biographique...op. cit.*

[25]C. Solomon, *Biblia dela Bucuresti (1688), Contributiuni noua istorico-literare* (Tecuciu, 1932).

[26]Cartojan, vol. II, 217.

[27]*Noului Testament* (Alba Julia, 1648).

[28]This work was entitled: *Enchiridion sive Stella Orientalis Occidentali splendens, id est, sensus ecclesiae orientalis scilicet graecae, de transubstantione Dominii allisque controversiis,* published in *Perpetuité de foy de l'Église catholique touchant l'Eucharistie,* ed. A. Arnauld, and P. Nicole, (Paris, 1669), vol. II, 50-54.

[29]Cf. supra, Part II, on the Greek Church that deals with the literary publications of Dositheos in Rumania. Between 1690 and 1716 Dositheos managed to have printed 31 works in Greek to strengthen the Orthodox theological position in Rumania and elsewhere.

[30]Cf. D. Russo, "Elenizmul in Romania," *Studii istorice greco-romane,* V, II (Bucharest, 1939) 487-542; Cartojan, 203.

[31]Antim is well known in the history of Rumanian religious literature for his *Didahii,* a book of sermons written in a very artistic language that contributed as much by its style as its theological content to the formation of a theological literature. This work has been edited by I. Comoi, *Antim Ivireanu, Din Didahiile tinute in Mitropolia din Bucuresti* (Bucharest 1895).

[32]Typical of his published works in his noted pioneer work on the

philology of the Rumanian language, *Elementa linguae daco-romanicae sive valachicae* (Buda, 1780). On his works and life see, Gh. I. Moisescu, "Samuil Micu Clain," *Biserica Orthodoxa Romina,* 74 (1956) 1057-1077; Iacob Radu, *Samuil Vulcan episcopul romin unit al Orazii-Mari (1806-1839) si Biserica ortodoxa Romina* (Oradea Mare, 1925). For a description of his main theological works cf. Bianu-Hodos, 272, 274, 287, 325, 380, 382, 385, 386, 397, 425, 429, 430, 434, 451, 452, 465, 476, 479, 481.

³³Cf. Bianu-Hodos, 251, 281, 282, 310, 325, 363, 479, 481, 525, 526.

³⁴Cf. A. M. Marinescu, *Viata si operele lui Petru Maior* (Bucharest, 1883).

³⁵For a description of some of his liturgical and theological works, cf. Bianu-Hodos, 154-158; also, A. Bunea, *Episcopii Petru Pavel Aron si Dionisie Novacovici* (Blaj, 1902).

³⁶Printed in Blaj in 1858.

³⁷Cf. *Istoria Bisericii...op. cit.,* vol. II, 499-510; also St. Berechet, "Reformele bisericesti sub Cuza Voda, dupa presa straina," *Biserica Ortodoxe Romina,* 43 (1925), 475-479.

³⁸His works include the following: *Mineele* (Blaj, 1853-1856); *Acatist, Teologia morala, Marturisirea ortodoxa* and *Chiriacodromiomul* (all printed in Blaj, 1855). *Istoria Bisericii ortodoxe rasaritene universale;* 2 vol. (Blaj, 1860).

³⁹For works on Paisii, cf. V. Cazanacli, *Paisie Velicicovski si insemnatatea lui pentru monahismul pravoslavnic* (1898); N. M. Popescu, "100 de ani de la moartea staretului Paisie Velicicovschi," *Mitropolia Oltenia,* 7 (1955), 41-47; St. Berechet, *Autobiografia staretuliu Paisie Velicicovschi* (Jassy, 1918); S. Tchetverikov, *Moldavskii staretz Paissi Velitchkovsky* (Petseri, 1938) [to be published in English by Nordland Publishing Company]; Anon., *Zhitie startza Moldavskago Paissia Velitchkovskago* (Optina ed., no date).

⁴⁰Cf. A. Stadnitkii, *Romini poluchivshie obrazovanie v Rosskikh duchovno uchevnikh zavedekiyakh* (Cernauti, 1891); N. Iorga, *Histoire des relations russo-roumains* (Jassy, 1917); Gh. I. Moisescu, *Bursieri romini la scolite teologice dine Rusia (1845-1856)* (Bucharest, 1947).

⁴¹Cf. I. Naniescu, *Istoricul pe scurt al inceputului Seminariilor* (Bucharest, 1893); *Istoria Bis. Rom.... op. cit.,* 441-443.

⁴²For his life and works, cf. N. M. Popescu, *Viata si faptele parintelui Grigorie Dascalul mitropolitul Tarii Rominesti* (Bucharest, 1934); I. Ionascu, *Mitropolitul Grigorie IV si intrebuintarea unor venituri in vreme a pastoriei lui (1823-1834)* (Bucharest, 1940).

⁴³*Catehismul ortodocs* (Jassy, 1857).

⁴⁴*Scurta introducere in cursul stiintelor teologice* (Jassy, 1854).

⁴⁵*Teologia dogmatica a Bisericii ortodoxe de rasarit* (Jassy, 1855).

⁴⁶*Manual de Tipic* (Jassy, 1854).

⁴⁷*Introducera in Sfintele carti ale Scripturii Vechiului si Noului Testament* (Jassy, 1860).

[48]*Dreptul canonic, Ermineutica* (tr. from a Latin edition printed in St. Petersburg).

[49]*Teologia pastorala* (Jassy, 1863).

[50]*Liturgica* (Jassy, 1853; Bucharest, 1862).

[51]His works in Rumanian include: *Catihisis* (Jassy, 1846); *Istoria Sfinta pe scurt* (Jassy, 1847); *Morala crestina* (1855); *Ermineutica* (1856); *Istoria bisericeasca pe scurt* (Jassy, 1858); *Marturisirea ortodoxa* (tr. of Peter Mogila's *Confession of Faith*) (Jassy, 1842).

[52]*Catihisis* (Jassy, 1838).

[53]*Sfinta istorie a Noului Testament* (Jassy, 1854); *Omiletica* (1856).

[54]On didactic theological compendia, cf. O. Ghibu, "Din istoria literaturii didactice romînesti," *An. Ac. Rom.,* 38 (1915); I. Georgescu, "Manuale didactice, teologice in veacul XIX," *Studii Teologice,* 9 (1957), 710-725.

[55]On the history of Rumanian periodicals, cf. N. Hodos and A. Ionescu, *Publicatiunile periodice rominesti* (Bucharest, 1913); N. Iorga, *Istoria presei romine* (Bucharest, 1922); I. T. Vasiliu, "Cea dintii revista religioasa din tara," *Bis. Ort. Rom.,* 46 (1928), 980-982.

[56]Cf. M. A. Plamadeala, "Preocupari dogmatico-simbolice in literatura teologica contemporana," *Ortodoxia,* 2 (1957), 297 ss.

[57]Cf. for a description of these publications, the short work, *The Rumanian Orthodox Church,* edited by The Bible and Orthodox Missionary Institute (Bucharest, 1962), 68-70.

[58]On the seminaries of this time, cf. C. Chiricescu, *Trei institutii bisericesti din Rominia* (Bucharest, 1902); I. Popescu-Malaesti, "Facultatea de Teologie din Bucuresti," *Studii Teologice,* 3 (1932), 3-19; T. G. Bulat, "Contributii la istoricul Facultatii de Teologie din Bucuresti," *Bis. Ort. Rom.,* 75 (1957), 1071-1217.

[59]Dr. Popan, Flaviu & Draskovic, *Orthodoxie heute in Rumänien und Jugoslawien* (Vienna, 1960), 56.

[60]Bucharest, 1948-61.

[61]Bucharest, 1960.

[62]F. Popan, *op. cit.,* p. 67.

[63]Cf. N. Chitescu, "Taina Bisericii in gindirea lui Alexei Homiacov (1804-1860)," *Biserica Orth. Rom.,* LXVI (1948), 5-8.

[64]Androutsos' Δογματική...was translated into Rumanian with the title, *Dogmatica Bisericii Rasaritene* (Sibiu, 1930). Justin Moisescu translated his Συμβολική with the title, *Simbolica Bisericii Ortodoxe Rasaritone* (Craiova, 1954).

[65]Published in 1855.

[66]*Invatatura ortodoxa din religiunea crestineasca* (Vienna, 1862).

[67]*Prelegeri Academice din Dogmatica Ortodoxa* (Cernauti, 1899).

[68]*Manual de Teologie Dogmatica ortodoxa* (Caransebes, 1907).

[69]*Manual de Teologie Dogmatica* (Bucharest, 1916); *Dogma soteriologica* (Bucharest, 1926); *Catehismul crestinului ortodox* (Bucharest, 1930); *Die Bekenntnisse und die wichtigsten Glaubenszeugnisse der griechischorientalischen Kirche* (Leipzig, 1904).

[70]*Teologia Dogmatica si Simbolica*, part I: *Teologia Dogmatica General sau Principiala si Simbolica* (Bucharest, 1958); part II: *Teologia Dogmatica Speciala si Simbolica* (Bucharest, 1958).

[71]Cf. A. Johansens, *Theological Study in the Rumanian Orthodox Church under Communist Rule* (London, 1961), 4.

[72]*Teologia Dogmatica...op. cit.*, vol. I, 1942.

[73]*Ibid.*, 202 ss.

[74]I have been rather dependent upon A. Johansen's study, *op. cit.* for my statements concerning the textbooks of biblical studies, ethics and canon law, pp. 10-47.

[75]Neaga's work deals exclusively with Christ in the Old Testament and was printed in Sibiu in 1940.

[76]Johansen, *op. cit.*, 12-13.

[77]*Viata si invatatura Sf. Grigoire Palamas* (Sibiu, 1938).

[78]*Filocalia*, vol. I-IV (Sibiu, 1946-48).

[79]Johansen, *op. cit.*, 15-16.

[80]*Ibid.*, 29-32.

[81]Cf. D. V. Sadeanu, "The Ecumenical Movement and the Russian Orthodox Church," *Ortodoxia*, no. 4 (1949), 161-172, in Rumanian.

[82]Cf. Cl. Lialine, "Anglicanisme et Orthodoxie, quelques apercus sur leurs relations," *Istina* (1956), 32-198; 183-190.

[83]Cf. the excellent articles of Goia, "L'Orthodoxie roumaine et le Mouvement oecumenique," *Istina*, vol. IV (1957), 55-84.

[84]Cf. "Les Chrétiens en Roumanie," *Informations catholiques internationales*, no. 233 (1965), 25.

[85]*Ibid.*, 24.

[86]In an interview with the French newspaper *Figaro*, November, 1964, Patriarch Justinian claimed "in present-day Rumania there are only .5% unbelievers in contrast to the 40% in France. Cf. "Les Chrétiens en Roumanie," *Inf. cath. intern.*, art. cit. 25.

NOTES ON PART SIX

[1]Hans von Campenhausen, *The Fathers of the Greek Church* (N. Y., 1959), p. 155.

[2]G. V. Florovskii, "Patristics and Modern Theology," *Procès-Verbaux du premier Congrès de Théologie orthodoxe à Athenes—29 novembre-6 decembre 1936* (Athens, 1939), ed. H. S. Alivisatos, p. 240.

[3]*Vvedenie v pravoslavnoe bogoslovie* (St. Petersburg, 1847); *Pravoslavnoe dogmaticheskoe bogoslovie* (St. Petersburg, 1849-1853).

[4]Galatians 3:28-29.

Index of Names

A

Aaron, Bishop Petru Pavel, 281
Abbot, George, 138, 194
Acyndynes, 93
Adalbert, 12
Adam of Tsernikov, 172
Adrian, Patriarch, 35, 40
Afanas'ev, Nikolai, 77, 79, 316, 317
Agallien, Theodore, 156
Akilonov, 61, 316
Aksakov, K. S., 57
Aleksandr, Tsar I, 50, 51, 52, 315
Alekseev, P. A., 67
Alexander (of Crete), 109
Alexander the Great, 16
Alexander of Hales, 117
Alexander, Tsar Ioan, 222, 225
Alexander, Bishop of Rodostolou, 209
Aleksei, Tsar, 38, 39, 146, 147, 308
Alemannos, Nicolas, 168
Alivisatos, Hamilcar, 61, 201, 202
Allatios, Leo, 91, 153, 155, 168
Ambrazis, Nicolas, 198, 318
Amfiteatrov, Antonii, 35, 53, 70, 196, 237
Amici, 37
Anastasiou, I., 201
Andreas, 101, 103
Andrievici, Metropolitan Silvestru of Bukovina, 291
Androutsos, Chrestos, 35, 99, 141, 155, 197, 199, 291, 292, 318
Anfimus, Metropolitan of Valachia, 224
Angel, Bishop Athanasius, 280
Angelar, 212
Anichkov, N., 55
Anselm of Canterbury, 240
Anthimos, Patriarch IV, 189
Anthimos, VII, 195, 196
Antim, 296
Antim (of Vidin), 235